ANTHONY Q. ARTIS

THE

SHUT UP AND SHOOT

FREELANCE VIDEO GUIDE

ANTHONY Q. ARTIS

THE
SHUT UP
AND SHOOT
FREELANCE VIDEO GUIDE

A

PRODUCTION

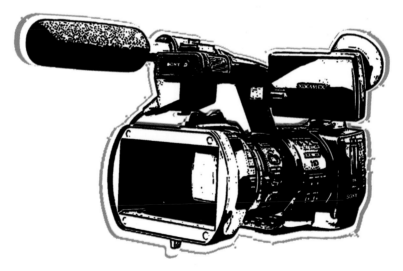

ELSEVIER

AMSTERDAM · BOSTON · HEIDELBERG · LONDON
NEW YORK · OXFORD · PARIS · SAN DIEGO
SAN FRANCISCO · SINGAPORE · SYDNEY · TOKYO
Focal Press is an imprint of Elsevier

Focal Press is an imprint of Elsevier
225 Wyman Street, Waltham, MA 02451, USA
The Boulevard, Langford Lane, Kidlington, Oxford, OX5 1GB, UK

Notices

Knowledge and best practice in this field are constantly changing. As new research and experience broaden our understanding, changes in research methods, professional practices, or medical treatment may become necessary.

Practitioners and researchers must always rely on their own experience and knowledge in evaluating and using any information, methods, compounds, or experiments described herein. In using such information or methods they should be mindful of their own safety and the safety of others, including parties for whom they have a professional responsibility.

To the fullest extent of the law, neither the Publisher nor the authors, contributors, or editors, assume any liability for any injury and/or damage to persons or property as a matter of products liability, negligence or otherwise, or from any use or operation of any methods, products, instructions, or ideas contained in the material herein.

Library of Congress Cataloging-in-Publication Data
Artis, Anthony Q.
  The shut up and shoot : freelance video guide : a down & dirty DV production / Anthony Q. Artis.
      p. cm.
  Includes bibliographical references and index.
  ISBN 978-0-240-81487-2 (alk. paper)
1. Video recordings--Production and direction. I. Title.
  PN1992.94.A77 2011
  778.59--dc23
                                                                    2011032055

British Library Cataloguing-in-Publication Data
A catalogue record for this book is available from the British Library.

ISBN: 978-0-240-81487-2

For information on all Focal Press publications
visit our website at www.elsevierdirect.com

11 12 13 14 15   5 4 3 2 1

Printed in the United States of America

Typeset by: diacriTech, Chennai, India

This book is dedicated with loving memory to my mother, Norma Elizabeth Artis, who did not live to see its completion, but whose legacy is on every page in the form of the knowledge and wisdom I'm able to share with you courtesy of the opportunities and education she provided for me as a single mother. You are appreciated, loved and missed.

CONTENTS

CRAZY MAD THANX.. xix

WEB SITE PAGE.. xxi

HOW THIS BOOK IS LAID OUT.. xxiii

PREFACE... xxv

INTRODUCTION... xxxi

CHAPTER 1—IMAGE CONTROL..1

GETTING STARTED

- Video Tech Specs—The Necessary Evils... 2
  - Intro: My Low Definition of High-Definition Video 2
  - Pixels.. 2
  - Resolution 2
  - Progressive vs. Interlace Scan Lines... 3
  - Refresh Rate 3
  - Frame Rate.. 3
- Important Menu Settings 4
  - Check Your Menu...First.. 4
  - Video Format.. 4
  - Timecode Menu Settings 5
- Freelancers Camera Guide 7
- Why DSLR Cameras Are Lame.. 20
  - Intro.. 20
- Why DSLR Cameras Are Da Bomb 23
  - Intro.. 23
  - Conclusion.. 24
- DSLR Workarounds and Fixes.. 25
- Anatomy of a DSLR Franken Rig 26
- Digital File Chart.. 27

- Digital Media Chart 29
- Hot Tip: A Down and Dirty Raincover 31
- Exposure and Zebra Stripes 32
  - Zebra Stripes 101 32
  - Zebra Stripes Are Your Friend 32
- Underexposure and Gain 33
  - Gain 33
- What It Looks Like: Gain 34
- White Balance 201 35
  - Changing Mood with White Balance 35
  - Secrets of the Color Wheel 35
- Making the Most of Any Camera 36
- How to Shoot Handheld 37
- Focusing 38
  - The Problem with HD 38
  - Using a Monitor 38
- Focusing 39
  - Peaking...Focus Pocus! 39
- Zooming 40
  - Introduction: Who's Zooming Who? 40
  - Pushing In 40
  - Pulling Out 41
  - Smooth Like Butter, Baby! 41
- The Three Ways to Zoom 42
- Shutter Speed 43
  - Shutter Speed 101 43
- Hot Tip: 5 Cool Shutter Speed FX 44
- Focal Length 46
  - Crowds 46
  - Cityscapes 46
  - People and Faces 47
- Hot Tip: Shooting Time-Lapse Scenes 48
- Anatomy of a Green Screen Interview 50
- Working with What You've Got 51
  - Constructing an Interview Space 51
- Working with What You've Got 52
  - A Bare Conference Room with a Great View 52
- 4 Reasons to Enhance People's Looks 53
  - Why Make People Look Good? 53
- Makeup Makes Money 55
  - Introduction 55
  - Brands 55
- Hiring Makeup Pros 56

What to Expect 56

Cutting Makeup Costs 56

- Makeup Supplies 57

Translucent Powder Makeup 57

Premium Brush 57

Apron or Towel 57

Brush Cleaner 57

- Applying Powder Makeup in Five Easy Steps 58

- Common Facial Issues and Fixes 59

- **Been There, Done That:** Seven Practical Tips on Shooting Sports 61

CHAPTER 2—AUDIO TECHNIQUES 67

GETTING STARTED

- Introduction 68

Why Your Audio Is More Important than Your Video 68

- Sound Tools of the Trade 69

- Sound Tools of the Trade 70

- Sound Tools of the Trade 71

- Sound Department Crew 72

Sound Mixer 72

Boom Operator 72

Mixer/Boom 73

- Audio Recording Strategy 74

My Mic Sounds Nice...Check One, Two, Three! 74

- **Been There, Done That:** Mic Choice, Meters and Miking Pianos 76

- Analog versus Digital Measurements 78

Exceptions to the General Rules 79

Why Are There Two Different Digital Standards? 79

- Setting Proper Audio Levels 80

My Mic Sounds Nice, Check 1: Audio Levels 80

- Hot Tip: Bracketing Your Audio 81

- Wireless Mic Units 82

- Five Wireless Mic Tips 83

- Taming Wind Noise 84

Wind Noise Is Most Likely... 84

Blocking Out Wind Noise 84

- Dealing with Shorts 85

Beware Shorts 85

Detecting Shorts 85

- Hot Tip: Two Mics are Always Better Than One 86

- Audio Troubleshooting Guide 87

- Other Audio Trouble Spots 92

- **Been There, Done That:** Location Recording Issues and Post Tools 93
- Fixing Location Audio in Post 95
- Hot Tip: Graphic Equalizer 96
- Voice-over Narration 97
  - Casting 97
- Directing Narration 98
  - Directing Voice-overs 98
  - Voice-over Setups 98
- Anatomy of a Down and Dirty Voice-over 99
- Five Sound Rules to Live By 100
  - Rule #1 100
  - Rule #2 100
  - Rule #3 100
  - Rule #4 101
  - Rule #5 101
- **Been There, Done That:** The Secrets to Recording Great Audio 102

CHAPTER 3—LIGHTING: GETTING YA SHINE ON...............................103

GETTING STARTED

- Practicing "Safe Sets" 104
  - Introduction 104
- Hot Tip: 10 Ways to Practice Safe Sets.. 105
- **Been There, Done That:** How Many Lights Can I Plug Into This Circuit? 109
- Basic Lighting Safety... 112
- Light Is Good 113
  - A Word (or Two) about Low Light Conditions 113
- Reflectorology 114
  - Let God Be Your Gaffer 114
  - Reflector Flavors 114
- Reflectorology 115
- Hot Tip: Chromatte Greenscreen Tips... 116
- Lighting Cookbook 2.0 117
- Lighting Cookbook 2.0 118
- Lighting Cookbook 2.0 119
- Lighting Cookbook 2.0 120
- Lighting Cookbook 2.0 121
- Lighting Cookbook 2.0 122
- Lighting Cookbook 2.0 123
- Lighting Cookbook 2.0 124
- Lighting Cookbook 2.0 125
- Lighting Cookbook 2.0 126
- Lighting Cookbook 2.0 127

CHAPTER 4—MARKETING AND PROMO VIDEOS 129

GETTING STARTED

- Intro: Solving Clients' Problems 130
- **Been There, Done That:** Video Marketing Ain't For Everybody 131
- Conceptualizing the Video 132
  - Creative versus Effective 132
- Start with an Outline 133
  - It All Starts with an Outline 133
  - A Simple Outline 133
  - A Detailed Outline 134
- Creating a Script 136
  - The A/V Script Format 136
- Sample A/V Script 137
- Storyboards 138
- Creating a Storyboard 139
- Hot Tip: 7 Tips for Working with "Real People" 140
- Load-in Procedure 143
- Setup Procedure 144
- Rehearsal Procedure 145
- Shooting Procedure 146
- Wrap-out Procedure 147
- Teleprompters 148
  - Working with Teleprompters 148
- **Been There, Done That:** Commercials 101 149
- How We Do 151
  - "Differenter" Campaign 151
  - Project Details 152
  - Breaking the Fourth Wall 153
  - Traditional Cutaways 153
  - Third-Party B-Roll 154
  - Text Treatments 154
  - Multiple Camera Angles 155
  - Using Different Lens and Focal Lengths 156
- Text and Storytelling 157
- Hot Tip: Five Ways to Get B-Roll 158
- **Been There, Done That:** Commercials 201 162
- Getting "Broadcast Standard" 165
  - Slate/Title Screen 165
  - Color Bars 165
  - Tone 165
- Slating a: 30 Commercial 166
- How We Do 167
  - A Web Promo Campaign 167

Project Details 168

- How We Do 169

Graphic Text 169

Music 169

Transitional Visual FX 170

Illustrative Visual FX 171

Retro Film Look 172

Student Group Interview 172

- Hot Tip: Shooting Group Interviews 173

- The Freelance Video Workflow* 177

CHAPTER 5—MUSIC VIDEOS 179

GETTING STARTED

So, Why Make Music Videos? 180

- 5 Good Reasons to Make Music Videos 181

- 5 Tips for Finding Your First Act 182

- Before the Gig Starts 185

Things to Keep in Mind Going into the Gig 185

Cost/Benefit of Using Your Own Money 185

Be Reasonably Transparent 185

- Preproduction—The Pitch 186

Preparing to Pitch 186

First things first... 186

- Preproduction—The Budget 187

A Word on Budgets 187

Under-Promise and Over-Deliver: Words to Live By 187

Do It for Real 187

Be Honest with the Act and Yourself 188

Mo' Money, Mo' Problems 188

- What Goes into a Budget? 189

Preproduction 189

Production 189

Postproduction 189

Contingency 189

- Sample Music Video Budget 190

- Dreaming Up a Video 192

Dreaming 192

Get to Know the Song Super Well 192

- Brainstorming Notes 193

Some Things I Did Well When I Wrote These Notes 193

Some Things I Could Have Done Better 193

An Aside 193

- The Treatment 194

Distill Your Ideas 194

Your Treatment 194

• Putting the Treatment Together 195

Put It All Together 195

• After You've Been Approved 196

What Do I Need to Do to Prepare? 197

• Scripting Your Video 198

The Patent-Pending Benjamin Ahr Harrison Music Video Scripting Process 198

Fundamentals of the Process 198

In Preparation, Hire an A.D. 198

The Four Key Documents 198

• Scripting: The Outline 199

Outline 199

• Scripting: The Location-Based Outline 200

Location-Based Outline 200

• Scripting: The Shot List 201

Shot List 201

• Scripting: The Shooting Schedule 202

Shooting Schedule 202

• Prepping Your Music Video Shoot 203

A Few Things to Consider as You Prep Your Shoot 203

Locations 203

Studio Space 204

Test Shooting 204

• Production 205

The Day Before 205

The Day Of 205

• 5 Things to Always Do On Set 206

• 10 Pro Tips for Shooting Music Videos 208

• Postproduction 212

Introduction 212

Kill Your Baby 212

Notes on Media 213

• Managing the Postproduction Process 214

• The 3 Review Edit 215

• Review Edit #1: Rough Cut 216

Getting Synced 216

Getting Rhythmic 217

Send It to the Client 217

• True Music Video Confessions 218

• Review Edit #2: Compositing 219

Review Edit #2 219

The Basics of Compositing 219

• Music Video Tools of the Trade 220

- The Process of Keying 221
- Review Edit #3: The Final Cut 223
  - Review Edit #3 223
  - Intro to Color 223
  - My Approach to Color 223
  - Nota Bene 223
- Down and Dirty Color Terminology 224
- Color Grading Options 225
- What It Looks Like: Color Correction 226
- The End of the Edit 228
- Music Video Exhibition 229
  - Television 229
  - The Internet 230
- Going Viral Online 231
  - Okay, Go!—"Here It Goes Again" 232
  - Beyoncé—"Put a Ring on It" 232
  - Rebecca Black—"Friday" 232
- Ben's Final Thoughts on Music Videos 233
  - In Conclusion 233
- How We Do 234
  - Project Details 235
  - Establishing Shots—Adding Movement 236
  - The Bridge—Enhancing the Look and Fixing My Screwup 236
  - The Murals—Adding Production Value with Location 237
  - Documentary Street Scenes—Film Look 237
  - The Studio Scenes—Projection FX 238
  - Special FX in Postproduction 239
  - The Abandoned Harbor Pier—Baltimore Money Shot 239
- Hot Tip: ~~Stealing~~ Borrowing Locations 240

CHAPTER 6—WEDDINGS 241

GETTING STARTED

- "Introduction: The Video *Is* the Memory" 242
- In the Beginning 243
  - The Golden Rule of Wedding Videos 243
  - The "How They Met" Montage 243
- Approach and Style 244
- **Been There, Done That:** Wedding Video Approach 245
- Scouting the Wedding Venue 247
- The Wedding Video "Cast" 248
  - Get a Point Person 248
  - Identifying Key Characters 248
- Before the Wedding 249

The Rehearsal 249

The Celebrant 249

• Wedding Lighting Conditions 250

• Tips for Shooting in Low Light 251

Add More Light 251

Shoot Wide 251

Decrease Your Shutter Speed (Slightly) 251

Use the Gain Function 251

Use a Camera Light 251

Use a Fast Lens 251

• Positioning Your Camera 252

• Covering the Ceremony 253

Anatomy of a Good Camera Position 253

• Establishing Shots 254

The Establishing Sequence 254

Setting the Mood 254

• Capturing the *Whole* Wedding Story 255

The Bride's Preparation 255

Candid Interactions 255

The Guests 255

• Stealing Cutaways and Reaction Shots 256

• Smooth Moves: The Reveal 257

The Pull-Out Reveal 257

The Rack-Focus Reveal 257

• Transitioning from Point A to Point B 258

A Simple Transition 258

• A Dozen Ways to Get Artsy with It 259

• Details Details Details! 261

• **Been There, Done That:** Capturing the Key Moments 262

• The Ceremony Money Shots 263

The Rites and Rituals 263

The Vows 263

The Kiss 263

• Handheld versus Tripod Camerawork 264

Why You Should Use a Tripod 264

Why You Should Go Handheld 264

Why You Should Split the Difference 264

• Wedding Audio Strategies 265

Wireless Lav Mics 265

Plugging In 265

Placing Hardwired Mics 265

• A Few Words about Wedding Video Music 266

• Other Things to Keep in Mind 267

The Most Important Part: The Vows and Kiss 267

Tape and Media Card Changes 267

Getting Establishing Shots 267

- **Been There, Done That:** 10 Wedding Video Best Practices 268
- Capturing Intimacy 269

Look Out for the Little Tender (Semi) Private Moments 269

Hang Back and Zoom In 269

- Storytelling Sequences 270

The Groom Awaits His Bride-to-Be 270

The New Couple Steals Away for a (Semi) Private Walk 270

Bridal Prep Close-up Montage 270

Capturing the Fun 271

- Getting Paid 272
- Covering the Reception 273

Covering the Spread and Decor 273

- Incorporating the Photo Shoot 274
- Wedding Videographer and Video Checklists 275

Wedding Videographer Checklist 275

Wedding Video Shotlist 275

CHAPTER 7—LIVE EVENTS **277**

GETTING STARTED

- Introduction 278
- Hot Tip: 5 Questions to Ask the Venue 279
- Shooting Live Music Shows 281

The Performance Versus The Video 281

Audio Quality 281

- Live Event Audio Cookbook 282
- Live Event Audio Cookbook 283
- Live Event Audio Cookbook 284
- Live Event Audio Cookbook 285
- **Been There, Done That:** Recording and Mixing Live Music 286
- Hot Tip: Miking Instruments 288
- Make 'Em Move! 290

You're in the Band Now, Baby! 290

- Live Event Camera Techniques 291

Pull-Out from Instrument CU 291

Push-In for Solo 291

Push-In from Performer's POV to Audience 291

Handheld High Angles 292

Raise It Up 292

Showing Off Technique 292

Lens Flare 293

Rack Focus to Pull-Out 293

Whip Zoom 294

Whip Pan 294

- The Art of the Close-up 295

    Getting Up Close and Personal 295

    Detail Close-ups 295

    Emotion Close-ups 295

    Action Close-ups 295

- Hot Tip: Mounting Shotgun Mics 296
- Miscellaneous Live Event Camera Tips 297
- Covering a Musical Performance 298

    Making Single-Camera Coverage Work 298

- Hot Tip: Neutral Shots and Cutaways 299

    Do One Just for the Camera 299

- The Anatomy of "Shooting for the Cut" 300
- The Anatomy of "Shooting for the Cut" 301
- Covering the Whole Performance 302
- 3 Single-Camera Coverage Strategies 303
- Shooting the Audience 305
- Seven Tips for Shooting Stage Plays 307
- Hot Tip: Shooting Projected Images 312

CHAPTER 8—HANDLING YA BUSINESS 315

GETTING STARTED

- Business Basics 316

    Get an Employer Identification Number (EIN) 316

    Form a Business Entity 316

    Bank Account 317

    Production Insurance 317

- How to Get Paying Clients 319

    1. Do the First One for No Money 319

    2. Develop Strategic Partnerships 320

    3. Offer a Kickback 320

    4. Hand out Cards and Brochures 320

    5. Create a Website 321

- **Been There, Done That:** The Client "Dance" and Crafting a Proposal 323
- 5 Things to Clarify with Clients from Go 324

    Will You Just Shoot or Also Edit? 324

    What Is the Rate? 324

    When Is Payment Due? 324

    What Will You Shoot? 325

    What Do *They* Have to Do? 325

- What Should You Charge? 326
- Hot Tip: Setting Your Rate 327

- Calculating Your Crew's Rate 329
- **Been There, Done That:** Calculating Your Crew's Rate................................ 330
- Hot Tip: Working Remotely With an Editor... 331

GLOSSARY...**333**
ABOUT THE AUTHOR **353**
CREDITS **354**
INDEX **355**

No endeavor like this comes together from a single person. It simply takes way too much physical work, knowledge, research, mental and emotional investment to go it alone, so I want to thank some of the many people and entities that have helped me pull this off.

To my beautiful wife Sonya, my #1 fan and cheerleader. Without you holding down everything I dropped to write this book and educate the peoples, there would be no Down an Dirty DV. (So if y'all want more books, thank her too when you see her, 'cause she's the invisible contributor to all the books, DVD's and seminars.)

To Pete Chatmon who kept a constant (and nagging) foot in my butt every step of the way to finally write this book and played the Oscar-worthy role of Devil's Advocate as I shaped the content and tone of this book.

To "Big" Ben Harrison who crafted the entire music video chapter, you were my student, but now you're one of my teachers and inspirations. Keep flipping the script and cranking out those hot videos, man. Thanks for sharing your hard-won knowledge in this book. Big things to come, no doubt.

To all of my filmmaking colleagues at NYU's Tisch School of the Arts who supported my last book and so generously shared their time, knowledge and filmmaking wisdom with me, especially those that took the time out of their busy schedules to give interviews and advice for this book.

To my N.A.B. "entourage" Dan "The Man" Shipp and Maxie Collier who've always watched my back and pumped me up to keep growing Down and Dirty DV. It means a lot to have you both still in my corner for more than 15 years now.

To Dean Sheril Antonio whose encouragement and confidence in my abilities has been a constant source of motivation and inspiration to really delve deeper into the world of freelance video, which provided me with much of the material for this book.

To Alex "Rev. Al" Houston, my Spiritual Technical Advisor. I'm so glad you understand and generously share the details of all this stuff, so I can just ask you. (Too much tech, makes my brain hurt. I just wanna make movies.)

To The Double 7 Squad, you guys are the most talented and straight-up coolest group of collaborators I've the pleasure to work with. I look forward to the projects of the future. It's great being down with a hardcore filmmaking gang. (Throwing up my D-7 sign.) Let's keep building this thang up and out.

To digital whiz, Giga Shane, whose After Effects skills have helped me take my visual storytelling to a new level and populates many of the illustrations in this book. Great working with you.

To Dave DiGioia who was one of my first mentors and didn't even know it. Your tough love video lessons are the very foundation of the knowledge base I share with thousands of students every year (albeit at a few decibels lower). I remain grateful.

To Zully, David, Mordy and all my peeps at B&H, Thanks for all your continued support of Down and Dirty DV from day one and inviting me do my thang in the Event Space.

To my literary agent, Jan Kardys, one of the hardest working women in publishing. Thanks for believing in me from the start and all the great advice you've given me. Your Unicorn Writers Conference is an incredible resource for up and coming writers.

To the generous staff, faculty and students of the Clive Davis Institute who allowed me to tell their inspiring story on video and share it in this book.

To the good people at the Coda Bar and Grill in Maplewood, NJ and the South Orange, NJ Starbucks who provided a stimulating atmosphere and the nourishing fuel needed to help me crank out this book in record time.

To all the students and people who've attended my workshops, talks and seminars, and all the fans of my first book, *The Shut Up and Shoot Documentary Guide* you continue to be my biggest inspiration. Your emails and kind words are the only thing that can keep me going for six hours straight with a laptop burning my crotch while I crank out just one more page.

And last, but by no means least, all my Focal Press peeps: Elinor Actipis, Stephen Bradley, Michele Cronin, Melissa Sanford, Amanda Guest, The Notorious Scotty B, Melinda Rankin, Cara Anderson St. Hilaire, Big Jim, Dennis, and the baddest book sales team on the planet. I love rolling with the best in the film book business and have nothing but love for y'all. Keep putting a foot in the ass of film book publishers everywhere and raising the bar, baby. We got much more work to do.

The Crazy Phat Bonus Website

Be sure to check out the website for more info and resources! On the site, you'll find:

- Forms
- Checklists
- Cheat Sheets
- Videos
- Internet Resources
- And a whole lot more!

www.freelancevideoguide.com

HOW THIS BOOK IS LAID OUT

This book is written and designed to be ultra user-friendly. So, just as I did in my first book, *The Shut Up and Shoot Documentary Guide*, I have attempted to break down the most common elements of freelance video into a comprehensive collection of clearly-illustrated simply-worded bite-sized chunks of practical production techniques and storytelling strategies that anyone can understand, digest and apply quickly to their own work. Most sections are laid out in just one to four pages. Also, because this is a visual medium populated by visual thinkers, I've tried to illustrate most concepts to make it even clearer and easier to understand. Here's how it breaks down:

Been There Done That

Even moreso than in my first book, I've included the sage wisdom of some of my most talented colleagues that work in the various freelance video genres in sections entitled "Been There, Done That." These filmmaking professionals serve up some crucial lessons, perception and insider tips that they themselves only learned through years of experience.

How We Do

This time around I've also added some new sections entitled "How We Do" where I share with you specific case-studies of freelance video projects that I have produced and/or directed, as well as an additional case-study of a project directed by my partner in grind, Pete Chatmon.

Hot Tips

Back by popular demand are my Hot Tips pages, which give quick illustrated overviews of insider tricks and solutions to everyday filmmaking problems.

Anatomy Of...

The *Anatomy Of...* sections give simple illustrated overviews to help you quickly understand certain concepts laid out in the book in a visual format...you know, the way filmmakers actually think.

Charts

This book also includes several charts of useful reference information on common tools such as cameras, sound gear, and digital media. These charts provide basic specs, notes and sometimes pricing information on many of the most common tools of the freelance video trade.

Why I Wrote This Book and Who I Wrote It For

This book is a sequel of sorts to my first book, *The Shut Up and Shoot Documentary Guide*, which covers many basic concepts and techniques of video production. *The Shut Up and Shoot Freelance Video Guide* builds on the information in my first book and breaks out into more genre-specific storytelling strategies. It is designed to be a tutorial and reference guide for those that create or aspire to create marketing, wedding, live event or music videos. Despite the legions of veteran and new filmmakers now shooting these video genres, there is a severe lack of guidance on the technical logistics, business and storytelling aspects of shooting videos for hire. Now that more people than ever have access to high-quality video cameras, maintaining quality control and professionalism are real challenges. In other words, a lot of people out there are now making whack (i.e. bad, lame, weak) videos. I don't fault them 100 percent for this.

The biggest issue in my opinion is that not enough experienced filmmakers are taking the time to inform and instruct others on how to make good freelance videos – not in film school, not in books and not in independent seminars, so you have this funky situation where everybody's doing it, but nobody's really *teaching* it. To complicate matters, the technology and instruction can also be over-complicated and confusing even for people like me who have been in the video game for a while. Admittedly, I'm no Rhodes Scholar, but I didn't ride the short bus to school either, so I know I can't be the only one who's been routinely confused and intimidated by many of the new tools and practices of the video trade.

So, I wrote this book for all the non-techies that still need to understand and do technical things and for the non-video geniuses that still need to exercise their *creative* genius on video. Whether you're a filmmaker who's striving to make a living or earn some extra money doing freelance video work, an aspiring filmmaker or student who wants to fill in these gaps or just taking on the new role of video director for your company or church, I hope you will find plenty of valuable advice and knowledge in this book that will help you to efficiently create better videos with fewer heartaches and greater production value.

Indeed, Down and Dirty DV was founded on the very idea that filmmaking should not be needlessly complicated or complicated simply for the sake of creating a greater barrier to entry. I've learned most of what I've written in this book the hard way- by screwing it up first, and having painful, frustrating and expensive filmmaking lessons seared into my memory. If I had more clear, concise and practical instruction at the time, I think my work (and income) would've improved exponentially faster. That is the goal of this book: to smooth out the learning curve and give you a hand up the ladder whether you happen to be on the bottom, middle or top of that ladder. It explains almost everything I wish someone would've told me when I started

> This book picks up where *The Shut Up and Shoot Documentary Guide* leaves off. It includes genre-specific storytelling strategies and techniques.

shooting videos for hire. And it's all illustrated and spelled out clearly in plain English with little dashes of slang and humor thrown in just to keep it real and have some fun along the way.

A Shocking Filmmaking Reality Check

Okay here's a reality that I think many new filmmakers fail to grasp:

You *aren't* James Cameron.

And to be clear, you are also not Jane Campion, Todd Phillips, Ang Lee, Spike Lee, Steven Spielberg, Kathryn Bigelow, Michael Moore or whatever other successful director you happen to idolize at the top of the film industry...Yes, I know it's a shocker, but there are still bright-eyed film students with diplomas in-hand and self-taught auteurs with a full video rig and a few films under their belt that think that Hollywood is gonna come knocking on their door and cut them a fat check to turn their visions into films. For some of you that will happen... but chances are it won't be in a few weeks or months after you feel you've "arrived" or paid your dues, but more like a few years, if not a full decade or longer. In the meantime, before Hollywood cuts you those big checks, you've gotta find a way to make a living and stay on your game. If film and tv is your passion, then you'd better find a way to make a living doing something related to film and tv. If you are just starting out on this journey (and it truly is a journey moreso than a career), then your choices are limited to pay the bills and still remain true to your craft.

A Filmmaker's Choices to Pay the Bills

Work for a film/tv company.   Work in the mainstream.   Freelance for hire.

A Show of Hands

Okay, let me see a show of hands: How many people reading this book right now actually make their daily living by creating their own original films and videos?...Now look around- there are like 3 people with their hands up (and one of them is lying). It's most filmmakers' dream to make our living entirely by writing and creating original films and videos that would somehow generate enough income to sustain us or even prosper. The reality of the situation is that only a small percentage of filmmakers actually *make a living* by simply making their own films.

The rest of us are helping other people and companies make *their* films, documentaries and tv shows in one capacity of another. And still another huge faction of filmmakers is working a regular day job completely outside of the industry and making films and videos on the side. My point here is that buying film equipment, learning and making films costs plenty of money and personal filmmaking simply does *not* pay the bills. And after the warm glow of film school or your first successful filmmaking endeavors wear off, the realities of everyday life settle back in and the rent has to be paid. So, all of that is to say: You ain't James Cameron…yet. And until you are, I advise you to find a viable way to keep one foot in the industry, steadily building actual film producing and directing experience and pay the bills all at the same time. One of the industry arenas that can allow you to do all of the above is freelance video.

Tools vs. Skills and Knowledge

I don't care about the much-debated issues of Final Cut Pro 7 vs. Final Cut Pro X vs. Avid…I only care that I am able to tell my story through editing. I don't know or care much about the difference between cameras that record in long GOP video vs. short GOP video – (whatever that is)… I only care that the video quality looks good to my clients and my audience. In other words I am not caught up in the *tools* and *technology* of the trade. I am caught up in the trade itself. And our chief trade as filmmakers is *storytelling*. We should be caught up in moving an audience. We should be caught up in effectively communicating a message. We should be caught up in realizing our creative visions. These are the constants that actually matter.

I'm pretty sure that at the time I attended, I was the brokest student at NYU film school. Back then I hopped subway turnstiles to avoid paying the fare and went to art openings and happy hours for the free appetizers. My consistent lack of money forced me to become more creative and learn to effectively use the limited resources that I *did* have. So I am always most concerned with gathering skills and practical knowledge that can be applied to any budget, any camera, any time. That's what Down and Dirty DV is all about… getting professional video results despite limited resources.

Whether it's a corporate promo piece for a website, a wedding or your favorite local band's debut at a big venue… all we are doing at the core is telling a story, painting a picture of the event, product, performer or client's business for the audience. We are artists and as such I believe we should focus on our brush strokes and not the chemical composition of the paint. I believe we should focus on what's on our canvas, rather than the type of canvas itself. Picasso could paint the hell out of a napkin and it'd still be great art- and sell. The paint (equipment) and the canvas (format) is not what makes a creation great. It's *the content*. The *skill* of the artist. The *effect* it has on the people watching.

The world is full of technical achievement over the most basic and inexpensive element of all- story. But if you learn to master the elements of story *first*, you can collaborate with master technicians. And with experience and education you will gradually improve technical results. The audience will tolerate a great story with technical shortcomings, but they won't tolerate whack and uninteresting video under any circumstances. Freelance video is a training ground – correction: it's a *paid training ground* for film and video storytellers. I know some filmmakers and film professors poo-poo and dismiss this kind of work – and I really like those people, because they leave that many more paying clients for those of us that have immediate financial responsibilities to meet and see the big picture of the unique opportunities presented by creating freelance videos.

> Just because you are getting paid to create a work for hire, doesn't mean that you aren't being *creative*.

Just because you are getting paid to create a work for hire, doesn't mean that you aren't being creative. Sure, some projects will just be straight-forward dry video documentation of a simple event or speaker, but many others will offer ample opportunities to show off and push the limits of your creative talents, if you go in with this goal and mindset, if you truly are a talented filmmaker (or aspire to be one), then you can apply your skills and talents to many projects beyond your own personal work and earn the money and experience you will need to further your loftier long-term filmmaking goals.

I say work on creating videos – any kind of videos – that impact people, that move them, that excite them, that makes them laugh, cry, ponder the ideas you've presented them with...any kind of videos that tell a story. Work on them as often as possible and preferably for pay and you will more rapidly gather practical real-world skills and knowledge that you can apply to *all* of your filmmaking endeavors, be they documentary, narrative, personal or commercial.

Do It. Learn It. Share It. Repeat.

I have discovered that I'm powerless to fix my own filmmaking mistakes of the past, but *because* of them, I've become incredibly empowered to help anyone who wants to listen avoid them. I urge all filmmakers to constantly share, rather than covet the hard won knowledge and lessons they pick up on their filmmaking journey. If everyone shared their knowledge and filmmaking "secrets" more openly, we'd all have an easier go of it and there wouldn't be so many bad videos out there.

I've made it part of my life's mission to share those invaluable filmmaking lessons with anyone who'd rather learn them the easy way. Helping fellow filmmakers is my day job (teaching at NYU's Tisch School of the Arts), my night job (creating instructional books, DVD's and seminars) and my hobby (the Down and Dirty DV Blog and Double Down Film Show podcast). And when I'm not teaching, I'm actively shooting what I teach. And occasionally when time allows, in between all of this, I manage to squeeze in something that resembles a personal life.

Understand this: Done right, filmmaking isn't a just an art form, craft or career option, ...it's a never-ending journey of learning, discovery and practice. And I believe creating videos for hire can be an important, educational and even profitable part of that filmmaking journey.

I truly hope this book will help you somewhere on your own filmmaking journey wherever it takes you. May all your shots be in focus and all your clients be happy. Godspeed and good luck.

Peace, Love and Video
Anthony Q. Artis
Down and Dirty Filmmaker

8:09 a.m. Wednesday, July 13, 2011
Manhattan-bound NJ Transit Train #1013

INTRODUCTION

What Can Freelance Video Do for *You*?

While people may not (yet) be willing to shell out cash for you to create your own original films, if you've developed enough *skills* there are companies and people who will gladly pay you to write, direct and produce custom videos to suit their personal and business needs. While creating marketing, wedding, live event or music videos may not be your end goal (and there's certainly nothing wrong if it *is*), you should still recognize that moreso than the other rent-paying options I mentioned above, freelance video work (even when done for free) provides you with golden opportunities to:

- better hone your directing craft
- finance the cost of your equipment
- gather more filmmaking experience
- learn and master your own equipment
- experiment with new techniques and gear
- build a network of professional crew people
- build a solid reel of professional work

...all while getting paid and keeping the security of your day job. Imagine that–getting paid to become a better filmmaker. When you look at freelance video from this perspective, it's a no-brainer.

Understand that there is absolutely nothing to prevent you from pursuing your career as a bonafide feature or television filmmaker just because you *also* shoot corporate or wedding videos on the side. While it may not always be the most exciting or glamorous work, these endeavors can help you develop the confidence, experience, network and skills you'll need to successfully execute that first feature. (Not to mention that in tough economic times or competitive markets it is those filmmakers that are the most *versatile* in genre and skills that will manage to keep getting paid to create films and videos.) I say be like Clint Eastwood in a Western with your camera...a gun for hire. If it's not against your personal ethics and the clients have a check- shoot it. You have everything to gain and nothing to lose except inexperience.

The Great Con of the Noble "Starving Artist"

Let me be clear, another big reason I wrote this book is because I don't believe in any such thing as a [expletive deleted] "starving artist". That very notion is a horrible con that was played on many of us very early on...we somehow let the prevailing culture convince us that as film and mediamakers we must suffer and be broke and uncomfortable and actually relish in it as some noble romantic idea of being an "artist". It's one of the stupidest notions I've ever heard in my life. And for a brief while I too actually believed it, but like many others I was flim-flammed, bamboozled, conned, tricked into buying into a philosophy that makes no common sense at all...unless you are one of the many entities that makes their money from exploiting the talents of filmmakers.

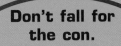

**Don't fall for
the con.**

There is nothing noble about staying
broke after you've invested so
much in learning your craft.

Let me get something straight, if you've paid thousands of dollars for your gear, spent even more on a formal education, toiled and struggled for hundreds of hours to learn your craft- there is nothing "noble" or romantic about being a "starving artist". That's called being a "sucker" where I'm from, particularly when we are working in a multi-billion dollar industry and plenty of other people are making money off of the work we do.

We deserve and should strive to be just as prosperous as anyone else (lawyers, engineers, nurses, etc.) who worked hard to learn and master a specialty craft. We need to get out of the "starving artist" mindset and start thinking like a "prospering artist" and look at all the many ways we can make our hard work actually pay off some of those student loans and B&H equipment invoices.

In *The Shut Up and Shoot Freelance Video Guide* I am sharing with you my perspective, methodologies and specific tips to help you not just make better media, but to make more money while doing so. It's not selling out or a crime to actually make money doing something you love. In fact, I think it's a crime *not* to make money off of something that you're so passionate about and have invested so much in. The freelance video opportunities I discuss in this book are open to anyone with the knowledge, skills and hustle to go after them.

So, what are you *waiting* for, baby?! Time to make it happen. All those stories aren't going to tell themselves. You wanna direct? Produce? Then start directing and producing whatever you can. Read the book, tighten up your film game, then grab your camera and make it do what it do while you learn and earn at the same time. That's Down and Dirty y'all!

CHAPTER 1
IMAGE CONTROL

"Good things come to those who wait, but only the things left by those that hustle."

—Abraham Lincoln

"Always be patient in filmmaking, but don't <u>wait</u> for [anything]. Waiting implies inaction and aspiring filmmakers should always be in action."

—Anthony Q. Artis

Intro: My Low Definition of High-Definition Video

In as much as I like to focus on content and story and stay out for the bottomless rabbit-hole of confusion that is the technical specs and terminology of video, it is necessary to give some basic explanations of certain video concepts and definitions in order to better understand certain camera and TV settings and specs.

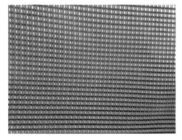

Pixels

Pixels are all the little red, green, and blue microdots that make up the image on a TV or monitor screen. The more pixels there are, the sharper and clearer the picture will be, the better the quality of the image.

Resolution

Video resolution refers to the size of the image in pixels. In camera and TV specs resolution is listed as the number of horizontal pixels × vertical pixels. The most popularly used resolutions are 1920 × 1080 and 1280 × 720 for HD cameras. Standard definition (SD) cameras have a resolution of 720 × 480. When listing HD resolution, most manufacturers simply state the vertical pixels: 1080 or 720 followed by the type of scanning (interlaced or progressive) as in 1080i, 1080p, or 720p. (See next page.)

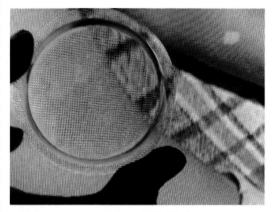

Pixels as seen magnified on a 720p HD plasma screen.

Pixels as seen magnified on an old-school (circa 1976) 480i TV set.

> Pixels are the colored dots that make up a picture on a screen. And resolution is the size of the screen in pixels.

Progressive vs. Interlace Scan Lines

Images are created on a screen by scanning vertically from top to bottom to refresh the picture a specified number of times per second, known as the refresh rate. The two flavors of video scanning are progressive (Yeahhhh!) and interlaced (Boooo!). Progressive scanning goes straight down the vertical rows of pixels to form a complete picture on each frame of video. Interlaced scanning skips every other vertical row of pictures—making one pass on the odd-numbered pixel rows (1, 3, 5, etc.), then a second pass on the even-numbered pixel rows (2, 4, 6, etc.) and alternating between these two half images known as video **fields** to form a single interlaced frame of video. The end result of interlacing is a less detailed and less smooth image than progressive video. This is most noticeable in text displayed on-screen and when pausing an interlaced picture, where funky jagged lines can often be seen in a freeze-framed image.

Refresh Rate

Lastly, we have monitor refresh rate, which refers to the number of times per second an image is scanned on a screen to form the picture. This number is measured in units called Hertz (Hz). So a TV with a 60Hz refresh rate scans the image on-screen 60 times per second to form the image we see. At the time I'm writing this, common refresh rates in Europe are 50Hz and 100Hz, and in the U.S. refresh rates are 60Hz, 120Hz...and most recently, refresh rates have gotten as high as 240Hz on the very baddest HDTV sets or monitors on the shelf. (Not bad meaning "bad", but bad meaning "good"...Michael Jackson bad.)

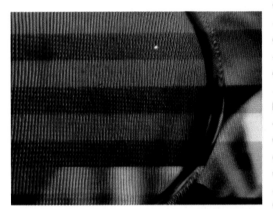

Refresh rate scan lines from CRT (cathode ray tube) TV's and monitors are often visible when shot with a still or video camera. Adjusting your cameras shutter speed a few settings up or down will usually solve the problem.

As technology improves, so will the maximum refresh rates, so by the time you read this, it could be even higher. Just like pixels, a higher refresh rate is a good thing to have on a TV.

Frame Rate

Frame rate refers to how many frames of video you are shooting each second. Frame rates are usually shown in camera specs followed by a designation of "p" for progressive or "i" for interlaced scanning as explained above. So typical frame rate specs are expressed in terms such as 24p, 30p, and 60i. Video frame rate accounts for a good deal of the aesthetic look and feel of the video. For example, film is shot at 24 frames per second (fps), so video that is shot at the same 24 frames per second looks more cinematic and film-like. Video shot at the 30fps looks more "broadcasty," like the local news.

Check Your Menu...First

The first thing that I advise you to do when you pick up any camera before a shoot—is to thoroughly check the *menu settings*. I understand that this can be a tedious and boring exercise. However, impatient shooters should be aware that there are some crucial settings in any video camera menu that can make for some big headaches in postproduction and even during shooting if you are not familiar with what your camera is doing to your footage "under the hood."

One thing you become keenly aware of with experience is that as brilliant as the people who make cameras are, they are *not* filmmakers or cinematographers—they are engineers. And as such, they occasionally make some nonsensical design decisions, so key features important to us are sometimes unintuitive, buried deep in a menu system or otherwise awkwardly arranged. Let's take a look at some of the most crucial menu settings:

Video Format

This is the very first thing you should check, because choice of video **format** will have the greatest effect on the *quality* of your captured image. Prosumer cameras generally have a choice (often a wide choice) of format configurations that you can shoot in. The video format section of the menu is also where you will choose your frame rate—the number of video frames recorded per second (abbreviated as "fps").

This is where you will decide which type of HD footage you're shooting: 1080 vertical lines of resolution × 1920 pixels of horizontal resolution or 720 vertical lines of resolution × 1280 pixels of horizontal resolution. (And just to add a layer of confusion, HDV format cameras shoot 1080 × 1440 pixels!)

Common frame rates are 24fps, 25fps, 30fps, 50fps and 60fps. And just to go a little deeper down this rabbit-hole, this spec might also be followed by an "i" for interlaced scanning or a "p" to indicate progressive scanning.

The first thing you want to do is set your video format in the menu.

Video format settings are typically listed in a menu as **1080p/24**—which means you'd be shooting 1080 vertical lines × 1920 pixel progressive high-definition video at 24fps. (Some models may also list the exact same setting as 1080/24p, preferring to indicate progressive video after the frame rate.)

Shooting at 24fps will give you the most cinematic film-like video, since this is the same frame rate that film is shot at. Shooting at 30fps will give you a traditional broadcast video look.

Generally, it's a good idea to shoot at the very highest quality video format your camera is capable of. The only time you'd switch this up usually is when you are going for a different look, such as a more video or film-like appearance.

Whether you understand all of this or not, the most important thing is that you check with two parties to make sure what you are giving them is compatible with their end needs and/or in-house systems: (1) your clients and (2) the editor. The clients will often be completely clueless, so you want to check with the people serving their technical needs on the other end such as a projectionist, editor, cable station, webmaster, etc. The bottom line is that anyone who will be handling the footage after you shoot it is someone you want to have a conversation with **before** you shoot. They will marvel at your foresight.

Timecode Menu Settings
Record Run
Record Run timecode is the setting you should use most of the time. This means that whenever you start recording, the camera is going to start running and recording timecode, and whenever you hit the record button to stop recording, the timecode is going to stop. When you start recording again, the camera will resume recording timecode at the very next frame.

Time Code: 00:23:14:17	Time Code: 00:23:24:19	Time Code: 00:23:24:20
Recording starts	Recording stops	Recording starts again

Free Run
Free Run timecode, on the other hand, runs continuously like a clock, no matter when you start or stop the recording. So when you are in Free Run mode and press record, then stop for one minute and start recording again, there will be a one-minute jump in the timecode, resulting in a ***timecode break***, which can make your nonlinear editor very unhappy when shooting on DV tape. (For tapeless cameras, it's not such a big deal.)

Time Code: 00:23:14:17	Time Code: 00:23:24:19	Time Code: 00:23:25:19
Recording starts	Recording stops	Recording starts again

…"That seems like a real unnecessary pain in the butt, Anthony. Why would I ever want to shoot in Free Run timecode then?"…I'm glad you asked. Allow me to pontificate.

Free Run timecode is good for one very important function- *multicamera recording*, which is standard for many live events. If you are recording a band performing live with three different cameras all shooting Record Run timecode, you are going to have a real editing nightmare on your hands when you load the footage on your laptop and realize that you also have three different sets of timecodes and no reliable way of matching up the close-up from camera 1 with medium shot from camera 2 or the audience shot from camera 3. If you have a timecode generator and cameras that allow you to **jam timecode** or jam-sync, then you would shoot with all those cameras in Free Run mode, and every shot from the same point in time would have the exact same timecode, so you know precisely where to cut from one camera to the next, and every frame will match regardless of the camera it was shot from.

Timecode Preset

In Timecode Preset mode, the timecode runs the same as in Record Run, except in this mode you can preset the value of the timecode. For example, if you were shooting with your second media card, you could preset the value to 02:00:00:00 as an easy way to tell which card your clips were from in postproduction.

Timecode Display

The Timecode Display function lets you choose what type of timecode information is displayed on your LCD screen or monitor. You have three standard choices on most cameras: user bits, duration, or timecode. Timecode Generated displays timecode on the LCD. (That's what you want.) Duration just keeps a running count of the elapsed time of the recording, so you can know exactly how long a shot is. And user bits are an archaic way of writing some simple alphanumeric **metadata** into your timecode. Most recent generations of cameras have much easier ways to write metadata into your footage, so we ain't gonna be using these bits.

Gain

On many popular prosumer models such as Panasonic's HVX-200 and HMC150 cameras or Sony's EX-1, you can go into the menu to manually assign values to the generic gain settings of Low (L), Medium (M), and High (H). The switch for video gain appears on the side of the camera with three positions marked "L," "M," and "H." The ability to assign specific gain values to these positions is a very nice plus that will make it easier for you to set up the camera for your specific shooting situation or personal preference. Following is a chart of common configurations for a few different situations:

SETTING VIDEO GAIN IN THE MENU

LOW (L)	MED (M)	HIGH (H)	WHEN TO USE IT
0	+6	+12	Normal shooting at "0dB" with option to turn on some gain for moderate low light situations.
0	+12	+18	Normal shooting at "0dB" with option to turn on heavier gain for very low light conditions.
+6	+12	+18	Normal shooting at "+6dB" for continuous low to very low light conditions
−3 or −6	0	+6	Normal shooting at "−3dB" or "−6dB" negative gain to reduce overall picture noise some. (At the expense of some shadow details.)
0	0	0	For normal shooting at "0dB" under continuous well-lit conditions when you don't want to worry about accidentally shooting with any gain on.

FREELANCERS' CAMERA GUIDE—ARRANGED BY BUDGET.

MODEL	SPECS	NOTES
CANON  EOS Rebel T2i DSLR—$1000.00 (body only $700.00)	■ 18.0 MP CMOS (APS-C) ■ 18–135mm ■ 1080p ■ 720p ■ 3" LCD screen	■ Records in H.264 (.mov) format ■ Records to memory card SD/SDHC/SDXC ■ ISO 100–6400, expandable to 12800 ■ 67mm filter ■ Optical image stabilizer ■ Advance live view ■ No XLR inputs ■ Weight = 18.7oz. incl. battery
NIKON D90—$1200.00	■ CMOS ■ DX ■ 3" LCD screen ■ 18mm–105mm	■ Record to SDHC/SD cards ■ 5.8x zoom lens ■ 67mm filter size ■ 12.3 megapixel stills ■ ISO 100–6400 ■ Weight = 1.4lbs

Continued

FREELANCERS' CAMERA GUIDE—ARRANGED BY BUDGET.—CONT'D

MODEL	SPECS	NOTES
PANASONIC  Lumix DMC-GH1—$1500.00	■ AVCHD/ MJPEG ■ 4/3" type MOS ■ 1080p @ 24fps ■ 720p @ 60/30fps ■ 16:9 & 4:3 capable ■ 28–280mm ■ 3" free angle LCD screen ■ 14–140mm ■ mirrorless system	■ Records in H.264 (.mov) format ■ Record to SD or SDHC cards ■ Micro 4/3" system ■ 12.1 megapixel stills ■ 62mm filter size ■ Continuous auto focusing capability ■ 10x zoom ■ HDMI output ■ No XLR input ■ Weight = 13.6 oz (*body-only)
CANON  EOS 7D DSLR—$1,600.00 (*body-only)	■ 3:2 Native ■ 16:9 and 4:3 capable ■ 3" LCD Screen ■ 1080p @ 24/25/30fps ■ 720p @ 50/60fps	■ Video encoded in H.264 (.mov) format ■ 60fps slow motion capable in 720p mode ■ Takes 18 megapixel stills ■ No XLR inputs! ■ Internal Mic/Mini-stereo mic input ■ Separate audio recorder recommended ■ Max video clip length = 12 min. in HD ■ No autofocus in video mode! ■ Follow-focus and support rig recommended

SONY

NEX-VG10—$2,000.00

- AVCHD
- 23.4 × 15.6MM HD CMOS
- 18-200mm—11x zoom lens
- 1080/60i
- SD/SDHC media
- Memory Stick PRO Duo/ Pro-HG Duo
- 11 lux minimum
- 3" LCD screen

- NO XLR inputs
- Interchangeable lenses
- 67mm filter size
- No variable frame rates
- HDMI output
- 14MP still images
- Manual image controls
- Weight = 18.5 oz

PANASONIC

AG-HMC40—$2,400.00

- AVCHD
- 1/4" 3MOS
- 1080p and 720p
- 4-48mm
- 16:9, 4:3, and 3:2
- 1 lux minimum
- 2.7" LCD screen

- Optical Image Stabilizer
- 3.1 lbs (with battery)
- 12x zoom lens
- HDMI output
- Takes 10.6-megapixel stills
- Detachable handle
- Records directly to SD and SDHC memory cards
- 43mm filter size

Continued

FREELANCERS' CAMERA GUIDE—ARRANGED BY BUDGET.—CONT'D

MODEL	SPECS	NOTES
JVC GY-HM100U—$2,400.00	■ ProHD ■ 1/4" CCDs ■ .44" viewfinder ■ 1080p, 24p ■ 3.7-37mm ■ 5 lux minimum ■ 2.8" LCD screen	■ Records to SDHC cards ■ Optical Image Stabilization ■ 46mm Filter size ■ 10x zoom lens ■ Lightweight ■ Poor in low light ■ Poor still image ■ Weight = 3.2 lbs
JVC GY-HMZ1U—$2500.00	■ CMOS ■ PROHD 3D ■ 24p or 60i ■ Twin F1.2 HD lenses ■ 3.5" LCD touch panel	■ 5x zoom (10x in 2D) ■ Built-in timecode ■ SDXC/SDHC flash media card slot ■ XLR inputs ■ 3D digital still recording ■ 3D time lapse recording

CANON

- 3:2 Native
- 16:9 and 4:3 capable
- 3" LCD Screen
- 1.07" CMOS
- Full 35mm frame
- 1080p @ 24/30fps
- Mount-CanonEF

EOS 5D Mark II–$2,500.00 (*body-only)

- Video encoded in H.264 (.mov) format
- 60fps slow motion capable in 720p mode
- Takes 21.1 megapixel stills
- No XLR inputs
- Internal Mic and Mini-stereo mic input
- Separate audio recorder recommended
- No autofocus in video mode!
- Follow-focus and support rig recommended

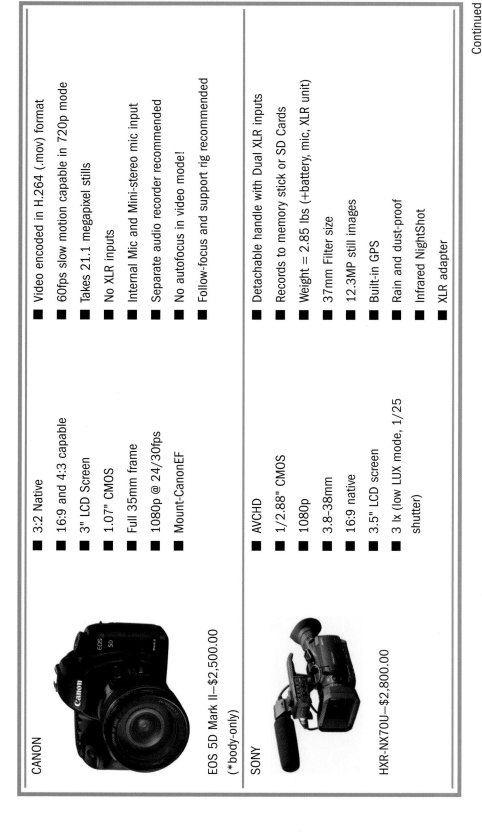

SONY

- AVCHD
- 1/2.88" CMOS
- 1080p
- 3.8–38mm
- 16:9 native
- 3.5" LCD screen
- 3 lx (low LUX mode, 1/25 shutter)

HXR-NX70U–$2,800.00

- Detachable handle with Dual XLR inputs
- Records to memory stick or SD Cards
- Weight = 2.85 lbs (+battery, mic, XLR unit)
- 37mm Filter size
- 12.3MP still images
- Built-in GPS
- Rain and dust-proof
- Infrared NightShot
- XLR adapter

Continued

FREELANCERS' CAMERA GUIDE—ARRANGED BY BUDGET.—CONT'D

MODEL	SPECS	NOTES
CANON XF100 /XF105—$3,000.00/ $4,000.00	■ 1/3" CMOS ■ 4.25–42.5mm ■ 16:9 ■ 4.5 lux (full AUTO mode) ■ 1.6 lux (Manual mode) ■ 0.24 Color viewfinder ■ 1080p/720p mode	■ XF105 *only*—HD/SDI out, SMPTE timecode, Genlock ■ Dual XLR inputs ■ Records to CF and SD cards ■ Built-in 3D assist features ■ 58mm filter size ■ Optical image stabilizer ■ 10x zoom lens ■ Small and lightweight ■ 2.4 lbs ■ Limited zoom ■ Poor sound
SONY HXR-NX3D1U—$3,400.00	■ AVCHD ■ 1/4" Exmor R CMOS ■ Double HD lenses ■ 2D/3D Recording mode ■ 1080p ■ 3.5" LCD glasses-free screen	■ Full HD Steroscopic 3D ■ Timecode recording ■ Side-by-side 3D output via HDMI ■ SD/SDHC/SDXC cards ■ Double HD lenses ■ 12x zoom lens, 10x zoom in 3D ■ Removable audio pod with XLR ports ■ Active SteadyShot in 3D ■ Weight = 1.5 lbs with battery/2.5 lbs with all add-ons

PANASONIC

AG-HMC150P—$3,500.00

- AVC HD, 24p
- 3.9–51mm
- 1080p mode
- 3.5" LCD screen
- 0.44" color viewfinder
- 3 lux minimum

- Records directly to SD and SDHC memory cards
- 72mm filter size
- Weight = 3.7 lbs (4.3 lbs with battery)

SONY

HDR-AX2000—$3,500.00

- AVCHD
- 24p
- 4.1–82mm
- 1/3" CMOS
- 1080p mode
- 3.2" LCD screen
- 0.45 color viewfinder
- 1.5 lux minimum

- Weight = 5 lbs
- Dual XLR ports
- Records to PRO Duo or SD/SDHC cards
- 3 built-in ND filters
- 72mm filter size
- 20x G-lens

Continued

FREELANCERS' CAMERA GUIDE—ARRANGED BY BUDGET.—CONT'D

MODEL	SPECS	NOTES
SONY HVR-Z5U—$4,000.00	■ 1/3" CMOS ■ HDV/DV switchable ■ 1080p/24p ■ 4.1-82mm ■ 1.5 lux minimum ■ 3.2" LCD screen ■ .45" color viewfinder	■ 72mm filter size ■ Weight = 5 lbs ■ 20x zoom lens ■ 1.2MP still capture ■ Records to MiniDV or Compact Flash or CF (with optional add-on) ■ Good in low light ■ 24p
SONY HXR-NX5U—$4000.00	■ AVCHD ■ 3 1/3" CMOS sensors ■ 1080i/1080p/720p ■ 4.1-82mm ■ .45" color viewfinder ■ 3.2 LCD screen ■ 1.5 lux minimum	■ HD-SDI and HDMI Output ■ SMPTE timecode in/out ■ Dual XLR inputs ■ 20x zoom lens ■ 72mm filter ■ Simultaneous HD/MPEG-2 SD capture ■ Memory stick Pro Do/SDHC cards (solid-state storage) ■ Built-in GPS ■ Active SteadyShot ■ Weight = 5 lbs

Continued

PANASONIC

AG-AF100—$ 4,800.00
(*camera body-only)

- AVCHD
- 4/3-type MOS fixed pickup
- 1080p
- 3.45" LCD color screen
- .45" viewfinder

- HD-SDI, HDMI output
- Timecode, waveform
- Uses still and cinema lenses
- Records to SDXC, SDHC, and SD memory cards
- Depth of field similar to 35mm
- Optical ND filter wheel
- Interchangeable lenses
- Excellent image quality
- Record button awkwardly located where zoom rocker would normally be
- Handgrip gets bad reviews
- Overall issues with design choices
- Weight–2.9 lbs

PANASONIC

AG-HPX170—$5,200.00

- DVCPRO HD
- 3.9mm–51mm
- 1/3" CCDs
- 16:9 native
- 1080p mode
- 3.5" LCD screen
- Color viewfinder
- 3 lux minimum

- HD-SDI output
- Weight = 5 lbs with battery
- Records to solid-state P2 cards
- 13x zoom lens
- Optical image stabilizer
- Highly compressed video

FREELANCERS' CAMERA GUIDE—ARRANGED BY BUDGET.—CONT'D

MODEL	SPECS	NOTES
NIKON D3S—$5200.00 (*body-only)	■ 12.1 Mp FX CMOS ■ Native 3:2 ■ 720p @ 24fps ■ 3" LCD screen	■ Dual Compact Flash card slots ■ HDMI HD output ■ 12.1 megapixel stills ■ Auto focus tracking ■ Fully weather sealed ■ Video fixed @ 24fps (no 29.97 or 30 option) ■ Limit to 5 minute clips of HD video ■ No image stabilization ■ No XLR inputs ■ Weight = 2lbs (body only)
SONY HVR-Z7U—$5,300.00	■ HDV/DVCAM/DV ■ 4.4-52.8mm—12x zoom lens ■ 1/3" CMOS sensor ■ 1080i/24p mode ■ 3.2" LCD screen ■ 1.5 lux minimum ■ Uses Compact Flash cards and MiniDV tapes ■ 72mm filter size ■ Weight = 5.3 lbs	■ Interchangeable lens ■ HDMI output ■ Dual XLR audio ■ A bit front-heavy ■ 1/3" bayonet mount

PANASONIC

HVX-200A—$5,500.00

- 1/3" CCDs
- 16:9 native
- 4.2mm-55mm fixed lens
- 1080p
- 3.5" LCD screen
- 0.44" monochrome / color switchable viewfinder
- 3 lux minimum
- 82mm filter size
- Records to solid-state P2 cards
- Weight = 5.2 lbs
- DVCPro HD

SONY

NEX-FS100—$5600.00
(body only $5000.00)

- AVCHD
- 18-200mm
- 1080p
- 3.5" lcd screen
- .28 lux minimum
- S35 CMOS
- Color viewfinder
- Slow & quick motion
- E-mount interchangeable lens system (most others via adaptor)
- Records to SD/SDHC/SDXC
- 67mm filter size
- 11x zoom lens
- Geotagging with built-in GPS
- Dual XLR inputs
- HDMI Output
- No built in ND filters
- Weight = 2.3lbs (body only) 6.1lbs (w/lens)

Continued

FREELANCERS' CAMERA GUIDE—ARRANGED BY BUDGET.—CONT'D

MODEL	SPECS	NOTES
CANON XF300 /XF305—$6,500.00/ $7,500.00	■ 3 × 1/3" CMOS Sensors ■ 4.1–73.8mm 18x HD L Series Zoom ■ 1080p ■ 16:9 Native ■ 82mm filter size ■ 4" LCD color screen ■ .52" color viewfinder ■ 4.5 lux minimum ■ Weight = 5.8 lbs	■ XF305 model ONLY—HD/SDI out, SMPTE timecode, Genlock ■ Records to Compact Flash (CF) cards ■ Slow-motion and fast-motion modes ■ SuperRange Optical Image Stabilization system ■ MXF file format ■ MPEG-2 50Mbps Codec ■ Dual XLR inputs
JVC GY-HM750—$7,000.00	■ 1/3" CCDs ■ 1080i/p 720p ■ 4.4-61.6mm ■ 4.3" LCD screen ■ .45" viewfinder ■ 1.25 lux minimum	■ Records to SDHC cards or optional SxS adapter ■ HD/SD-SDI, FireWire output ■ Variable frame rates ■ 82mm filter size ■ 14x zoon lens ■ Shoulder Mount Form Factor ■ Native MOV, MP4, AVI Capture ■ Weight = 7.5 lbs (includes lens, viewfinder, mic, batter)

PANASONIC

AG-HPX370—$7,200.00

- 1/3" 2.2MP 3-MOS
- 16:9 native
- AVC-Intra/DVCPRO HD
- DVCPRO 50/DVCPRO/DV
- 0.4 lux minimum
- 3.2" LCD screen
- .45" monocrome/color switchable viewfinder

- Interchangeable 17x Fujinon HD Zoom Lens
- Timecode, Genlock
- HS/SD-SDI
- Improved noise sensitivity
- Records to P2 and SD memory cards
- Scan reverse function for use with film lenses
- 4 channels of audio
- Camera can be remotely controlled
- Weight = 11 lbs

SONY

PMW-F3K—$19,000.00

- Super 35mm Exmor CMOS
- 35mm, 50mm, and 85mm
- Full HD, native 23.98p
- 3.5" color LCD screen
- .45" color viewfinder
- Lux not specified
- Weight = 5.3 lbs (camera only)

- SxS ExpressCard/34 (x2)
- PCM Uncompressed 1-bit audio
- HD-SDI output
- Genlock, Timecode
- Records using MPEG-2 long GOP
- PL Mount Adapter for compatibility with 35mm Cine lenses
- Slow and quick motion function
- 3D system link option
- Supports Look-up Table (LUT) for dailies and on-set color management

Intro

I think there are equally compelling arguments both for and against shooting video on DSLR cameras. (DSLR = Digital Single Lens Reflex) I'll try to share both arguments and let *you* decide whether it's a good choice for you. DSLR video cameras are essentially high-quality ***still photo cameras*** that now have added HD video functionality. As such, DSLR cameras are designed first and foremost with still photo shooting in mind–**NOT** video. This means they have some major limitations and require you to jump through a few more hoops than if you were to just shoot with a traditional video camera.

Here are some of the biggest DSLR issues as I see them....

1. Major Audio Limitations

One of the biggest drawbacks of DSLR cameras right out of the box is that they do not have XLR audio inputs. Instead, they come with a single mini-stereo audio input. This means you can't plug in any of your professional-quality mics if you only have a camera. Instead, you will need some type of audio adapter to feed sound into the camera, or you will need to record sound on a separate device. Not only that, but many popular DSLR models, such as the **Canon 7D** do not allow you to manually control the audio. They have **autogain** audio only, which is simply unacceptable (i.e., whack) for professional-quality work. Also, if you go the route of a separate audio recorder, you will also need to sync the sound with the picture in postproduction–film style, which is an extra step you don't have to take when shooting with a dedicated video camera. Most DSLRs do have a tiny built-in onboard mic, but it's not good enough for professional-quality audio capture. It's primarily useful for a **"dirty track"** for syncing or just recording personal home video. And to top it all off, as of the time I'm writing this, there are no on-screen audio meters to show you your audio levels. Lame!

2. You Need to Assemble a Franken-Camera

Because these are still cameras first and foremost, they are shaped and held like still cameras, which are normally way too shaky for motion-picture photography, so you need to assemble what my fellow author Kurt Lancaster refers to as a "Franken-Camera" in his book *DSLR Cinema: Crafting the Film Look with Video*. This means shooting with some type of third-party support system that usually involves some combination of a shoulder mount, grip handles, support rods, mounting rods, and often a counter weight. If you've only been shooting video with traditional prosumer video cameras, this is a whole other way of holding and operating a camera that will take some practice and getting used to. (It's actually much more like shooting with a film camera.)

3. Great Danger of Soft-Focused Shots

All the DSLR cameras have one chief asset that makes them extremely attractive: a big, beautiful video imaging chip. The size of the video chip is to a video camera what the size of a negative is to a film camera–so the bigger the chip, the better and more high resolution the image, also the greater the natural **shallow depth of field** (DOF). However, what comes along with high resolution and extremely shallow depth of field is hypercritical focus, meaning you've gotta get it right every time all the time, baby, or your clients will definitely notice. And unfortunately, the built-in LCD screens on the backs of these cameras are even smaller than those found on most prosumer video cameras, so you have no accurate way to judge this very critical element of focus on these super high-res HD images. Not to mention that on one of the most popular models, the Canon 7D, the focus assist, which magnifies the LCD screen image to help you focus, is disabled during recording.... Like I said, whack.

4. Overheating and 12-Minute Clip Limit

Another limitation of DSLR shooting is that you are limited to a maximum shot length of 12 minutes. The problem is that the camera automatically cuts itself off and stops recording after 12 minutes to avoid overheating that giant imaging chip. This probably isn't a big deal for narrative and scripted projects where the average take will probably run well below 12 minutes. However, in the world of freelance video where some of our easiest and lucrative gigs are event videos, a chief requirement is that we must shoot *continuously* for a long time, such as in the case of concerts, speeches, wedding ceremonies, etc. I don't care how dope it looks—your client is not gonna be happy if you missed part of the wedding vows or 10 seconds in the middle of their encore performance of their signature song, so this issue has to be carefully considered in the context of what you'll be shooting, especially when dealing with live events.

5. It's Really Not That Much Cheaper

I suspect that the biggest reason DSLR cameras have exploded onto the indie, student, and freelance scene is the price. At $1800–$2500 each, they are considerably cheaper than the average HD prosumer video cameras, which are more in the $3,000 to $7,000 range and don't offer nearly as much raw image quality as popular DSLR models such as Canon's 5D Mark II. However, here's the catch…if you want to routinely shoot with a DSLR camera in any professional capacity at all, you will ultimately want to add on a bunch of accessories to just to make it fully functional and more practical for video shooting, most typically:
    a. Audio Recorder or Adapter ($300–$500)
    b. Support Rig ($500–$1,800)
    c. External Monitor ($200–$600)
    d. Follow Focus ($200–$1,800)
    e. Matte Box ($500–$1,100)

So by the time you complete your Franken-Camera rig, you've laid out about as much money or very possibly more than if you just had purchased a dedicated video camera to begin with.

6. Rolling Shutter Issues

The first few generations of prosumer video cameras were powered by CCD imaging chips. The new crop of DSLRs are powered by cheaper CMOS imaging chips that allow manufacturers to pack a lot more bang for the buck in chip size. However, like anything else that does the same thing for less, there's a drawback. In this case the drawback to CMOS technology is that it's more prone to an issue called **rolling shutter**. What this means in practical terms is that if you tilt, pan, or otherwise move the camera swiftly, there's a good chance that the resulting image will blur, distort, and/or appear "stuttery." So camera moves with DSLR cameras are best limited only to those that are slow and steady.

7. The Depth of Field Is Too Shallow

Sure, shallow depth of field looks more cinematic and film-like, but there's such a thing as too much of a good thing in my opinion. There are plenty of times when it works well for the genre and the story, but there are also plenty of times when it doesn't. A bride standing at the altar or a close-up of an ice-cold beverage on a table looks great in the super-shallow depth of field of DSLRs. However, seeing only one skier clearly out of a pack of 12 racing down a slope or watching a motivational speaker giving a speech at a podium are situations in which super-shallow depth of field can be awkward and impractical for the content. Not only that, but heavy use of shallow DOF is essentially an aesthetic style, and like all aesthetic preferences, it can also go *out of style*. (Remember the frenetic handheld style popular in indie films in the '90s like Laws of Gravity, Clerks, El Mariachi? Don't see so much of that style anymore, do you?) Any stylistic choice such as shallow depth of field, should be motivated by the content and story on screen and not done just because you could. Shallow depth of field is a powerful visual storytelling device that can be used to great effect to shift the audience's attention, give meaning to props and characters or visually create certain emotional states. So if you can't answer the crucial question as to *why* a given shot has extreme shallow depth of field in terms of **the story** you are telling, you are probably overusing it and diluting the real impact of the technique. As these cameras find their way into the hands of more and more clueless amateur shooters, heavy use of shallow depth of field may become real old real quick and ruin it for us all, that's all I'm saying.

...So those are all the main reasons I think DSLRs are whack. However, there are two sides to every issue. So in the interest of being fair and balanced, let's look at the flip side of shooting with DSLRs as I lay out all the reasons why DSLR cameras are da bomb on the next page.

Intro

So I just told you how whack and impractical DSLR cameras are, but now I'm gonna share all the genuine reasons I think DSLR cameras are the bombdiggity....

1. You Can't Beat the Image Quality for the Price

As of the moment I'm writing this, you simply cannot beat the superior image quality of DSLR cameras for the entry-level price of less than $3,000. For a fraction of the cost, you can shoot images on a chip that is more than 10 times the size of dedicated video cameras that cost triple the price.

2. Super-Duper Stealth Mode

When you're "borrowing" sensitive locations (i.e., NYC subway train, Beverly Hills Mall, etc.), shooting in a hostile environment (i.e., Middle East protest, inner-city 'hood, etc.), or are in any other situation that requires you to shoot covertly, DSLR cameras are a good choice because they draw considerably less attention and look just like still cameras. The lower-profile innocent appearance of a video-capable DSLR camera versus a full-fledged video camera could ultimately help you avoid being kicked out (the subway), captured (Syria), or punched in the mouth (inner-city 'hood). So if you regularly shoot in risky places, a DSLR is an ideal choice. (See also "Borrowing Locations" on page 240.)

3. You Can Build the Rig as You Go

Yes, sooner or later, you will want to buy some accessories to make your camera fully video-friendly–such as an audio recorder or adapter, a monitor, a support system, and perhaps a follow-focus and all the little bells and whistles you'll need to make the camera actually do what it do. But the beauty of DSLR shooting for broke filmmakers is that you don't have to get everything all at once. You can save up for the initial camera purchase and then buy some "bells" one paycheck and maybe get some "whistles" for Christmas and slowly build your rig as your finances allow. The most important thing is that you just get into the game, and the low entry-level price of DSLR cameras offers easier access to filmmaking and the ability to slowly and steadily build a formidable **"Franken Camera"** with full video functionality and superior image quality.

4. More Practical Options for Multicamera Shoots

Again, the math is real simple here. It's a lot easier to buy or hustle up three affordable $2,000 cameras than it is to pull together three $6,000 cameras. The rental rates for DSLR cameras are considerably cheaper than their prosumer and professional video counterparts. Also, because these cameras have become so popular so fast, chances are if you are tied into any filmmaking community or group at all, there are probably at least two other people who have DSLR cameras, particularly Canon 7D's, 5D's, or T2i's, which are the most popular models as I write this. So not only is it easier to gather three DSLR cameras, but you can also probably get three cameras of the exact same brand, so you won't have to worry as much about matching up the images. This popularity also means it's easier to find experienced operators if you rent or borrow the cameras from friends.

5. You Can More Easily Borrow the Lenses

Borrowing lenses is even easier than borrowing cameras. Because these are still camera lenses and not dedicated video lenses, they are much more affordable and in greater supply around you. For every one person you know who's a videographer, you probably know two who shoot still photos and have a few decent lenses that you can borrow. Some of my friends have even formed informal DSLR and lens co-ops. Each has invested in a different set of lenses, and they simply borrow and trade them back and forth whenever they shoot, as well as loaning and borrowing each other's cameras for multicamera shooting. (The stakes aren't as high with the costs of DSLR cameras, so in general I've noticed that people are a little more generous with a Canon 7D than, say, their $25,000 Red camera package.) And again, even if you don't have any friends with compatible still camera lenses you can borrow, these lenses are also much cheaper to rent and save up for as you go. So DSLRs offer you an affordable option to swap out and shoot with superior prime and zoom lens versus many popular prosumer video cameras which have fixed lenses that you can never change.

6. Great Low-Light Sensitivity

Another major advantage of having a big, beautiful imaging chip is that the big chip doesn't need nearly as much light as smaller prosumer video chips. This means it performs much better in low lighting conditions—a huge advantage for indie, low-budget, documentary, and international filmmakers who often have to rely more on natural lighting conditions and stealth shooting to pull off their projects. Fewer lights means less time, hassle, and money spent lighting and more time spent shooting your project.

7. Super-Duper Shallow Depth of Field

Apart from price, video-capable DSLR cameras offer extremely shallow depth of field. Shallow depth of field is the cinematic look that shows your subject in sharp, clear focus while the background behind them is completely soft-focused (or the opposite if you prefer). While you can achieve decent shallow depth of field from any prosumer camera under the right conditions (primarily long lens and open aperture), you can achieve an even greater shallow depth of field under almost any circumstances with a DSLR camera just by virtue of the larger chip size. This look is associated with the cinematic look of 35mm film, which also naturally has a much more shallow depth of field because it uses a big negative. DSLR cameras can achieve such an extreme depth of field that you could easily show someone's eyes in focus while their nose and ears are out focus...if you're into that sort of thing.

Conclusion

...So those are all my basic pros and cons of DSLR shooting. The extra hoops you have to jump through to make DSLR cameras truly video-friendly may not work for everyone, but make no mistake about it, DSLR cameras are a revolutionary game-changer in the world of indie film. They are the very definition of a "disruptive" technology. Suddenly, the entry bar was lowered, and the video quality bar was raised simultaneously, opening the flood gates for a new generation of Down and Dirty filmmakers to do what we do with better image quality than ever. The DSLR movement may be just an intermediary step to more affordable large-format prosumer video cameras. Time will tell, but for now, I think the long-term future of these powerful and awkward new filmmaking tools is still to be determined.

When it comes to video shooting, DSLR cameras have some "issues." But hey, don't we all? However, just as in life, "issues" are only a big problem when you don't deal with them (or bury them deep deep in your soul). So here's how to give your DSLR camera some much needed video therapy or at least hide its worst shortcomings....

ISSUE	PROBLEM	SOLUTION(S)
No manual audio control	■ You can't record professional-quality audio if you can't have 100% control over your levels. ■ Cameras autogain boosts hiss when it's quiet on set.	■ Use a preamp or adapter that has XLR inputs and manual control. ■ Record audio separately on a digital audio recorder. ■ Record audio separately on a digital video/audio recorder.
No XLR inputs	■ You can't use professional XLR mics and sound gear. ■ Unbalanced mini-stereo audio is more noisy.	■ Use a preamp, digital recorder with XLR, or external video/audio recorder. ■ Use an XLR to mini-stereo adapter cable.
No on-screen audio levels	■ It's impossible to accurately judge your audio levels. ■ You can't adjust tone from a mixer.	■ Use Magic Lantern firmware, which adds on-screen audio levels. ■ Use an external video/audio recorder with on-screen levels.
Depth of field is too shallow	■ You would actually like a person's nose and eyes to both be in focus at the same time. ■ You want the background and foreground to be in focus.	■ Shoot with wider lenses or wider zoom lens settings. ■ Shoot at a higher F-stop (F8 or above). ■ Avoid ND filters if you don't absolutely need them.
12-minute clip limit	■ You may need to record longer than 12 minutes at a time. ■ You may miss part of a wedding, speech, or performance.	■ Shoot with multiple cameras ■ Stagger the start time when multicamera shooting so all cameras don't run out at the same time.
Hard to judge focus	■ Big picture—little LCD screen makes it hard to tell what's sharp. ■ There's a high risk of soft-focus shots.	■ Use an external monitor—the bigger and sharper, the better. ■ Use Magic Lantern firmware, which adds peaking functionality.

ANATOMY OF A DSLR FRANKEN RIG

Image courtesy of B&H Advertising

VIEWFINDER

This little add-on magnifies the LCD viewfinder and can be used in lieu of a monitor.

ONBOARD MIC

You'll want something better than the camera's little built-in mic for better audio quality.

FOLLOW FOCUS

This is an expensive but useful tool to make focusing smoother and more accurate. You can mark exact focal points on a follow focus and have an A.C. pull focus for you.

HD MONITOR

The most essential accessory in order to better judge your image quality and focus.

MATTE BOX

A matte box has two important functions: to hold filters and to shade the lens from sunlight.

ARM MOUNT

This an adjustable support arm that can be used to easily move your monitor to various viewing positions.

SUPPORT RIG

DSLRs are small and less steady when handheld, so you'll need a support rig—rods or some other type of handheld apparatus. You'll also need something sturdier than your camera body to mount all these accessories to—hence a support rig.

XLR AUDIO ADAPTER

Professional mics have XLR connections. DSLRs don't. So you'll need an adapter box to connect pro mics and mixers to your DSLR and help you manage the audio quality.

EXTENSION	NAME/TYPE	COMMENTS
.mp4/.avi/.h264	H.264	■ High quality ■ Standard for video podcast ■ iPad, iPhone, iPod playable ■ Good for client delivery online ■ Relatively small file size ■ Cross-compatible with Macs and PCs ■ a.k.a. AVC (Advanced Video Coding)
.mov	QuickTime	■ High quality ■ Has a wide range of compression formats from its cousins .mp4 or H.264 to uncompressed 10bit ■ Can be used for broadcast television
.wmv	Windows Media Video	■ Used for Microsoft proprietary compression ■ Compatible with PCs and Microsoft devices ■ Flip for Mac and VLC Player can be downloaded in order to play WMVs on a Mac.
.mp4	MPEG 4	■ Similar to H.264 ■ Utilizes similar compression methods within QuickTime Pro ■ Some portable devices require .mp4 files ■ Can be played and converted to another format using QuickTime or MPEG Streamclip.
.pict, /.pct, /.pic	PICT	■ Used for stills or video
.tiff	TIFF	■ Used for stills or video ■ High quality ■ Often used for graphics delivery
.jpeg	JPEG	■ Used for stills and web graphics ■ Used to retain quality but avoid large file sizes

EXTENSION	NAME/TYPE	COMMENTS
.png	Portable Network Graphic	■ The file extension seen when "screenshots" are taken on a Mac computer ■ An option to be used in graphics if there are no alternatives such as JPEGs or TIFFs
.gif	Graphic Interface File	■ Replaced by PNG files, as well as other image formats such as JPEG/TIFF/PICT ■ Can still be seen on old-school websites ■ At times used for small, low-resolution animations/movies embedded within websites
.acc	Advanced Audio Coding	■ The default audio standard for Apple devices like the iPad, iPod, iPhone, and iTunes ■ Meant to be a replacement for MP3s ■ Keeps audio file size low but high quality when compared to an .aiff
.wav	Wave or Waveform Audio File Format	■ Often the audio file type used on professional production audio recording devices due to its high quality
.mp3	MP3	■ Standard format for music files ■ Playable on iPad, iPod, iPhone, Mac, PCs, and many other MP3 devices ■ Many .mp3 files can fit on a CD.
.aiff	Audio Interchange File Format	■ High-quality standard for audios ■ Often used on professional production audio recording devices for its high quality ■ Noncompressed CD-quality audio ■ Lossless format, similar to .WAV files ■ Commonly used to burn audio CDs
.amr	Adaptive Multirate Codec File	■ Primarily used for speech recording ■ Used for voice memos on some cell phones

MEDIA	CAPACITY/SPEED	COMMENTS
 SD Card	8GB–16GB Slower than SDHC	■ Cannot be used in SDHC card devices ■ Used in consumer still and video cameras ■ A reusable efficient media over tape
 **SDHC Card**	4GB–32GB (*New SDXC can store up to 1TB!) Speed varies by card class.	■ Cannot be used in SD card devices ■ Used in prosumer video cameras ■ Used in a variety of digital still cameras ■ A reusable efficient media over tape ■ Protection tab to avoid accidental erasure
SxS Card	8GB–64GB and growing 800 MB/sec. 11 (megabits per second)	■ Aka PC Express Cards ■ Used in prosumer and professional cameras from Sony (XDCAM) and Arri (Alexa) ■ Comparatively pricey ■ Mounts directly into older Macbook Pro laptops ■ Adapters are available to use on later Apple Macbook Pro models ■ Used in prosumer and professional cameras from Sony (XDCAM) and Arri (Alexa) ■ A reusable efficient media over tape ■ Like tape, each card comes with a protection tab to avoid accidental erasure
 **P2 Card**	4GB–64GB 1.2 GB/sec.	■ aka P.C. Cards (type 2) ■ Used in prosumer/pro Panasonic cameras ■ A reusable efficient media for recording instead of tape ■ Record protect tab to avoid accidental erasure

MEDIA	CAPACITY/SPEED	COMMENTS
Compact Flash Card	32GB-128GB and growing Speed varies by manufacturer up to 100MB/sec.	■ Popular in Canon prosumer video cameras ■ A reusable efficient media better than tape ■ Protection tab to avoid accidental erasure ■ Used in a variety of high-quality still cameras
USB Drive	4GB–128GB and growing 60 MB/sec. speed varies by computer	■ aka "thumb drives" ■ Very small and pocket portable ■ Available in a variety of different styles ■ Convenient way to share demos with clients ■ More efficient than data DVDS
Bus Drive	Up to 1TB and growing 5400rpm = good for data transfer, NOT for editing 7200rpm = good for data transfer and light editing	■ Small and portable ■ Powered by USB port on computer via a USB cable ■ Does not require AC power ■ Perfect solution for remote locations ■ Good to have for run-and-gun shooting ■ Good option to deliver/ship projects
Solid State Drive	Typically 40-120GB	■ Aka SSD ■ Flash memory w/ no moving parts ■ More durable and faster than HDD's ■ Comparatively very expensive
Hard Drive	Up to 4TB and growing 5400rpm = good for data transfer, <u>NOT</u> editing 7200rpm = good for data transfer and all editing	■ Best option for video editing ■ Largest storage capacity ■ Good for long-term project archiving ■ Backpack portable ■ Different ports for different transfer speeds ■ Insanely fast Thunderbolt ports avail. soon for compatible devices are 10 GB/sec.

A DOWN AND DIRTY RAINCOVER

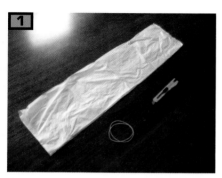

Get a clear plastic trash liner or a plastic bag from the vegetable section of the grocery store if it's big enough. Cut about a 4" slit in the side of the bag (just big enough for your hand to fit through).

Place the camera inside so that the lens is facing out the opening of the bag and the slit you cut is at the bottom of the camera.

Secure the bag around the lens hood with a rubberband so that only the lens glass is left exposed. Smooth out the plastic over the LCD screen and secure with a separate rubberband.

Slip your hand in through the bottom slit and shoot like normal.

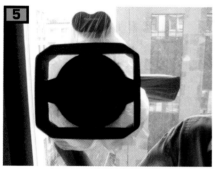

Front View: Ready for drizzle and snow.

OTHER TIPS FOR SHOOTING IN WET WEATHER

1. It's always best to *still* have an assistant with an umbrella for heavy rain.
2. Use two bags for extra protection.
3. Dry off any exposed parts of the camera that get wet ASAP after shooting.
4. Consider a pro raincover or water-resistant camera like the **Sony HXR-NX70U** for regular shooting in bad weather.

Professional Raincover = $200
Down and Dirty Raincover = $0

Zebra Stripes 101

Let me be clear: *overexposing an image is the absolute worst thing you can do when it comes to image quality*. When you overexpose a shot, crucial details such as skin texture, words on paper, surface textures, etc., are rendered on video as blobs of white nothingness.

Once those crucial visual details of texture, words on white paper, skin tone, etc., are lost to overexposure, they are gone forever, baby, and they ain't coming back. So you need to always be vigilant and mindful of keeping a good exposure on your subjects. Whether it's a person, place, or thing- it's gotta be properly exposed. It's very easy to misjudge exposure on a little camera LCD screen, especially when shooting in daylight. Lucky for you, there are **zebra stripes**.

Zebra Stripes Are Your Friend

Zebra Stripes (like Anthony Artis) are your *friend*. We are both here to tell you when you're doing something wrong and help you correct it…before it's too late. *Zebra stripes* are a camera function that helps you judge exposure by superimposing vibrating diagonal stripes on the overexposed parts of the image. These stripes are only seen on your camera's viewfinder or LCD screen and are *not* recorded to tape. Look for a switch or check your camera's menu for a "zebra" function. Set the zebra stripes function to "100%." Now, whenever you point the camera at anything that's *more* than 100% of the acceptable video level (i.e., overexposed), you will know without guessing.

You don't want to close down the lens to get rid of *all* of the zebra stripes in the image. There should be some zebra stripes on the natural highlights in the image such as lights, jewelry, the sun, shiny objects, oily skin, etc. Where you *don't* want to have a significant number of zebra stripes is on your subject's face or important details in the frame. If there are zebra stripes on your subject(s) face or on important details of the image, try these remedies: (1) Stop down your lens; (2) use an ND filter (or a graduated filter for an overexposed sky); (3) recompose the shot to include less of the overexposed area.

You can take some steps to fix an overexposed shot like this in post…

…but the visual details in her clothing and the pavement are gone forever.

Gain

Your camera's video gain function allows you to get a better exposure in low-light situations. It's a way of artificially brightening the image. You aren't really letting more light into the lens as you do when you open the iris or lower the shutter speed. Instead, you are *electronically* brightening the picture, which works to boost exposure, but has one big drawback: it adds video **noise.**

Just like audio noise, gain is measured in decibels (dB). And just like it sounds, the "noise" that comes along with using gain is not a good thing. It's essentially grainy static that degrades your image. It's a permanent part of the recorded image and cannot be removed in post, so

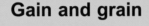

Gain and grain

0dB – 3dB – 6dB – 9dB – 12dB – 15dB – 18dB

what you see is what you get. Most prosumer cameras have gain settings that increase by increments of 3dB and run the range of 0dB (no gain) to 18dB (very grainy and degraded). The higher you set the gain, the more noise you'll add to the picture.

The fact that gain degrades the image doesn't mean that we don't want to *ever* use gain. It just means that we don't want to ever use a decibel more of gain than what we need to get a decent exposure. Think of gain like salt: sometimes you'll absolutely need it to make something taste good, but if you use *too much*, you can ruin your food completely.

Occasionally, you will be in a situation that requires a full 12dB or 18dB of gain, but better to get a grainy shot of the lead singer as he's crowd-surfing the audience or a grainy shot of the bride and groom's first dance in a dim ballroom than to completely *miss* a golden moment because it's too dark. If you have control over the lighting in a low-light situation, it's always preferable to add more light first or lower your shutter speed slightly, but this will often not be a practical reality, so we have to use gain when the situation calls for it.

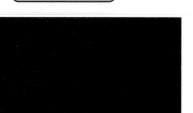

0dB Gain

3dB Gain

6dB Gain

9dB Gain

12dB Gain

18dB Gain

Gain is just like salt: you need it sometimes, but if you use any more than what you need, you can ruin the dish!

Changing Mood with White Balance

In my lighting workshops, I often see young filmmakers put a great deal of time and effort into experimenting, switching, and finding just the right colored lighting gels and effects to set a certain mood. There's nothing wrong with this, and experimenting is truly the only real way I know to effectively learn and master the craft of lighting. However, there is also an easier, cheaper, and faster way to dramatically alter the color and moods of any given scene that should be experimented with as well, especially when you are tight on time: manipulating white balance. By learning to effectively manipulate your camera's white balance, you can achieve a variety of dramatically different feels for a scene with nothing more than the right color "white card" and the push of a button.

Natural White	Sickly Green	Cool Blue

Here, the scene was white balanced to the natural "daylight" (actually a 5600K HMI light) spilling onto the subject.	In this shot, the students white balanced on the pale pink wall behind the subject to create a cool, sickly green feel. Notice the wall now looks white.	In this shot the filmmakers white balanced to a white card under very warm tungsten light to create an extremely cool blue look.

Secrets of the Color Wheel

In addition to a standard white card, you can also white balance on a **warming card**. A warming card is simply a pale blue or pale green card. When you white balance to either of these pale cool colors, it will make the overall color tone of your scene appear warmer. This generally has a pleasing effect on skin tones and feels more warm and fuzzy, as opposed to cool and sterile. As always, whether or not you use a warm card should be dictated by the story being told. A touchy-feely family dinner scene lends itself to warm tones. A slick futuristic-looking science lab lends itself to cooler tones. You can also do more extreme color shifts by white balancing on other colors. Soft pastel-like colors will result in more subtle color shifts, while saturated colors will produce an extreme shift. If you want your whole scene to be really red or blue or something extreme like that, you are better off doing the color effect in postproduction, because if you white balance to achieve anything other than a subtle shift in tone, you are "married" to it and it can't be easily undone in post (if it can be undone at all).

White-balancing on a color will give you the opposite color on the color wheel.

WB on very pale blue (or green) to warm a scene.

Note: There are two warm cards that you can download and print out on a color printer on the Superfly Illmatic Bonus website at: www.freelancevideoguide.com

Down and Dirty guerrilla filmmaking ain't about the tools—it's about acquiring the *skills and knowledge* to maximize whatever tools you do have. Whether that's a $1,500 fixed-lens camcorder or a $19,000 super cam, you gotta know how to make it do what it do. Here are some tricks of the trade to get more bang for your buck in production value from any camera...

Shallow Depth of Field

Use shallow depth of field (DOF) to create a more cinematic big budget look from any camera. To do this effectively, you'll need a large enough space to get some real depth in your frame and separate your subject from the background. The more depth, the greater the effect. (See "Focal Length"pg. 46.)

Multiple Camera Angles

Shooting with multiple camera angles will make your project much more dynamic and professional looking with a variety of shots, camera angles, and focal lengths. You can use multiple cameras or, with some forethought and few more takes, give the illusion of multiple cameras. (See "Covering a Musical Show" pg. 302.)

Great Lighting

Great lighting will give you more bang for your buck than just about anything else. Hire a good gaffer; or experiment and learn to create artful pockets of light and shadow, make your subjects pop, soften features, hilight props, and "paint" a frame with light. Lighting makes the image even more so than the camera itself.

Keep It Moving

A static shot on a static tripod is the height of boredom and public access TV production values. If you want your images to feel dynamic and hold an audience's attention, sporadically work in some well-timed pans, tilts, zooms, rack-focus moves, dolly shots, and solid handheld camerawork in between those rock-steady tripod shots.

Basic Handheld Technique

1 Keep both elbows against your body to brace the camera. Use your free hand to steady your camera hand or to steady the camera by gripping the lens.

2 Keep your lens zoomed out as wide as possible.

3 Assume comfortable footing and lower your center of gravity slightly as you twist left or right to follow the action.

4 Avoid zooming *IN*. Move in closer or further away to adjust the composition of your shot.

Standard

Best all-around handheld position. Very stable and easy to pan or tilt. Good for holding on closer, more intimate shots. Also best position for heavier cameras.

Up High

Use this position to shoot over crowds when you get blocked out of the action. Also good for shooting over obstacles such as cars and fences. Use for a more dramatic overhead angle on a scene.

Down Low

Good for creative POV shots. Use to show anonymous legs and feet as people enter or exit a location. Rest on floor for a dramatic wide shot. Fun move for dancing subjects.

Cradle

Very steady position. Switch to cradle position to give your arms a break. Good position for funky active "MTV-style" camerawork. Use to shoot shorter subjects and people who are seated.

The Problem with HD

Today's crop of prosumer HD cameras offers us unprecedented image quality comparable to cameras that cost two to three times as much just a few years ago. We can now shoot crisp, clean HD footage with 720 or 1080 lines of horizontal resolution (more or less *double* standard definition resolution) that rivals the image quality of much more expensive cameras.

However, there's one HUGE problem that comes with this brave new world of inexpensive high-res HD...we're still shooting with little tiny 3" LCD monitors. So we're using a 3" picture to judge focus on video that will be viewed on a 50" screen. The end result when you get back home and view your footage on that 50" flat screen TV is often an embarrassing number of soft, fuzzy, and out-of-focus shots that can make your clients seriously wonder if you are legally blind. (This is a particular problem on DSLR cameras such as the Canon 5D and 7D, which have even *more* resolution and *smaller* LCD screens than most dedicated video cameras.) Here are three *solutions* to the problem...

Using a Monitor

One thing I would recommend adding to your kit once you get your camera and sound gear squared away is a decent monitor. The bigger, the better to judge image quality, but for many jobs– especially with limited crew and a lot of mobility–a small battery-operated portable monitor about 7" to 15" is more practical. These portable monitors are considerably better than the tiny little LCD screen for judging focus, a dirty lens, and noise from gain, just to name a few things, so they are an excellent all-purpose choice if your budget allows.

An external monitor is vital for sharp focus on DSLRs.

However, if you are still building your rig and haven't yet made enough money freelancing to cover the cost of your camera and audio gear, there are some Down and Dirty solutions that will allow you to better judge your image and keep more your money in your wallet. While a "professional" video monitor will have more advanced features, such as **BNC** connections, built-in color bars, etc., it is by no means the only option to remedy the basic limitations of having a small screen.

A regular old HDTV works just fine as a production monitor.

A regular old HD flat-screen TV, portable color TV, or even those inexpensive little portable DVD players/monitors can be made to serve as field monitors. Just about anything with a video screen that has a component, HDMI, or RCA input jack will work as a makeshift monitor. It is highly preferable that the display be HD if you're shooting HD, but even a 10" standard-def image is better to help judge picture quality than the tiny LCD screen found on prosumer cameras.

A small HDTV with the component inputs can also be enlisted as a cheapie monitor for under $100.

Focus assist (also known as **expanded focus**) is a simple camera feature to help you better judge focus. The button to activate this feature on your HD camera will likely be right near the record button. When you activate this feature, it will magnify the image on your LCD screen (and likely also in the **viewfinder**), making it easier to tell if your shot is actually in sharp focus. This magnification occurs only on the LCD screen. This magnified image is *never* recorded and will also *not* be seen on an external monitor, just the LCD.

Normal Camera LCD image.

LCD image with Expanded Focus.

Peaking...Focus Pocus!

Focus assist and monitors are helpful for using your naked eye, but there's an even greater and more reliable tool that helps you keep your HD image in crisp sharp focus: **peaking**. Peaking is similar to zebra stripes (see "Zebra Stripes 101" page 32), but it helps you judge focus rather than exposure. I can not overstate how I feel about this feature. I think it is hands down the single most useful extra feature to look for in a prosumer HD camera if you are a video freelancer.

When you activate peaking on a camera, it shows a colored outline around everything that's in sharp focus. So instead of squinting and scrutinizing over a giant HD image displayed on a tiny little LCD screen, all you have to do is look for a very visible colored outline around your subjects. Abracadabra, focus pocus, as you shift focus from one object to another, the peaking lines shift as well, allowing you to instantly tell *exactly* what part of your image is in sharp focus. Peaking is a very handy feature for pulling off precise **rack focus** moves,

shooting with a **shallow depth of field**, or quickly adjusting focus as you shift to different subjects within a scene. It's more reliable and faster than using your naked eye and allows you to shoot on the go without a monitor and still be confident that your scene will be in clear, sharp focus. However, just like most camera image control features, peaking does *not* perform well in low light. (Hey, you can't have everything, baby!)

Peaking can help you easily (and quickly) manage focus even when zoomed in from a distance.

ZOOMING

Introduction: Who's Zooming Who?

The *primary* reason you should use the zoom control on your camera is to readjust your frame from wide to medium to close-up. I say that's all it should be used for 90% of the time. More seasoned event and documentary camera people learn to resist the newbie temptation to constantly push in and pull out of shots for no *story-driven* rhyme or reason. If your finger is pushing the zoom control for any reason other than adjusting your shot, you should be clear what that reason is. Any zoom move (in or out) should be *motivated* by the scene you're trying to visually communicate.

> *Any zoom move—in or out—should be clearly motivated by the action and story of the scene.*

Pushing In

We generally push in to draw the audience's attention to something specific in a larger scene. Every time you zoom in or out, your camera is "talking" to the audience to communicate some piece of visual information. Here's what your camera's saying in various situations...

PUSH IN TO	WHAT YOUR CAMERA'S SAYING
A *particular person* in the room	■ Hey, look! There's Mike Tyson in the front row of the ballet. ■ This scowling congressman does not like what his colleague just said. ■ This happy hippie is really into this band.
A *particular detail* in the large shot	■ Wow, check out the size of that "rock" on her finger! Is that from Tiffany's? ■ That is a very nice statue in the corner. This must be a classy joint. ■ Who would've guessed she had a tattoo *there*? Now, you don't see that every day.
Get more *intimate* during an interview	■ This is the climax of a dramatic story. ■ It's getting emotional now. Here come the tears. ■ Come a little closer; I want to tell you something important now.
Show a close-up of some *action*	■ Now she's adjusting the engine bolt clockwise with a #12 Rawley's wrench. ■ Notice how he's holding the peeler to create those cute little decorative lemon peel flowers. ■ Check out what he's doing to those piano strings with his teeth. That's crazy!

Pulling Out

If we are starting off on a tight medium or close-up shot, we generally pull out to reveal *new* information to the audience. This is a playful way to create some tension and engage the audience by holding their suspense. People are psychologically accustomed to anticipating where you are going with a pull out. You are communicating that there is something *more* than meets the eye at first composition…and now you're about to show it to them.

Here's the mental dialog that runs through my head whenever I'm smoothly executing a well-thought pull-out move to reveal some new piece of visual information to the audience: "Here we go…niiice and smoooth…Wait for it…wait for it…wait for it…Bam! There it is, baby! Bet you didn't know I was gonna show you *that*, did you?" (Then I usually imagine wild applause as I rise to accept my Emmy for best cinematography.)

The point is that you want to give your audience some little visual *surprises* along the way…something to look forward to. Keep their eyes glued to the screen for fear they might miss something good. That's where the pull-out comes in. Pull-outs are best used to dramatically reveal some new piece of visual info. Just like a good joke or anecdote, a good pull-out always has a good payoff.

> A pull-out (aka "zoom out") move builds suspense by slowly revealing new visual info.

PULL OUT FROM	TO REVEAL
From: A bikini-clad sunbather rubbing on tanning lotion	To: The sunbather is in the middle of a city tanning lotion roof on a snow-covered day
From: A Native American on horseback riding over a ridge	To see: The ridge overlooks an illegal dumping ground in the desert.
From: A clown performing magic tricks for a child	To see: The child is one of many young patients smiling in a cancer ward.

Smooth Like Butter, Baby!

Whether you are zooming in or out, there's one constant: your move has to be smooth like butter, baby! That means it should be: slow, steady and controlled. This means you absolutely need to be familiar with the sensitivity of your particular camera's zoom control. If you are shooting with an unfamiliar camera, always allow yourself a few minutes to play around and practice with the camera's zoom control until you have a good feel for its sensitivity. The zoom control on every model of camera performs a little differently.

If you ever botch a zoom by accidentally letting up the pressure on the rocker control so that your smooth move comes to a dead halt midway through, don't immediately continue with your intended move. It will look very obviously like a mistake. Instead, if there's an unintended pause in your zoom move, just stop and let the shot rest there for a few moments. No one will ever know that that was not what you originally intended. I call this "doing a Pee-Wee Herman." "Ha! Ha! I meant to do that!"

1. Semi-Automatically

This is the method you'll probably use most often—using a standard pressure-sensitive **rocker control** near the record button. The harder you press it, the faster the zoom. You'll need to practice some to become familiar with your particular zoom control's "sweet spot" to pull off a smooth move using just the right amount of pressure. It's very helpful if your camera has some type of on-screen scale to measure zooming, as this will allow you to practice the move and then start and stop at the same points every time.

The lighter you press, the slower and smoother the move—the harder you press, the faster.

Use a zoom scale (if your camera has one) to execute precise zoom moves.

"Servo" is a fancy word for a zoom motor. Servo = automatic zoom.

2. Fully Automatic

Some cameras also have smaller zoom control on the handle. These controls are not pressure sensitive, but instead can be preset in the menu to operate at a constant speed. This is ideal for very long smooth and/or precise zooms.

Some cameras, such as the Canon XA-10 have a second zoom control on top.

Turn off the handle zoom control to avoid accidentally hitting it when not in use.

On many cameras you can adjust the speed of the handle zoom control.

3. Fully Manually

To zoom this way, you'll need to set your zoom control to "Manual" and use the little lever on the zoom ring to operate the zoom lens. It's difficult on most cameras to pull off a full manual zoom that's smoother than a semi- or fully automatic zoom, so this technique is most useful for quickly adjusting your frame, **"jump-cut style"** shooting popular in some reality shows and **whip zoom** moves. (See below and "Whip Zooms" on page 294.)

Switch your camera from manual to servo. This button is usually near or under the camera lens.

Use the zoom lever to move the zoom lens entirely by hand. Flick for a whip zoom.

Flick this lever up or down to do a whip zoom, but not too hard.

Shutter Speed 101

Shutter speed is one of those filmmaking concepts I heard a hundred times in film school, but honestly never knew what the hell they were talking about or how I should apply it to my shooting. So let me attempt to make the concept of shutter speed accessible for nontechno geeks.… The primary purpose of manipulating your shutter speed is to control how motion is portrayed in a scene. In other words, how do moving things and people look on video? Normal (i.e., the way your naked eye sees it)? Blurry? Or sharp strobe-like and surreal?

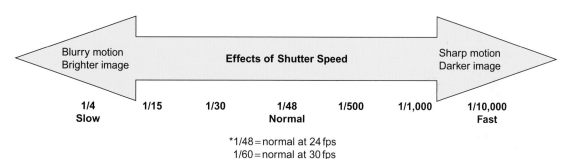

Blurry motion
Brighter image

Effects of Shutter Speed

Sharp motion
Darker image

| 1/4 | 1/15 | 1/30 | 1/48 | 1/500 | 1/1,000 | 1/10,000 |
| Slow | | | Normal | | | Fast |

*1/48 = normal at 24 fps
1/60 = normal at 30 fps

To best understand shutter speed, think of a still film camera that actually has a little mechanical shutter or door that opens and closes to expose each frame of film for a given amount of time–such as 1/48th of a second or 1/1000th of a second. The longer the shutter stays open, the more light *and motion* are captured on that particular frame of film. A racecar zipping by shot at 1/48th of a second will be blurry, whereas the same race car shot at 1/10,000th of a second will be much sharper and clearer because it didn't move nearly as much in that shorter span of time. The shutter speed simply indicates the length of that moment in time that is captured on each individual frame of video.

Once you've got this basic concept down, you can start to apply it to the all-important goal of telling your visual *story* in new and creative ways that compliment, manipulate, and play with motion. For normal shooting where you want things to look natural, like your naked eye, your shutter speed should be set to double your frame rate. So if you are shooting at 24fps, you should set your shutter speed to 1/48 for normal motion. If you are shooting at 30fps, you should set it to 1/60 for normal motion, etc.

Shutter = 1/32
1. Motion appears more blurry
2. Lets more light into the lens
3. No good for slo-mo or freezes

Shutter = 1/48
1. Motion appears normal
2. Some blurring occurs
3. No good for slo-mo or freezes

Shutter = 1/2000
1. Motion appears strobe-like
2. Less light allowed in lens
3. Good for slo-mo or freezes

So you know that you adjust shutter speed to control how motion is portrayed on video, but you may be asking, "How do you actually *apply* shutter speed to the art of telling a dynamic visual story?" Well, ask no more....

1 SLOW-MOTION IN POSTPRODUCTION

Even if your camera does not have built-in slow-motion ability like that found on many higher-end prosumer cameras, you can still achieve smooth slow-motion shots by adjusting your shutter speed and then slowing down the footage in a nonlinear editing program such as Premiere or Final Cut Pro. To do this, shoot *only* the particular scene to be slowed down at a very high shutter speed— anywhere from 1/1000 to 1/10,000. You'll want to experiment first to find what works best in slo-mo.

The faster the action that you want to slow down or freeze frame, the higher you'll want to set the shutter speed. So kids on a merry-go-round could probably be shot at a shutter speed of 1/2000 and still look good when slowed down in post. However, to get clean slow motion of a goalie stopping a flying hockey puck, you'd want to shoot at a very high shutter speed (closer to 1/10,000) in order to actually see the puck in mid-flight. One thing you should keep in mind before using this technique is that a higher shutter speed, by necessity, will result in a much darker image than a normal shutter speed, so you will need to shoot in full daylight, in a very bright studio environment, or with the camera's gain cranked up (the least preferable).

  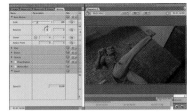

Set your shutter speed to a high setting (at least 1/1000). | Shoot just the scene to be slowed down or frozen at that high shutter speed. | Use your NLE to slow down the footage or display a freeze frame.

2 STROBE-MOTION ACTION

Another way you can use shutter speed as a story-telling device is to shoot your scene with a high shutter speed (try 1/500 or higher) and *not* manipulate the speed of the footage in post. The end result will be footage that appears very surreal or strange and disturbing. It's surreal, because things and people that aren't moving will pretty much look the same as on normally shot video. However, anyone or anything that is moving in the same scene will appear as if it's under a strobe light. Waving a hand in front of the lens will appear as if you are waving four hands (the Ganesh effect, I like to call it). In the past decade, many narrative action films have employed this effect to create a feeling of surrealism and/or jar the audience—specifically, the big beach battle scene in *Saving Private Ryan*, the zombie attack scenes in *28 Days Later,* and the bank robbery sequence in *Inside Man* all used high shutter speeds to mess with people's heads. This technique is most useful for sports, music videos and narrative projects where it compliments the story/scene at hand.

3 BOOSTING EXPOSURE IN LOW-LIGHT SITUATIONS

Probably the most common reason camera people manipulate shutter speed is to compensate for low-lighting conditions. The primary purpose of shutter speed is to control how motion is portrayed on video, but the secondary purpose is to manipulate exposure. It's standard practice for many videographers to lower their shutter speed one or two settings below normal. So instead of shooting with a shutter speed of 1/48 when shooting at 24fps, they might instead set the shutter speed to 1/32 or even 1/24 (if they were feeling really wild and crazy). This means each frame of video is exposed longer and therefore brighter. Unlike using gain, lowering your shutter speed *naturally* lets more light into the lens, so it's like being able to shoot a full stop below your lowest f-stop, without any video noise side effect. Because it's only a notch or two down from your normal shutter speed setting, this has a minimal effect on motion that results in slightly more image blur. I do this automatically just about any time I'm shooting an event that takes place at night.

4 TRIPPY, DREAM-LIKE, AND SURREAL RE-CREATIONS

Lowering your shutter speed way below normal, say in the 1/4 to 1/15 range, will make still objects and backgrounds appear normal, but *moving* things will appear as colorful blurs. This creates a very surreal, dream-like, or hallucinogenic effect. This makes shooting at very slow shutter speeds a popular choice for flashbacks, dream sequences, and POV shots for characters under the influence. Similarly, handheld or roving POV camera work moving through a setting is a popular choice for reality TV and documentary re-creations. Another popular way shooters use this technique is to have a character hold perfectly still. While the entire world zips by around them, they appear as if they were frozen in time.

5 STILLS IN THE DARK AND "GHOSTS" ON VIDEO

Shutter speeds of 1/4 or lower let *a lot* more light into the lens than shooting at a normal shutter speed or slightly lower shutter speed. When you use these super-slow shutter speeds of **1/4 and lower**, a dark room will appear on video as if it were fully lit or even overexposed—with no video noise added to the picture. In order to avoid overexposing your shot in this mode, you'll need to close down your lens or possibly even use an ND filter. (Yes, it's that bright.) At these super-slow shutter speeds, motion appears *extremely* exaggerated. So rather than just getting a trailing image, moving subjects and objects are delayed by several seconds and fast-moving subjects become barely perceptible phantom-like blurs.

So how and what can you apply this to? The most practical use I've found for these really long frame exposures is shooting cutaway *still* shots in the dark. Let's say there's a cool poster on the wall of a dark nightclub or a mural on the dark ceiling of a mosque. Then (1) frame your shot, (2) lock down your tripod, (3) set your super-slow shutter speed, and (4) adjust your iris until the shot looks normal and record. As long as it's a still shot with nothing moving, it will look as if the scene is fully lit. The second application of this effect is pretty specialized—faking ghost footage. (As opposed to catching a *real* ghost on video, which is considerably harder.) To do this, just follow the same procedure as above in a darkened room and have an actor run or walk quickly through the scene.... Pretty freaky, right?

FOCAL LENGTH

An often overlooked aspect of composition and storytelling is focal length. Whether you shoot with a wide, medium, or close-up lens has a HUGE impact on how your scene and subjects are perceived by the audience. By doing nothing more than zooming your lens in to full telephoto or pulling out to full wide, you can make the *exact same* street scene feel desolate and sparse or jam-packed and dense. Here are some common ways to tell your story using focal length....

Crowds

Here's the exact same crowd on a street corner shot with a fixed-lens camera at the mid-zoom point (1) and then again a few seconds later zoomed all the way in to telephoto (2).

One subject matter that really benefits from careful selection of focal length is crowds. Whether it's protesters in the streets of Greece, Christmas shoppers in New York City, or onlookers at the X-Games, a telephoto lens can be used to emphasize and exaggerate the size of the crowd....even if it's really not that crowded. A telephoto lens visually "compresses" any mass of people so that even if they are 10 feet apart, it appears to the lens that they are right up on top of each other. It also helps bring the audience right into the crowd. Clients that have shelled out loads of cash to put on some big event want the video to reflect that their event was a jam-packed success. And with a little video know-how and a carefully chosen camera angle, we can usually give that impression.

Cityscapes

It's fairly typical for many projects to start off with some establishing shots of the city where the project takes place. Visually, shooters typically try to make city scenes appear dense and compact by using a telephoto lens. However, focal length—like just about every choice we

A telephoto lens can make the traffic on any street look jam-packed and put the audience "right on the street" (1) A wide lens can make the exact same street seem much more empty and desolate (2).

make when shooting—should be dictated by the ***story*** we are trying to tell. So if you were shooting a video for a client that wanted to make the point that jobs are leaving the city, you might choose to shoot city scenes with a wide lens to visually show that the city is empty. Pictured here is the exact same group of cars shot five seconds apart at different focal lengths. Note the *apparent* distance between the black SUV and the double-decker bus.

People and Faces

Almost as much as cityscapes and landscapes, focal length is a handy tool to manipulate how people are portrayed on video as well, particularly when it come to close-ups. Just about any scene where you want to isolate the subjects from their background and make the audience feel intimate, up close, and personal with the subjects is a good choice for a telephoto lens. The big benefit of shooting close-up and medium shots with a telephoto lens is that you get much greater **shallow depth of field**, making the shot all about the subjects in the foreground. This is also a great technique to minimize a busy background, such as a carnival or casino floor. All the distractions from our story are blurred out, and the audience's attention is directed entirely to the people you want to focus on…literally. You should be aware that telephoto lenses also tend to flatten out faces and make your portrait appear more two-dimensional, which may not be a desired effect.

A normal lens (mid-zoom for fixed-lens cameras or 50mm if we're talking 35mm DSLR camera prime lens) is the standard for close-up portrait shots of faces. A normal lens looks the most natural, and if you are shooting on a DSLR camera, you will still have ample shallow depth of field.

Telephoto lens

Normal lens

Wide lens

For music videos or comic subject matter, we can go full wide and put the camera right in the subject's face for a funny, distorted effect that makes the mouth and nose appear much larger and three-dimensional. To push this comedic visual effect even further, if your camera has a detachable lens, you can rent or purchase a super wide **fish-eye lens** to get an extreme distorted effect, as popularized by the videos of Busta Rhymes. ("Woo-haa!" You got ya lens in check!)

Time lapse is a cinematic technique that allows us to manipulate time with our cameras so that events that unfold over the course of hours, days, or even months can be condensed down to a few dramatic seconds or minutes of fast-motion video. From a the sun setting over a valley to a skyscraper going up to an artist creating a painting on a blank canvas—time-lapse video will condense the whole event to a single short captivating sequence.

1 INTERVAL RECORDING MODE

Some prosumer cameras offer an **interval recording** mode to shoot **time-lapse** footage. In the interval recording mode, a camera can be set-up to shoot anywhere from a frame to a few seconds of video at set intervals of time. Your choice of shot length will vary from camera to camera but will generally fall in the range of one frame to several seconds per interval. For the smoothest time-lapse effect, the shorter the shot, the better, so one frame is ideal. If your camera doesn't have single-frame recording, set it to the shortest length of time available.

2 INTERVAL TIMES

Next, you need to set the interval time. Choices will fall in the range of 1 second to several hours. Typically, setting the time of your intervals somewhere between 1 to 10 seconds will yield a pretty cool effect, but you might find that longer intervals work better for the feel you want to create for your particular subject matter and how much screen time you want the event to take up when played back. So if you were shooting **24P** video of a 10-minute event with the interval recording mode set to record one frame of video every second, you would end up recording 60 frames of video for every minute that you shot for a total of 600 frames of video. When the video is played back at 24 frames per second, the 10-minute event you shot would be condensed down to just 25 seconds of fast-motion footage.

3 USE A TRIPOD

If you're shooting time-lapse video, your camera has to be on a tripod and **locked down** the entire time. The whole effect is blown if your camera is bumped even slightly somewhere during the shot. For this reason, it's important that you place your camera in a secure spot that won't be disturbed by people in your vicinity, curious pets, or anything else.

Put your tripod on lockdown.

4 PLUG INTO POWER

One thing you'll definitely want to do for any lengthy time-lapse shot is use AC power instead of batteries. Remember, if your camera's going to be on for hours on end, you don't want the batteries to die out in the middle of making the magic.

5 BEWARE OF DAYLIGHT SHOTS

If you will be shooting outdoors or otherwise relying on daylight to illuminate your subject matter, the level of lighting will shift with the moving sun and clouds, resulting in uneven exposure. This may or may not be a desired effect, depending on the exact subject matter and lighting conditions. For example, if you want to record a sunset going into nightfall and have set up your camera manually exposing for full daylight, once the sun starts to set, your shot may quickly become very underexposed, if not completely dark. Similarly, if you manually expose for times when the sky is cloudy, and an hour later the clouds clear up and the sun comes out, you will probably end up with a completely blown-out shot. Because of these potential issues, I recommend using autoexposure, so your camera adjusts to the scene as the lighting changes throughout the day. Autoexposure can often be fine-tuned in the menu.

6 USE AUTO-WHITE BALANCE

For the same reasons as just described, you should also put set your camera on auto-white balance. Throughout any lengthy day-lit scene, color temperature will likely shift. In the case of sunrises and sunsets (perhaps the most popular time-lapse subject matter), it will shift dramatically from cool to warm or vice versa. So auto-white balance is crucial to capturing these scenes well.

7 SLOW DOWN THE SHUTTER SPEED

Lowering the shutter speed a little may help smooth out the time-lapse effect, particularly if your camera can record only 0.05 seconds of footage in this mode (as opposed to one frame, which is preferable). Otherwise, cameras with longer interval recording times such as 0.05 seconds will produce a more choppy time-lapse effect.

A FINAL NOTE

If a time-lapse shot is a particularly important element of your project, the best thing I think you can do is set aside some time beforehand to do some time-lapse test shoots that experiment with the key settings of interval time, shutter speed, and exposure. You can also play around with playback speed and blurring effects in postproduction to get closer to your desired time-lapse effect. The bottom line is that time-lapse is not an exact science here, because the end effect is largely dependent on a combination of your camera's capabilities, the subject matter, and the feel you want to give this part of your story. So take the time to play around with it some and discover which combinations of settings works best for any given scene.

1 Hair light should be placed behind and a little above the subject to provide greater separation from the background.

2 Bright, soft, even lighting on the green screen background. If using a cloth backdrop smooth it out to avoid big wrinkles which cause shadows.

3 Adequate lighting on the subject. Should be consistent with the look or lighting of the scene to be keyed into the background. (i.e., If you were keying in an outdoor scene, then the color temperature and relative brightness of your lights should match daylight.)

4 Interview subject with wardrobe that does not match the green color to be keyed out. Beware that subjects with glasses may be particularly tricky to work with. If their glasses pick up a green reflection it may key out along with the green background.

5 Apple boxes, chairs, or other platforms that you do not wish to be seen should also be painted green, pulled out or cropped out of the frame.

Constructing an Interview Space

One of the more difficult challenges you will face on a routine basis is finding a decent room to shoot an interview. Often the facility, office, store, or client-owned location where you will be shooting will be less than ideal for interviews. At a minimum, it must be good for audio and a space that you can have as much control over as possible. The next thing you also want to strive for is an interview location that helps to also *visually* tell your story with an appropriate setting and props. However, in practice, you will often be limited to less than ideal settings or even worse—settings with little more than plain white walls. (One of your worst nightmares.) Below is a typically tricky interview situation I found myself in when shooting a pilot for a reality series.

These pictures represent pretty much all we had to work with to stage an interview. (The two corners of the room not shown here were even less cinematic.)

We only had a few hours to shoot some B-roll and an interview in a boutique dog-grooming and exercise facility. The facility was open for normal business, which meant that dogs and customers were coming and going throughout the day and employees still had to be free to move about and conduct their normal course of business. The business office was way too small and lacked any personality whatsoever, so that left only one quiet room—the grooming room. In these situations, you have to really use your imagination just to create a workable solution. This usually means moving around some furniture, wall décor, and props to pretty up the location and, more importantly, *visually* tell the story you came to tell. In this case, my frame had to say, "We love and care for dogs."

We did four key things to make this shot work: (1) brought in a small cabinet with a plant, (2) added a cute dog poster to cover a plain wall, (3) added a variety of colorful dog leashes to the rack, and (4) removed the big ugly jugs of pink shampoo.

The end result was a shot that helped tell the story with a few dog-related props and just enough items to break up the flat, industrial background. (This is also a good example of positioning for a formal two-person interview. Subjects must be seated unnaturally close to appear naturally positioned *on camera*.)

A Bare Conference Room with a Great View

If you are shooting corporate video, one of the common challenges you will likely come up against sooner or later is the dreaded corporate conference room. Many business offices these days are open cubicle workspaces. So often the only quiet space available away from ringing phones, conversations, and visual distractions will be a conference room, which will often have just plain white walls—the freelance videographer's *kiss of death*. Apart from a decent poster or artwork, a window with a nice view may be your only attractive option.

Pictured here are the three other visual options I had to choose from in this room...lame and lamer.

For the conference room interview below, there was a perfect view of the Empire State Building, so it was a no-brainer. However, the colossal challenge to capturing any scene out of a window is *exposure*. The daylight will always be considerably brighter than your indoor lighting, so this setup requires A LOT of light on your subject. And if your subjects are dark-skinned, they will need a *massive* amount of light. To pull this shot off in the 20 minutes I had to work with, I used a fluorescent Kinflo Diva 400 light, plus two 500-watt omni lights at an uncomfortably close distance just to get a decent subject exposure. Finally, I used the translucent window shade to act as giant makeshift **ND gel** over the window, which helped cut down the overexposure of the sky. Even so, I still had to blow the sky out a little to properly expose for my subject's face. The lights were also uncomfortably close and bright on the subject. I got away with this because it was a very short interview and the subject was an understanding filmmaker.

With more time and resources, I could've also neatly taped a giant sheet of (real) ND gel on the windows to get the outside exposure perfect and not use as much light inside. Conversely, I could've used the ND filter on the camera and *roasted* my subject in light. (Mind you, he'd be temporarily blinded and sweating bullets, but, man, that *skyline* would look good!)

4 REASONS TO ENHANCE PEOPLE'S LOOKS

Why Make People Look Good?

One of the very first things anyone will ask you when they get before the camera is, "How do I look?" The degree of your success as a freelancer hinges on the honest answer to this question. To get repeat business and compete in this field, you need to become well versed at knowing how to make *anybody* look their best on video (regardless of whether they actually look good or not to begin with.) This is one of the freelancer's *most vital* skills. People hire you to show them, their company, products, and events all in their best light. Understand this: if *they* don't look good, *YOU* don't look good. Here are four good reasons you need to master the art of enhancing people's appearance on camera.

> Enhancing appearances is a *VITAL* skill. If they don't look good, *YOU* don't look good.

1 Correcting the Harsh Hyper-realities of Hi-Def

HD video is great for sharp, crisp, clean pictures, but when it comes to close-ups of people's faces, it's a little too sharp and too clear. Coupled with video lighting, having 1080 or 720 pixels of HD video actually makes people look a lot *worse* than in real life if certain corrective steps aren't taken. One could argue that HD is just better capturing reality, except in real life, we don't have a conversation with the other person standing a foot away from us and a 500-watt light shining six feet from our face. So with HD video, we can now see *all* the super sharp details. (And I ain't talking about the good details.) I mean all the things people *don't* want us to see: every pock mark, crater, pimple, wrinkle, unsightly facial hair, mole, bump, blotch, freckle, scar, eye bag, and blemish is put front and center on giant 50" HD screens for all the world to see.

These are the "dirty details" (i.e., imperfections) that don't stand out to us nearly as much in-person under normal lighting or when shooting standard definition video. So HD, while providing a superior picture, is also magnifying our imperfections. Not only that, but when people are on camera, under these hot lights, they can get hot or nervous–often both. Either way, the end result is sweat. That sweat creates an extra shine. So now we have *shiny* pock marks and craters in ultra-sharp hi-def close-ups. Nasty. I know some of you want to be purists, but when it comes to video, it's all subjective in the end anyway. Because how you look at any given time depends on the lighting, depends on how far away we are, depends on the angle, etc. All we're really trying to do for starters when I say enhancing people's looks, even if you're dealing with documentary, is simply correcting or restoring the cosmetic "damage" caused by HD video. I think the corporate videographer's first oath, just like doctors, should be "Do no harm." (Second oath: "Make it look *hot*, baby!")

A shiny forehead is not "natural" or "real" if your lights are the actual cause of the shine.

2 Professionalism

The second reason that we want to enhance people's looks is that it's standard *professional* practice. Enhancing people's looks when they appear on camera is an aesthetic form of "broadcast standard." What I mean by my use of "broadcast standard" here is that it's what's *expected*. When you turn on your TV and see a host, spokesperson, actor, etc., 95% of the time some measures–usually *many* measures–have been taken to correct their appearance on camera. (If you've ever seen your favorite TV personality in-person on the street, then you probably know *exactly* what I'm talking about.) Nobody really looks as good as they do on TV. We are used to seeing people looking their best or even better than they do in real life. That's also exactly what clients expect (and should get) when they hire a video "professional." Not only do clients expect it, but professional talent who are used to being on camera also expect it. If you aren't versed in the standard enhancing measures of video, your production will seem less professional, talent will have less confidence in you and may not want to work with you in the future. You want to develop a reputation as someone who knows how to make people look good. Reputation is everything.

3 Psychology

The third reason that you want to become well versed in enhancing people's looks is pure psychology. It's real simple. People who look good feel good. People who feel good perform better. Avoid showing your subject the picture on the monitor until you've got everything all set and perfect....Work all of the video voodoo from this chapter on the image; *then* right before you're ready to shoot, turn the monitor around and let your subject take a look at themselves. If I've done your job properly, more often than not, you'll be able to make them look better on video than they look in real life. When they see how you've craftily softened their imperfections, taken 10 years off their age with makeup, how you've found the perfect angle that hides their double-chin, all of a sudden they realize that you are somebody who knows what they're doing. Now they are going to sit back, relax, and focus on the questions that you're asking them or the performance they are giving, rather than constantly worrying about how they look.

> You'll never do BAD making somebody look GOOD. *Never.*

4 Mo' Money

All of these reasons go to the fourth and final reason to enhance people's looks: to make mo' money. You'll never do bad making somebody look good. Never. Why do corporations make videos anyway? Why does a client make a video? More often than not, if somebody's hiring you to make a video the reason is that they want themselves or their company or their product–they want something, whatever it is–to look *good*. That means that the people on camera need to look good. That means that their spokesperson needs to look good. The CEO on camera needs to look good. Looking good makes clients happy, plain and simple. Happy clients are returning clients, and that's what this whole book is about: how to make your clients happy, how to get them to come back...how to make more money.

MAKEUP MAKES MONEY

Introduction

Translucent powder makeup is definitely one of the secrets of the pros. It is a big part of the movie-making magic that goes into making people look much better than real life. (Fellas, don't be intimidated by makeup. You don't need to be a professional makeup artist to put this stuff on. It's only powder. It's not that complicated. So, if you've never handled it before, read the tutorial on the next page and/or get one of the women in your life to show you the basics.)

Before makeup

After makeup

Brands

I am all about cutting corners and saving a buck when and where appropriate, but makeup is not one of those areas where it's appropriate. You gotta get the good stuff. I like the Ben Nye, Nars, Sephora, and L'Oreal brands. All are acceptable and good brands of translucent powder makeup, but Ben Nye is what I personally use most of the time. They specialize in theatrical stage and TV makeup. Comparatively, these brands are not cheap, but we're talking about how we *make* our money here. We're talking about the crucial act of making our clients look good.

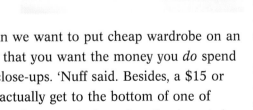

We don't want to get cheap makeup any more than we want to put cheap wardrobe on an actor or put a cheap lens on our camera. I always say that you want the money you *do* spend to show up *on the screen*. Well, makeup makes your close-ups. 'Nuff said. Besides, a $15 or $20 jar of powder will last you forever. (I have yet to actually get to the bottom of one of these jars without it getting lost or stolen first.) It's more than worth the value. I've invested less than $100 in the makeup and supplies that I've been using for the last two years. So it's a very cost-effective investment.

> Translucent powder makeup works wonders. Don't be cheap. Get a good name-brand powder.

What to Expect

If you do decide to hire a professional makeup artist, make sure that you check out their portfolio or website first. Look at their previous work to make sure their style(s) and sensibilities match what you're looking for. Find out what requirements they might need of you on set. (See the list below.) Also, it's standard for makeup artists and certain other professionals on set to charge an additional fee known as a **kit rental**. That means that you're paying for their services, but you're also paying for the use of their supplies—in this case, makeup. Kit rental prices will vary some from professional to professional, depending on how big their kit is and how big your job is. Ask up front.

Cutting Makeup Costs

In lieu of paying a makeup artist a full kit rental or their normal fee, I have sometimes been able to simply purchase the makeup and supplies for the shoot with the understanding that they would *keep* all the makeup and supplies after the shoot. If you want to try to save some cash, you might also consider makeup school students. You can contact your local makeup academy directly, put a flyer up at the facility, and/or send them an email to seek out advanced students who are looking for some professional experience for *some* pay, albeit less than the going rate. If you're really hard up for a makeup budget and you have somebody in your family or somebody in your immediate circle of friends who is always glammed up, chances are they know many of the same beauty secrets as the professional makeup artist and fit the bill. Just make sure they don't overdo it. Always specify whether you want a natural look or greatly enhanced look.

What a Makeup Pro Needs

If you are hiring a professional makeup artist for a commercial or other big job with multiple people to be made up, they are going to need a few basics. Ask them first, but here's a typical hit list:

1. **Dedicated Makeup Area**—A dressing room is ideal, but if that's not practical, make sure they have their own dedicated space on set to set up all of these items.
2. **Large Mirror**—They may have their own, but you want to make sure that there is a decent sized mirror on set to check their work.
3. **Stools or Chairs**—The taller, the better, so stools with backs or tall chairs are preferable for makeup artists to stand while working on talent who are sitting comfortably.
4. **Running Water**—Having a clean sink nearby is important for washing hands, faces, and supplies as needed.
5. **Ample Light**—Makeup artists need lots of bright light to see their subjects' faces as the camera will see them—bright.

Translucent Powder Makeup

You want a premium brand of translucent powder makeup in at least three different tones: cocoa, cream, and mocha (or as I prefer to think of it—Black, White, and Mexican). Your kit isn't very useful if you don't have enough shades to cover every skin tone you will encounter from dark brown to very pale Caucasian. By blending any two of these three basic shades, you can cover every ethnicity in between. It's better to have no makeup at all than to make up someone in a shade that is clearly darker or lighter than their natural skin tone.

Premium Brush

Again, same as with the makeup, we don't want to cheap out on the brush. Cheap brushes may feel coarse on a subject's face, won't last as long, and worst of all, are more likely to clump and cake powder makeup. I recommend a good organic animal hair brush such as pony hair or softened goat hair. These brushes are super soft and plush and the same as the pros use. (Don't worry. They don't kill the animals to make these brushes; they just give them a haircut.)

Apron or Towel

A simple smock or apron that covers up the front of their clothing up to the neckline is fine. This is particularly necessary for keeping stray powder from smearing and staining clothing. Solid black or white clothing is especially prone to stains. This is a supply that you can cheap out on and substitute a simple towel or any large piece of cloth as long as it covers the whole outfit. (If possible, your talent shouldn't get dressed in wardrobe until after they are made up.)

Brush Cleaner

It's important to clean your brushes between applications to avoid contaminating your brush or makeup with bacteria, which could cause talent to break out. You can use professional makeup brush cleaner, or mix your own homemade solution.

Cleaning a Makeup Brush

Use brush cleaner *or* mix some water and a little baby shampoo and stir gently. Avoid too many bubbles.

Dip the brushes into your solution until the color starts to drain into the water.

Rinse them in a 50/50 alcohol/water solution. Rinse again in water only.

Pat them dry with a paper towel and lay them flat to dry to avoid excess water draining down into the handle.

APPLYING POWDER MAKEUP IN FIVE EASY STEPS

Step 1—Clean

We want to make sure that the skin is free of oil and dirt, so first have your subject clean their skin with mild soap and water or some other gentle cleanser. Pat the skin fully dry with a clean towel or paper towel.

Step 2—Choose Your Powder

Select the shade of powder that best matches the natural skin tone of your talent's face. You may find that you need to blend two different shades of powder to match their exact skin tone. If so, blend on the back of your clean hand or other clean palette or surface. If you want to apply the powder right after moisturizing, just make sure you blot the skin with a tissue to prevent the powder from caking on wet areas.

Step 3—Powder Your Brush

Apply the powder with your choice of a plush makeup brush or a disposable powder puff or pad. I recommend using a large brush for the best results, but disposable applicators may be more practical for making up multiple subjects. Put a little powder onto a palette and twirl your brush in the powder; then tap it on the side to remove excess powder. If using a powder puff or pad, dip it in the powder and gently shake it above the palette to get rid of excess powder.

Step 4—Apply the Powder

Lightly brush the powder onto the talent's face starting with the normal shiny spots—the forehead, nose, and chin—then cover the rest of the face evenly. (Gently press when using puffs or pads.) If the subject has dark circles under their eyes, or any undesirable wrinkles, freckles, acne, blemishes, etc., give these a few extra applications of powder until they are diminished or disappear altogether. Sweep the brush over their face once more to remove any excess powder, so the makeup doesn't look too heavy.

Step 5—Reapply as Necessary

Reapply as necessary throughout shooting to keep down any shininess that develops. If you desire, this also the point where you would add blush. Finally, set the lights and the camera angle just right and show your subject how great they look; then listen.… Hear that?… "Ca-ching!" That's the sound of you making money with makeup!

Note: Some male subjects, in particular, may be reluctant to be made up, and that's fine, but see if you can at least convince them to let you powder away the unflattering shiny spots.

Large Noses

The key to shooting a subject with a large nose in the most flattering light is to avoid shooting them from profile (i.e., side) angles and also from below. Instead, shoot and light them more dead on. This helps avoid a large nose shadow and makes the nose flatter and less three-dimensional. Normally, you would avoid lighting and angles that flatten out faces, but this is a case where we break one rule to enforce another: always show your clients in the most flattering light.

Double Chins

The secret to getting rid of or avoiding the appearance of a double chin is to make the "second chin" invisible or much less noticeable. You can do this in any one or combination of several ways: (1) Raise the key light and aim down to create a shadow under the chin. (2) Raise the camera and shoot from a slightly higher angle than normal. (3) Make up the area under the chin one shade darker.

Darker Skin Tones

Simply put, dark-skinned brothas (and sistas) need more light. When shooting a Caucasian person sitting next to a Black person with a single light source, try using an ND gel, scrim or net on the lighter-skinned person so that they will both be better exposed for their individual complexions. Also, dark skin looks best on camera with a little bit of sheen, so don't overdo the powder.

IMAGE CONTROL | 59

Taking Off 10 Lbs.

Contrary to popular belief, the *camera* does not "put on 10 pounds"...*bad camera people* do. To make people look slimmer or better yet, avoid making them look fat to begin with, do all these things:

BEFORE

1. Shoot them from a slightly higher angle than eye-level.
2. Also, light them from a slightly higher angle and *never* from below.
3. Next, you want to make sure your key light is focused on the side of the face that is turned *away* from the camera. This is called *short lighting* and creates a shadow on the near side of the face, which slims down the subject's appearance. (ex. After 1) Also, note that a subject's hair can also be positioned to further slim the face. (ex. After 2).

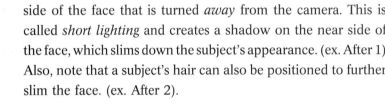

AFTER 1

(Conversely, if you ever want to *broaden* the face of a thin person, put the key light on the side of their face closest to camera, known as **broad lighting**.)

AFTER 2

Pale Skin

Pale skin is a pretty quick fix. Here are several ways to go from pasty to tasty in 10 seconds flat:

1. Add an amber or **CTO gel** to your key light (seen at right).
2. Use makeup one or two shades darker than their skin tone.
3. White balance to a warm card.
4. Manually adjust the color temperature in the camera menu.

BEFORE

1/2 CTO GEL

FULL CTO GEL

Note: Options 3 and 4 will make the entire image warmer, whereas options 1 and 2 will affect only your talent's face.

Seven Practical Tips on Shooting Sports

ALEX HOUSTON, INDEPENDENT DIRECTOR/D.P., FIAT LUX PRODUCTIONS, LLC (fiatluxproductions.com)

1. The Difference between Shooting Sports and Narrative

The main difference between shooting sports and narrative production is you can't usually have your subjects do something over again, which you can do when shooting narrative. Even in documentary, sometimes you can ask people to repeat what they are doing. However, in sports, you have only one shot to get it right. If you don't make that shot, that's lost *income* right there. So, you have to be 100% on your "A game", and you have to know all of your equipment like the back of your hand. It should be an extension of your body. You have to be 100% completely comfortable with all of your gear.

2. Lens Choice

It's also nice to have a variety of lenses to take with you, particularly if you're shooting more extreme sports like snowboarding, skateboarding, or mountain biking. Wide lenses let you get right up on the action. It's a little more consistent with the style of footage you usually see in those kinds of sports videos. The imagery from those sports is very strongly defined. Skateboard and snowboard videos are often shot by people who have small handy cams with a wide angle or fish-eye lens added

You can play with compressing space with a long lens, but it's also trickier to follow the action and keep it focused.

on, so the audience comes to expect that look and feel. Also having a wide lens and getting right in the action allows the audience to really identify with those athletes more closely. For those kinds of sports, I recommend getting as wide a lens as you can possibly get.

With other sports where proximity can be a danger, like horse racing or auto racing, you definitely want a long lens especially if the action is coming toward the camera. You can have a lot of fun with the compressed depth of field that you get from a long lens. The challenge of that, of course, is that you have to be spot on with pulling your focus. In those situations, you really have to find a way to scout and test shoot beforehand. If you're using a long lens, rehearse your focus pull and try to mentally find some visual reference marks, the same way you would have focus marks on the ground on a feature film. Use railings, poles, flags, or other objects along the path of action to rehearse focus pulls if you can get to the location beforehand. The disadvantages of bringing a bunch of glass (a.k.a. lenses) with you in the field are that (1) glass is heavy, and (2) environmental conditions may prevent you from changing lenses without contaminating the optical path, even if you have a camera assistant to help carry the cases.

3. Camera Position and POV Shots

If you have the time or if you can get the action to happen more than once, you want to try to get cutaways and move the camera to different positions. From a continuity perspective, this introduces the danger that the athlete is not going to do the exact same thing twice, particularly with the more extreme sports like snowboarding or skateboarding. Those guys are notorious for riding "in the moment," so you can't guarantee that they're always going to hit it the same way—even if they *want* to. Sometimes they want to, but a slight variation in speed or line can easily put them out of the same position. Sometimes they also get tired, and aren't comfortable doing something again if they feel they might get hurt doing it. Also from a documentary perspective, to try to put together different runs and make them feel like they're the same run is ethically a little bit in a gray area. However, if you're doing a montage or something creative like that, then I think it's fine.

It's always nice to have two cameras running. It's helpful to have a FlipCam or other small secondary camera with a wide angle lens adapter. You can point the smaller consumer camera in the same direction to get a wide angle shot and then use your main camera to get medium and close-up shots. Obviously, the cameras aren't going to look the same, so they aren't going to intercut well in terms of color and resolution. But with the fast pace and editing style of extreme sports, it's now pretty common and accepted practice to include some quick shots from less-professional cameras.

There are a lot of new point-of-view cameras out there. The GoPro Hero Cams are one option. I've seen them used in mountain biking and snowboarding. They're waterproof and very durable. A company called Liquid Image makes a camera that is actually embedded into athletic goggles. They make scuba, motocross, and ski/ snowboard goggle cameras. The advantage with that

Liquid Image makes HD camera goggles for extreme sports and scuba.

particular camera is that the camera is literally right between your eyes. It's an extremely wide-angled camera. I think it's a 135° field of view. It is literally taking a picture of whatever it is you are looking at. It's also not sticking out from you in any way, so there's much less chance of a Liquid Image POV camera getting lost or damaged during an extreme activity or wipeout. Wherever the goggles go, that's where the camera's going to go, even during a crash. And if you crash hard enough that your goggles fly off, I'd say you've got way bigger problems than worrying about the camera!

The GoPro Hero Cam can be mounted onto helmets, cars, handlebars, surf boards, etc.

4. Extreme Cold

Remember, batteries lose their ability to store energy at lower temperatures. So always go into it with extra batteries and assume they'll last half as long. If you can, keep your spare batteries inside your coat or indoors nearby. There are also camera jackets out there that have heating elements in them. You could also use some air-activated hand warmers or camera warmers in extremely cold environments; those are good to keep on hand. Stuff them around the camera if you can, particularly around the battery section or near areas with moving parts, per the manufacturer's instructions, of course. Just be careful to keep them from coming in direct contact with batteries, so they don't *overheat* your batteries or melt the plastic because they can get pretty hot.

Another thing I would recommend is to protect the gear. Make sure that you bring some camera body armor or a camera glove. Portabrace makes some. Those are really handy to have. When I was recently in Ghana, we were shooting at a construction site where there were pools of water and mud. The camera strap broke, and the camera went tumbling down a 35 or 40-foot hill and landed in the mud. The Sony EX-3 we were using has a breakaway view-finder, so part of the diopter viewfinder can pop off without damaging the rest of the camera. We had the Kata camera glove on the camera, and none of the mud got in the controls. We ran down, picked it up, wiped it off, snapped the diopter on, and kept rolling. I'm convinced that if the camera did not have the glove on it, we would have lost the camera. That glove saved the shoot. You don't want to have gear problems in the developing world. Portabrace makes what they call "camera armor" out of ballistic nylon. The camera is pretty much completely covered. It's like a winter coat. The one that Kata makes is Neoprene, so it's more like a glove. It fits the camera more snugly.

The other thing about shooting in really cold environments is you have to be aware that your viewfinder or lens might fog up if temperatures change too quickly, particularly in going from a cold to a warm environment. If you're following your subjects from the cold to indoors, keep a microfiber lens cloth or something else soft and lint-free, so you can just wipe the lens off. To keep the viewfinder from fogging, I use one of those chamois eyecup covers. There are fewer and fewer people shooting tape or film these days, but remember that condensation also happens inside the camera, and can prevent it from working properly, and in extreme cases can damage sensitive electronics. It's a good idea to allow your rig (and the media you're shooting on) enough time to acclimate to the conditions before you start rolling. It's also good to keep a rag or small towel handy to wipe off snow, mud splatters, and water that can get on the camera sometimes.

5. Snow and Exposure

Generally, on "bluebird days" (i.e., bright, sunny days) the snow is a little bit hotter exposure-wise than a blue sky, believe it or not. So, I'm usually exposing to keep some detail in the snow, which gives me a really nice beautiful cobalt-blue sky with fluffy clouds. The biggest problems that I've run into regarding exposure and snow have been on overcast days where you have flat, soft light and it's hard to pull detail out of the really bright areas when exposing for the overall image. Sometimes things are a little bit blown out, and you don't get a lot of detailed white clouds in the sky. The way I solve that is if the sky isn't that interesting, I try to frame it out of the shot as much as possible.

The snow-covered ground is the biggest reflector in the world. Generally, I have found that if there's enough *light* out to shoot, even on a bright day or an overcast day, there's enough *light* bouncing up from the snow that you're not going to run into too many underexposure issues on people's faces. As a matter a fact, a lot of times I've found that even people wearing hats with a bill or a brim don't have too much shadow in their eyes.

6. Audio

It's always nice to have wireless mics for sports coverage to get the close-up intimate sounds of a sport—grunts, cheers, heavy breathing—all the most intimate sounds that even the live spectators don't get to hear. It really gives the audience the athlete's POV and puts them in the event. If it's windy and you're outdoors, make sure you have a "fur coat" or "dead cat" (aka windjammer) for your shotgun mic because you're going to pick up a lot of wind noise at many sporting events. You also need a good shock mount because you're going to be moving the camera around a lot, and you're going to get a lot of bumps and unwanted extraneous noise. The built-in camera mic mounts aren't really designed for the rough handling that happens in sports and extreme shooting.

7. Safety

If you're going to be in situations, specifically extreme situations, where you, as a shooter, are a participant in the action—for example, a follow cam on skis—you want to make sure you are not just in good physical shape (that should be a no-brainer) but also a *competent* practitioner of whatever sport you're doing. Also realize that even if you're a highly skilled athlete, carrying heavy, expensive gear will wear you out sooner, both mentally and physically. Pack water and a couple of energy bars. Those are *your* extra batteries! Staying fueled up will help you maintain your "A-game".

It should go without saying, but safety is absolutely paramount. You definitely don't want to collide with the athletes, spectators, referees, or obstacles that could get in your way. Whenever possible, wear a helmet. If it interferes with the eyepiece, flip up the diopter and shoot from the raw screen (obviously, you can't do this with a film camera without the right kind of eyepiece and a video tap). This also lets you use both eyes to scan the environment around you, which helps you not only avoid dangers, but also anticipate what's coming into the frame. And if you absolutely have to use the eyepiece, learn to shoot with both eyes open and separately process what your viewfinder and naked eye see.

Shooting with both eyes open is also generally a good skill to develop in any run-and-gun situation, whether sports, documentary, or ENG (electronic news gathering). (To train yourself how to do this, start by opening your naked eye for short periods of time; then gradually keep it open for longer periods. Eventually, you'll be able to shoot with both eyes open most of the time, only closing your naked eye when you have to do something that requires your whole attention on the viewfinder, like checking critical focus.) But when things get really gnarly and you need both eyes wearing their birthday suits, just go wide, point the camera in the right direction, estimate the focal distance, and hope for the best. And don't forget to hit the record button!

Insure your gear, because if it breaks and you can't replace it, you're out of business. Also make sure that *you* are medically insured, because if you get seriously hurt, you're not going to be shooting for a long time. If you are employing anybody, make sure that those people have signed releases and waivers that relieve you of any liability or damage to them; their equipment; your equipment; or any other people, property, or objects that are around them. You don't want someone suing you, because they or their gear got run over by a BMX bike when they got too close to the track, so make sure you protect yourself liability-wise. If somebody is using your gear, make sure they take responsibility for it. If your insurance policy won't cover loaning, your waiver should probably have some sort of "you break it you buy it" clause. Don't DIY and copy somebody else's legalese. Get an attorney to review and prepare these kinds of documents for you. A couple hundred bucks is worth the peace of mind. Finally, remember that no single shot is ever going to make or break a production. You should never risk injury or your life to get a particular shot. It's not worth it. Ultimately, the quality of a sports production is the result of many factors well beyond your control. There are a lot of other people who have creative input and their skills can make up for any shortcomings.

CHAPTER 2
AUDIO TECHNIQUES

Why Your Audio Is More Important than Your Video

I said it in my first book, *The Shut Up and Shoot Documentary Guide,* and I'll say it again: **Your audio is more important than your video**.

   I realize that this is an earth-shattering concept for some—the equivalent of saying that aliens really DO exist. However, it's extremely important to me that everyone I teach actually gets this concept, as controversial as it may be. Here's the reality: with most of today's generation of prosumer HD cameras, it really isn't *that* hard to create beautiful images with just a little bit of knowledge. What you see is what you get. And even if you screw up the visuals, there are still multiple ways to correct, cover up, or substitute another image, and in most cases the audience will never know you screwed up.

Witness a pro at work. Detailed attention to audio always separates the pros from the hacks...*Always*.

However, to achieve consistently crisp, clean audio, you better believe that someone knew exactly what they were doing, because much more so than your image, audio is fraught with potential problems and it's very unforgiving. You either get it right at the time of recording, or you don't. Most audio mistakes or issues are not easily fixed — if they can be fixed at all — and audio issues are much more noticeable to your audience. Not even your own mama will sit through an entire project with crappy over-modulated or low-level audio. (Remember that lop-sided clay bowl you brought home in the first grade? Well, she'll give you that same sad look and patronizing pat on the head. "Well, you tried your best, dear.")

   Rack your brain real hard.... Think of how many times you've seen a blurry shot, shaky camera work, a dirty lens, or a boom mic dip into frame on your television or in the theater. My guess is many times. Okay, now think of all the times you've been watching TV or been in a movie theater and heard a production with bad overmodulated (too loud) or undermodulated (soft, barely audible) audio. My guess is

> If you have bad *audio*, you have a bad *project*. Period. Your clients won't forgive it, and TV stations won't air it.

you've *never* heard bad audio in any project that's been screened on TV or even just an indie film festival because it's just too noticeable and annoying. Bad audio is an *unforgivable* video sin. It sabotages everything else. People stop noticing great images, acting, or story when there's bad audio because it stands out like a sore thumb.

   If you have bad audio, you have a bad project. Period. Your clients won't forgive it. Film festivals won't accept it. And TV stations won't air it. Fixing bad audio is expensive and time consuming, and many problems such as overmodulation or audio shorts simply *can't* be fixed in postproduction. So for aaaaaall of those reasons and more, I'm going out of my way to tell you that your audio is more important than your video, and you'd better get it right every time, all the time. 'Nuff said. (Oh, and while I'm at it, aliens really DO exist.)

MICROPHONES

Shotgun Mic

Shotgun mics aka hypercardioid mics are mics designed to pick up audio primarily in the direction they are pointed, while ignoring or minimizing sounds coming from the sides and rear of the mic. Essentially, their narrow-focused pickup pattern allows you to primarily pick up your subject's voice while curtailing background noise. Because of this ability to record clean dialog and minimize unwanted background noise, shotgun mics are the primary mics for all types of filmmaking from narrative to corporate to docs. If you can afford only one mic, make it a shotgun mic. It's the most versatile and practical mic.

Hardwired Lav Mic

A hardwired lav mic is indispensable for recording formal interviews. These tiny unobtrusive mics are out of sight and out of mind, which makes for a better more natural interview with a more comfortable subject. Hardwired lavs are also great for hiding in a scene.

Wireless Lav Mic

Once you have a shotgun mic, a lav mic and a decent mixer or pre-amp, you will want to pick up a set or two of wireless mics. (Each unit features one mic and one receiver.) These are indispensable for certain shooting scenarios, specifically: moving subjects, wide shots, concealed recording, intimacy, demonstrations, and anything else that isn't practical to boom or be tethered by a wire.

Headphones

You need the padded kind that completely cover the ear. The Sony 7506 headphones pictured here are an industry standard. Professional-quality headphones should cost at least $50 to $200. Make sure the plug (stereo or mini) is the right one for your mixer or camera. If not, you may need to use an adapter plug. Your iPod ear phones won't cut it. However, if you need to shoot more low key, you could go with professional sound-isolating earbud headphones, which completely plug your ear holes.

XLR Cables

Take at least three 6' cables for every mic. You can't have too many XLR cables. Beware, with rough handling, XLRs may develop shorts, which cause static and sound dropouts. If you will be recording live events such as concerts or public speakers, extra-long 20' to 40' XLR cables are practical.

Accessories

You'll need an assortment of cable ties, gaffer's tape, and a stack of sound reports. Get gaffer's tape from a film/video supply store. Don't use electrical tape as a substitute! It'll leave a sticky residue on everything!

MIC SUPPORT

Boompole 	The lighter and longer the pole, the better. A decent shock mount is a must-have for location audio. It's okay to cheap out on the boom pole if you have to. A heavier, homemade paint pole boom will get the mic just as close as the $500 models. Search the Internet for do-it-yourself boom pole designs if you go this route.
Shockmount 	If you have a boompole, you'll also need a decent shockmount. A shockmount is a shock absorber for your shotgun mic to keep it from banging around as you move the boom. You can get simple models with rubberband-like suspensions that mount on a boompole and/or directly on the camera, like the shockmount on the left, or you can go with my preference—a pistol grip shockmount that can be mounted on a boompole, fitted with a blimp and windshield, or handheld sans boompole.
Windscreen 	This is the bare minimum when it comes to wind protection, but it still beats a naked mic. Windfoams are good to prevent and cut down mild breezes, but for anything more, you want one of the solutions below. You should always keep a windfoam on your mic, even indoors, to prevent breath noise and help absorb some of the blow if your mic is ever accidentally dropped.
Blimp 	Also known as zeppelins, these little mic housings are pricey, but they are hands down the most effective solution for blocking wind noise when shooting exteriors. The pistol grip has a sound shockmount at the top for the mic and also allows you to use mics that are normally boom-mounted in small spaces without a boom pole.
Windjammer 	To make your zeppelin even more effective at blocking wind noise, slip on a windjammer (also affectionately known as a "dead cat"), and you can still shoot on moderately windy days. Use a hairbrush to fluff it before shooting for maximum effect. This is an item that you can go cheaper with a guerrilla substitute, if you are handy with a sewing machine and have a piece of faux fur. Look online for DIY windjammer instructions.

PRE-AMPS, MIXERS, AND RECORDERS

Sync Digital Recorder

There is a new generation of high-end digital recorders that have replaced the DAT tape machines of yesterday. These devices digitally record to flash media cards, and the higher-end versions such as the Sound Devices 702T even lay down timecode. The media files generated are edit ready.

Digital Mixer

Just like recorders, many mixers have now gone all-digital. This is vital accessory for your second round of purchases when you are ready to get more serious about audio. Mixers allow you to use multiple mics, offer greater and remote control over audio, and have much better pre-amps.

Analog Mixer

If a digital mixer is just out of your budget range, for a little less cash, you can get an analog mixer with peaking needles instead of peaking lights or LEDs. The Shure FP-33 mixer here is an old-school workhorse three-channel field mixer that's been around for decades.

Handheld Recorder

For the DSLR set, there is now a whole cadre of small portable digital recorders such as the Zoom H4 that will help you overcome the severe audio limitations of DSLR cameras by recording on a completely independent device and syncing the audio tracks later in postproduction. Any audio recorder for filmmaking purposes should have XLR inputs like this model, so you can hook up professional microphones.

Pre-Amp

A pre-amp is similar to a mixer, only without as much functionality or the ability to route three or more channels of audio. Instead, it has one core function and that is to process and amplify audio signals from mics and other sound devices much better than the camera's pre-amp. The Sound Device's Mixpre is seen at left.

Juiced Link

Another popular device for the DSLR set, the Juiced Link box is a pre-amp that allows you to feed XLR mics and devices into a DSLR camera and consumer cameras that only have a little mini-stereo audio input jack. This box employs a unique trick to override the Canon 7D's autogain and give you manual audio control, but this trick also makes it impossible to listen back to audio until you're in post.

Beachtek Box

Similar to the Juiced Link box above, Beachtek Boxes have been around for a long time as the go-to solution to allow you to use pro XLR audio equipment with cameras that have only a mini-stereo mic input. They provide phantom power and have mic/line settings and external knobs that allow you to control levels as well.

Sound Mixer

The sound mixer's main job is setting the audio levels by operating a mixer and/or separate audio recorder. The mixer is in charge of maintaining the quality of the audio and coming up with audio strategies to best capture each scene.

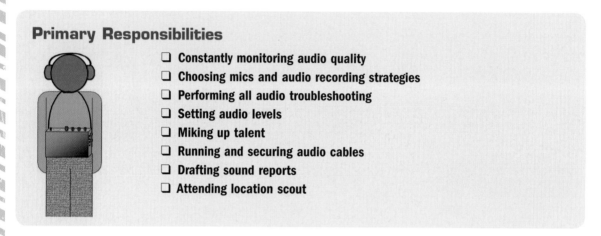

Primary Responsibilities

- ❑ Constantly monitoring audio quality
- ❑ Choosing mics and audio recording strategies
- ❑ Performing all audio troubleshooting
- ❑ Setting audio levels
- ❑ Miking up talent
- ❑ Running and securing audio cables
- ❑ Drafting sound reports
- ❑ Attending location scout

Doing It Well: A good sound mixer needs to have a wealth of knowledge and experience. The two most crucial aspects of the job are the ability to quickly devise effective audio strategies for a wide variety of shooting situations and to be able to quickly detect and troubleshoot audio problems–which are common.

Boom Operator

The boom op's job is pretty simple on the surface: hold the boom. However, it's by no means a job that anybody can do. The boom op is the right-hand person to the sound mixer and generally should have much of the same expert knowledge as a sound mixer. The job of boom op requires stamina; careful attention to what's happening in real-time; and a certain amount of expert knowledge about boom positions, mic patterns, and the needs of the camera.

Doing It Well: The key to doing this job is knowing multiple techniques to hold the boom and *anticipating* what's going to happen audio-wise and with camera...and then always being one step ahead of the action.

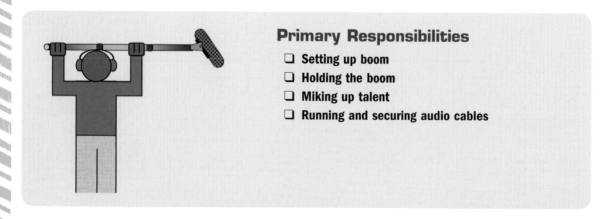

Primary Responsibilities

- ❑ Setting up boom
- ❑ Holding the boom
- ❑ Miking up talent
- ❑ Running and securing audio cables

Mixer/Boom

Just as it sounds, the mixer/boom position combines all the duties of the mixer and boom op as just listed. This person is a one-man (or one-woman) band of audio expertise, stamina, and multitasking. While it's not uncommon, pulling off this hybrid position is considerably more difficult than doing either job alone, as it requires the audio person to deftly hold a boom and still keep their eyes on the levels. The reality is that booms dipping into the frame, soft sections of audio, or other common audio mistakes are more likely to occur with so much responsibility on just one person.

Primary Responsibilities

- ❑ Constantly monitoring audio quality
- ❑ Choosing mics and audio recording strategies
- ❑ Performing all audio troubleshooting
- ❑ Setting audio levels
- ❑ Miking up talent
- ❑ Running and securing audio cables
- ❑ Drafting sound reports
- ❑ Setting up the boom
- ❑ Holding the boom
- ❑ Attending the location scout

Doing It Well: Pulling off double-duty on audio calls for someone with enough knowledge and experience to stay on top of both jobs at once. Because there's only one set of eyes and ears on audio, attention to detail is crucial. This double-duty position is *not* recommended for newbies.

My Mic Sounds Nice...Check One, Two, Three!

Check One!—People

Look at the scenario, script, etc., and think about how many people you have to record at the same time, how those people will be situated, and what types of mics you have at your disposal. For example, if you have three people talking around a table, you could cover their dialog in several different ways. The simplest way if you have a small package is to just have a boom op cover whoever is speaking at any given moment. For the greatest control over the audio in a three-way conversation, putting lavs on all three speakers and feeding the audio into a mixer would allow you to set each individual's ideal level. If you have a larger group of people, say six or more, you might want to consider using two boom mics to cover all the conversation. If it's more of a controlled conversation in a larger group, such as a group interview, you can instruct people to pause for a moment before speaking to give the boom op time to get into position. **(See "Group Interviews" page 173.)**

SITUATION	MIC CHOICE
Stationary Subject	■ Boom mic
	■ Boom mic on stand
	■ Hardwired lav mic
	■ Handheld mic on stand
Moving Subjects	■ Wireless lav mic
	■ Boom mic
Multiperson Conversation	■ Boom mic
	■ Lav mics
Subject at Desk	■ Hardwired lav mic
	■ Boom mic on stand
	■ Plant mic
In Car	■ Wireless lav
	■ Hardwired lav on subject or hidden in a car
	■ External shotgun mic on camera
	■ Shotgun on pistol grip
Wide Shot	■ Wireless lav
	■ Plant mic
Group at a Table	■ Hardwired lavs
	■ Table mic

Check Two!—Pattern

The next thing you want to consider when picking a mic is its pickup pattern. Pickup pattern on a mic is similar to focal length on a lens in that it determines the range and space that a microphone can record. Here are the most common pickup patterns:

PICKUP PATTERN	COMMON IN	RECOMMENDED FOR
Hypercardioid	■ Shotgun mics ■ Handheld mics	■ Recording dialog ■ dialog in noisy environments ■ Foley sound FX ■ Booming
Cardioid	■ Handheld mic ■ Short shotgun (as plant/ desktop)	■ Stand-up interviews ■ Talk formats ■ Audience Q&A ■ Recording voice-overs
Omni	■ Lavaliere mics ■ Stick mics	■ Sit-down interviews (lav only) ■ Ambience (stick mic only)

Check Three!—Position

Finally, you will need to choose a boom position. Boom positions should be chosen, for practicality based on the particular scenario you are recording.

Overhead
Pro: Easy to twist mic axis and
follow moving subjects
Con: Hard to hold for long time.

Shoulder
Pro: Easy to hold/switch to
Con: Clothing noise; slower to move.

Below
Pro: Easy to hold for long time
Con: Plane/vent noise; gets in the way of
moving subjects.

Pelvic
Pro: Can hold one-handed long time
Con: Can cut off frame angles moved diagonally.

Pistol Grip
Pro: Very mobile, low profile overhead time
Con: Shorter reach; limited angles.

Mic Choice, Meters and Miking Pianos

JOCELYN GONZALES, FREELANCE AUDIO PRODUCER, *NEW YORK TIMES*
(JocelynGonzales.net)

DYNAMIC VERSUS CONDENSER MICS

Most music venues have a combination of mics—condenser and dynamic. The Shure SM57s and SM58s are a popular choice. They are dynamic mics, which means that they don't need phantom or battery power. Often they are used in a lot of club situations because they can handle high SPLs, or loud volumes, sudden transients, and screaming without distorting. Dynamic mics are less sensitive and more rugged. You can drop them. (Although it's not *advised*.) You can put them in front of a drum kit. They just have a lower sensitivity to bigger sounds. They have a pretty flat frequency response, so what you put in is pretty much what you get out. They are not going to "color" the band's sound that much.

Condenser mics are great too, but I personally don't see them used in live situations that much simply because the actual electronics inside make them a lot more fragile. If you drop a condenser mic, you are likely to see little chips fall out. They usually need another power supply, and you might easily forget that and it might go dead or someone might trip over it. We have crates of dynamic mics for most gigs. The reason people buy a lot of them is that they are only about $110 apiece, so you can invest in several of them. They will be good in front of a vocalist. They will be good on a drum kit. And they will be good on a guitar. Because of the flatter frequency response, they are very versatile and can be used for a pretty wide variety of instruments and voices.

RECORDING A PIANO

With any type of piano, whether it's an upright or grand piano, I recommend generally starting by opening up the top, so you can mic the strings. You want to mic the upper and the lower half of the strings inside as the mallets hit them. But you don't want to go all the way down or up to the extreme ends of the piano because you're going to miss anything that's played in the center and pianos have a wide mid-tonal range. Instead, you want to mic the low-mid and upper-mid range of the strings. You would also tend to record a piano in stereo, so you need two microphones; that's the best way to mic the piano. You can mic a piano with just one mic if you're short on mics, but you have to know the music. You have to know *what* they are going to play because you might actually have to move that one mic around the piano for each song in order to get it placed just right. You don't want it to be pointing at the lower end (bassy) when the next song is all high notes—because you wouldn't be catching any of that. So I would always try to use two mics instead. I have recorded a piano with both two Shure dynamic mics and with two AKG 414 condenser mics. The condensers suck up more sound and give you more harmonic overtones and detail on each note. Anytime a string vibrates on a piano or a guitar, it has its own frequency, but it's also setting off other vibrations in the other strings that are mathematical multiples of it. So you get a "fat" sound from it. It's not just one frequency; it's several frequencies sounding together in tune for every string. The condensers will pick up more of that "fat" sound. But they both work well.

ANALOG VERSUS PEAKING METERS

It's sometimes harder to read these digital LED meters than it used to be with analog needles. The hardest thing for people to understand with digital meters is that once you go over, *you go over*. There is no repairing it. You have run out of bits. There is no more digital information to assign to the size of the signal you just recorded, so it's garbage.

Analog meters show you a peaking average, so if you see something peaking or pinned constantly in an analog system, you are being very obnoxious with your levels. If you peak once or twice on an analog system, you might not hear the distortion, and it will usually absorb that momentary peak. You won't see red lights blinking like you would in the digital system, and it's more forgiving in that way. Typically, if someone wants sound to be their career, they would study how to read both analog and digital peaking meters at the same time.

I think the easiest way to understand digital versus analog audio measurements is to think of it as the difference between the metric system (meters, milliliters, etc.) and the English system (yards, inches, etc.) of measuring. They are simply two very different scales to measure the exact same thing. However, just like the metric and English systems, the important point is to always be aware of exactly which one you're dealing with and to know how to translate one into the other. So let's start with how you can generally tell the difference.

Don't screw it up.... When you're using an analog mixer and a digital camera, tone should be sent from the mixer at 0/VU but set on the camera at −12dB or −20dB.

DIGITAL VERSUS ANALOG AUDIO

COMPARISON	DIGITAL AUDIO	ANALOG AUDIO
Ideal Peaking Level:	−12dB or −20dB*	0/VU
Audio Measured In:	dB (decibels)	VU (volume units)
Display Type:	LED Lights, LCD	Moving Needle
Scale Ends In:	0/dB	+3VU or +5VU
Response:	Instantaneous	Slight delay

*See "Why There Are There Two Different Audio Standards?" next page.

On *digital* equipment, you want your audio
to peak at *−12dB or −20dB*.
However, on *analog* devices, your levels
should peak at *0/dB*.

Exceptions to the General Rules

Now mind you, not everything on the previous chart is a 100 percent hard-and-fast rule, as devices vary from manufacturer to manufacturer. For example, some modern analog equipment may actually use LED lights to measure VU levels, such as the Sound Devices 302 Mixer, and some scales will end past +3dB.

Exceptions to the Rule—Some modern analog equipment like this mixer has LED peaking meters instead of a peaking needle.

However, if you look at the where the peaking scale ends and whether it's measured in VU (analog volume units) or dB (digital decibels), you can pretty easily tell what type of audio scale you are dealing with and know where to set your levels. If you are ever completely clueless or working with a scale that has no markings (common on consumer equipment), you generally won't go too wrong keeping your levels a few marks to the right of center on horizontal meters or a few marks above center on vertical meters.

Why Are There Two Different Digital Standards?

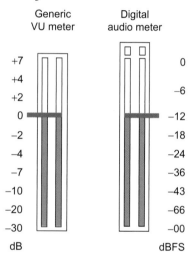

Generic VU meter

| +7 |
| +4 |
| +2 |
| 0 |
| −2 |
| −4 |
| −7 |
| −10 |
| −20 |
| −30 |

dB

Digital audio meter

| 0 |
| −6 |
| −12 |
| −18 |
| −24 |
| −36 |
| −43 |
| −66 |
| −00 |

dBFS

In short, the reason digital equipment is set at −12dB *or* −20dB (as opposed to strictly one or the other) is personal preference. If you want to play it pretty safe and have a little more headroom in case of sudden loud noises, you should let your audio peak at −20dB. If you like to live life a little more on the wild side, you can do what I do and let that baby peak out at −12dB to give yourself a better chance of capturing healthy levels for quieter sections of speech.

If you ask any two audio people, they'll each have their own preference and reasoning why they go with one or the other. Even though the two numbers sound vastly different, if you actually look at the distance between −12dB and −20dB on a digital audio scale, it's actually fairly negligible.

SETTING PROPER AUDIO LEVELS

Camera mistakes we can fix and cover up in a variety of creative and often easy ways. However, audio mistakes are unforgiving; we have to get the audio right the first time, every time. Getting it "right" starts with getting healthy levels—not too soft and definitely not too hot, but juuust right in the audio sweet spot that I like to call the "Super Happy Fun Sound Zone."

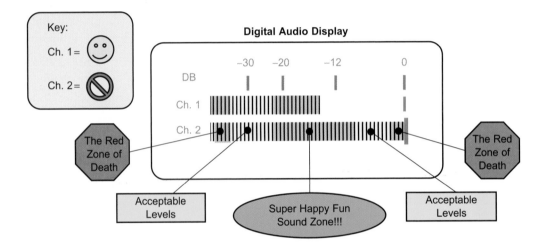

THE DIGITAL AUDIO SWEET SPOT

On *digital* quipment (such as your camera or digital recorder) you want your audio levels to peak roughly between **–20dB and –12dB** on average.

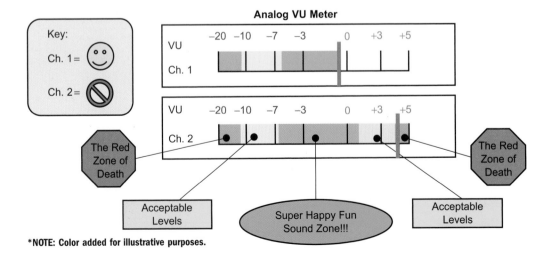

THE ANALOG AUDIO SWEET SPOT

On *analog* equipment (such as certain models of mixers) you want your audio levels to peak at **0 VU** on average.

*NOTE: Color added for illustrative purposes.

BRACKETING YOUR AUDIO

Bracketing in action on a Sony EX-1

One practical recording technique that you can use to help cover your butt when recording audio from a single mic or other single audio input is bracketing. Bracketing is a term that refers to recording the *same* audio signal to two different channels at slightly different levels. The idea is that if there are sudden rises or dips in the sound level (or if you just flake out for a moment and allow a stretch of dialog to overmodulate), at least one of those channels is likely to capture that section of audio more clearly, and *that's* the one you'll use. Remember, you can easily copy and paste to mix either (or both) audio channels in your NLE during postproduction.

CHANNEL 1	CHANNEL 2	USE WHEN:
Set manually at normal levels	Set manually a little higher than normal	...you anticipate many *quiet* sections of audio. Examples: ■ Soft-spoken subjects ■ Ambient sound ■ Shy people
Set manually at normal levels	Set manually a little lower than normal	...you anticipate many sudden loud rises in audio. Examples: ■ Audience laughter ■ Stage acting ■ Boisterous conversation
Set manually at normal levels	Set to AGC (automatic gain control)	...you are recording in an unpredictable situation, a situation where it's difficult to monitor audio, or where there are a lot of fluctuations in the audio level. Examples: ■ A public rally ■ A concert ■ A stage musical

When you are ready to expand your sound kit, one of the first things you'll want to consider is whether you should purchase a wireless mic kit. The next thing you'll want to consider is whether you can *afford* to purchase a wireless mic kit, because at $500 to $4,000+, they ain't cheap, but they can often be invaluable in certain shooting situations. Wireless mics are among those pieces of equipment that you don't need that often, but when you need them, you really need them because there just isn't any substitute that can do the same thing. So when do you really need them? Let's take a look...

When to Use Wireless

1. Moving/Active Talent

If your talent is a chef giving a cooking demonstration or a college dean taking you on a walking tour of the new building, they are going to be on the move. While a shotgun mic on a boom pole is a common workable solution here, a boom operator stands to get in the way or distract the talent and could also restrict wide shots. A wireless mic won't slow down the action or hinder your subjects in anyway.

2. More Distant Talent

Because of the golden sound rule of always getting the mic as close as possible without getting in the shot, wide shots and boom mics don't mix. When the subjects speaking are further away from the camera, as in a wide shot of a couple walking and talking on the beach, there's no room to get a boom operator close enough to get decent sound. So you've got three real choices (and the first two suck): (1) **ADR** the whole thing in post, (2) boom it from far away, or (3) go wireless...And the winner is - (3) go wireless!

3. Intimacy with Talent

This particularly applies to documentary-style shooting of people in real-life situations such as a personal conversation or a real interaction with a customer.

4. Secret or Sensitive Recording Situations

Wireless lav mics are also handy for those rare situations where it's not appropriate or advisable to use a camera. Examples of this are investigative journalism when you want to covertly record a conversation. Or sensitive situations where the presence of a camera (but not necessarily audio) might be undesirable, such as a meeting, job interview, or audition. Any decent professional wireless mic can easily be picked up from 50 yards or more away with crystal clarity through most building walls, even a from few floors down, so audio can be recorded to camera from a distance. Even without picture, the audio recording will effectively tell the story. Laws vary state-to-state and obviously, there are potential legal and ethical issues involved here, so you should consult an attorney before recording anything without someone else's knowledge.

1 Use Fresh Batteries

Always use fresh premium-brand batteries when starting a new shoot. If you've been recording a clean signal for a while from the same distance but then start to get hiss, static or dropouts (periods of no sound at all), then the most likely culprit is low batteries. If it's not the batteries, it may be interference, and you can usually fix the problem by switching frequencies.

Make absolutely sure that the transmitter unit with the mic on it is turned on and has full battery power just before the shooting starts. One of the worst audio nightmares you can ever experience is to have that mic signal break up and then go dead in the middle of an important moment or performance, forcing you to interrupt the proceedings to change batteries or forcing you to capture the rest of the event with just your camera mic. Both options truly suck. Do your best to avoid either situation.

2 Don't Embarrass Your Clients

People on wireless mics often forget that they are broadcasting everything they say back to the camera. Be careful about inadvertently recording any embarrassing comments or private conversations that your clients would not wish to hear and share with their loved ones, colleagues, or bosses on video for the rest of their days. If you do happen to record anything less than flattering to the clients, make sure it's edited out before the video is turned over.

3 Avoid Cheap Wireless Models

Good and reliable wireless mic units are not cheap. On the lower end of the price scale is the popular Sennheiser Evolution G3 model, which goes for about $500 as I write this. Don't waste your money on cheap VHF wireless mic units, which are much more prone to interference. You're better off sticking with more affordable hard-wired mics than risking CB truckers' colorful commentary breaking into your soundtrack.

4 Scan to Find Open Channels

The golden rule for setting up a wireless mic and receiver is that they must both be on the exact same channel. However, it's possible that other wireless devices such as walkie-talkies, local radio signals, etc., might also be on or very close to the same channel. Many wireless mic models have a "scan" feature that can scan the local area for open channels where you are least likely to get interference. If your wireless unit has this feature, use it.

Wireless mic receiver and transmitter unit.

5 Have an Audio "Plan B"

It's a good idea to test your wireless mic units at the actual location during the rehearsal. And it's equally smart to always have a backup plan and hard-wired mics on standby to capture sound in case you do have any nasty wireless issues. Don't get got. Be prepared for whatever.

TAMING WIND NOISE

The most common audio problem you'll encounter when shooting exteriors is wind noise. Any large open space without sufficient obstacles to block the wind is going to be most susceptible to wind noise. City rooftops can be a particularly deceptive location because down at street level everything could sound perfectly fine, but six stories up on a rooftop, it's often much windier than on the ground, since there are no longer any buildings to block the wind.

Wind Noise Is Most Likely...

on rooftops...   on waterfronts...   at the beach...   ...and on open fields.

Blocking Out Wind Noise

1. Use a Zeppelin with a "Dead Cat"

A simple windfoam slipped over your mic will offer some protection against wind noise on a normal, calm day, but the hands-down best solution to stop wind noise is using a zeppelin with a windjammer (aka "dead cat"). The plastic blimp-like housing of the zeppelin protects the mic from most moderate wind, but with the furry windjammer fitted over the zeppelin, you can shoot in heavier wind conditions with only a fraction of the wind noise you'd get from a bare mic.

2. Use a Building or Other Obstacle to Block Wind Noise

A quick and simple fix to your wind noise blues is to block out wind noise using any large obstacle or structure on location. Strategically position your boom next to a dumpster, large sign, corner of a building, or any obstacle. Even holding up a large piece of cardboard near the mic will do the trick.... It really doesn't matter as long as whatever you're using is in the right

position to *block* the wind from the mic. (Hey, production solutions don't have to be complicated or high-tech; they just have to be *effective*. That's Down and Dirty.)

3. Filter It Out Onset

The third solution to wind noise—filtering—can be used in conjunction with any or all of the above. Most mixers and some mics have a built-in lo-cut filter, which cuts out the low-frequency rumbles of wind hitting the mic. Similarly, you can also cut out the same low frequencies in postproduction using a graphic equalizer or any of the simple audio modules built into most computer editing programs. (See "Hot Tip: Graphic Equalizer" on page 96.)

DEALING WITH SHORTS

Beware Shorts

One of the audio issues that you want to be particularly vigilant of is shorts. An audio short results when a cable or wire that transmits the audio signal is not connecting fully or consistently and results in crackling or popping on your audio soundtrack or even ***dropouts*** in your audio, which could eventually devolve into getting no sound at all from that cable or connection.

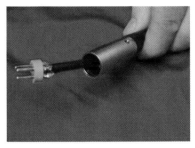

The soldered wires inside an XLR cable.

Shorts are caused by a loose wire somewhere in an audio or video cable connector or port. Shorts are a common result of wear and tear on a cable's connections or ports for cables. Rough handling, extra strain, people tripping over cables, and routine abuse are all contributing factors that make it much more likely that your gear or cable will develop a short.

Having an audio short is a particularly dangerous problem because it's an *intermittent* problem, so sometimes it's there and sometimes it's not. It all depends on which position the cable and/or your equipment is in whether or not the tiny wire connects at a given moment and transmits the signal. This is dangerous because it's very possible that you could do a full audio check and everything could sound fine and then start dropping out on you an hour or so later in the middle of your crucial shoot.

Detecting Shorts

The easiest way to detect a short is to connect a mic and then hook up all your audio cables, end to end, and plug into your camera or mixer. Then you can listen with headphones as you jiggle the cables around some–particularly near the connections–and listen for crackles and dropouts.

Avoiding Shorts

❑ **Don't Drop Cables**–Repeatedly dropping or throwing an XLR cable head on the ground can knock loose the little wires connected to the prongs inside the cable head, giving you a one-way ticket to Short City. Population–YOU.

❑ **Don't Strain a Cable**–Pulling cables tightly or tripping over the cable and yanking them can short the cable or the camera's XLR port. (Yikes!)

❑ **Avoid Heavy/Awkward Adapters**–Plugging large adapters directly into an XLR port could cause a short in the worst place: your camera audio port. Use L-shaped adapters when necessary to take some of the strain off the XLR port.

❑ **Secure Cables**–Secure your cables to the tripod leg with tape or Velcro ties for stationary shots, so cables don't strain the port if they are pulled or tripped over.

TWO MICS ARE ALWAYS BETTER THAN ONE

One big thing you can do to increase your chances of quickly recovering from an audio mistake is being redundant in your setups. Even if a scene only calls for one mic, I still recommend using two mics as often as possible. These dual-mic setups take more time and effort, but once you've been burned a time or two with bad audio, they won't seem like nearly so much trouble as reshooting the whole scene or slinking over to the director with your tail between your legs.

Here are a few common tricks of the trade that can save the day. If there is a cable short, low batteries, an actor accidentally hitting the mic, wind noise, or any other unfortunate (but not uncommon) occurrence that may ruin a take, a second mic may still get the shot crisp and clean...or at least usable. Your options will be limited by your equipment and shooting circumstances, but here are a few Common Backup Mic Strategies.

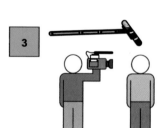

Mic #1 – Shotgun Boom
Mic #2 – Lav Mic

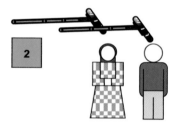

Mic #1 – Shotgun Boom
Mic #2 – Shotgun Boom

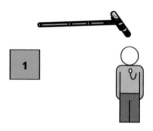

Mic #1 – Camera Shotgun Mic
Mic #2 – Shotgun Boom Mic

Mic #1 – Shotgun Boom
Mic #2 – Hidden "Plant" Mic

Mic #1 – Camera Shotgun Mic
Mic #2 – Lav Mic

Mic #1 – Camera Shotgun Mic
Mic #2 – Handheld Mic

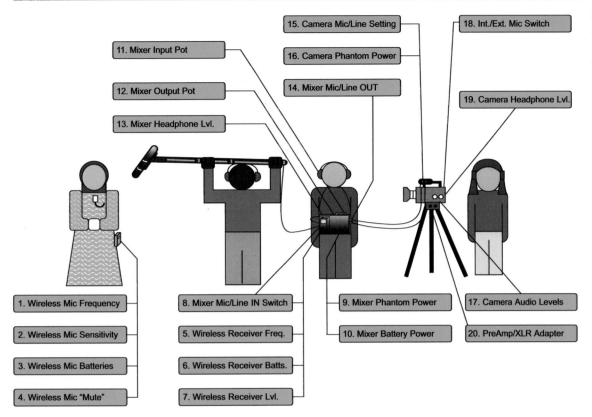

15. Camera Mic/Line Setting

18. Int./Ext. Mic Switch

11. Mixer Input Pot

16. Camera Phantom Power

12. Mixer Output Pot

14. Mixer Mic/Line OUT

19. Camera Headphone Lvl.

13. Mixer Headphone Lvl.

1. Wireless Mic Frequency

8. Mixer Mic/Line IN Switch

9. Mixer Phantom Power

17. Camera Audio Levels

2. Wireless Mic Sensitivity

5. Wireless Receiver Freq.

10. Mixer Battery Power

20. PreAmp/XLR Adapter

3. Wireless Mic Batteries

6. Wireless Receiver Batts.

4. Wireless Mic "Mute"

7. Wireless Receiver Lvl.

When I say, "Your audio is more important than your video," I don't mean in terms of the storytelling–*all* the elements of storytelling are important. What I really mean is that you have to always pay careful attention to your audio because there is much greater potential for things to go wrong. And when audio problems do occur, they are usually much harder to detect, cover up, or fix (*if* they can even be fixed at all)....so to me that makes audio more important.

There are anywhere from 6 to 20 possible points of failure that might cause you to have bad audio or no audio at all. In most cases, it's simply a matter of a single switch being on the wrong setting. The best and fastest way to diagnose the problem is to physically trace the path of your audio signal (aka "audio chain") **in order** from the mic all the way through *ALL* the audio devices, settings, and switches until you get to the final signal being recorded to your camera.

1. Wireless Mic Frequency

Check to make sure that your wireless mic transmitter unit is on the same frequency as your receiver unit. If the frequencies don't match exactly (including the number after the decimal points), you will get no audio signal at all or a weak signal that fades in and out.

2. Wireless Mic Sensitivity

Make sure that you have adjusted the sensitivity on the wireless mic transmitter unit to reflect healthy levels, which should be somewhere just to the right of the middle. If your sound is too low or too hot, this is the first place to check in the "audio chain."

3. Wireless Mic Batteries

Check to make sure that your mic transmitter unit has sufficient battery power—at least two bars or more. It's always best to start out with fresh premium-brand batteries.

4. Wireless Mic "Mute" Switch

Another simple but common mistake is not to realize that the mute button is turned on for the mic unit. (It is a "duuuuh" mistake that I have made on more than one occasion.) Check the "mute" switch on the mixer and look out for a mute indicator on the display screen before you waste a bunch of time checking all the other settings below.

5. Wireless Receiver Frequency

Your wireless receiver is the other half of the wireless mic unit that's picking up the signal being sent by the mic transmitter. It too must be on the *exact* same channel as the transmitter, or you will get a degraded signal, static, or no audio signal at all.

6. Wireless Receiver Batteries

Next up, check to make sure that your receiver unit has enough juice to last the gig. Low battery power on ANY sound device is like local TV— nothing but bad news.

7. Wireless Receiver Level Out

Next up, make sure that your wireless receiver unit is being sent out to your mixer or camera at good and healthy levels—generally described as somewhere just right of center.

8. Mixer Mic/Line IN Switch

If you are using a mixer (highly recommended), then the receiver gets plugged into the mixer input, which can be set to receive a mic or line level signal. Generally, if you are plugging in a microphone, this will pretty much always be set to "mic." For anything other than a mic it will probably be set to "line." (Imagine that; something in video that's actually intuitive for a change!)

9. Mixer Phantom Power

Most shotgun mics are condenser mics that require **phantom power** to work. The phantom power comes from whatever device they are plugged into, be it a camera, mixer, or other device. However, phantom power is yet another switch that must be turned on when using condenser mics or "There shall be NO sound for YOU!".

10. Mixer Battery Power

Always periodically check to make sure that your mixer still has plenty of battery power throughout shooting. Ideally, your mixer will just stop working if the batteries run low, but beware—some models such as the Shure FP-33 field mixer won't just cut off, but actually start to record crappier and crappier audio as the audio signal dies a slow and ugly death. (Think of a scene from the movie *Saw*.) You won't always catch this quickly in your headphones in a live performance situation, so make it a habit to check routinely. I recommend always starting with fresh premium-brand batteries for every shoot.

11. Mixer Input Pot

Now that we've established that the mixer has good battery levels and that the input jack is set to receive the right kind of signal—mic or line—the next thing is just to make sure that the input **pot** (aka knob) is turned up sufficiently if you are still getting no audio or low audio.

12. Mixer Output Pot

From the mixer's input pot, the audio signal is sent over to the mixer's output pot, where the level can be adjusted again for whatever device will be recording the final signal—likely a camera or audio recorder. Once you send tone to a camera or recorder and set the levels, it's extremely important that you not change the output again. (Note that some mixers may not have an output pot, which is fine, because that's one *less* thing to worry about right.)

13. Mixer Headphone Level

Often your audio signal will be getting through to the camera just fine, and you'll be checking all the knobs and meters trying to figure out what's wrong, and the only problem will be that you didn't have your headphone volume (aka monitor volume) turned up. If you see strong audio levels on your peaking meters but are still *hearing* low levels, you probably have your monitor volume turned down too low.

14. Mixer Mic/Line OUT

Make sure that the "mic/line" setting going out of the mixer is set to the exact same setting as the mic/line switch on your camera. The "Line" setting is the stronger of the two types of signals, so set it to "Line" whenever you have that option on your camera or recorder. If these settings don't match between mixer and camera, your signal will be extremely weak or horribly over-modulated. As NAS would say, "It ain't hard to tell."

15. Camera Mic/Line Setting

Same thing I said in #14 above, but now you're checking for the correct switch setting on the camera.

16. Camera Phantom Power

If you are going straight into the camera from an external mic and getting no audio signal at all on your LCD screen, you probably have the phantom power turned off. Look for a setting (usually right under the XLR input port) that says "Mic +48V." That's the phantom power. Dynamic (i.e., unpowered) mics and mixers do not require phantom power to operate. Note that you want to always turn OFF the phantom power on your camera or audio recorder for a signal coming in from a mixer or other device (such as a Beachtek or Juiced Link XLR adapter) that already has its *own* power because having phantom power turned on unnecessarily could cause funky audio problems or even damage some equipment.

17. Camera Audio Levels

Now that you are sure that the little black box on your camera has all the right settings, check to make sure that the levels for audio channels 1 and 2 are actually turned up. (Some models may use L–left and R–right instead of channels 1 and 2) Many earlier generation prosumer cameras were designed such that these dials could easily get acciden-tally bumped during production, which resulted in many amateur audio disasters. Most designs these days have recessed dials or a little plastic shield, making it much harder to accidentally change the levels during normal camera handling.

18. Internal/External Mic Switch

Another little switch to look out for is the internal/external mic switch, which selects between recording a signal from the camera's internal (i.e., built-in or onboard mic) and any external mic or device plugged into the XLR ports. A very common and dangerous mistake is to have another mic plugged in, but to inadvertently have this switch set to "INT" (internal). It's dangerous because filmmakers are often fooled since they will be getting audio levels and sound from their headphones, but it will actually be the audio from the *onboard mic*, when they thought they were recording from a boom or lav, and it usually sounds pretty bad compared to what they should've been getting. The easy way to avoid this everyday audio disaster is to always *listen* as you give your mic a gentle tap or rub to make sure that the mic you think you're hearing really is the mic that's being recorded.

19. Camera Headphone Level

Yes, this should be a no-brainer, but sooner or later, we all get temporarily stymied by the old headphone volume being turned down low—the audio equivalent of leaving the lens cap on. Just as with the mixer, always check the camera's monitor (aka headphone) volume level if you are hearing very low levels or no levels. It's a simple but common error, especially since we often turn down the headphones when we record bars and tone to camera during our audio setup.

20. PreAmp/XLR Adapter

Although it's not actually hooked up (or needed) in the diagram here, filmmakers shooting on DSLR cameras or cameras without XLR ports, usually will have some sort of audio device such as a pre-amp or XLR adapter that allows them to hook up professional XLR audio mics and devices into their camera's mini-stereo audio input. Make sure these units are turned on, fully plugged in, have sufficient battery power and the proper mic or line level settings—or once again, you could easily end up with no audio or bad audio.

> **A Final Note:** So now that you've read all *that*, I think it's a little more clear why I always say, "**Your audio is <u>MORE</u> important than your video.**" There are many more potential points of failure with audio—some tricky to detect. However, you will learn them all with painful experience, or by having the wisdom to read this book...Smart choice.

Yet another source of potential audio frustrations can be found in the camera's menu. Make it a habit to check key settings on the camera menu system, including the audio menu set. Specifically, check these things:

1. Audio Monitoring Setup

These settings affect only how you *hear* the audio through your headphones, not what's actually being recorded. Nevertheless, if you inadvertently have them on a wrong setting, you may panic (on the inside) that you are not recording audio on one of the channels or mistakenly listen to the opposite channel you intended to. (This can occur with the "CH1" or "CH2" settings on the following chart.) Audio pros monitor camera or mixer audio in **Stereo – CH1/CH2**, so they can hear Channel 1 in their left ear and Channel 2 in their right ear to easily pinpoint any issues with either channel.

AUDIO MONITORING SELECTION

MENU	TYPE	WHAT YOU HEAR
CH1/CH2	Stereo	Channel 1 will be heard in the left ear while Channel 2 will be heard in the right ear.
CH1+CH2	Mono	*Both* channels 1 and 2 will be heard equally in *both* ears at the same time.
CH 1	Channel 1 Only	Only Channel 1 will be heard in *both* ears.
CH2	Channel 2 Only	Only Channel 2 will be heard in *both* ears.

2. External Channel Select

Some cameras have menu settings that allow you to enable or disable one of the external mic channels. When it is disabled in the menu, the XLR port simply won't work no matter what switches you change. If your camera has such an audio menu setting, I think it's a good idea to just leave both ports always turned on to avoid any confusion.

3. Audio Trim

Another new (and very useful) feature that has started cropping up on some prosumer cameras is audio **trim,** which allows you to amplify or decrease the level of a signal being fed into the camera from a mixer, mic, or other audio device. This means you can quickly adjust a weak or hot signal, particularly when you are plugging into a mixing board or other audio device. If your camera has this feature, check the manual and make sure it's still on the factory default setting when you *aren't* trying to adjust the incoming signal before it gets to the normal audio level controls.

4. External Power Sources

More often than not, the mics you use will run off phantom power, but you may occasionally use some units that run off an external power source, such as a T-Power capsule or PS-1 box that holds a 9-volt battery. Make sure you've got a good battery. If you touch both terminals of a 9-volt battery to your tongue and get a good little shock, they're good. No shock or just a very mild buzz means your 9 volt is bad. (Probably best *not* to try this if you have a pacemaker.**)**

Location Recording Issues and Post Tools

JOCELYN GONZALES, FREELANCE AUDIO PRODUCER, *NEW YORK TIMES*
(JocelynGonzales.net)

LOCATION AUDIO RECORDING ISSUES

One of the main problems with the footage that I get back from my reporters is that they do not get close enough to whomever they are talking to. Because we have audio people working with video people, sometimes there is a disconnect. They think that if the picture looks good, the audio must sound cool too. But they forget that a camera person can zoom in and make it look like they were standing close, but the audio person has got to come in closer or boom from underneath to get decent audio. Lavalier mics are quite useful for these situations as well. At the end of the day, we end up having to fix less than stellar audio with a number of noise reduction and gain plug-ins and trying to EQ it. Another common problem is distortion. Sound people need to constantly watch the levels when someone gets excited or starts shouting. If they are taping a rally or public gathering, and people yell and cheer, that tends to distort and overmodulate. So those are things you can't always anticipate; you do the best you can and try to edit around it in post. Another thing is wind distortion. If wind noise is really obvious, you can EQ *some* of it out with a bass roll-off filter, but if it really tore up the mic head, you can't do anything with it. You can try, but more than likely you're still going to have broken up audio and dropouts.

KNOW WHAT THE SOUND DEPARTMENT NEEDS

As a director, you should be aware of the issues of the sound department—both out in the field and in post. Even if we don't hold the mic ourselves or set the level ourselves or hit "play," we know what our sound people need and we make room for them. We have respect for those challenges and issues and address them. And we know enough about the issues to be able to communicate with the sound editor or sound mixer effectively. Over the years, I have heard some very wacky conversations between directors and their mixers. Since you're a technical person, sure sometimes people think you are crazy or you are just being anal, but you know that you need to take care of certain issues in order to make your job complete. And some filmmakers don't understand that. Unfortunately, I think sound people experience this scenario *a lot*.

ROOM TONE

In interview situations, room tone lets me patch over edits that I might have to make to fix bad dialog. So, if I have a particularly nasty breath or somebody drops something or someone is talking, I can replace that with clean room tone and it's like it never happened. Also, room tone is useful to connect the edits. When there is a room tone track, edits from different sections of the raw audio will actually knit together better when they sit in the same room tone bed. A good example of when this is most useful is when we are working on a journalistic documentary-type piece and we are interviewing someone. More times than not, we need to grab this section of the interview and connect it to that section, but when you put them together, they kind of jump a little bit. In this situation, you can try and smooth out those cuts or make cross-fades using the room tone loop. When I'm recording on location, not only do I want clean room tone to loop for editing, but I also look for ambience that has some dynamic elements. This helps me create a sense of place, transitions, or a sense of activity. I actually use this a lot for masking. I don't just use ambiance to try and make a constant audio bed. I will actually look for something in the ambiance that's more active, like a dog barking or a car going by, and I will use that underneath the edit. It's a little audio fakeout that helps smooth out a rough cut.

AUDIO POST

For audio post I use ProTools and most of the tools that are included with the ProTools software. (**www.avid.com/US/products/Pro-Tools-Software**) The only thing I would buy extra are various Waves (**www.waves.com**); that's a bundle of very powerful audio plug-ins for compression, EQ, limiting, etc. They do get very expensive, it's true, but when you hear what they can do, they are worth the money. The other postproduction tool that I rely on is iZotope. (**www.izotope.com**) I cannot live without iZotope, which is a suite of plug-ins and a standalone application that helps you remove noise and clipping and assists with additional types of audio repair. For example, I use it for removing ground hum, rumble, pops and clicks—all very common problems that we have with audio.

Pro Tools

Waves

Izotope

FIXING LOCATION AUDIO IN POST

It's a long-running joke on many sets whenever someone says, "We'll fix it in post." This is often the mantra of an inexperienced, overly optimistic, or just plain delusional filmmaker, because more often than not, production mistakes and problems simply *can't* be "fixed in post." And even when they can, fixing the problems generally requires 10 times the amount of time, effort, and cost it would've taken to plan and capture the shot *correctly* on location. However, there's a notable exception to this general rule when it comes to many common location audio problems.

While we always want to capture our audio as clean as possible, in reality it ain't always possible. There will often be some hisses, hums, rumbles, and other audio annoyances that you just can't avoid or won't always catch in the heat of shooting. Thankfully, there is a fairly easy way to deal with many of these common location audio irritations: using a graphic equalizer. Just like all different sources of light have their own specific color temperature, all sounds have their own individual frequency. A graphic equalizer is a type of software or hardware device that allows you to hone in on a specific frequency and either increase or decrease the sounds in that frequency on your soundtrack.

No doubt some directors think they can "just remove" the background noise of these thundering waves when recording dialogue on the beach... They're probably in for a long and expensive post process.

So the trick to minimizing unwanted noises (such as hiss) and increasing desirable sounds (such as dialog) is to figure out what type of frequency you're dealing with–low, mid, or high– and then just bring the level of that frequency a little up or down. I wouldn't tweak any frequency more than 30–40 percent either way, because overdoing it can make your audio start to sound unnatural and weird. You can't always eliminate the noises you want to get rid of, but you can usually decrease their presence enough that it won't be nearly as noticeable. And if you are going to be playing music or narration over that section of the project, it will be *much* less noticeable. Whether or not you realize it, you've been using a simple form of graphic equalizer your entire life whenever you've turned up the treble or bass on your car stereo.

Peep my book, *The Shut Up and Shoot Documentary Guide* for more audio advice on:

❑ **Hooking Up a Mixer**
❑ **Mounting Lav Mics**
❑ **Boom Techniques**
❑ **Location Audio Hazards**
❑ **Audio/Video Cable Guide**
❑ **And More!**

GRAPHIC EQUALIZER

Just like audio mixers, graphic equalizing was traditionally possible only with hardware devices, but now there are also a variety of affordable software-based graphic equalizers that can do the job from the convenience of your computer. Not only that, but almost all nonlinear editing programs also have a built-in function to equalize audio and help you filter out the bad stuff and turn up the good stuff. Whether it's hardware or software, the concept works the same....

SECRETS OF THE GRAPHIC EQUALIZER

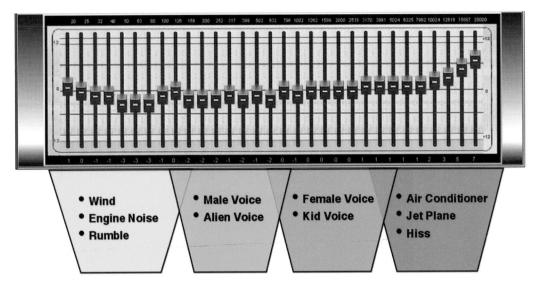

• Wind
• Engine Noise
• Rumble

• Male Voice
• Alien Voice

• Female Voice
• Kid Voice

• Air Conditioner
• Jet Plane
• Hiss

FINDING JUST THE RIGHT AUDIO FREQUENCY

This illustration gives you a general idea of which frequency to find certain sounds, but you still have to hone in on the *exact* frequency to cut or boost a specific sound. You can do this by simply "auditioning" each of the faders on the equalizer. To audition the faders, play the problematic section of audio from your project. Then, starting with the first fader in the frequency range you suspect—low, mid, or high—one by one bring the faders all the way down until the sound disappears or cuts out significantly. Then slowly bring it back up some so that your overall section of audio still sounds natural, but the offensive noise is eliminated or greatly reduced. To boost the sound of something that you want to be louder and be more prominent on your soundtrack, use the same auditioning process, but bring the faders up instead of down.

Equalizers built into mixing boards have pots (i.e., knobs) instead of faders to adjust various frequencies, but the concept works the same.

VOICE-OVER NARRATION

There's a pretty good chance that if you are shooting commercials or corporate videos, you are going to need a narrator sooner rather than later. If you went to film school, you were probably taught to avoid narration because it's like cheating when it comes to storytelling. Instead, you were told to find a nonverbal way to communicate the same story. That convention has its place in narrative filmmaking, but in commercials you have a very limited amount of time to get your message out, and it must be 100 percent clear, not nuanced.

It's hard to communicate that "ribs are 50 percent off every Wednesday night" in 30 seconds, so we show it visually and in text and say it at the same time to reinforce it. *That's* a clear message that will stick with people who often tune out when there's advertisement. The audio is very important to grab their attention. If they're tuned out, but still *hear* an interesting message, they're more likely to stop and watch for 30 seconds. However, if the message is only visual, they're less likely to take notice. Therefore, narration is a common convention in corporate, informational and marketing videos.

Casting

The first consideration for voice-over narration is the actual voice. *Who's* going to be delivering these golden lines of dialog? Unless you have a background in acting, and are also actually *good* at it, you really shouldn't do this yourself. (And even if you *think* you're good at it... you still really shouldn't do it yourself.) Voice-overs are an art that really shouldn't be treated any different from any other talent you'd put on-screen. You want to find someone who has previous acting and voice-over experience and who also has a voice-over demo reel. You want to cast for your voice-over the same way you cast for a role. Give some thought to what is appropriate for the project in terms of age, sex, race and viewpoint. A 22-year-old with a sultry voice is probably a bad choice for a retirement home commercial, but she's the exact right voice for a hot new nightclub commercial. Ask yourself questions such as these:

Casting Voice-overs

- ❑ Which voice is more credible—a male or female?
- ❑ Would a certain *ethnicity* be more appealing to my target audience?
- ❑ Do I need a voice of *authority* such as a doctor or policeman?
- ❑ Should the *voice* be soothing, commanding, or more humorous?
- ❑ Who would most appeal to my *specific* audience?
- ❑ What do the voice-overs for *similar* projects sound like?

Directing Voice-overs

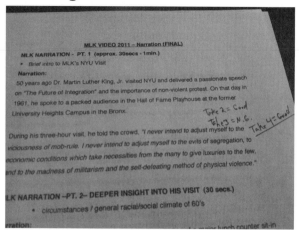

Read along and take notes directly on the script as to which takes are good or will need correction later. This will save you or your editor tons of time in the edit room, which is so especially important for tight deadlines.

I recommend wearing headphones and closing your eyes when someone's giving a voice-over reading so that you can focus on just the words and the delivery. This will also help you catch common issues such as popping p's, which occur when a person is pronouncing a word that starts with the letter "p" and their breath hits the mic sharply, or slight overmodulation that can occur when an actor gets too loud or the mic is too close or turned up too high. It is not enough to just have an actor come in and read the lines. Carefully listen to the delivery of the words.

- Are they emphasizing the most important elements of the script–such as a special price, new feature, specific date?
- Are they delivering the lines too fast for the audience? Too slow?
- Do they sound enthusiastic enough? Are they too enthusiastic and over the top?
- Are they changing tone at the appropriate moments in the script?
- Are they smiling when they speak? (Smiles come across in the voice.)

I find that it really helps to mark up the script with the actors ahead of time by underlining words of emphasis, noting pauses, and phonetically spelling out tricky names or words when necessary.

Voice-over Setups

There are many different setups you could use to record a voice-over. Ideally, you'd be in a nice studio somewhere that's set up just for voice-overs. However, chances are you are working with a less than ideal budget. If that's the case, your primary ingredients will be a microphone and a decent digital audio recording device or audio recording software such as Pro Tools or GarageBand and maybe a mixer. On the simplest level, I've gotten good results with little more than a mic running straight into camera in a quiet environment. To be clear for the audio purists reading this, by "good results,"

A pop filter is very effective for preventing common popping p's and breath noise. You can make your own with panty hose and wire.

I don't mean that it was 100 percent comparable to the rich, professional quality of a voice-over studio recording. I mean that it worked for the level of the project; my clients and the audience were happy with it and gave me the same accolades and check they'd have given me if I *had* recorded in a studio.

1 Talent

Cast talent strictly for voice quality and ability to deliver the lines as needed. Sex, age, ethnicity, and authority/credibility should all be casting factors.

2 Mic

A dynamic mic or cardioid condenser mic is preferable, but a shotgun mic will also work. Use a pop filter or windfoam (seen above). Talent should be 1.5' to 2.5' away from the mic.

3 Camera (or Digital Recorder)

Direct to camera is the *easiest* way, but you could also run through a mixer first—the best way, or record directly to a dedicated audio recorder.

4 Quiet Room

The location doesn't have to be soundproof, but record in the quietest environment you can find that's free of echo, noise, or unnatural acoustics.

5 Water or Hot Tea

Make sure you have some fresh water and/or hot tea with honey nearby. Voice-over sessions can be taxing on the throat.

6 Slate

Name and slate each take to save tons of time when editing. If you don't have a slate, paper is fine. Name each take out loud if just using an audio recorder.

5 SOUND RULES TO LIVE BY

I know I already listed these in *The Shut Up and Shoot Documentary Guide* and made an accompanying DVD, but this advice is so crucial that I wanted to make sure it isn't lost on anyone. Some rules were meant to be broken. The following were **NOT**. Break these rules at your own risk.

RULE #1 — Get the Mic as Close as Possible

The most basic rule for recording dialog is to get the mic as close to the action as possible without being in the shot. The closer the mic, the better the quality of the recording. This is why boom mics so often end up creeping into scenes; the sound person was trying to get as close as possible and accidentally allowed the mic to enter the frame. The sound person should always confirm the frame line with the DP before shooting starts to avoid this problem.

RULE #2 — Always Use Headphones ... Always

There are a wide variety of things that can ruin your sound that can be heard only by listening to your sound with professional over-the-ear headphones. Simply watching sound levels on a meter or relying on your naked ear will not reveal the following: a cable clunking against the boom pole, air conditioner noise, hum from a computer, a distant plane, a loose mic in the zeppelin, excessive street noise, etc.

If using a mixer, you should monitor the sound being recorded by the camera, as opposed to monitoring the sound coming from the mixer. The sound could come out of the mixer perfectly but still be ruined by bad levels or other settings on your camera. Many mixers have a setting to monitor sound from the camera. The bottom line is to always listen to the sound from its final recording destination, regardless of whether you run through a mixer or other sound equipment.

RULE #3 — Monitor the Sound Levels from the Camera

Not even the most skilled sound technician can do anything to fix overmodulated sound in post. If you record sound that is too loud, you've just jumped on a one-way train to Stinktown. If you are using a mixer, remember to match levels between the camera and mixer. Once your levels are set, use the mixer controls. Be sure to monitor sound from the camera by feeding it back to your mixer through the

"monitor in" or "return" jack because that's what's actually being recorded to tape and that's what counts. If you can't feed it back, keep an eye on the sound levels on the camera LCD.

RULE #4 | **Scout Your Locations for Sound**

It is vital to carefully observe every location, inside and out, for any source of noise or sound problems that could interfere with your shoot. Murphy's Law—whatever can go wrong will go wrong—is always in full effect when it comes to location shooting. If you don't take sound into full consideration when location scouting, or even worse, if you haven't observed your location beforehand, you are personally inviting Murphy to wreak further havoc on your shoot. Always think about sound in addition to those beautiful images in your head. Do that cool director viewfinder thing with your hands...then cup your ears and *listen* to your location.

Above: The Staten Island Ferry made for great *visuals* of the New York Harbor, but difficult *dialogue* recording due to the considerable engine noise.

RULE #5 | **Always Record "Wild" Sound**

Recording wild sound or room tone is simply recording the natural sound of any location—all the little buzzes, hums, birds, traffic, and background noises that often go unnoticed in production. The purpose of recording wild sound is to smooth out audio inconsistencies in editing. This comes into play in two primary situations:

- **Situation A:** You need to do additional dialog recording (ADR) after a scene was already shot. The ambient sound under the dialog that you record during ADR will not match the shots you recorded on location unless you lay in the ambient sound from location or "room tone."
- **Situation B:** You discover background noise elements that you had no control over or failed to notice when you were shooting, such as air conditioners or computers, are present in certain takes but not others. You'll need to restore that particular noise for certain shots for them to sound the same as the other shots when edited together in the same scene.

The procedure is simple. During a break or as soon as picture is wrapped, have everyone on location be silent and freeze where they are. No packing or adjusting equipment—no nothing for at least one full minute while the sound recordist captures the natural ambient sound of the location that will save your butt in the edit room. (Note that room tone should be recorded with the same mic used for dialogue at that location.)

The Secrets to Recording Great Audio

JOCELYN GONZALES, FREELANCE AUDIO PRODUCER, *NEW YORK TIMES*
(JocelynGonzales.net)

THE SECRET TO RECORDING GREAT AUDIO

The secret to recording great audio is listening…just listening. There is a lot of stuff that I get in my classes and so many other projects where they figure if the levels are hot, and the content is good, then the sound must be okay. They don't *hear* that it is distorted coming right into the mic. With the equipment these days, audio has become very visual, and people have stopped listening. It's all waveforms and LEDs. So that's the hardest thing to teach. The only thing to make you a better sound recordist or editor is to listen a lot more and listen closely.

Clearly defined audio and a little bit of design can go a long way to fill out your story. Always think about all the psychological effects that sound and speech have on the audience and how it can help improve any type of project; whether it's a web project or a podcast or a video or film, we should always remember and pay attention to what sound can do. Pay attention to it; hire the right people who have good ears and people who can get you clean audio from your set, from your live show, or whatever it is you are after. This way, you don't have to do that much in postproduction. You can really start to concentrate on things that are done for transition or emotional cues. Realize that sound can have as powerful an impact on your audience as the visuals. It is a different medium, with unique properties, but the storytelling impact is equal in my eyes.

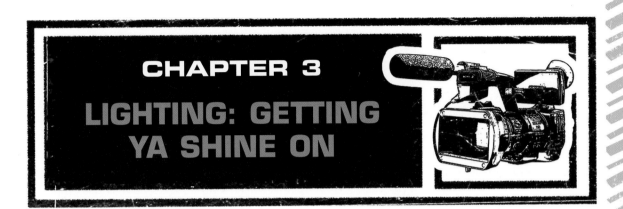

CHAPTER 3

LIGHTING: GETTING YA SHINE ON

Introduction

Often in our rush to get the shot, we overlook the single most important consideration—*safety*. If you aren't already, you need to get into the life-long habit of what I like to refer to as practicing "safe sets." Let me keep it 100 percent real with you in bold fonts for a minute...

There is not a shot, scene, expensive piece of equipment or big pay check in the world that is as important as the safety of everyone on your set.

I have witnessed foreheads split open, hands gashed, toes smashed, rental vehicles wrecked... you name it. I have personally come close to very seriously injuring—if not killing—*myself* while shooting a film. (I'll spare you the details here of that incident, but you can hear the whole story in the first half of Episode #70 of the "Double Down Film Show" podcast.) And sadly, since I wrote my last book, some young filmmakers I know have even experienced a tragic accident that resulted in a death on set. So needless to say, safety is something that all filmmakers need to take very seriously and set aside time in their busy shooting schedules to do basic safety checks.

In almost all of the incidents I'm referencing here, I really don't think it was a matter of the set not being safe or the filmmakers not being responsible. Rather, in almost every case, it was the very real (and common) occurrence of filmmakers just being caught up in the moment and the *seeming* importance and urgency of getting the job done. As in my case, I suspect most film set accidents are just a momentary lapse in judgment—a brief failure to recognize the potential danger of the moment in an everyday filmmaking situation, whether it's one too many lights plugged into an outlet, a gas-powered generator draped with sound blankets to quiet the noise, or the unsecured leg of a light stand sticking out into a walkway. These mundane little situations can turn into an injurious or even tragic accident if everyone on set doesn't constantly *stay* vigilant of safety concerns. Also keep in mind the unexpected expenses and hassles of paying for damaged equipment, filing insurance claims, scrambling for replacement equipment, and just trying to finish the project you started...with a considerable damper on morale I might add. Always be extra careful when things start getting tense and hurried on set. Stop and just slow everything down and ask yourself if everyone is still being *safe*. And if the answer is "no," STOP everything on set until you can make it safe again. Real enough for you?

> **Nothing is *more* important than the safety of everyone on your set... *absolutely nothing*.**

10 WAYS TO PRACTICE SAFE SETS

Hey, clearly, I am Mr. Down and Dirty when it comes to production. I believe in doing whatever you gotta do to get the shot and finish the project, but I draw a clear and distinct line when it comes to safety on set. Stealing a location or risking arrest is one thing, but risking your (or anyone else's) personal safety for the sake of a film or even a very well-paying music video or commercial is just plain stupid. And when serious accidents happen, it's never worth the shot. Read on for my tips to stay clear of this scenario and always practice "safe sets."

> Risking safety for the sake of a shot is NOT "Down and Dirty." It's just plain dumb!

1 DON'T BE STUPID

A reader once sent me a picture of some guerrilla filmmakers she saw on the side of the road that are the very essence of what I *don't* believe in. These filmmaking fools were 100 feet off the ground; on the wrong side of a highway overpass; and completely unsecured by a tether, safety chain, and apparently, also by common sense. Let me be clear here: This type of stuff is *NOT* "Down and Dirty." It's just sheer "dumbassery." I really can't put it any other way. Your camera and brain should always be fully engaged—at the same time—when it comes to filmmaking.

Photo courtesy of Linda Maxwell

Witness two filmmaking idiots risking their lives to get a shot from the open ledge of a highway bridge 100+ feet off the ground. This ain't Down and Dirty filmmaking; it's just dumb.

2 SLOW IT DOWN

The pressure on a film set can be tremendous when the dollars are ticking away on a piece of equipment due back at the rental house, you're about to lose that last bit of golden sunlight, or the lead actor has to leave in two hours to catch a plane. These are the panic times. Bad things are more likely to happen when everyone is tense and rushing to get things done. Remember, the best filmmakers panic only on the *inside*, so take a deep breath and mentally (if not physically) slow down the pace long enough to make sure that everyone is still safe, because if they aren't, you still won't get the shot; plus you'll have a whole new set of problems to deal with. As Kanye West put it, "Drive slow, Homey. You never know, Homey."

3 ALWAYS KEEP A FIRST-AID KIT ON SET

Even in the safest of environments, little accidents can and will happen—cuts, bruises, burns, and such. When these things do happen, be prepared with the basic supplies to take care of the people who take care of you: your talent and crew. When a gaffer slices his palm trying to set up a light for your scene, it's so much classier and caring to have a large bandage and some Neosporin on hand than to have the poor guy walking around the rest of the shoot with a blood-soaked paper towel held on by a piece of gaffer's tape. Apart from bandages and standard medical supplies like rubbing alcohol to clean and treat basic wounds, you also want to stock things like instant hot and cold packs,

BenGay, tweezers, gauze, aspirin, or ibuprofen (lots of it), cold and allergy medicine, and relief for upset stomachs...whatever you keep in your medicine cabinet. You can get a fully stocked first-aid kit at any drugstore or pharmacy.

4 PUT UP SIGNS, ROPE IT OFF, AND MARK THE DANGER SPOTS

Another simple thing you can do is put up signs in big, bold print on bright-colored paper on and around everything on set that is of potential danger: "WARNING—Do not plug lights in this outlet!!!" "WATCH YOUR STEP," "PLEASE *STAY OFF* BALCONY," "DO NOT COVER GENERATOR WITH *ANYTHING!!!*" etc. (A safety sign cannot be big and obnoxious enough in my opinion.) Similarly, from

any big-box hardware store you can purchase some iconic yellow caution tape that has the word "caution" printed on every inch to rope off areas of the set that you want to keep people away from. If a potentially dangerous area does need to be accessed, limit access to only those crew members who need to deal with it directly, such as the grips or gaffers. And although they went out fashion in the '80's, neon colors are always in fashion when it comes to safety. Use bright, obnoxious neon pink, yellow, and green tape and paper signs to clearly note areas of caution and catch people's eyes.

Bright neon colors are always fashionable when it comes to safety. People can't help but see this light stand on the floor now.

5 KNOW WHERE THE NEAREST HOSPITAL IS

The producer or A.D. on set is normally responsible for this standard precaution. Knowing how to get to the nearest hospital emergency room is as simple as doing a Google Map search. Equally important is knowing the fastest route to get there. For a serious emergency, you may have to decide which is faster: driving versus calling an ambulance. Having the hospital's address already punched into your production vehicle's GPS unit will save you those extra excruciating minutes of trying to punch in the address and make navigation decisions while someone in your passenger seat needs urgent medical care.

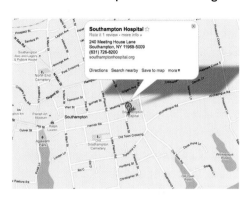

6 GOT PHONE SERVICE?

While we're speaking of hospitals and ambulances, you should be very wary and extra cautious of shooting at any remote location with no phone service at all. The ability to be able to call 9-1-1 and get emergency medical help on set within minutes is not one that you want to be without. In the very worst-case accident scenarios, the inability to make a quick phone call can become a life-or-death situation. You need to have a full medical emergency plan and know all the nearest emergency healthcare providers and their hours of operation when you are shooting in remote and isolated places. It would also be wise to let those emergency care providers (i.e., paramedics, fire dept., etc.) know exactly where you will be shooting beforehand, so they can quickly get to your remote location if there is an unexpected emergency...and all film set emergencies are always "unexpected," but they should never be *unprepared* for.

7 SECURE EVERYTHING

Wherever possible, all heavy equipment should be safely secured in place so that it does not fall over or onto someone. Securing things is not only a safety issue, but also an equipment issue. Equipment that's not held in place is more prone to getting dropped, broken, or knocked over accidentally. By secure *everything*, I mean

- Put sandbags on lights and C-stands.
- Always double-check the security of your tripod and tripod plate.
- Make sure any overhead lights are securely fastened down and have safety chains or wires as well.
- If your tripod has spreader legs at the bottom, sand bag those, too.
- If someone needs to climb a ladder, the ladder should be secured in place by another crew member.

In other words, secure *everythang*.

8 HAVE A SAFETY BRIEFING

Whenever you shoot whatever you shoot, you should take a few minutes to make sure that the entire crew—from the bottom to the top—has been briefed on basic safety concerns for the day. This doesn't have to be a special safety meeting per se. You can just set aside a few minutes during your normal preshoot briefing with the talent and crew. (You do normally have a preshoot briefing with your talent and crew, *right*?) The A.D., producer, or director needs to brief everyone on safety concerns with any specific

props, scenes, or vehicles; how to navigate (or avoid) any dangerous areas on location; and any dangerous equipment, lights, or rigging on set.

9 MAKE SURE EVERYBODY KNOWS WHAT'S UP

If you are doing a stunt or dealing with any unusual scenario, prop, or vehicle, such as using a helicopter; staging a Samurai sword fight or a gun battle; shooting on a boat; or rigging a camera car or anything else out of the norm with potential safety implications, make sure that everyone on set—from the production assistants to the talent to the craft services people—knows exactly what the scene is going to entail, who will be involved, when it will happen, and how everyone else can stay out of harm's way.

10 AVOID THE UNTRAINED, INEXPERIENCED, AND INCOMPETENT

When it comes to dangerous equipment and activities on set, there should always be an experienced professional who routinely deals with any of those types of props, equipment, vehicles, or stunts on set whenever these riskier scenes are scheduled. People who are untrained, inexperienced, and incompetent with specialty props, equipment, vehicles, or physical stunts are a big potential liability for injury and even lawsuits when all the dust clears.

If you feel like you have no choice but to have someone with little to no experience handle something on set that is potentially dangerous, I strongly recommend that you both do as much homework as possible on the subject matter and try to get some sort of training session with a professional beforehand. If you can't arrange for some one-on-one guidance by a professional, at least make sure you've taken the time to consult someone with previous experience in the issues at hand. Even a 20-minute phone consultation with someone who's already been there and done that successfully could save you immeasurable amounts of unforeseen and unfamiliar trouble on set and help protect your crew from potential danger. Also, be honest and straightforward with everyone on set about any possible risks that you think they could incur. Everybody needs to be 100 percent comfortable and okay with anything they are asked to do on set. (And if they aren't, it's a clear indication that what you are asking for should probably not be done and be completely rethought, replanned, or reconceived instead.)

How Many Lights Can I Plug Into This Circuit?

BY STEVEN BRADFORD, DIRECTOR OF PHOTOGRAPHY (SEANET.COM/~BRADFORD)

You're on location, in a house built in the 1940s. But you're worried about blowing fuses or popping a circuit breaker with the bright and hot lights from the nice Arrilite kit you brought.

You need a way to tell in advance, how to know when the next light you plug in will blow the circuit. You're not an electrician, you heard there was a formula, by some Ohm guy, but you have no idea what it is.

No matter—There is a simple way to figure this out, and keep out of hot water (and in the light) with the homeowner.

It seems confusing, because the electrical draw of your light fixtures is expressed in Watts, while circuit capacity is marked in Amps. Ohm's Law is an electrical formula that electricians use to make this conversion, but in practical application, you don't really need to use a calculator for this sort of simple situation.

Let's start by looking at the situation in the house. A circuit is a single line of electrical supply, that is usually shared by several outlets or lights in the home. Each outlet is NOT a circuit! Instead, multiple outlets are shared by one circuit. Also, normally, all the outlets or lights in a room are not dedicated to a single circuit. They are usually spread across several rooms. In a two story house, the lights will usually be on circuits shared between floors. This seems illogical, until you realize what happens if the circuits were divided by floor. If that circuit blows, all the lights on that floor go out, and no one can see, until they can find the a flashlight, and get to the circuit breaker.

Fortunately, discovering the capacity of a circuit in a home is easy. First, find the circuit breaker panel. *(The following refers solely to 120 Volt electrical service as commonly found in North America.)* It might be in a utility closet or it might be on the back porch. If the home has a garage, it is often found there. Upon opening the panel, you'll normally find two rows of black switches, the circuit breakers.

These have two digit numbers printed on them, normally a a *15* or a *20*. That number is the number of Amps the circuit can safely handle, before the breaker trips off, cutting off the power. If the circuit breaker didn't do this, the wiring in the walls would overheat, and start a fire. This is a special effect we normally want to discourage—and there are better ways to meet firemen.

	Outlets		20	Separate Circu
	Outlets		22	Separate Circu
	Outlets	*Hall Light*	24	Separate Circu
	Outlets	*Entrance Light*	26	Separate Circu
	Outlets		28	Separate Circu
	Outlets		30	Separate Circu
	Outlets		32	Separate Circu

Ideally, the circuit box will be labeled inside, but often the it will be blank.

If the house is older, built before the 1960s, and never been re-wired, it may have fuses. These are very often only 10 amps. *NEVER replace a 10 amp fuse with a higher number fuse, this is very unsafe!* If you're blowing fuses, it's for a reason. More current is being drawn than the circuit can safely handle without overheating.

The next puzzle is to figure out which outlets in the house are assigned to which circuits.

If you're very fortunate, sometime in the past, someone else already figured this out for you, and filled in the blanks in the circuit description on the circuit breaker panel door. Sadly, we often find that we're the first persons to bother filling in this card. If that's the case, you have little choice but to experiment, and turn breakers off and on to determine which plugs they control. Before you start, make sure there is nothing plugged in or turned on that might be harmed by the loss, or sudden resumption of power. Home electronics, computers etc. Now you could have another crew member walk around the house with a light, plugging it in to every outlet, yelling out when the light is extinguished, as you flip breakers in turn. A slightly more elegant solution is to use a cheap AC outlet powered radio instead of a light. That'll preserve your vocal cords. It also works well if you don't have an assistant—although with a lot more steps as you walk back each time to move the radio's plug. But you needed some exercise anyways, right?

Circuit breaker switches inside the circuit box. Note that the middle circuit has been "tripped" and is in the "OFF" position.

You'll notice too that in addition to the breakers marked *15* and *20*, there are other breakers, with higher numbers, and ganged together as one switch. You don't need to test those, they're for high power items that are hardwired, or not plugged into standard outlets, such as clothes dryers, ovens and heaters. If you're lucky, all the outlet breakers will be 20 amp circuits, and the 15 amp breakers are just assigned to ceiling lights. As it is, you may discover that all the outlets in the house are assigned to as few as two or three breakers.

Now that you know what outlets are available on each circuit, all that's left is to figure out how many of your lights you can plug in to each circuit, staying safe, and not popping a breaker!

I use this simple rule of thumb—each amp is "equal" to 100 watts of 120 volt power. Now this isn't correct—but this rule of thumb leaves a nice safety factor, as it's not really a good idea to load a circuit all the way up to its maximum amperage limit.

So if you plug in a 600 watt light, that takes up 6 of the amps on a 20 amp circuit. And if you plug in two more 600 watt lights, the total is 1800 watts, or 18 amps; you're still under the limit, and won't pop a breaker. But if you start with a 1000 watt light, you only are safe for one more 600 watt light—another 600 watt light would be 2200 watts, and that's over 20 amps, using our rule of thumb with a built in safety factor. But you could plug in another 400 watt light. If you need more than this, you should find a stinger (AC extension cable) and move on to the next circuit.

A word of caution—Always keep an eye open for what else might be plugged into the circuit. They need to be taken into account too. So if there's a computer that needs to be left on, on the circuit you need for a light, you have to accommodate it's load also. If the computer draws 500 watts, and it's a 20 amp circuit, then you only have 1500 watts available on that circuit. I really really recommend against sharing lights and a computer on a circuit though.

Also, look out for tell-tale signs of damaged wiring or outlets in old houses.

Watch out for these appliances, that draw much more power than most people realize: Hair dryers and curlers, laser printers, coffee pots etc. Laser printers are particularly sneaky, as they don't draw much power till they print, then suddenly you will see a 600 watt surge, and your lights go out!

Most all of this applies also to offices and commercial bldgs—These often have sub breaker panels on individual floors. Be vigilant about not overloading circuits that might be shared among rooms, or down a hall. You don't want to shut down someone's computer when they're trying to meet a deadline! A gotcha you'll find in offices is a coffee pot on the other side of a wall in a break room you don't know about, but is on the same circuit you've plugged a 1000 watt chimera into!

I already covered lighting safety in more detail in *The Shut Up and Shoot Documentary Guide*, but here are a few quick reminders worth repeating:

Always call "Striking!" as a warning to the crew before you turn on a light.

Use only heavy-duty extension cords in the 12–16 gauge range.

Make sure all lights are securely tightened onto the stands.

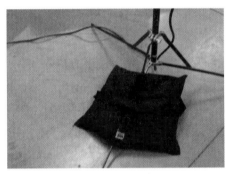

Use sand bags to weigh down all lights to keep them from falling.

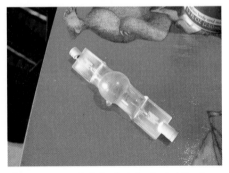

Change any quartz bulbs that develop bubbles from being touched with bare hands. Bubbles may pop.

Use only open-faced lights with safety screens in case bulbs shatter.

LIGHT IS GOOD

A Word (or Two) about Low Light Conditions

Here's a common misconception: *Today's prosumer cameras perform great in low light.* This is a true statement. However, it's also a *relative* statement—meaning that today's cameras perform "great" in low light *relative* to the crappier low-light performance we had a few years ago. Just think about how some otherwise average people look when they are standing with their ugly friend—great…but that "great" is *relative* to the company they're in. (Hey, let's be honest here; some nights we're *the average person,* and some nights we're *the ugly friend.* It's all relative, baby.)

So, I want to be clear: no camera performs at its best in low light. The new generation of cameras is simply more capable of performing in low light, but low light is still an *undesirable* shooting condition if you can avoid it. So what I'm saying is that light is *always* good. The more light you have to work with, the better you can get your camera to perform. We have quick and easy ways of dealing with an abundance of light, but *low* lighting conditions require us to jump through a few more hoops and often make some image-quality compromises (i.e., video noise from using gain or underexposure).

> Just because your camera is *capable* of shooting in low light, doesn't mean it's something you *want* to do. More light is always good.

Let God Be Your Gaffer

One thing I recommend shooters do as often as possible is to take advantage of the natural light you have on location. Let God be your gaffer. And when I say *natural* light here, I don't just mean sunshine; I mean whatever type of lighting that is already naturally occurring in the location you are in—be it daylight, halogen lamps, or street lights. Of course, sunlight is king here, so any time it's practical for the shot, I look for practical ways to shoot with sunlight because it (a) is gorgeous, (b) requires no setup, and (c) requires no electricity, and as an added bonus—it's 100 percent organic. (If you're into that sorta thing.) While there's no real setup involved, you will need at least one key tool to fully harness the awesome power of the sun: a reflector.

Reflector Flavors

Reflectors can come in a variety of shapes and flavors, but just remember a reflector is as a reflector does. (Yes, I'm resorting to *Forrest Gump* wisdom here.) So what I'm saying is that you can invest in a cool $70 fold-out reflector with interchangeable surfaces if your budget allows, or if you are broke and just getting started, you can make your own **"ghetto-flector"** out of cardboard, aluminum foil, and gaffer's tape. They will both reflect light equally well. The only real downside to using a ghetto-flector or other makeshift reflective device is that it won't make that really cool "whoosh" sound when it unfolds, and your little arts and crafts project certainly won't impress paying clients, but it *will* do the job the same as the so-called professional devices. Peep the recipe...

Ghetto-flector Recipe

Ingredients:

- ❑ **Sturdy piece of cardboard**
- ❑ **Heavy-duty aluminum foil**
- ❑ **2"–3" wide gaffers tape**
- ❑ **Invisible tape**

Substitutes:

- ❑ **White paper instead of foil**
- ❑ **Masking tape instead of gaffer's tape**

The foil surface can be smooth for hard light or crinkled for soft light.

Tape all the edges down with a thick roll of gaffer's tape.

Neatly tape seams of paper or foil with invisible tape.

A white paper surface can also be used to get a softer reflection.

Gold Poster Board

Color: Shiny Gold   **Surface:** Smooth Flat
Light Type: Hard   **Color Temp:** Warm

When to Use It:
- To quickly warm up skin tones/scenes
- On overcast days
- Low light indoors
- Bouncing soft light indoors

Silver Bead Board

Color: Shiny Silver   **Surface:** Smooth Flat
Light Type: Hard   **Color Temp:** Neutral

When to Use It:
- On overcast days
- When shooting in shadow
- Bouncing low light indoors
- Bouncing soft light indoors

White Bead Board

Color: Soft White   **Surface:** Smooth Flat
Light Type: Soft   **Color Temp:** Neutral

When to Use It:
- On bright sunny days
- Bouncing bright light indoors
- At close range to a subject's face
- For very subtle soft fill

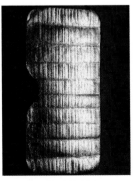

Silver Car Windshield Protector

Color: Flat Silver   **Surface:** Textured
Light Type: Soft   **Color Temp:** Neutral

When to Use It:
- On overcast days
- Bouncing low light indoors
- Far away outdoors on clear days
- Bouncing soft light indoors
- If flat gold texture; same as above, but warmer look

CHROMATTE GREENSCREEN TIPS

Chromatte is a special reflective fabric that works in conjunction with special colored LED ring lights to create a greenscreen effect. Here are some quick tips to get the most out of a Chromatte greenscreen on set:

Shoot from a frontal angle for the cleanest effect. When the colored LED hits the Chromatte, it will appear the same color as the lights on camera.

One drawback of the Chromatte system is that the LED lights can be uncomfortably bright to subjects, and you need to be extra wary of green reflections in glasses.

With a greenscreen, you will generally be limited to shots from the waist up. For full body shots, you'll need to shoot in a special type of studio space called a cyc (aka cyclorama), which has all green walls, floors, and curves—not corners.

Use a large monitor or TV on set to easily spot any problems with greenscreen, such as green spill or funky shadows on your backdrop.

Avoid zooming when shooting greenscreen footage because your background perspective will *not* change with the zoom move and it will look weird and cheesy.

The high resolution of HD footage allows you to "blow up," or magnify, your greenscreen subject some for a medium close-up. If you do this, magnify your high-res background to match the new composition.

Window View Setup

THE RECIPE:

SKILL LEVEL: Beginner
PREP: 20 mins.
INGREDIENTS:

Key light   Prop light   Window light

Amber gel   Dimmer

OPTIONAL INGREDIENTS:

Color gels   ND filter

NOTES: In situations where you are shooting the head of an organization, a celebrity, or a V.I.P., time will usually be tight. Simple setups are a particularly practical and effective solution in these scenarios. Here, I used two diffused 500-watt open-faced Omni lights and took maximum advantage of the scene outside the window and the natural objects on location to tell the story. When using a window view, first expose your shot for the scene outside (since you can't adjust the sun); then adjust the intensity of your set lights accordingly. The subject's dark hair and brown skin tone juxtaposed against a white sunlight building gave me enough separation from the background that I didn't need to add a hair light. I also did a little set dressing to move specific props that were in the office into the frame. Most notably, I moved the costumed mannequin to simultaneously hide a plain white sliver of wall and balance the frame with a burst of regal purple color and interesting textures. I also moved her nameplate to the corner of the desk so it would be in the shot. I positioned the subject in front of, rather than behind, her desk for a more intimate conversation and feel for this interview discussing people's personal stories about the legacy of Dr. Martin Luther King, Jr. Alternatively, I could've used a large piece of window ND gel to decrease the brightness outside and shoot with lower lighting inside.

Courtesy of Son #1 Media

Entertainment TV Setup

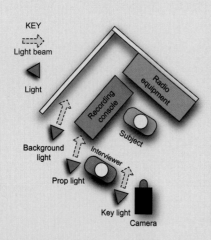

SKILL LEVEL: Intermediate
PREP: 30 mins.
INGREDIENTS:

Key light   Prop light   B.G. light   Color gels

OPTIONAL INGREDIENTS:

Dimmer

NOTES: For this interview about the music business shot at a radio station, there was plenty of visual equipment that communicated the setting and subject of the interview, but there was very little in the way of color or texture. Worst of all, I was once again face to face with my video interview arch enemy—plain white walls—the single most boring background in the world. To defeat this common foe, I lit the walls with a little splash (okay—it wasn't a splash but more like a whole *bucket*) of bright saturated color. Apart from adding more of a flashy music television feel to the interview, the purple on the control panel versus the red on the rear wall help provide a feeling of greater depth to the shot by clearly separating the console from the wall. Similarly, because our subject was wearing a light gray shirt and lit with standard white light, he now pops out from the otherwise bland background, and the audience's eyes are visually drawn to him. The D.P. framed the shot with the camera facing the corner to further complete the sense of depth and three dimensions. Again, the ideal is that people should be able to look at your frame and get a clear sense of your subject, tone, and subject matter just from a freeze-frame shot. You can't always pull this off for practical reasons, but it is a goal I say you should strive for every time.

Courtesy of Son #1 Media

Desk Setup

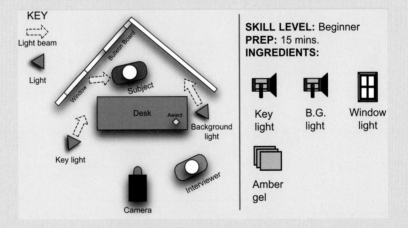

KEY

Light beam

Light

Bulletin Board

Subject

Window

Desk   Award

Background
light

Key light

Camera   Interviewer

SKILL LEVEL: Beginner
PREP: 15 mins.
INGREDIENTS:

Key
light

B.G.
light

Window
light

Amber
gel

NOTES: A common setup that comes up in corporate video interviews shows a CEO or other employee behind their desk. This more formal setting communicates authority and emphasizes the subject's role in the company. The gray wall on the right side of the frame was undecorated, but it wasn't plain. It actually had a very nice visually interesting texture but still needed some light on it, so I just added a diagonal beam from above. By angling this diagonal beam more toward or away from the wall and playing with the spot/flood controls on the light, I was able to control how wide the beam flanges out and its intensity. Remember, lighting is as much about shadows as it is about lights, so you want to avoid things being flat and evenly lit across the board. Another element of this setup was the deliberately mixed color temperatures of the cool blue light from the window, contrasting with the warm amber light on his face. D.P. Eric McClain white balanced for the dominant tungsten light in the scene. Lastly, he incorporated at least three "props" that communicate that this is the CEO of a music organization: two music awards and a concert seating chart on the bulletin board. Ideally, I would have also pulled the subject away from the wall some to avoid the shadow on the wall, but time and the space was too tight (and that desk was too heavy).

Courtesy of Son #1 Media

Monitor Set Up #2

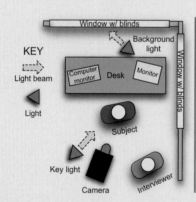

SKILL LEVEL: Intermediate
PREP: 30 mins.
INGREDIENTS:

Key light   B.G. light   Monitor

Color gels

NOTES: We aren't just painting our scenes with light; we are also "painting" with the color of our subjects' clothes, hair color, choice of background, and props. All these things come together to form the full color palette of the frame. You can choose a palette that compliments (i.e., matches) or contrasts (i.e., stands out from) your subject...it doesn't matter, as long as the end result looks good and visually matches the larger story you want to tell. I usually start with a subject's clothing, skin tone, and hair color and build the interview and lighting setup from those because they represent the elements of color that I can't really change (although you will occasionally have the flexibility of having a subject change a top or put on or remove a jacket or sweater). So here we started with the subject's festive red Hawaiian shirt, white hat, and amber skin tone and decided to go with a contrasting cool blue/purple color scheme for the background. In this set-up the background light is on the floor pointed up at the shades to form a slash of light that flanges out at the top. Keep in mind that the D.P. could have decided to white balance for daylight and gel the lights to match it, which would have made the light shining through the blinds appear a more complementary natural and warm white rather than cool blue. Note that we used the Avid edit station with a title screen and time-code burn-in over his shoulder as a prop to visually communicate that the subject is a filmmaker.

Unorthodox Two-Camera Setup

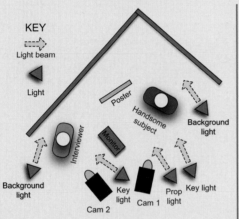

KEY

⇢ Light beam

◀ Light

Poster

Handsome subject

Background light

Interviewer

Monitor

Background light

Key light

Cam 2

Key light

Cam 1

Prop light

Key light

SKILL LEVEL: Advanced
PREP: 1 hour
INGREDIENTS:

Key light 1   Prop light   B.G. light 1   Key light 2

B.G. light 2   Poster   Monitor   Color gels

NOTES: For a formal interview with this handsome author (yours truly) that also included the interviewer, we set up one light on my face, a bold slice of red light on the shadowy rear wall to break up an otherwise flat background, and one bright light on the key prop: a giant poster of my first film book, *The Shut Up and Shoot Documentary Guide*. (A little subtle product placement.) For the interviewer's setup, we just went for a single key light and a background light forming a green slash on the brick wall behind her. Although the end result on-screen looked great, this particular two-camera setup was fairly unorthodox in the way we executed it. Normally, you'd shoot a two-camera interview with one camera on the subject and one on the interviewer by simply having the cameras shoot criss-cross. For reasons of the narrow space we were in, wanting to keep the same brick wall in the background and getting a good eyeline, I was not able to look directly at the interviewer or make eye contact as we spoke, which made it EXTREMELY difficult to have a natural conversation. (I highly advise that you avoid asking a subject to do this, if you possibly can.) I've been in this situation before, so after a few frustrating minutes of trying to make this setup work unsuccessfully, we hooked up camera 2 to a TV monitor and placed the TV in position so that I could maintain a natural eyeline and still see the person I was talking to. I then completed a fun interview with no problems while looking directly at my interviewer on the monitor and responding to her questions and the all-important visual feedback of her *facial expressions* and *body language*.

Library Bookshelf Setup

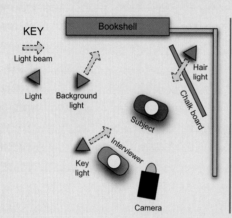

SKILL LEVEL: Intermediate
PREP: 30 mins.
INGREDIENTS:

Key light Hair light B.G. light

Amber gel

NOTES: The old "bookshelf in the background" interview setup is a pretty standard setup for academics, experts, and other smart and authoritative people—professors, doctors, lawyers, congressmen, etc. In fact, this setup is so popular as a go-to choice for busy videographers that it is actually available as a fake backdrop from many companies, so even if you don't have a real library shelf to work with, you can set up your fake background and throw it out of focus using shallow depth of field, and the audience will never be the wiser. (Look carefully behind the interviewee next time you see this setup on TV; there's probably a 50/50 chance it's fake, but let's just keep that secret to ourselves in the industry.) Again, just glancing at the lighting and setting for a minute gives us visual clues as to the specific subject and tone of what's being said. The books say he's a man of knowledge. The chalkboard tells the audience it's an educational setting. The straight, formal lighting and the subject's suit tell us this is a probably a serious interview. Apart from the setting, this is a standard 3-point light setup. Note that the hair light here really serves to separate the subject from the background and add a sense of three dimensions to his face.

Color Slash Setup

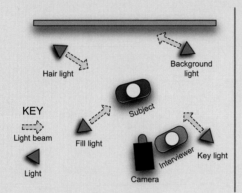

Hair light

Background
light

KEY

Light beam

Light

Fill light

Subject

Interviewer

Key light

Camera

SKILL LEVEL: Intermediate
PREP: 30 mins.
INGREDIENTS:

Key
light

Hair
light

B.G.
light

Color gels

NOTE: This is a pretty standard setup I use all the time: find a wall with some decent texture or decoration on it and add a slash of color behind your subject. This does three key things: (1) allows you to "paint" the scene whatever color you'd like to set the tone and feel, or contrast or complement your subject's clothing; (2) helps you bring out the texture in the wall and use it to separate your subject from an otherwise flat background; and (3) allows you to have interesting lighting and shadows. I often use this setup when I've got multiple interviewees lined up for the same project. I simply switch the colored gel on the background and alter the direction the various subjects are sitting from interview to interview. Again, to create a slash, just close your barn doors down to a narrow slit and experiment by twisting the light more toward or away from the wall, moving it closer or farther away, and spotting and flooding to get variations on the look of your light slash.

Frame-in-Frame Setup

SKILL LEVEL: Intermediate
PREP: 20 mins.
INGREDIENTS:

Key light B.G. light 1 Umbrella light (B.G. 2)

Amber gel Color gels

NOTE: In this setup at a hair salon, the goal was to have the activity at hand—hairdressing—be going on unobtrusively in the background. An active background is always a nice touch as long as you take steps to make sure it doesn't attract too much attention. This setup probably would've worked okay with just natural white light in the salon behind her, but I think it would've put the background on too much of an even level with the subject—the person we always want to notice first and foremost. So to draw a more stark contrast between the subject and background and add a healthy coat of color for this interview, we went with a bold blue light setup on the people in the background and a more natural warm white light on our subject, the owner of the salon. The large space allowed the D.P. to get some decent depth, so the separation of subject and background is further aided by a more shallow depth of field, which puts the potentially distracting background more out of focus. The extreme color contrast here also helps play up the frame-within-a-frame composition. A second more dim background light was used to pick up the marble wall texture on the right.

Pete Chatmon - Director

Chromatte Greenscreen Setup #1

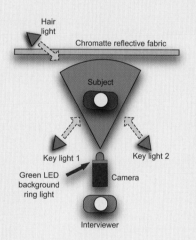

Hair light
Chromatte reflective fabric
Subject
Key light 1
Key light 2
Green LED background ring light
Camera
Interviewer

SKILL LEVEL: Intermediate
PREP: 45 mins.
INGREDIENTS:

Key light 1   Key light 2   Hair light

LED ring light   Chromatte reflective fabric

NOTE: Greenscreen lighting is the one situation in which your goal is to actually light everything as flat and evenly as possible. Shadows and greenscreen keying don't always get along very well, so you want to generally avoid the moody lighting you see in some of the other setups in this section. Instead, use soft bright lights such as the Kinoflos we used here. However, to keep things from getting too flat and one-dimensional, try adding a hard hair light. For a little variation, on the hair light, you may wish to add a splash of light color like amber, magenta, or light blue, but I recommend always consulting your editor first or doing some test shots and keying them right there on your laptop to determine if your color choice is going to be a problem in the editing room later. In this particular scene, we used a new type of greenscreen technology that uses a green LED light ring and a special reflective gray fabric called Chromatte that turns green on camera when the green LED light hits it. (See "Hot Tip: Chromatte Greenscreen Tips" on page 116.)

Chromatte Greenscreen Setup #2

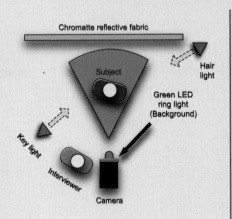

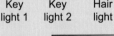

SKILL LEVEL: Intermediate
PREP: 45 mins.
INGREDIENTS:

Key light 1   Key light 2   Hair light

LED ring light   Chromatte reflective fabric

NOTES: For this greenscreen setup also using the Chromatte reflective backdrop and camera ring light, Down and Dirty D.P., Ben Harrison (who wrote the music video chapter of this book), *was* able to achieve a little more three-dimensional and moody look by using only a single Kinoflo Diva fluorescent light as a key. Our editor and Visual FX artist, Giga Shane, shot an extreme close-up of a spinning turntable for this interview for the Clive Davis Institute of Recorded Music. With greenscreen setups, you have the ultimate control over your choice of a "storytelling background." The brown/gray/black color palette is an example of complementing the colors of your subject's clothing and skin tone. The hair light (aka "kicker") on his head and shoulders keeps the subject from getting lost in the background. Notice that we also used an extreme shallow depth of field for the background plate of the turntable to minimize the distraction from our subject in the foreground.

Low-Angle Setup

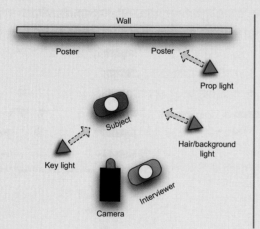

SKILL LEVEL: Intermediate
PREP: 45 mins.
INGREDIENTS:

Key light   Hair/B.G. light   Prop light

Color gels

NOTE: This is another unorthodox setup. Shooting and lighting from a lower angle can give your subjects a more authoritative presence. Shooting from a low angle makes them appear larger and more powerful. Conversely, higher angles can make them appear more vulnerable and less imposing. If the CEO is announcing an aggressive new marketing plan, I may choose to shoot them from slightly below for a greater visual feel of authority and power. If he's giving a public apology for destroying the local environment in an oil spill, I'd probably shoot from a little above to give a visual sense of a little more humility and humbleness. Placing key lights at a low angle is a stylistic choice that works for some subject matters and subjects, but be careful when lighting people from lower angles. If you overdo it and go too low, you get into the realm of spooky horror lighting. (Everything looks scarier when lit from below—even puppies.) Here, I went with more of a black, white, and gray palette and added just a tiny splash of color across the record plaque in the background—to break up the shadow and balance out the frame.

CHAPTER 4

MARKETING AND PROMO VIDEOS

INTRO: SOLVING CLIENTS' PROBLEMS

People enlist your video services because they have some challenge that requires the services of a video professional. (That's you.) They need more people to come to their store, they need to let everyone know about their new product, they want to promote their special event, they need to change their image, etc. Whatever it is…they are betting a wad of cash that you are just the person who can help them do it, so you need to make sure to deliver the goods.

There are a few questions I ask every client at the very first meeting for a commercial or corporate video project. I use some variation or combination of these simple questions to try to determine the direction of their project:

GOAL:
WHY do you want to make this video?

AUDIENCE:
WHO are you trying to reach?

CALL TO ACTION:
What do you want the audience to feel or *DO*?

END RESULT:
What do you ultimately want to *happen* as a result of this project?

In other words, we're back to my guerrilla film mantra of "the end result." I ask these questions because once I know where the client wants to end up, it's a lot easier to craft an effective path to get there. You will have some people who know exactly what they want and exactly how they want it and exactly what they want to happen. If it's compatible with your skill set, then you'll just give them exactly that, and everyone's happy.

But just as often (and probably more so), you will have clients who really have no clue at all as to what they actually need or want. They just want "a commercial" or "a promo video" for their website. These jobs are often the most challenging of all, but they can also be the most rewarding when you get it right because an open-ended situation offers many creative possibilities for you to shine as a creator.

The key here is to actually spend some real time talking with the clients and thinking about their business, their customers, their company culture, and what worked in the past. What crashed and burned? How would they like to grow as a company? Get a clear sense of who they are as a company and the message they want to send; whether it would be effective to meet their goal; and whether you can find a clear, effective, and hopefully *creative* way to convey that message.

VIDEO MARKETING AIN'T FOR EVERYBODY

PETE CHATMON, CEO, DOUBLE7 IMAGES—MEDIA + MARKETING COLLECTIVE (double7images.com)

Video marketing is taking responsibility for the future of someone's company into your hands. It's not just something to do because you have equipment and a team. You have to understand story and company objectives and whether those objectives are quarterly or yearly, so when you come up with an idea, it's in direct support of what they need to accomplish. Bringing you on is just adding another platform to accomplish company initiatives. Once you've accepted that responsibility, distinguishing yourself from all the other video producers out there is about really being true to your own approach or your own style. What people often do in the beginning stages of their company is try to satisfy whatever needs the client might have. Whatever the potential client is buying becomes the product they are selling.

That's a recipe for disaster because you won't always do your best work if you are just there to fill any gap. If you know that your skills are in making short films for brands, then that's what you should push. And you should push that hard so you get hired to do what you do *best*. If you don't take jobs where your core skills lie, you're probably going to end up with an unhappy client. You're not going to have your heart in it and probably aren't getting enough money for it to be worthwhile anyway. That doesn't bode well for the longevity of your career because people should engage you with the work that you're most engaged by.

You shouldn't take a job when your heart's not in it or your skills aren't for it. It's a tough decision to make. That's one of the things you should know before you even reach out to clients: what you *won't* do. Over the course of a campaign, oftentimes the job evolves and people will throw stuff at you weekly, daily, hourly, and you might find yourself doing something that, had

TAMEKIA FLOWERS-HOLLAND
FOUNDER / HIP HOP FOR LIFE

you thought about it beforehand, you wouldn't have agreed to. All you end up doing is something that is not what you want to do, are suited to do, or what your company is about. All your client decisions should be guided by, "Am I the *best* vendor for this client?" If you really honestly can't say that you are, then you should pass on it.

Creative versus Effective

I prefer to have a little fun and try to get creative where appropriate, but you don't always have to reinvent the wheel. You want to create a video that is both creative *and* effective as often as possible, but make no mistake about it, *effective* always trumps *creative* when it comes to works for hire. If something works, it works. If a certain simple approach has been effective for you or the client in the past and they are happy with it, you're probably better off giving them what they want, unless you are very confident that your new concept will give them even better results.

That polished and ultra-witty award-winning commercial you did with a B-list celebrity won't mean anything if the client does not get the *end results* they want, so stay focused on the goal, not just on a new addition to your demo reel. In the best-case scenarios, you will find a way to meet the client's needs with a video that challenges you creatively and still delivers exactly what the client wants.

It All Starts with an Outline

Once you know the end goal and general direction you need to take a project, the easiest way to begin any writing endeavor—whether it's a commercial, corporate video, or music video—is to start with a simple outline that touches on all the points you want to cover. Of all the things that were drilled into me in school, few have been more useful in filmmaking than understanding how to make an outline. The ability to organize your ideas and plans into a hierarchal outline form is a vital skill for writers, producers, and filmmakers and one that you will call on again and again.

Creating an outline is a great way to brainstorm and get a quick sense of the scope of any project. Once you break it down by topic, chronological order, or key points to hit, you will have a clear overview of the project condensed down to a single page or two that can easily be digested. Now you have a simple vision that you can share with clients, collaborators, and talent in your initial meetings to plan the project.

A Simple Outline

Following is a sample of a simple outline for a project I created for an event celebrating the 50th anniversary of a speech that Dr. Martin Luther King, Jr. gave at New York University. This is essentially what I would give to the client in a first proposal or statement of work to show the general content of a video. As the project develops, elements may be added or taken away, but this ensures that we all share the same basic vision of the project.

MLK at NYU Anniversary Video

1. Introduction (1–2 mins.)
- ❏ Brief intro to MLK's NYU visit

2. Deeper Insight into Dr. King's Visit (2–3 mins.)
- ❏ Political and social climate of U.S. in '60s
- ❏ Circumstances of visit
- ❏ Climate of NYU campus at the time

3. The Speech (3–4 mins.)
- ❏ Content of Dr. King's Speech

4. His Legacy (2–3 mins.)
- ❏ Dr. King's legacy on campus
- ❏ End quote

A Detailed Outline

Simple outlines are good for broad first strokes and simple projects, but later you'll want to flesh out the whole project with a more detailed outline that will become the main blueprint for the final video. Following is the detailed outline that I used to create a series of six videos for The Clive Davis Institute of Recorded Music. In addition to the standard outline, I also included a bullet point outline of the core production elements for each video. This outline became the basis for choosing interview subjects, production scheduling, the budget, and the edit.

The Clive Davis Institute of Recorded Music Promo Video Series

1. About the Program (3 mins.)
   a. Goals of the program
   b. Mission
   c. Basic history
   d. What makes it unique among music programs
   e. An interview with Clive Davis

Production Elements:
   ❑ Clive Davis interview (re: starting program)
   ❑ Exterior shots
   ❑ Administrator interviews
   ❑ Archival NYU photos
   ❑ Candid action B-roll of students

2. Virtual Department Tour (3 mins.)
   a. Guide through the department
   b. Classrooms
   c. Facilities
   d. Basic stats and facts

Production Elements:
   ❑ 30-second high-speed "flash tour" through entire facility
   ❑ Interview with staff and administrators
   ❑ Interior tour of empty facilities
   ❑ Recording studio
   ❑ Classrooms and student lounge
   ❑ Graphic overlay of notable REMU stats

3. Course Offerings (3 mins.)
   a. Clive Davis 101
   b. Introducing the curriculum
   c. Talking to alums
   d. Getting a sense of the "feeling"

Production Elements:
- ❏ Candid student interviews
- ❏ Classroom instruction
- ❏ Quick scroll through all course listings
- ❏ B-roll student videos

4. The Business Curriculum (2.5 mins.)
a. Business curriculum
b. Business faculty
c. Program expectations

Production Elements:
- ❏ Candid student interviews
- ❏ Classroom instruction
- ❏ Instructor interview
- ❏ Clive Davis interview (re: business)

5. The Production Curriculum (2.5 mins.)
a. Introducing the production curriculum
b. Production faculty
c. What aspiring producers and engineering students can expect to get out of the program

Production Elements:
- ❏ B-roll making music (planning, production, and post)
- ❏ Candid student interviews
- ❏ Classroom instruction
- ❏ Instructor interview
- ❏ Production equipment
- ❏ B-roll student projects

6. The History Curriculum (2.5 mins.)
a. Introducing the history and journalism curriculum
b. Program expectations
c. Teaching Approach

Production Elements:
- ❏ Music history montage
- ❏ B-roll archival music photos
- ❏ Classroom instruction
- ❏ Instructor interview

Once you have a detailed outline, drafting a script is simply a matter of expanding even further upon your concept with the fine details. The script will be as close to a full written representation of the final product as you can get, including dialog, narration, and description of the visuals. Things always change on set and in the editing room, so your script serves as a blueprint to help you stay on track and make sure you are being true to your original intentions.

The format for corporate and commercial videos is different from that of narrative screenplays, which most filmmakers are already familiar with. The format for commercial videos is called **A/V screenplay format**—"A" being audio and "V" being video. This type of script shows the audio and video content side by side. The audio column includes anything we hear in the video—dialogs, monologues, narration by off-camera talent, and any important sound FX. The video column includes anything visually depicted on-screen, which may include straight video footage, titles, animation, still photos, or special FX.

Although it's desirable and it can make the job faster and easier, it's not mandatory to run out and buy a dedicated A/V script-formatting program, especially if it's a stretch for your budget. The A/V format isn't as detailed and formal as narrative screenplay format, so you can just create a simple two-column table in a program like MS Word or Pages. Following is a sample of the A/V script from the production of my *Down and Dirty DV Audio Crash Course* instructional DVD... which just happens to be available at **DownAndDirtyDV.com**—just in case you were wondering... (I'm just sayin').

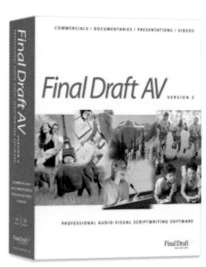

Final Draft AV makes formatting easier...for a price—$150 retail.

The A/V Script Format

I also like to color code my A/V scripts to make it even easier for anyone reading to quickly tell what's going on...and that's the most important part of any script: do the people reading it—your clients, crew, and talent—all easily understand everything you are trying to communicate visually? If the answer is "yes," then your script is good to go. So here's a basic look at what goes in each column.

AUDIO
Character dialog
On-screen narration
Voiceover narration
Music
Major sound FX

VIDEO
Shot description
Titles
Graphics
Special FX
Animation

DOWN AND DIRTY DV'S AUDIO CRASH COURSE DVD

AUDIO	VIDEO
The Right Mic for the Job	**TITLE SCREEN:** The Right Mic for the Job
There are four basic types of microphones to consider for location production: boom mics, lavaliere mics, handheld mics, and wireless mics.	**VIDEO:** Anthony's Stand Up
Each has unique advantages and drawbacks depending on the specific production situation you are in.	**POP-UP GRAPHIC:** One by one each mic pops up and stays on the lower part of the screen.
Boom mics are microphones that are mounted on a boom pole, which is held by a boom operator. Although you can use any type of mic that will fit on a boom pole, **shotgun mics** (aka hypercardioid mics), which have a very directional and narrow **pickup pattern**, are most often used on boom poles.	**VIDEO:** Mic put in a shockmount and screwed onto boom pole **ANIMATION:** Shotgun mic with sound waves in hypercardioid pattern (live video overlay)
Shotgun mics focus on sound only in the direction they are pointed and greatly diminish most sounds from the rear and sides. Because of this, they are great for isolating your subject's voice from a noisy or crowded environment. They are also ideal for recording dialog in narrative filmmaking.	**ANIMATION:** Wide shot—shotgun mic on boom pole with shockmount pointed at subject in crowd of people (gray blobs are fine for "people"). Subject is red; sound waves are yellow or green.

Note: When editing an A/V script in an MS Word or Pages table, you will have to pay careful attention to spacing between lines and repeatedly adjust the entries in your video column to stay lined up with your audio. To make this a little easier, you can add more rows to your table to keep things better separated. You will have to weigh the hassle of this against the purchase price of script formatting software like Final Draft A/V, which keep things in line automatically.

STORYBOARDS

The necessity and value of a script is obvious. However, storyboards that lay out the project visually can be just as vital, depending on the complexity of your project. I am a huge fan of storyboarding. Storyboards always make any project go smoother, even if they are just stick figure drawings. The mere act of visualizing your ideas on paper will help you anticipate production problems, get a better handle on your story, and communicate your vision more clearly to everyone involved. The purpose of employing storyboards is two-fold: (1) to previsualize the project to help you and the technical team better plan each scene, and (2) to make sure that you and the client are on the same page.

There are several approaches you can take with storyboards. You can storyboard just the more complex camera moves and angles, such as dolly and aerial shots. Or you can storyboard every shot of the video. For commercials, you may want to use a format that also includes the dialog below each shot, or it can be purely visual. (See the Superfly Illmatic Bonus Website at FreelanceVideoGuide.com for a blank commercial storyboard form.)

Another form of storyboarding that's more involved is creating **animatics**, which are essentially simply animated storyboards that mimic the basic visuals of camera and character movement. There are a number of photo and stock image–based software programs that can help you create storyboards and animatics, including some programs that allow you to craft storyboards using your smartphone or iPad. I think these programs can often be overkill for amateur filmmakers who can easily find themselves spending many hours crafting cool and colorful semi-animated storyboards when a good old-fashioned black-and-white drawing would be faster and communicate the same info just as effectively, if not more so. I think these programs are most beneficial for narrative filmmakers doing complex action sequences. (But I must admit they are very fun to play with...but that's the main problem.)

If you have some artistic skills or a friend with drawing skills who does comics, then you can come up with some sweet storyboards. However, from my very first film in film school until now, I have always used simple stick figure drawings, and they've always done the trick.

You don't have to be a great artist. The only purpose of a storyboard is to get the shot across and that doesn't take much. Of course, if it *is* a big job with a big budget and you want to get the vision on paper just right, you can also hire a professional storyboard artist. The difference between a "storyboard artist" and a regular old "artist-artist" is that a storyboard artist understands the language of filmmaking. It's much more akin to drawing comic books. Just like

Storyboard Composer by Cinemek, Inc., is an iPhone/iPad app that can create and animate photo-based storyboards.

scripts, storyboards have their own visual language to denote the various camera moves and shots that are common to the commercial filmmaking genre, and professional storyboard artists know exactly how to communicate those shots on paper. The bottom line is whatever format you use, storyboards are a powerful tool to help you see, plan, and prethink your projects more clearly.

A storyboard is as a storyboard *does* however you create it:

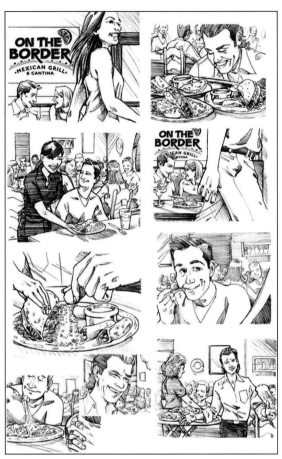

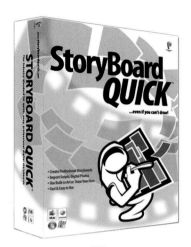

A professionally drafted commercial storyboard.
(By Clark Huggins, courtesy of StoryboardsInc.com)

Storyboard Quick is one of several programs that import photos and require no drawing.

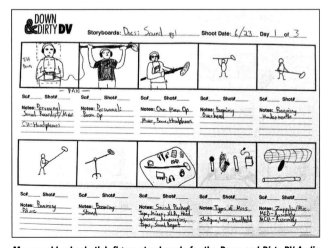

My own old-school stick figure storyboards for the *Down and Dirty DV Audio Crash Course* DVD. Storyboards don't have to be slick; they just have to do the job of visually *communicating* the shot.

Often even the best performance by an Oscar-worthy actor won't be as convincing as the genuine emotion, first-hand reports, and sincere words of someone who is obviously spontaneous and unrehearsed. Just think of how you feel about the professional TV hosts pitching you a product versus the unscripted reaction of people on the street who have actually used the product in everyday life. Audiences trust and better relate to "real people." And often the very nature of your project will *require* that you shoot with a predetermined group of people who've probably never been on camera before in their lives.

As a director, you always have to distinguish between professional actors or personalities who are used to speaking and being on camera and "real people," i.e., documentary-style subjects who are enlisted to be in a particular project. While it's always easier to work with professionals who know how to consistently deliver lines, hit their marks, and stay in the light, many projects will require that you use real people to share their real experience with a certain company, product, or event. However, there are two very different approaches to working with these two kinds of talent. Here are some things to keep in mind:

1 KEEP THEM RELAXED AND INFORMED

Nervous people are people who're not going to think or speak at their very best. So, if possible, I first of all try to keep them out of the room when I'm doing my setup. I tell them to continue to talk on the phone, go get a coffee, or do whatever they'd normally be doing for at least the next half hour and then bring them in for the last few minutes when I need them to adjust lights and sound. If they have nothing to do, it's a good idea to have a producer or other talent casually conversing with them while they wait. This makes people more relaxed, rather than just building up tension about speaking on camera while sitting there watching the crew fuss over a big setup.

Once you've got them in the room, the next thing you'll want to do is humor, educate, and inform them about the fascinating world of video. Chat with them about their work, kids, favorite TV shows—whatever. Keep it conversational as you set up. Let them know what you are doing and why you're doing it. Explain to them what some of these otherwise intimidating gadgets and doodads actually do to help you create video magic. This all helps to put people at ease since all of our equipment and fussy preparations tend to make "real people" nervous.

So, just like a good dentist doing a new procedure with a patient, take a little time to explain to your subjects what's going on. "Do you mind taking a seat for minute, Carolyn? I'm going to adjust your hair light now. This is the special light that gives your favorite starlets like Zoe Saldana (sigh!) that magic glow of beauty whenever they are on-screen." And BAM!—With that few seconds of conversation, I've just educated them, involved them in the process, made them smile and feel like a superstar...I want them to know that I'm not just lighting them; I'm lighting them just like a Hollywood superstar, baby. And that's *exactly* how I want my real people on camera to feel—relaxed and confident that they are being handled by a team of video professionals who all know exactly how to make them look, sound, and feel their very best on camera.

2 GIVE THEM *CONSTANT* VISUAL FEEDBACK

One thing you want to always do is maintain good eye contact when you are interviewing or conversing with people on camera. This means you can't continually stare at your own questions, script, or notes. Instead, you'll come in already familiar with them, and occasionally glance at your notes briefly between answers or whenever the subject glances away for a second or two. Apart from that, every single time they look over, they should see your smiling face and deeply engrossed eyes and approvingly nodding head looking right back at them and hanging on their every fascinating word (whether it's truly fascinating or not).

Ask a question; then nod and smile. By the end of the interview, you may feel like a goofy grinning bobble-head doll on the dashboard for a bumpy ride. However, when your subject sees your pleased face and encouraging nod every time they look over at you, they will feel confident and encouraged to tell you *more* of their fascinating story with even *more* details and sincerity. (They know it's fascinating because you *look* fascinated as they are telling it.)

Always maintain eye contact and remember to smile and nod at your subjects answers to *show* approval.

3 CHEER THEM ON WITH VERBAL FEEDBACK

Responding to what people are saying lets them know you are actually interested and paying attention. Nodding and smiling is good for starters, but to elicit even stronger answers from your subjects, try raising the inflection of your questions and giving them a little exaggerated verbal feedback as well. You'll find that your subjects will usually match your more excited tone. You don't want to overdo it, but you'll want to occasionally challenge them to give you more emotion, with little lines like "Get out of here?!" "Really?!" "You're kidding me?!" "I don't believe you?!" "No freaking way?!" "You did whaaat, girlfriend?!"...all of these phrases raise the excitement level and illustrate your desire to hear *more* of their fascinating story. And now that you've egged them on and gotten them to turn up the enthusiasm, it really *will* be a more fascinating story on camera. When necessary, get your subjects to turn up the emotional volume, and I promise you, you'll get better sound bites every time.

4 WORK WITH MORE NATURAL OR SIMPLE LIGHTING

The lights are probably the single most intimidating aspect of being on camera. Subjects literally feel the spotlight and all eyes on them. So, if it's appropriate and works for your video, you may want to go with more natural lighting or keep the lighting fairly simple. A sunlit window or the soft comforting glow of a simple China ball is considerably more familiar and much less intimidating than the bright hot glare of professional lights on stands. Natural lighting also offers the added benefits of considerably less setup time, manpower, and electricity.

Soft, warm China balls make your set feel more like a cozy Ikea bedroom than a witness chair.

5 TURN OFF THE RECORD LIGHT AND BEEP

Go into your camera's menu and turn off the little beep function that makes the camera beep every time you hit the record button. Also turn off the record tally light that comes on whenever you are recording. Both of these can only serve to make people more self-conscious on camera. There's absolutely no advantage whatsoever to having people in front of the camera (whether it's narrative or documentary-style shooting) knowing the exact moment that you're recording on the other end.

6 AVOID BOOM MICS IF YOU CAN

The other thing I would say as far as keeping it real is if you have the option of using a lav mic instead of a shotgun mic on a boom pole, you'll probably get a more relaxed subject. Having someone stand there holding a giant phallic symbol just above your head while you try to think and speak spontaneously can get very distracting and intimidating if that's not the kind of thing you're used to. Even if you are used to it, it still takes a certain amount of discipline to ignore this giant mic hovering just above your head. So, I recommend working with tiny, unintrusive lav mics instead. Lav mics tend to make people much less self-conscious because they have the *opposite* effect of a boom, in that people quickly forget that they are wearing them. The biggest worry you'll usually have with a lav mic is that people may forget they have it on and suddenly get up at the end of shooting and accidentally rip the wire out or yank your equipment onto the floor. If you must use a boom mic or just prefer the sound quality, try mounting your boom mic on a stand or otherwise rigging it so it stays in position without needing someone to hold it. (See photo below.)

7 MOVE THE CAMERA FAR AND AWAY

Another technique you could use to get more natural and relaxed performances from nonprofessionals is to get the camera farther away and zoom in from a distance to compose your medium and close-up shots. This is a technique commonly employed by the big network interview shows such as *60 Minutes* and the nightly world news shows.

If you can back up your camera a good 20'–30' away from your subject, this will give you two big benefits: (1) The camera will be farther out of sight and therefore further out of mind, so you don't have to worry about subjects being intimidated by the camera. If you have a three- or four-point professional light setup in the center of a big room, subjects often can't even see the camera because it will be in

The farther away your camera is, the more normal your conversation will seem.

the shadows, and the exchange with your subject will feel more like an intimate conversation between two people. (2) If you zoom in your lens all the way to the telephoto setting and move the camera back to compose your desired frame, your shot will have much more cinematic and shallow depth of field, so your subject will be in sharp focus in the foreground and the background behind them will be soft and out of focus. Take note that this technique will require more or longer audio cables and/or monitor cables to reach from the setup to the camera and could also make it more difficult for an interviewer to subtly communicate with a camera person...but all intimacy has its price.

LOAD-IN PROCEDURE

Equipment Pickup	All equipment needs to be picked up from its respective sources before the shoot. Equipment that's personally owned should be checked and prepped the day before the shoot. Arrangements for equipment rentals should be made at least a week or two (if not a month) before the shoot with proper time to check the equipment at the rental house.
Location Greeting	The location manager or producer should be the first to arrive on set, greet the location owners, and make sure the location is prepared to receive the production. A written location agreement with the location owners should already be in place well before the shoot.
Crew Call	Crew call should be scheduled at least an hour before talent call. You don't want actors on set well before they are needed or the crew is prepared to receive them.
Craft Services	Nothing moves on an early call time without caffeine, so a crafts services table should be set up just prior to the full crew's arrival with fresh hot coffee and tea ready to greet them on set. A simple continental breakfast of bagels, pastries, and/or fruit is standard.
Production Meeting	Have a brief final meeting with your crew to fill them in on the plan for the day, last-minute changes since the last meeting, and any specific location issues and safety concerns, such as warning of any potentially dangerous scenes, props, or areas; and pointing out which bathroom to use.
Load In	The location manager or producer should direct the crew as all equipment is loaded onto the set. Each department should have its own **staging area**.

Note: This page and the next few pages show charts that outline the general procedures for a typical shooting day on the set of a marketing video or commercial. However, with a few exceptions, the procedure is pretty much the *same* for music videos and other scripted genres.

Talent Call	Actors and other on-screen talent should be scheduled to arrive on set with an hour or so to eat quickly, get dressed, and made up. Consult your wardrobe and makeup department for how much time they will need.
Talent and Releases Signed	I always recommend getting talent releases up front before the camera even rolls, so you don't forget at the end, and just in case a funky actor "situation" develops later, you're covered to use the footage you've shot.
Makeup and Costume	Talent should get their hair and makeup done and get dressed and ready for shooting.
Set Dressing	The set should be rearranged and dressed as needed for shooting—furniture moved and props put in place. Always take a few digital pictures on your phone beforehand, so you can place everything back exactly where it was when location shooting.
Camera Setup	The camera should be built and hooked up to a monitor with all needed accessories added on. You can't properly set lights without seeing the picture from the camera, so picture must be ready early.
Lighting Setup	All lights should be set up and placed in position. You need to look at the monitor and set your lights one at a time so that you can actually see what each light is doing on camera; then turn them all on for the full picture.
Audio Setup	The audio department should start assembling and hooking up their gear, running cables, and testing mics. For single system setups, the audio should also be hooked up to the camera. Record **bars and tone**.

Blocking and Rehearsing Talent	The director walks the actors through their physical motions and actions (aka blocking) without speaking lines first. The goal is to familiarize the actors with their movements and work out the logistics of the physical character and set interactions. Diagrams of the set and prep time spent prethinking blocking decisions are an important part of a director's preparation. In fact, most of the director's job takes place before they ever even step foot on set.
Blocking and Rehearsing Camera	Now the director blocks the cameras by working out specific shots, composition, and camera movement as well as which camera will cover what actions as the actors walk through their blocking. Initial camera blocking will be based off your storyboards or shot list, but often changes will need to be made on the fly based on the actual set and other logistical issues that may present themselves (otherwise known as "reality").
Block and Rehearse Camera with Talent	Now that the actors know their movements and the cameras know how they'll be covering those movements, it's time to put your brilliant on-the-fly blocking plan to the test and have the actors and camera rehearse the scene with full lines and actions. Again, adjust each as problems become apparent on the monitor.
Placing Mics and Audio Adjustments	Now that you know where the actors and cameras will be, the audio department can make final decisions about how to best mic the scene and cover the dialog accordingly. The audio department will also want to set levels at this time.
Final Adjustments and Rehearsal	Lastly, run through the whole scene with actors, camera, and audio all rehearsing their respective jobs. Again, adjust the equipment and blocking as needed according to the realities you encounter on set.

Director Calls for Take	Call for cameras, audio, and talent to be ready and make sure all set lights are turned on. Call "Roll camera! Roll Sound!" (Note: Keep your eye on *the clock*. A classic mistake is to over-rehearse and then run out of time to adequately shoot the scene. Avoid this.)
Recording to Audio and Booming	The boom operator puts the boom in position. The mixer begins recording audio and calls "Speed!" if you recording **double system audio** or the mixer just calls "Ready!" if recording **single system audio**.
Recording to Camera and Shooting	The camera operators set their shots, start recording, and call "Ready!"
Slating Take	An A.D., A.C., or P.A. should mark (i.e., call out the info on) and clap the slate. Even if you are not shooting double-system audio and syncing audio in post, slating is still an important practice that makes it considerably easier to find and organize footage in post.
Script Supervising and Continuity	During each take, the script supervisor or continuity person takes careful notes on the placement of props, actors' positions, wardrobe, and line readings and informs the director of any issues, particularly those that will be a problem in post or in representing the brand.
Holding Talent	When they are not needed on set, actors should be in a comfortable nearby holding area so that they are out of the way and readily available when they are needed.
Downloading Digital Media	The digital assistant should be carefully tracking, organizing, and offloading the footage on the digital video cards (i.e., P2, SxS, SDHC cards, etc.) from the cameras onto a hard drive as the shoot goes so that you never have to stop shooting because all the cards are full. After verifying video and audio on a computer, the digital assistant should **wipe** (i.e. reformat) the cards and return them to the camera ops. Lastly, all the footage should be backed up on another hard drive as soon as possible after shooting.

Wrapping Out Talent	As soon as you are done shooting and have verified that you have no problems with the footage and are absolutely sure you have everything you needed to make the day, you should dismiss talent from set. Make sure you've gotten all necessary releases and filled out any **S.A.G. paperwork** if you are using union actors. If you are paying talent and they have already invoiced you for their services, now is a *great* time to pay them.
Striking the Set	Once the production is complete and the director officially calls it a wrap, the production designer and prop master should begin clearing the set of props and restoring any furniture, pictures, or other items that were moved from their original positions based on the photos taken at the beginning of the shoot. Try to make it look better than when you came. If the set was built on a sound stage, the crew would begin dismantling the set.
Load Out	At the end of the shoot, all the gear needs to be broken down and put back in the pelican cases and gear bags that it came in. It's extremely important to inventory everything as you break down to make sure that you leave with all the gear you came with and everything makes its way back to the rental house. Hurried crews often leave behind small accessories and parts of rigs that can be expensive to replace later. Everything should be neatly and logically loaded into trucks and production vehicles so that the first items that need to be unloaded are the last items loaded.
Thanking and Paying the Crew	The two most important words you can say on set are "Thank you"—to your crew, your talent, and location owners. More than anything, people want to feel that their hard work is appreciated—ESPECIALLY if they are working for free or very little. If you're paying and they've already invoiced you, cut them a check or give them cash on the spot after their job is complete. The most important thing you can do after wrap is pay your crew on-time and in full.
Equipment Return	Lastly, make sure you've designated who will return any gear that was rented or borrowed and that all returns occur as soon as possible after shooting to avoid late fees or extra rental day charges.

Working with Teleprompters

Teleprompters are invaluable for live presentations; long-form programs; or pretty much any scripted news, info, or reality-based project. Here's a little-known secret of some of your favorite TV talent: they are not nearly as fluid, natural, funny, or confident without a teleprompter directly in front of them telling them exactly what to say. If you've heard the term but aren't familiar, teleprompters are the special monitors rigged in front of (or right near) a camera to reflect a scrolling script on one-way mirrored glass. The camera lens shoots *through* the one-way glass from the nonreflective side, so the script is never visible to camera, only to the talent in front of the camera.

Talent

Although the two can be one in the same, "on-screen talent" generally differ from professional actors in that this "talent" also refers to people who are personalities. They are essentially portraying *themselves* (usually exaggerated, smilier, friendlier, and more amped-up versions of themselves, but it's still basically just who they are—amplified for the audience). The overwhelming majority of our favorite newscasters, pitchmen, athletes, talk show hosts, and TV personalities are just professional teleprompter readers.

That is not at all to say that they don't have talent, intelligence, or wit, just to say that a teleprompter is the single greatest tool that can help *anyone* on camera appear *much more* talented, witty, smart, and fluid. A teleprompter is to TV talent what Photoshop is to supermodels and what AutoTune is to a singer. Yes, they may be good already, but they don't look or sound nearly as good without their special little technological secret. If you do instructional, corporate, or any other kind of scripted nonfiction production, a teleprompter is a game changer. It is *our* little video secret. (Shhh!)

> ### Five Good Reasons to Use a Teleprompter
> ✔ **Keep the production on schedule.**
> ✔ **Make sure key points are covered.**
> ✔ **Give talent full confidence.**
> ✔ **Save time and maintain consistency.**
> ✔ **Make improv and humor more natural and easy.**

Apple's iPad Saves the Day

Only very recently, with the advent of the iPad, did filmmakers have an affordable option in the form of several inexpensive (under $10) teleprompter apps that do the job almost as well as their grossly overpriced predecessors. These apps allow you to import a script, change the font size and color, control the scroll speed, and even allow you to use an iPhone as a remote control. (Search for "iPad" on **DownAndDirtyDV.com** for a link to a DIY video on using an iPad with one-way glass.)

COMMERCIALS 101

CHRIS CHAN ROBERSON, PRODUCER/DIRECTOR
(COFOUNDER ETC PRODUCTIONS); facebook.com/etc.comedy

WHAT *IS* A COMMERCIAL?

A commercial is (ironically) not necessarily the selling of a product, but the selling of an *experience* that the product is going to bring you. My favorite recent commercial is the Old Spice commercial where clearly the guy is saying, "Ladies, you want your man to smell like me? Here are tickets to that show you like, whatever the show is." So, it's less about your buying Old Spice and more about your buying the experience Old Spice will provide. Commercials sell experiences. In the carpentry business, they say that people don't want drills; they want holes. Whatever can get them a hole is what they want.

They don't want to own anything; they want the *experience* of creating that hole. So, the commercial is the selling of that experience.

Commercials have gotten smarter over the years. Nike commercials are more about celebrating the physicality of the athlete as opposed to selling the shoe. The beer commercials are more about having fun than drinking beer. It's important that you create an atmosphere that's genre and product specific. Again, going back to the idea of selling an experience, like a short movie, you're trying to establish characters, drama, and *wants*. It's like creating a mini-movie. If you want to create commercials, yes, you want to sell a product. Yes, you want to make money, but you should really think about it like making a movie. How am I going to *engage* the audience, and how will I get them talking about it once the movie's over, once the commercial is over. So think about it commercially the same way you'd think about any other piece of creative work.... The success will follow if you think about how to make a better product as opposed to how to make money.

TELLING A GOOD STORY IN 30 SECONDS FLAT

Today's average young adult filmmakers are very savvy with their phones, being able to shoot a movie or to always have a video camera around. And that's fantastic. However, the idea of a shot ratio is really foreign to many young filmmakers because they didn't grow up with that ethos of shooting on film. I remember being an undergrad in NYU's Sight & Sound Film class shooting 16mm film, and when that motor ran, all I heard was dollars and cents. Shooting commercials is about being economical in thought. If you want to be a commercial director, you should try cooking. You should try stand-up comedy. You should try telling jokes—any medium that requires that you're *economic* in thought and execution.

You'll be surprised how it translates over. It's not easy. If it were easy, everybody would be doing it. That's the challenge. I find a lot of people that are good at telling a 30-second story fail at something else. I recently judged a commercial competition. There were some really clever 30-second spots, but they were poor at branding. Whether it was associating someone else's product with sexual abuse or with vulgarity, it was clever, but no one would want to associate their name with that kind of activity; or it was a great idea but poorly shot and executed. It's hard. It takes a lot of work. I would recommend that people go the opposite route and try to write a haiku. Try to do speed swimming—something that requires your brain to run faster than it normally does.

THE RULES OF COMMERCIALS

Know your brand. It is very important that if you are going to make a commercial for a company that is family-oriented, you're not going to get scantily clad women dancing around. If there is a brand that's geared toward young adults being very hip and very sexy, you're not going to go the route of elderly people driving around in a buggy. So, you've got to know their branding, know the group that they're reaching out to, and know their target audience. Work accordingly. Many people try to rebrand something, and it just doesn't feel like it's the same product. They're not going to like it, and the audience won't take to it.

STAYING ON THE SAME PAGE WITH CLIENTS

Keeping your client on the same page can be really tough. How savvy is your client? There have been really embarrassing times when I was making stuff for television where I put in some temporary credits. I put in a title that said I was going to color-correct something later. The producer got furious and said, "Why would we air something that has these titles on the bottom?" and I'm thinking, "Oh man, this guy's a moron!" So you have to know the client's skill set. If you're giving someone a version of anything that isn't color-corrected and has rough sound, you need to make it painstakingly clear that it isn't the *final* product. Sometimes clients are like, "Why isn't it color-corrected?" I say, "I'm not going to color-correct something in which you are not happy with the final product because these may not be the final shots."

Make sure that clients know what your process is. Make sure that there is a solid calendar that says, "By this Friday, we have to get this done." Sometimes a client may not know how to get you assets fast enough, so you may say you need music by Friday and they say they'll get it to you on Sunday. That may be too late because you may need to cut to it, or you may need it for an output. Make sure that there are clear calendar dates and that the client knows any jargon or industry speak that you're using if they're not already aware of it. Before anything is shot, before anything is edited, you want to get your obligations in a written legal format so that the client doesn't say to you, "Oh, by the way, I need 50 Digi-Beta copies by tomorrow." If you never talked about what the final deliverables are, you'd be obligated to give them to the client. I want to really stress the importance of a contract. There are great contract lawyers that get paid after you get paid, so it's not like they have to be held on a retainer. Legally protect yourself and protect your client.

"Differenter" Campaign

INNOVATORS OF CHANGE

Purpose:
To celebrate Black History month

Preproduction:
2 Meetings with Client
Preproduction Crew Meeting

Equipment:
3 Canon 7D DSLR Cameras
50mm Prime Lens
16mm–70mm Zoom Lens
70mm–200mm Zoom Lens
LED Lite Panel 1x1 Light
Omni Go Light Kit
2 Hardwired Lavs
Juiced Link XLR Audio Adapter

Clients: A Major New York Ad Agency
Subjects: 6 Community Leaders
Genre: Promotional Campaign
Director: Pete Chatmon
Web: vimeo.com/20441368 and
double7images.com/portfolio/differenter

Crew:
1 Director
2 Exec Producers
2 Producers
2 Writers
1 D.P.
2 Additional Videographers
1 Gaffer
1 Editor/Graphic Effects

Postproduction:
8 days post
Final Cut Pro
After Effects

Transportation:
NYC Subway
Cabs

Locations/Schedule:

DAY 1
Manhattan–Client's Office
Ryan Mack–3 cameras

DAY 2
Brooklyn in a library
Dr. Una Clarke–3 cameras
B-roll exterior library

DAY 3
Bronx–Office
Majora Carter–2 cameras
B-roll exterior Bronx streets

DAY 4
Manhattan–Client's Office
Jacques-Phillippe Piverger–2 cameras

DAY 5
Brooklyn–College
HipHop 4 Life–3 cameras
2 subject interview

Project Details

Concept: The "Differenter" campaign was commissioned by the diversity committee of a major New York City ad agency. They partnered with Double7 Images to deliver a media campaign spotlighting current Black "Innovators of Change" in NYC. Several hours of content had to be pared down to a compelling short documentary and a series of five "video signatures" that provided a glimpse into the worlds of the five extraordinary subjects. The short documentary premiered at a special live event at the agency's offices and was shared online via multiple social media platforms.

The Interviewees: The Differenter Committee selected the interviewees for the project. There were 12 people honored at the event, but 5 featured in the video with a goal of showing diversity in age, gender, and borough (Manhattan, Brooklyn, The Bronx, etc).

Crew: The project called for an agile crew that could handle a 3-camera shoot while limiting the "production elements" on set (gear, cases, etc). It was important not to bombard the locations with too many people or too much equipment. The actual crew selection was easy as Double7 Images is comprised of a creative collective from which they recruit the best talent for every client project.

Preproduction: Director, Pete Chatmon, decided the coverage approach as far as three cameras and what lenses to use, and then researched each interviewee to get a little more backstory on their accomplishments. This was a situation where the client actually provided the questions to ask, but by also doing his own research the director was able to be fully conversational with each interviewee and ensure that he got the client's desired answers even when he went "off book."

Production: For each interview, they pretty much walked into the location, found the best angle, and then lit for consistency. They had to work with what they were given, but even though it was a documentary, the crew still used the narrative tools of the trade. That meant moving a prop from another room onto the table in front of the subject or placing a plant behind them... anything to give the frame more volume and depth. They also made sure to grab footage while setting up and introducing themselves to the interviewees, as breaking the fourth wall was a creative element they wanted to exploit. Working with DSLR cameras required a new approach as far as breaking the shoot up into takes or sections to ensure they wouldn't run out of time. (The cameras can only shoot for 12 minutes straight). This meant they had to keep an eye on how long the questions and answers were running so they wouldn't have to make an interviewee repeat themselves due to technical limitations. Lastly, DSLR has its own sound challenges which were resolved with a Juiced Link Box. (You should consult with your sound recordist and editor as to what workflows they are familiar with and can best exploit before you shoot your project on a DSLR camera.)

Postproduction: This project had an extremely quick turnaround with editing of the short videos taking place immediately after each shoot, over a one- to two-day period. The advantage of this, however, was that they were able to set the graphic template early on while at the same time getting familiar with the footage. After shooting postproduction on the 15-minute documentary took four days. While the team would've preferred more time, their overall preparation allowed them to execute on such a short timeline.

Breaking the Fourth Wall

Here and there throughout the video we get glimpses of the behind-the-scenes filmmaking process. This is more commonly known as **"breaking the fourth wall,"** as in calling attention to the filmmaking process and the fact that there are cameras, lights, and crew members creating this experience. TV and video experiences are no longer the mysterious magical creations they were 30 or 40 years ago. Not only is the audience always fully aware that this is a manufactured experience, they occasionally appreciate being in on the making of it. This is commonly done in the popular news and television shows as a brief two- to four-second establishing shot at the very opening of an interview segment.

Breaking the fourth wall is a fun and creative way to spice up otherwise fairly static talking-head shots. With a **roving** second camera, grab a few shots that include elements of your setup—a wide shot over the shoulder of the cameraman, a glimpse of the image on the monitor, the clapping of the slate, crew members setting up, etc. To make it even more interesting and dynamic, try some rack focus moves and pans and tilts from equipment in the foreground to subjects in the background or vice versa. This practice will also help you remember certain elements of a spontaneous setup when you want to duplicate it in the future and also makes for good screen grabs for your own promotional material. (You are advertising *your own* services too, *right*?)

Traditional Cutaways

Sporadically throughout the video, a roving camera was used to also capture some more traditional cutaway shots—specifically, over-the-shoulder shots of the interviewer, interesting details of clothing, and hand gestures. Hand gestures are always a great all-purpose cutaway. Don't just let a talking head and mere words do all the work of telling your story. Hands can be extremely expressive of emotion—a fist pounding the table, the joyous clutching of one's heart, open palms moving in rhythm to their words...all poetic visuals to aid your storytelling. Best of all, these are all **neutral cutaways** that can be inserted anywhere to help you smoothly cut from one sound bite to another. If you have only one camera or miss these during your interview, you can always fake them at the end by re-asking your subject certain questions and shooting just their hands and body language this time.

Third-Party B-Roll

The "Differenter" Campaign had five different subjects' stories to tell and a tight shooting schedule and deadline, so it wasn't realistic that the New York–based Double7 Images production team would be able to shoot original B-roll for all the subjects, especially when some of the interviewee's work took place as far away as Haiti. The crew shot a few establishing shots and supporting B-roll in the Bronx and Harlem areas of New York City where several of the subjects lived and worked. However, the remaining video B-roll that was used in the project came from two pre-existing video projects or from news stories or television profiles of the subjects that had been shot years earlier. The trickiest B-roll to secure was getting shots to support the story of a company that did significant disaster relief work in Haiti. There was no pre-existing video of their relief work there, so the editor called upon a friend who had shot a documentary in Haiti, who supplied some beautifully shot and compelling HD images of the hurricane aftermath in Haiti. The subject's story wouldn't have nearly the resonance that it carried without these provocative shots taken hundreds of miles away. This is a classic example of being *resourceful* and working smarter and not harder to get the same end result.

Text Treatments

For the "Differenter" campaign pictured here, Double7 Images editor Giga Shane used Adobe After Effects to make the text come alive. Each subject's profile opened up with a simple white-on-black text screen that previewed a notable and inspirational quote from the segment of the interview to follow. After a few seconds, the name of the person quoted appeared on the screen. This slight teasing reveal of the person quoted is yet another way to further engage your audience's attention.

Each subject was also introduced to the audience with a unique animated title treatment displayed split screen. Some titles slid onto screen from the left and right, while others zoomed from the outer edges. In the sequence above, a spinning globe with the word "global" was animated in After Effects to add some energy to what otherwise could have been a standard (and much less interesting) lower third title. Careful listening to or reviewing transcripts will help you identify specific words and phrases that present excellent opportunities to add some visualization to text and/or simple animated sequences that can greatly enhance your storytelling imagery. A good director is constantly looking for ways to *show* the audience the story, instead of just telling them. Showing them can be literal, as in choosing the appropriate B-roll, but "showing them" also includes how we display text, the types of transitions we use to set a mood, the fonts we choose, the colors of backgrounds, and other techniques that translate mere words into vibrant images.

Multiple Camera Angles

A big factor in adding more production value and opening up any shot that's basically a talking head is to capture the action from multiple camera angles. All of the interviews in the "Differenter" campaign were captured from multiple camera positions with two or three cameras rolling at any given time. Switching angles regularly keeps the audience much more visually engaged. Also wider shots can be used to show a subject's hand gestures and body language. Apart from just adding some visual variety and showing the audience more of the space where the interview takes place, using multiple cameras has the very practical advantage of making it much easier to *edit* an interview or dialog sequence. If a subject misspeaks or says a few lines that you know you want to cut out, you can simply cut that part of the video and switch to another camera angle to smoothly and seamlessly cover up the fact that we are jumping to another point in time. With multiple cameras, you can do this all day long in the edit room. You are free to easily use any sound bite from any point in the process without the appearance of having a jump cut. Even things that would normally give it away, like different hand positions between shots, are much less noticeable when you cut to a completely different camera angle.

Using Different Lenses and Focal Lengths

Roving Camera 50mm Prime	Close-ups 70mm–200mm Zoom	Medium and Wide 16mm–70mm Zoom

One big advantage of shooting with affordable video DSLR cameras is that you can switch out lenses, whereas most dedicated video cameras at the prosumer price point ($3,500–$7000) have fixed lenses. Using Canon 5D and 7D model cameras allowed the team to simultaneously use three different cameras with three different lenses, to achieve a variety of big-budget looks and feels that more resemble film. In particular, they could achieve wider shots than you can get on most factory lenses, and they could also get more telephoto shots with very shallow depth of field.

TEXT AND STORYTELLING

One powerful weapon that can always help you create new visual elements to make a project more dynamic and interesting is text. Employed in the right way, text itself can become a fresh new visual that helps communicate tone, subject, and message in a clear, concise, and entertaining way. When animated with fly-ins, flips, dissolves, etc., mere words on the screen can be brought to life to help tell your story and keep it moving.

Simple animated text and title FX are readily available in just about every nonlinear editor. Even the more consumer-oriented editing programs like iMovie have *some* cool drag-and-drop title FX already built in to the program. Professional NLEs such as Avid, Final Cut Pro (FCP), and Premiere all have fairly robust text editors that will serve most needs. However, when you're ready to take your title game to the next level, you'll want one of the more powerful graphics FX programs, such as Adobe's After Effects or Apple's Motion

Even Apple iMovie offers a variety of ready-made text and title effects that can be customized. Pro NLE programs like AVID, FCP, and Premiere offer even more options.

software. In the hands of a skilled editor or graphics FX artist, these programs make it possible for multiple layers of text to dance, mirror, explode, spin, swirl, or all of the above, plus pretty much anything else your imagination can conceive. The Creative Cow community (**creativecow.net**) and the **Lynda.com** website are both excellent resources for advice and step-by-step tutorials on various animated text effects using the most popular programs.

Getting enough compelling and relevant B-roll is always a challenge for any corporate project, especially if it involves a wide variety of locations and events. The subject matter of your video will often be in another city, state, or even a whole other continent. But a Down and Dirty freelance video hustler should never let a little obstacle like intercontinental travel get in the way of telling a good video story. Try any of these easy creative solutions to your B-Roll blues....

1 SHOOT IT YOURSELF

Okay, before we jump into the more creative ways, let's look at the standard B-roll solution: if your project budget is big enough and you have enough time in your production schedule, you can shoot all the B-roll yourself—scheduling appointments, traveling, and gathering a crew to shoot whenever and wherever becomes necessary to capture as many relevant events and places as the subject matter (or client) dictates to bring your project to life. As often as possible, I recommend trying to gather supporting B-roll whenever you already have an interview scheduled. Arrange to shoot some B-roll immediately before or after a scheduled interview with a subject. You want to grab a few interior and exterior establishing shots of the general environment and atmosphere, but what you really want to try to get are shots of your subjects doing their thing in their natural environment—whatever that thing is. If your subject is a real estate agent, shoot them showing a house to a client, sitting at their desk scouring the new real estate listings online, conducting a meeting with their staff...*action*, baby! Shoot some "A-roll." Put some actual thought into it. Get creative and find ways to *show* the audience how your clients do what they do.

> Discuss upcoming events with your clients so you can be there to capture the most compelling visuals.

I recommend that you get B-roll just after an interview, so that if time gets tight, you've already shot the most important thing you need. You can always come back (or just send a shooter) at some other time to get more B-roll. You can often grab plenty of supporting images in less than an hour's time if you plan and time your visit correctly. Check with the client to get a sense of their daily routine and noteworthy upcoming events. Scrutinize which events will be the most visually compelling...a routine morning meeting may not provide much compelling imagery. However, a morning meeting where the company will be unveiling their fall lineup of new products to the full sales team or introducing their celebrity spokesperson will provide ample money shots to make the trip worthwhile.

When pressed for images in a boring setting like this classroom with plain white walls, look for the details in the scene to keep your B-roll varied and visually interesting.

Also, when faced with fairly mundane scenes, look for close-up details around the room for help that can help you tell the story at hand—a relevant graphic on a report cover, diagrams on a white board, an attendee's handwritten notes, engaged faces nodding in approval.... Spice it up with a few rack-focus moves from foreground objects to background objects or let your camera playfully rove across the details of the room to help bring that mundane scene to life. I think in most cases, if the B-roll is totally boring, it's because it was *shot* that way. Learn to visualize the details in any scene and think about how you can capture them in a more interesting way. Free your mind and your *camera* will follow.

2 ASK THE CLIENTS FOR B-ROLL

Notwithstanding all of the previous comments, a smarter, faster, and cheaper option that you should also consider is to get some of your B-roll from *the clients* themselves. (Yes, it's rarely true of anything in production, but this solution really is all three: smart*er*, fast*er* and cheap*er.*) This is particularly important to try if you're on a tight budget or timeline. These days many companies have some pre-existing video content—events they've archived in the past, various videos they've previously commissioned, marketing materials, etc., just sitting on a shelf or on a hard drive somewhere waiting—no *begging*—for you to use them to supplement the visuals in your project. Always ask your clients what, if any, relevant video they might already have that you can draw from. When you're conducting an interview or reviewing your transcripts, take note of all the things a subject mentions and note which ones are crying out for visualization. If you're interviewing a musician and they mention what a fabulous gig they played at a certain music festival, ask them if they have any footage of that event.

If the video footage provided by your clients is of a lower quality or format than your own, you can always get a little creative in editing to make it work for the project.

Even standard-definition camcorder footage or grainy cell phone video is better than nothing as long as it's not too shaky and amateurishly shot. With a little postproduction creativity by a skilled editor, even low-quality video can be treated with effects such as placed in a layer beneath an interview as an artistic blur, put in grainy black and white, included within HD footage as part of a picture-in-picture effect, such as showing the image within a TV or smartphone graphic—any of these solutions is better than not showing your audience a visual representation of a compelling anecdote, comment, or observation. Using similar post techniques as the ones I just laid out, you can pull footage from just about *any* source and creatively distort and obscure it in postproduction to create a supporting B-roll visual where none exists.

3 · RECYCLE OR BORROW THE B-ROLL YOU NEED

Getting lots of fresh new and original B-roll is always a good thing when you have the time and resources to pull it off. But let's be real here, you simply *don't* always have the time, resources, or budget to do what you'd *really* like to do creatively. Some clients hit us up to pull off big projects where the *starting* deadline is "yesterday" and the relative budget is "cheap." Nevertheless, we take the job because we need the cash, the client will add to our credibility, or just because it's a fun and interesting project to expand our range and reel.

General B-roll shots like this busy street scene can be used for different projects.

Even under less than ideal circumstances, I say you should still strive to turn out a compelling piece of video that gets the job done, albeit cutting a few *strategic* corners in the process. One of those strategic corners you can cut is to borrow the B-roll you need from one of your previous projects. Don't re-invent the wheel—recycle it! Having lived and worked in and around New York City for more than a decade now, I have gathered ample shots of life in the big city that I can draw upon to round out the establishing and atmospheric B-roll of any NYC-based video project. It's also a good idea to occasionally just shoot some general B-roll of your city, nature, public events—cool and interesting multipurpose visuals to build your own personal stock footage library. And, if you're pressed for time and don't have the right shots in your own video arsenal, perhaps you could also call upon your editor or one of your freelancing friends to dig into their personal archives as well. (You have *already* been doing plenty of favors to help out your fellow filmmakers, right?)

> **Start to build a library of multipurpose visuals. Cityscapes, nature, crowd scenes, etc., will always come in handy.**

4 · BUY THE B-ROLL YOU NEED

Yet another option to add more gripping and exciting B-roll to your project is to use stock footage houses and stock footage DVD collections. You are by no means the first person to shoot a project that calls for visuals of nature, Wall Street, cityscapes, sunsets, time-lapse footage, snow, or kids playing on a playground. Almost any atmospheric or routine corporate video visual you can think of (plus a bunch you can't) has probably already been shot and catalogued by one of dozens of a stock footage houses around the globe. Stock footage houses are companies that collect all sorts of video footage just to fill in the gaps for production companies just like yours.

Many of the money shots you'd love to have in your video are probably already burned on a DVD or sitting on a server somewhere awaiting nothing more than your credit card number to access or download them. Yes, I said *download*. Once upon a time, you had to go in person and comb through a stock footage house's archives tape by tape, but nowadays, you can review clips online and then have a high-quality digital file or DVD mailed to you. Or easiest of all, if you've got a fast Internet connection, you can download video clips in full-HD quality (720p or 1080p) from many different stock footage websites.

FootageFirm.com sells a variety of royalty-free stock footage video collections on DVD.

The biggest advantage of using preshot stock footage is that you can quickly and easily get exotic shots that you could never otherwise afford, such as helicopter swoops over Rio de Janeiro, beautifully shot time-lapse footage of a wild beach at sunrise, Polar Bears swimming underwater, the inner workings of a massive factory floor in Shang Hai—you name it. Shooting just one of these shots yourself would probably break your whole budget, but through the convenience of stock footage, you can get a whole slew of interesting big-budget visuals to open up

ArtBeats.com sells stock footage clips for instant download—very convenient for late-night edit sessions on a tight deadline.

your video for a small fraction of the actual costs. Same as with everything else, you want to use only footage that fits your project and enhances your story. Don't put in a shot of an exploding volcano just because you can; put it in because it's just the right image to tell your *story*... Boy, that word "story" just won't go away will it? Hmmm? Must be **important**. (See the Superfly Illmatic Bonus Book website at FreelanceVideoGuide.com for links to these and other sites that sell and license stock footage.)

5 STILL PHOTOS

If all else fails, I've got three words for you, baby: **Ken Burns Effect**. In the absence of video B-roll (or just to supplement it), the next best thing is high-quality still photos, which are usually also easier to come by. Always ask in the first meetings what, if any, pre-existing video and digital images clients have that could also be used for the project. Try to sift through this material *before* you shoot anything because the perfect shot or image to tell the story at hand may already exist. High-quality still photos can always be jazzed up with a little movement and visual treatment in post. The most popular technique is a series of digital camera moves in, out, and across digital pictures, known as The Ken Burns Effect, as popularized by the documentary filmmaker of the same name, that are preprogrammed into many NLE editing programs as well as photo programs such as iPhoto.

COMMERCIALS 201

CHRIS CHAN ROBERSON, PRODUCER/DIRECTOR (COFOUNDER, ETC PRODUCTIONS); facebook.com/etc.comedy

COMMON MISTAKES

The biggest mistake I see amateur filmmakers make is mis-branding. They'll try to make a product *too* sexy. They'll try to make a product *too* funny, or they just misrepresent a product altogether. If the company has a nun on the cover of their cereal, do not take us to a strip club. Improper branding has always been a problem.

The second biggest problem is not realizing their resources. I told my students that you're in New York. You can have the Empire State Building behind you. You can get on a ferry and see Manhattan Island. Use the city as a resource. A lot of guys were still shooting stuff in their dorm room. Really use location. Use the city as a character. Lastly, I think the thing people don't really wrap their heads around is that you want to create different versions of the same story. I told my students to make a 90-second commercial. Now edit it down to 60. Now edit it down to 30. Now edit it down to 15. With the same commercial, do four different versions. All of a sudden, it just opens up their eyes and it's like, "My God! I just told four different stories with the same footage."

Always think about how you can repurpose your material to have five or six versions. It allows flexibility for the client. By making a long version and a short version, they can advertise it more. Maybe they can't afford a 60-second spot, or they can't afford a 30-second spot. Also, it's a good exercise for a filmmaker to think small or think about different chunks.

THE COMMERCIAL WORKFLOW

So, let's draw a flow chart. The first question would be "Has this company ever had commercials made for them before?" If the answer is "Yes," then my next question would be "What were you satisfied with in the past and what were you dissatisfied with?" That way, I know what *not* to make or what to gravitate toward. Also, I would ask the clients to show me examples of previous commercials and tell me their strengths and weaknesses. If they have never shot anything before, or this is a new company and they never have been represented in the media, then I would ask them what are the "keywords" that they want people to think about their brand: Young? Fresh? Accessible? Inexpensive?... I get all those keywords, and I make them my statement of intent, which says that I'm crafting a commercial and the impression is that the brand is inexpensive, that it's accessible, that it's fresh. I would ideally script a couple of different scenarios. If a client is not really savvy with understanding a script format, maybe I'd get some friends together and follow them with my Handycam and shoot a mockup of it. That way, the client can be walked through on a low-key scaled-down version of what it might be like. I'd give them maybe three or four options with a low-end budget and a high-end budget and work with them on costs and a timeline. Then, I'd get to work.

The triangle of production is essential for anything that you do. There's fast. There's good. And there's cheap. You can only get two. I tell the client if you want it good and fast, it won't be cheap. If you want it fast and cheap, it won't be good. You can have it cheap and you can have it good, but it won't be fast. Those are the three things I say up front. If you need it right away and you want it to be good, it's going to cost you some money. If you don't really need it anytime soon, then I won't charge a whole lot, but it's going to take awhile. Find out the deliverable date from the client. If they need to air it on national television, then I'll need to put it to digital beta. If it's for the Internet, then it's going to be a digital file. I need to know from the client what they need because sometimes they may want a DVD. If you're airing this on television, they're not going to want a DVD. They're going to want a beta or HD cam master tape. I may have to walk the client through what the end product is and work backward from that.

EXPERIENCE COMMERCIALS VERSUS PROCESS COMMERCIALS

People have gotten savvier. One is a process commercial so you'll see people doing a process. Even in filmmaking, you have an intertextual read and an extratextual read. In an extratextual read, when you see *Saving Private Ryan*, no one has to explain to you *why* they're fighting the Nazis because you know about World War II from history class. Similarly, there are some products that need no explanation. You just need to establish the experience. A good example is the famous "1984" Apple commercial in which you see a woman running, and she throws a hammer, which breaks the screen. Oddly enough, there's no computer in that commercial. It's not about the Macintosh computer itself; it's actually about the *experience* of the Macintosh computer liberating you from being a PC tool. This kind of commercial is more about the experience and about creating a membership moment that they're going to attach to. These are called experience commercials.

Then you have intertextual commercials where you have to explain what's going on, what the characters are doing, and what the language is. You see this sort of thing in science fiction movies, too. For example, the film *Avatar* is completely intertextual: you have to explain what the Na'vi are, the language they speak, and what an Avatar is. The same *process* occurs in some commercials, and the viewer has to be walked through what the product does. For example, the commercials for some As-Seen-on-TV products like the Slap Chop or the ShamWow—in a 30-second spot, they communicate "Look-at-me-I-can-clean-anything!" Or OxiClean—you don't know what the product is, so you have to explain what the product does and why you need to own it. These are process commercials.

TESTING A SPOT

You don't want to show the final spot on the day before launch so that the clients have never seen what you've done and are like "What the [expletive] is *this*?!" To make sure that the products are being shown in the best light, make sure that your client has seen the commercial in the rough-cut stage and has approved it. It's also very helpful if you can get a test audience, so they can give you the thumbs up as well. I'll still relate commercials to filmmaking. Like you do with any film, you always have to show it to a test audience and get a vibe. Get it out there and see what people think about it. That's the best way, to me, to ensure that the product is seen in the best light: make sure the client is happy with it and that the test group gets it and would also be interested in the experience or product.

PREPARATION FOR BROADCAST

There isn't a hard and fast standard, so exact procedures differ slightly from company to company, but generally when you're editing you're going to start your timeline at 58:30, and you're going to give us 60 seconds of bars and tone. Then you put in 20 seconds of a slate, and then you're going to give us a 10-second countdown. Then your commercial will start at the one-hour mark. That's generally the standard—provide 60 seconds of bars and tone to make sure that they're calibrated. Twenty seconds of a slate, and the slate's probably going to state the product, the title of the spot, the run time, the date that you're laying it on the tape, who the producer is, and the producer's contact information. I've seen some crazy stuff where people put stamp codes in, but I think that's a little too high tech. You have a 10-second countdown where, after 3, you go blank and you have the blip on two, blank on 1, and start on 1 hour.

GETTING "BROADCAST STANDARD"

The term **"broadcast standard"** is a slippery one because there is no actual "standard." While there are many similarities, each network and broadcast platform has its own unique specs for how videos should be formatted and delivered. Always check with the company that will be receiving the final video well beforehand, so you'll know what you need to do in post and won't have any last-minute surprises. Allow for time and budget to transfer to the specified broadcast format such as Digi-Beta or HD Cam. Following are some basic elements that most broadcast outlets will expect on just about any video submitted for air.

Slate/Title Screen

Just like it sounds, this is just basic identifying info that should appear at the top of your video just after the color bars. This is not the fancy title sequence you may include for an audience, but a simple, clear, and easy-to-read screen intended only for the behind-the-scenes professionals who will handle the video after you hand it over. It consists of some basic info that anyone re-editing, broadcasting or projecting the piece will want to know:

- **Title, version # (if needed)**
- **Date of Edited Master**
- **Production Company/Producer**
- **Producer Contact Info**
- **Type of master (Broadcast, Dupe, Projection, etc.)**
- **Audio type channel 1 & 2 (mono, stereo, etc.)**
- **Total running time**

Color Bars

The very first thing that should come up after black on any video handed over for broadcast is one full minute's worth of NTSC color bars. This is the colorful pattern that you may

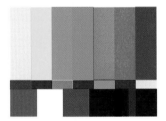

sometimes find broadcasting on your TV at 3:00 a.m. after normal programming has gone off the air. Much more than a cool retro pattern, color bars are used so that editors, TV station engineers, projectionists, and other video professionals can accurately adjust the colors on your video before broadcast. The color bars serve as a standard video reference point to help ensure that everyone's skin

does not look green and sickly, or your sky doesn't come up purple instead of blue. (You will find a how-to guide on setting color bars on the Superfly Illmatic Bonus website at FreelanceVideoGuide.com)

Tone

Running simultaneously with the color bars should be the 1kHz audio tone. This type of tone generated by a mixer or camera is the accepted standard reference for audio. Audio engineers, mixers, and editors use this tone to determine where to set the audio levels before a piece is screened or edited. Color bars are used to set the proper video and color levels, and tone is used to set the proper audio levels. Collectively, this practice is known as running **bars and tone** and should take up the first minute of the video after the simple identifying title screen.

30 Secs.—Black leader

58:00—58:30

30 seconds of
black leader

60 Secs.—Color bars

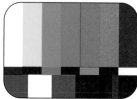

58:30—59:30

60 seconds of **color bars** and
1kHz **tone** so colors and
audio levels can be adjusted

20 Secs.—Slate

Jimmy's BBQ -: 30 spot
"Finger Licking Great"
Date: 4/4/11
Prod.: Rebekah Hotshot
Audio: ch 1&2 - mono

59:30—59:50

20 seconds of slate showing
title, run time, audio tracks
and production company info.

8 Secs.—Countdown

59:50—59:58

Count down from 10 to 3

2 Secs.—Black leader

59:58—59:59

Last 2 seconds of countdown
are blank screen with 2 seconds
of 1kHz audio beep.

30 Secs.—Spot

1:00:00—1:00:30

Content starts exactly at the
1:00:00 (1-hour mark).

A Web Promo Campaign
Project: Clive Davis Institute Web Promos

Client: Clive Davis Institute at NYU
Type: College Program
Directors: Anthony Artis, Pete Chatmon
Web: double7images.com/portfolio/clivedavis

Crew:
2 Director/Producers (alternating)
1 D.P.
1 Camera Op/Digital Assistant
1 Audio Mixer/Boom Op
1 Editor/Visual FX Artist

Equipment:
2 Panasonic HVX-200 Cameras
2 Tripods
1 Sennheiser 416 Shotgun Mic
2 Sennheiser Evolution G2 Wireless Mics
1 Kinoflo Diva 400 Light

Transportation:
NYC Subway
Taxicabs
By Foot

Postproduction:
Final Cut Pro
After Effects

Preproduction:
2 Meetings with Clients
Preproduction Crew Meeting
Location Scout with Still Photos

Videos:
1. "Production"
2. "Business"
3. "History and Criticism"
4. "Future Music Moguls"
5. "Virtual Tour"
6. "Program Overview"

Schedule and Locations:

DAY 1
1. 3 History Faculty Interviews
2. 1 Production Faculty Interview
3. 1 Business Faculty Interview
4. 1 Student Group Interview

DAY 2
1. 2 Administrator Interviews
2. Interview w/Clive Davis

DAY 3
1. Walk-and-Talk Facility Tour
2. Additional B-Roll
3. High-School Group Interview

DAY 4
1. Tour Reshoot
2. Walk-and-Talk Facility Tour
3. H.S. Program Faculty Interview
4. Exterior City B-Roll

DAY 5
1. Additional B-Roll
2. Classroom Footage
3. Production Footage

Project Details:

Concept: The Clive Davis Institute is a one-of-a-kind four-year program in recorded music that is part of NYU's Tisch School of the Arts. (FYI: At the time of production, it was called The Clive Davis Department of Recorded Music at Tisch New York University.) We set out to create a series of six videos for the web, each designed to highlight a different aspect of the school and its curriculum. We came up with a plan to produce six videos that covered the curriculum, a special summer high school program, and the facilities.

The Interviewees: After our initial consultation and proposal, the clients chose a handful of faculty members and administrators to represent each curriculum area and the department as a whole. In addition to these folks, they also selected two diverse groups of students: four college students to represent the main recorded music program and four high school students from their Future Music Moguls summer high school program.

Crew: As is my general preference, we stayed with a small skeleton crew and never shot with more than four crew members at one time. On the two biggest production days, which involved a series of interviews, we shot with a Director/Producer, one D.P., one camera op/digital assistant (who offloaded and managed the digital video files throughout the day), and one audio mixer/boom op. All the crew was drawn from our Double7 Images collective, a private group of independent NYC filmmakers who've banded together to produce commercial and personal video works.

Preproduction: After the initial simple proposal was submitted, we met the clients on two separate occasions. Based on the conversations at those meetings we drafted a new and more-detailed proposal based on the clients' feedback. We also shot photos and some video during our scout of the school to decide how we would shoot and light various interviews. Every interview location was decided beforehand.

Production: We had four standard production days and went back three more times for an hour or less to get B-roll of specific events such as a class meeting or studio session. (The follow-up B-roll was pretty easy to get because the facilities were within walking distance of our home base.) This shoot also marked my first major tapeless disaster when a 32GB P2 card became irreparably corrupt before it was off-loaded. We ended up having to reshoot the tour of the facilities–the most logistically complicated video of all. Murphy's Law is always in play when it come to production.

Postproduction: All the videos were cut on Final Cut Pro. Motion graphic text and animations were composed in Adobe After Effects. The editor also shot some supplementary B-roll such as album covers and greenscreen background plates to fill in some holes.

HOW WE DO

Graphic Text

In addition to the standard title and info screens we used, we also used graphic text elements to highlight some of the key aspects of the program. Editor/Visual FX artist, Giga Shane, always used movement to bring text onto or off the screen. Hardly anything just fades in. Every graphic in this piece slides, pops, or otherwise comes *seamlessly* in and out of the frame. One amateur mistake I see often is just getting a little too happy with the text effects and overdoing it. Don't use every other text FX on the list just because it's there and looks cool. Use it because it's *appropriate* for the look, tone, and subject matter of your story. Also, to maintain consistency and stay away from the bustling town of Amateurville, you want to create a **"style sheet"** for your text graphics and stick to it. Break your text elements down into groups such as lower thirds, main titles, info graphics, etc.; then choose a font style, size, layout, and color palette to apply to each. Generally, all similar elements should have the same look and feel and complement the video content and color palette on-screen.

Music

Obviously, the background music for a piece about a college for recorded music was extremely important. It was pretty much a no-brainer that we had to use only student-produced music, so we had students submit instrumental tracks for consideration. We were blown away by the quality of the music we received. In keeping with the visual music video theme, we placed music video–style credit screens at the end of each video, naming the students, their tracks, class year, and their websites. It's a cool surprise reveal at the end that says, "Oh and one more thing…you're listening to great student-produced music *right now*." BAM! Got 'em!

Transitional Visual FX

Marketing and promo videos need to be mean and lean. That often means condensing long passages of speech down to their simplest sound bites, which means you are going to be jumping from one section of an interview to another. You can accomplish this with jump cuts–jarring, but they work for some high-energy styles; dissolves–traditional and effective but somewhat boring and formal; or some other transitional visual effect that's just right. Every NLE, even at the consumer level, generally has a healthy selection of transition FX to get us from one shot to another. Again, same as with the graphic text FX I mentioned earlier–your shot transitions should always feel organic and never forced. Try to cut them in rhythm to the words, music, or general pacing of the piece. Each of these transitions that I've freeze-framed above lasts no longer than a quick second or two and goes by so fast and naturally that you *feel* it more than you notice it–just like a good camera move.

The organic feel comes from selecting transitions that complement the imagery, speed, and camera movement of the shots. In the screen grab shots below, the first shot is a whip zoom out to reveal the school's circular record-shaped logo, which then smoothly transitioned into a set of concentric circles expanding outward into the next shot. The transition naturally complemented the visual image of the circular record grooves and used that visual theme and a mimicking of the previous whip zoom shot to smoothly and organically take us into the next shot of our interviewee.

Transitions can also be used to help mask an audio issue such as a door slam in the background or a slight stumble or stutter in speech that couldn't easily be edited out. For example, in the first clip above, the picture jumps in a mock TV malfunction, so it "stutters." This type of effect could easily be used to turn a little verbal or accidental camera bump slip-up into an organic, well-timed visual/audio effect. Clever use of visual FX can help you flip the script and craft visual and audio imperfections into organic storytelling assets. And that, my friends, is the very essence of the entire Down and Dirty filmmaking philosophy: using creativity to turn limitations into advantages.

1. We open with a whip zoom out from a close up of the school's circular logo.

2. The whip zoom ends on a full-frame school logo shot.

3. Playing off the logo, expanding concentric circles transition us into the next shot.

Illustrative Visual FX

When I'm viewing the footage and reading through the transcripts for the first time, I always try to take notes on the very first visuals that pop into my mind to come up with ideas about how I can turn those words into imagery with B-roll, graphic text, stills, or, in this case, Visual FX, using After Effects. In this part of the video, an instructor describes a class exercise for a lesson about the music business in which students need to do the math to figure out how many tickets Lady Gaga needed to sell to recoup the cost of staging a major concert at Madison Square Garden after you account for all the expenses.

The editor/visual FX artist took advantage of an interview shot against a plain white wall to fill in the white space with simple animations of the arena seating chart, stadium chairs, and Lady Gaga tickets using Adobe After Effects. To plug in some live action visuals for the concert itself, he employed a classic re-creation technique by using footage from another band's concert he had on file (not Lady Gaga) and just posterizing, blurring, and distorting it enough that it was unrecognizable and therefore indistinguishable from actual Lady Gaga concert footage for the few seconds it flashes on the screen. Through the magic of editing, the audience is led to feel and believe that they are looking at footage of the concert in question. We could've jumped through the hoops to shoot the actual concert or license footage of it, but why leave your desk to shoot a mere five seconds of supplementary footage when you've got imagination and movie magic at your fingertips to tell the story just as effectively? Don't just work harder. Work smarter.

Another After Effects element, my Editor/Visual FX man extraordinaire, Giga Shane of Boat Safety Films, crafted based on my notes and style sheet was an animated visual math equation of the school's overall approach to career development. On a transparent layer of gold color over a live video pan across the music memorabilia that lines the school's walls, we see the simple equation presented twice: once in text and once in pictures. The gold theme here was meant to symbolize gold records (musical success) and gold itself (monetary success) *visually* searing the point into our audience's brains that this educational opportunity is golden. (At least that's what we were going for.)

Retro Film Look

The establishing exterior shots for the opening montage and all of the interview footage were treated with funky retro film FX reminiscent of old projected 16mm footage, complete with color fade, flicker, scratches, and dust marks. Apart from just looking cool (which it definitely does), this effect helped us achieve the edgy high-energy experimental music video look we wanted and was completely within keeping of the subject matter—the music industry—and the audience—high school students.

Student Group Interview

One technique I like to use, particularly when doing pieces that involve young people, is the group interview. This interview technique is practical, time efficient, and above all, effective. By shooting a group of individuals all at once, you are able to get multiple sound bites from different people in a single session. That means fewer setups and less budget for crew hours. This technique is effective with teenagers because they tend to be much more comfortable, confident, and forthcoming in a group of their peers, rather than one on one in front of a camera and lights. In a group environment, people feed off each others' comments and energy, so the person that normally can't think of anything to say on the spot suddenly has plenty to say a few minutes into the interview, sparked by the comments of peers. It takes on the feel of a group conversation with open trading and feeding of ideas rather than the usual solo interrogation, so there's a lot less pressure on the subjects, and it feels like a more natural conversation. (See "HOT TIP: Shooting Group Interviews" on the next page.)

1 WHEN TO SHOOT A GROUP INTERVIEW

Shooting a group interview is a good technique to get the input of multiple subjects all at once. This is a practical technique whenever you want to get different opinions and viewpoints on the same

subject from multiple people, particularly multiple people from a larger group. So rather than interviewing just one representative student, customer, or employee, you are interviewing a (hand-picked) "random sampling" of the larger group.

The practical advantage of this type of interview is that you can capture the opinions and input of a bunch of people in about the same amount of effort

and time (i.e., money) it would take you to interview just one of them alone. Group interviews are also particularly effective if you have to shoot ordinary people who tend to be more camera-shy. This is particularly true of many children and young people who find confidence and safety in numbers. It's much easier to think of intelligent things to say when you can feed off the collective thoughts, opinions, and energy of the group and gather your own thoughts while someone else is making their point. One good comment begets another and often sets off a chain reaction of good, usable sound bites and commentary.

Interviewing people in a group setting also tends to magnify the energy and emotion of the interview. Whatever type of energy your questions foster, be it enthusiasm for a product or anger against a public policy, know that it will usually be *magnified* when discussed in a group of people more so than in solo interviews.

2 CASTING THE GROUP

One thing I always recommend you do is to have your client produce as many elements of the project as possible with your guidance. Specifically, I mean tasks such as choosing the locations to scheduling to finding the subjects you will need to interview. Nobody knows their company, employees, and patrons better than your clients themselves. (And if anyone else does, it certainly ain't *you*.) So this method of finding subjects is much more practical than randomly picking or extensively prescreening dozens of people to find a representative handful. Discuss and give your clients clear and basic guidance in what you're looking for in terms of age, sex, race, background, etc. Generally, you want a diverse group of articulate people to give the appearance (if not the reality) of a random sampling of the larger group in question. Let them know how many people you need and when you need them. Depending on the clients, they may just give you the contact info for these people once selected, but when possible, it's even better to have the clients coordinate and schedule these people for you. This will save you immeasurable amounts of time in preproduction. Again, you want to work smarter, not just harder. I also point out to clients that by doing this casting legwork instead of having my team do it, they are also saving *money*. Lastly, if the people aren't very good or there is internal political fallout over who was or wasn't chosen, they take the heat, not you.

3 LIGHTING

In order to adequately light a large group of people, I recommend using a wide, soft, even source, such as a fluorescent Kinoflo, 2K softlight unit, an umbrella light, or a Chimera light bank, which converts hard light sources to soft, broad lights. To save even more time and hassle, if the look is appropriate for the project and the level of production value you want to achieve, you might even consider just using the natural practical light on location if there's a well-lit room that's not too flat. In the group interview pictured here, I split the difference by cutting off the main lighting for the room and using a fluorescent Kinoflo Diva Light for a key and the

We took advantage of the track lights already in the room as perfectly positioned hair lights.

track lights above as hair lights. If you really want to go au natural, a relatively private spot outdoors might also work to save you time and hassle with lighting, but be warned that you may be introducing new audio and sunlight issues shooting outside, so scout it first and think it through.

4 CAMERAWORK

I always try to use two cameras with this technique, so one camera stays on a wide shot to capture the entire group, including *reactions* to the commentary of the person speaking, while the main camera stays in tight for the close-up of the person speaking. More importantly, a two-camera setup allows me to avoid showing sloppy zoom-ins as the main cameraperson hunts for the person speaking for the first few seconds of the close-up. Instead, using two cameras I can just smoothly cut from the wide group shot to the close-up individual shot in postproduction. (When pressed for manpower, you can always just set up your wide shot on an unmanned camera—after carefully checking focus and exposure, of course). However, I think it makes for a more dynamic video to occasionally have the wide camera push in a little for slightly tighter group shots of three or four people at a time to better show the facial expressions (i.e., reactions) of the participants immediately around the speaker. In these moments, you might better capture a spontaneous smile, agreeable head nod, eye rolling, snicker, or other subtle reaction to the speaker that plays better on camera in a tighter shot.

Alternatively, a group interview can be covered with a single camera if that's all you have at your disposal. To cover a group more organically, you want the cameraperson to keep a steady hand on the camera, use

Shooting with a second camera is good to capture wide shots of group interviews that will also show the candid reactions of the other participants.

a fairly loose tripod, and very smoothly adjust the shot (either zooming in or panning over) to each speaker as they begin. By carefully observing body language in the group, an experienced camera operator will develop a pretty clear feel for who will speak when. You may occasionally have to ask someone to restart their answer if you weren't on a good shot when they started speaking or botch a camera move. But group interviews can be effectively covered with a single camera if you are carefully thinking through your edit on each shot.

Similarly, if you stage the group with just a little physical space between interviewees and/or frame your close-ups tight enough, you can even cut the finished video to appear as if you shot several individual interviews and never even reveal to the audience that those interviewees were shot all at once.

5 STAGING THE GROUP

Another important consideration of a group interview is how you will stage the group. In other words, *who* are you going to sit where? The first step of staging a group interview is scouting locations ahead of time. You are usually going to make your staging decisions based on the size of the group, the location seating, lighting limitations, group diversity in age, sex, height, race, and the color palette of the group as dictated by clothing, hair color, and skin tone.

In order to look natural and fit on screen, people in a group will often have to be sitting right next to each other.

Smaller groups of three to five people could be staged on a sofa, bench, or chairs lined up in a row or semi-circle, sitting at three positions of a square or round table. Some people could be in chairs while others sit comfortably on the floor for a casual home setting if this is something appropriate for your subjects and subject matter. College students, teenagers, and kids casually staged on a rug on the floor among other participants sitting on a sofa seems quite natural...while stockbrokers, doctors, or elderly people sprawled on the floor—not so natural.

For larger groups of 6–12 people, you will want to stage people in rows at different heights in order to get everyone in the shot at once. (Think back to all your group class pictures.) Any space with stadium seating such as a lecture hall or theater is great for this setup. A top row of people on tall stools and a bottom row of people on chairs is also pretty standard. A nice set of steps can also work for more casual subject matter. Again, use your Down and Dirty mindset (imagination and creativity) to find appropriate staging options at your location for rows of people.

Now it's time to look at the monitor and play musical chairs for a few minutes while you balance out the group for diversity, aesthetics, and compositional purposes. For aesthetic purposes, try not to have the only two people in the group in blue shirts sitting right next to each other. Don't put the tallest people in the front row or vice versa. You want to both mix and balance out the group based on all the factors I named here. People with darker skin tones or wearing all-black clothing and/or hair should be placed closest to the light source or given extra lighting. You want to find that perfect position for all the group members so that your frame looks balanced and we can see everyone's faces.

With some forethought, group interviews can be staged, shot and edited to actually appear onscreen as a series of individual interviews.

6 AUDIO STRATEGY

Another important part of pulling off a group interview is deciding how you will cover the audio of multiple people speaking at the same time. I think the best way to cover a group interview is with a boom operator who can quickly move the boom pole into position to pick up anyone in the group. A shotgun or cardioid mic is a good choice to mount on the boom. If you don't have a boom operator available, you could mount two cardioid mics on boom stands just out of shot. If you go the route of using unmanned boom mics for a group interview, avoid shotgun mics and use a mic with a cardioid pattern instead to ensure that you pick up all the speakers at a more even level. (Alternatively, if you have a smaller group or enough mics, you could put lav mics on *all* the participants and run them all into a mixer before feeding them into the two audio channels on the camera, but this is a lot more setup and work.)

7 INTERVIEW TECHNIQUE

There are two ways to go with a group interview. The first is to just let the conversation free-flow back and forth with participants occasionally overlapping or interrupting each other as enthusiasm and natural reactions take over the conversation—such as might happen during a heated political debate. The second approach is to conduct the interview a little more formally, so you can get good clean sound bites from everyone and preserve the ability to visually and aurally isolate any single person's commentary. If you wish to do this, right before the interview, tell the participants in the group to signal when they wish to speak and then pause for just a few seconds before speaking, to allow you the time to reframe your shot and move the boom mic into position. This goes really smoothly if you or the cameraperson simply gives them a quick hand signal to speak once the camera is set and focused on the shot.

The Client Dance

- ❑ Research the client's website and previous promo material.
- ❑ Set up initial client meeting
- ❑ Determine client's goal, budget, schedule, and if you can *deliver.*
- ❑ Submit a statement of work.
- ❑ Get client approval of statement of work.
- ❑ Get signed contract based on statement of work.

Preproduction

- ❑ 1st draft treatment
- ❑ 1st draft production plan and calendar
- ❑ Client's review and notes on treatment
- ❑ Client's review and notes on plan and calendar
- ❑ Revised draft treatment
- ❑ 2nd draft production plan and calendar
- ❑ Book rental equipment and vehicles
- ❑ 1st draft script
- ❑ Client review and notes of 1st draft script
- ❑ Complete 2nd-draft script
- ❑ Client review and notes of 2nd draft script
- ❑ Final draft script
- ❑ Create Storyboard

- ❑ 2nd client meeting
- ❑ Hire talent
- ❑ Hire crew
- ❑ Principal crew meeting

Production

- ❑ Principal production
- ❑ Reshoots and pickups if necessary

Postproduction

- ❑ Transcribe interviews
- ❑ Paper edit based on transcripts
- ❑ Editor's rough cut
- ❑ Director's review and notes on rough cut
- ❑ Editor's 1st cut
- ❑ Director's review and notes of 1st cut
- ❑ Editor's 2nd cut
- ❑ Director and client's review and notes of 2nd cut
- ❑ Editor's 3rd cut with titles and FX
- ❑ Client's final approval
- ❑ Minor corrections as necessary
- ❑ Delivery of final media

*You can download a printable version of this checklist on the Superfly Illmatic Bonus website at FreelanceVideoGuide.com.

CHAPTER 5
MUSIC VIDEOS

By Benjamin Ahr Harrison

A Quick Note from Anthony

So just for this chapter I'm actually gonna turn the book over to my man, Benjamin Ahr Harrison, whom I first met as an NYU film student where he worked for me in the Production Center. Over the years I watched Ben go from film student to a full-fledged film professional who consistently turns out some of the hottest and most creative music and marketing videos I've ever seen produced with limited resources. I've dibble-dappled in music videos (peep my case study at the end of this chapter), but Ben has fully immersed himself in the craft and hustle of music videos for the better part of the last decade, so I thought he'd be a much better source of music video knowledge than myself...and I was right. Listen and learn the game, baby.

—Ant.

So, Why Make Music Videos?

(**Hint:** There's no money in it.) Most filmmakers can't make a living sticking exclusively to one area, and that goes double for music videos. Michel Gondry does features, music videos, and advertisements. But he made a name for himself making some of the most creative music videos the world had ever seen. Music videos have a place in the world of filmmaking as a proving ground, a farm team for visionary filmmakers. If your goal is to ultimately direct austere, character-driven dramas, this might not be the world for you, but if you have a great visual imagination, love music, and want to make projects that let you experiment, directing music videos is an extraordinarily rewarding enterprise that will help your career, or if nothing else, make for a good conversations at parties.

I have been directing music videos for years now, and I would be remiss if I didn't warn you that this is a tough way to make a living. The filmmakers that land enough jobs to be full-time music video directors are few and far between, and based on what I'm seeing on YouTube these days, it's not always the most talented people who make it into that elite fraternity. I have made my living by including music videos in a constellation of other film gigs. Sometimes it was editing. In the early days, I took lots of PA jobs, which was always surreal when I went on a set and knew that I had a better reel and more talent than almost any of the people I was working under. I had to bite my tongue and do the work to get the

paycheck because the music videos weren't covering my rent. But eventually, I'd proven myself enough times to start getting other types of directing jobs, and the more diverse my portfolio got, the more people were interested in working with me. I think the most important thing I've learned through all of this is that I crave the satisfaction that comes with taking a project from inception to completion, and I get that satisfaction several times a year because I land jobs that allow me to pour my creativity into them.

See Ben's Music Videos at: double7images.com/author/benjamin-ahr-harrison

To answer the question at hand, here are some key reasons I recommend to get into the music video game....

1 Other People's Money

Music videos are one of the very few low-budget projects that young filmmakers can land that are entirely funded by somebody else. It's hard to raise a few thousand dollars to make a short film, but if you're being hired by a musician or a record label, the money comes out of their pocket.

2 Learning Opportunities

Music video shoots are a microcosm of big commercials and features. They are a great kind of project for newcomers to filmmaking because they give you an opportunity to learn the ropes while the stakes are lower. You'll come away from a few music video projects with a strong sense of your strengths and weaknesses as a director, a list of crew contacts, a reel, and a great understanding of the tools of the industry.

3 Exercise Your Creativity

Commercials and short films have very specific goals that must be met, but music videos are a totally experimental and open format. Having fewer restrictions on the decisions you can make will help you really flex your creative muscles.

Five Panasonic HVX-200s lined up for a funky music video visual effect.

4 Learn Your Weaknesses

Being a director can be shocking. Yesterday you were an artist with a dream. Today you're calling the shots, and you might have a crew of 30 people working under you. That's not something that's easy to prepare for, so the best way to get good at it is to do it often. Similarly, it's one thing to imagine what you'll do with a camera move in the planning stages and another thing to confront such a move on set when the pressures of budget and schedule are on you and you've just learned that you have 10 fewer feet of dolly track than you need. You'll be forced to improvise, and you will walk away from each project a better filmmaker.

5 Learn Your Strengths

By directing music videos, you can also get a handle on exactly what makes you unique as a filmmaker. Is it your amazing visuals? Your compelling narratives? Your style of magical realism? Your sense of humor? If you identify what makes you good, you can play those skills up in marketing yourself for other film projects.

5 TIPS FOR FINDING YOUR FIRST ACT

Okay, so you're inspired to try your hand at directing a music video, but where do you start? One of the hardest parts of directing music videos is getting gigs, and it's especially tough if you don't have any prior work to show. When I graduated from film school, I looked for restaurant jobs, but applying for the jobs was impossible because I had no prior restaurant experience. I wondered how anyone got restaurant jobs if there was no way to get them without having already had one? Music videos are the same, but I promise you that if you can land that first gig, it's about a million times more rewarding than bussing tables.

1 Hanging Around a Music Venue

You aren't going to book Metallica for your first gig, so start small. Chances are that if you're considering this, you're a music lover, so start with your favorite genre and work from there. Go to lots of local shows and talk to bands. Buy the bassist a beer after a good set. Make friends and be up front. Let them know that you're looking to make a video and that you would love to make it for them. I recommend you approach musicians whose work you respect because you will be more creatively turned on, and chances are your relationship with the band will be better.

A popular live music spot in Williamsburg, Brooklyn—the perfect place to connect with an up-and-coming band in need of a video.

2 The Internet

My first music video gig came through Craigslist.com. I was still a student and didn't have a lot to show for myself, but I had developed the right relationships with classmates who owned their own gear that enabled me to borrow equipment when I needed it, and I was able to offer much higher production value to my first customers than I otherwise would have. If you are looking to book an act that you haven't had a chance to form a relationship with, you need to sell yourself by telling them what sets you apart. Don't give up if the first few tries don't work out. I probably take 5 to 10 meetings with different bands for every one music video contract I get. I got my first gig through **Craigslist** (craigslist.org), but there are other sites like **Radar Music Videos** (radarmusicvideos.com; primarily UK bands), **The IdeaLists** (theidealists.com), and **Massify** (www.massify.com) that are set up with the intention of connecting young filmmakers to bands who need videos. I haven't had any luck with these, but you might. If you have a bunch of impressive work that you've done as a student or for yourself, having a well-executed YouTube presence can be a way to meet bands as well.

ABOVE: Sites such as Craigslist.com and Massify.com can be useful for finding music video gigs.

3 Do It for a Friend

You might already know your first act. This may be a little touchier in terms of budget, so be careful, but sometimes a friend's band is the best place to start. Patrick Daughters, one of my favorite music video directors, made his first video for his college friend's band. They happened to be the Yeah Yeah Yeahs. They happened to get huge! Some of my most important clients have been bartenders whom I struck up conversations with, meaning you might need to make new friends if you end up going this route!

4 Other Options

Do it yourself! A new trend with up-and-coming filmmakers is to make an unauthorized music video for a song that they like and put it out on the Internet. If you get enough attention, you might catch the eye of the band or the record label that put the song out, and if they're cool and like what you did, you might book a gig! You're shooting the moon, so don't go in to something like this with big expectations, but if you're inspired by a song, or even another music video, and you have the time and equipment to make your take on it, there's no stopping you.

5 Follow Through!

I can't stress this enough. The difference between getting the gig and not is making the phone calls and maintaining contact with the band in a persistent (but not annoying) way until there is ink on a contract. It's the difference between talk and action.

When a Band Has No "Skin in the Game"

I had the pleasure of taking a turn in the cinematographer position on a music video recently. This was the first music video by a young directing team (let's call them Mark and Michael), and they had convinced a band (let's call them *The Duds*) to give them a song to make a video for. Mark and Michael loved *The Duds*, and were excited to do a project for them, even though *The Duds* wouldn't be appearing in or providing any funding for the video. The mere fact that this would be an official music video when it was released was enough to make this directing team want to put a couple thousand dollars of their own money into the project.

We had an amazing shoot and produced something that I was really proud of. Mark and Michael started cutting the footage and eventually showed a cut to *The Duds*. And *The Duds*, in their infinite wisdom, hated the music video. This was a huge blow to Mark and Michael, me, and everyone else who had worked on the video. We'd spent a lot of time and creative energy on this thing, and *The Duds* had basically rejected it outright. How could they do that? They had approved the treatment and signed off on detailed storyboards. But they had no skin in the game. They hadn't put any time or money on the line, and it was easy for them to dismiss our work, having no sense of what had gone into it. They wanted to change the concept so completely that it would have been entirely unlike the music video that we had set out to make.

But Mark and Michael fought through this deterrence and told *The Duds* the deal was off. *The Duds* had no real stake in the video, so Mark and Michael saw no issue with taking it back. They had put all the money up, so it was up to them where the video ended up. They began to think about other bands, and eventually they found another band that was very excited by the idea. They re-edited the video to a new song from a band we'll call *Awesomesauce*, and *Awesomesauce* was completely psyched. *Awesomesauce* promoted the hell out of the music video, and Mark and Michael ended up with a successful project and a great new relationship with a band and a record label. This was all due to persistence and creative adaptability on their part.

BEFORE THE GIG STARTS

Things to Keep in Mind Going into the Gig

You are a creative artist with a vision and the talent to execute it, and this piece is going to go on your reel and be a calling card for you to get future gigs. That's all great; however, it can all get in the way of a simple fact that is important to remember: you are marketing the band. Your highest calling in this endeavor is to sell this band to their audience.

Music videos started as marketing material that record labels produced to hype their acts, and though they are also one of the most artistically interesting kinds of filmmaking, they're still basically just commercials. If you make a music video that doesn't do anything to market the band, then you've done them a disservice and you've shirked your responsibility. If you are able to keep that in mind, you have all the freedom anyone could ask for to create a reel piece for yourself and on someone else's dime. And remember, your band probably has a better idea of what public persona they're trying to communicate than you do, so they'll be your best collaborators. Talk to them about how they want to show themselves to the world!

Cost/Benefit of Using Your Own Money

Since it is really tough to get that first gig, sometimes filmmakers decide to use their own money to supplement the budget that the band brings to the table. I have never done this, but it's definitely not unusual. You just need to determine the cost/benefit of infusing the production with your own funds. Think of the amount of time you'll be spending on the video, and whether what pops out the other side is going to be worth everything you're putting in. I didn't make a dime from my first three music videos, but they gave me a track record of executing high-quality projects, and if that's what you need to establish yourself, then it may be worth putting some of your own money into your first production. (Hey, Michael Bay used his own money to pay for the big explosion at the end of *Bad Boys*, and look at him now!)

Be Reasonably Transparent

They say that you should never watch the legislative process or the sausage manufacturing process at work. Making a music video is like making sausage, and a lot of problems can arise from any kind of filmmaking. You will be working with musicians who won't know how extensively **Murphy's Law** applies to filmmaking, and since it's their money, this can be alarming for them. You need to insulate them from as much of the calamity of filmmaking as possible. At the same time, if

you keep them completely in the dark, they're likely to get just as skittish from that. I'll go further into this as this chapter progresses, but essentially, as you go through making the video, you need to keep the band updated on your progress, both good and bad, but spare them the gruesome details.

Preparing to Pitch

More than likely, your first time out you will be working with an act that has already picked you to make their video, but as you develop a reputation as a talented filmmaker, you may get opportunities to pitch in competition with other filmmakers, and the process for that is something I recommend you begin to familiarize yourself with early. Besides, you still need to sell the band on your idea for the video if it's your first time out, so why not do it right?!

First things first...

You need to know a few things in order to generate a pitch, and you should have a meeting or a phone call to establish the facts.

Process

You should make sure you're familiar with their timetable and goals. You should make sure they're familiar with how you work and what services you can and can't provide them with. Don't have the facilities to deliver on Digi-Beta? Make sure they know that going in. Do they absolutely need the final product in three weeks? You better find out!

Persona

This is a great time to have that conversation about the public persona of the band. You can bet 50 Cent isn't going to hire a director who wants to put him in a bunny costume...unless it's a gangster bunny costume.

Music

Get a mastered version of the song and the lyric sheet. Sometimes the mastered version isn't done yet. You need to be clear that all the timing and arrangement are going to stay the same if you have to swap in a new version of the track in later. It's really best to get the final version up front. Likewise, getting the lyric sheet will save you a lot of time and be really helpful in the planning process, especially if it's tough to understand the lyrics on the track.

Budget

If you've never embarked on a project like this, it can be hard to forecast what things will end up costing, but push the act to commit to spending as much as they can. Set a number so that you can keep that in mind as you develop your pitch.

A Word on Budgets

Writing a budget can be a challenge, especially if you're more creative minded. This is something that usually falls to producers and production managers, but we're trying to stay Down and Dirty here, and when you're working on tight budgets with skeleton crews, having a producer isn't always an option. But make no mistake, you're going to have a lot of expenses to keep track of, and if you want to be the one in creative control when it comes time to shoot, you should be the one holding the purse strings.

Under-Promise and Over-Deliver: Words to Live By

This can be a hard lesson to learn. I struggle with it every time I work. But believe me, this is the single best piece of advice I can give you when it comes to budgeting your projects. Be very conservative with how you allocate funds.

Going over budget or being forced to scale back on some aspect of your music video in the middle of production is extremely painful and can lead to serious rifts between you and your clients. Your reputation is all you have in this industry, so when you are committing to a project, don't stretch yourself too thin. If you are lucky, and you have extra resources because you've been so frugal, you can sink them into some cool surprises for the act, like an extra special effect or an added dolly shot, over-delivering on your promise, but if you sell them on every idea you have and can't make it work financially, you're going to disappoint people.

Dolly shots always eat up extra time (and therefore money) on-set, but can add considerable production value.

Do It for Real

What do I mean by "do it for real"? I mean track down the actual costs on everything you are going to be spending money on. Call the rental house and tell them what lens package you want to take out. Clients like to see real numbers on budget breakdowns, and they help you get an idea of what you can really afford, so if that lens kit costs $489.38 with tax, that's how you should write it. If you have to guess at a price, try to overestimate.

That said, there is a school of thought with pitching that says that you should give generalized budgets to clients and keep the line-by-line breakdowns to yourself. Usually, this means Preproduction, Production, Postproduction, and Total costs are listed in the pitch packet, with the Total being a number that approaches the round number that the client is budgeting for. If their budget is $10,000, your Total should be something like $9,998.73.

Be Honest with the Act and Yourself

You should be frank with them about the costs. They need to understand that their $3,500 music video budget isn't going straight into your pocket. You have real expenses: you're hiring crew, renting gear and locations, paying for gas and food. In my experience, your average musician or band manager hasn't got the foggiest idea of what it takes to put even a one-day film shoot together, so if you show them how you've broken the budget down, they will know what you're up against.

When you can, don't just tell them your ideas—*show* them using photos, examples from other videos and clips of your previous work.

Likewise, if your idea is a $20,000 idea, and you have a $1,000 budget to work with, you need to ask yourself if you're willing to let the remaining $19,000 come out of you in blood, sweat, tears, and time. I recommend you get really comfortable with the old filmmaking aphorism, "good, fast, cheap: pick two." You can't make a good music video if you don't spend any time or money on it. You can fake it if you throw a ton of money at the problem, but we all know that's probably not the position you're going to be in. Chances are this is going to take a long time to do on a tight budget.

My experience is that I often have a music video in postproduction that has to take a back seat to a more lucrative job. If my remaining budget for the video is $600 and I have about five days of real work left to do on it, I'm going to have to give precedence to a gig that pays a $500 day rate, even if it delays the completion of the music video. I try to be frank with my clients about this. If they want me full time, my prices change. I'm more than excited to make music videos for small budgets, but they take a lot of time to turn around. If this is your first music video and nobody is even getting paid, then your band is going to need to be patient in postproduction.

Mo' Money, Mo' Problems

A million dollar budget is a million potential mistakes. The bigger your budget, the more you have to keep track of and the more variables in your production. That means more potential for cataclysm and disaster. Hopefully, that doesn't happen, but keep that in mind as your career progresses and you start landing those bigger budgets.

WHAT GOES INTO A BUDGET?

Good question. Here's a handy checklist to make sure you are considering all of your potential expenses.

Preproduction
1. Man-hours of anyone who starts working on the video before the shoot day: director, producer, UPM, cinematographer, art director, etc.
2. Casting room rental? Production office?

Production
3. Day rates for crew
4. Cast
5. Equipment rental
6. Expendables for the camera and lighting departments
7. Location fees
8. Art department materials
9. Costume rentals
10. Production insurance
11. Transportation fees (i.e., van rental, gas, parking, etc.)
12. Meals and craft services

Postproduction
13. Edit suite rental
14. Editor
15. Graphics and special effects artists
16. Color correction
17. Hard expenses like tape stock, other media
18. Review uploads

> Try to budget conservatively. Make sure you set aside money for post plus contingencies.

Contingency
Add 15–30 percent of the entire budget up to this point. This will provide a much-needed buffer in case you go over budget or one of your P.A.s gets a parking ticket. Having a contingency is crucial on low budgets.

Pro Tip
Make sure you budget enough for post. It's easy to give post short shrift when you're getting excited about the camera crane you want to rent, but if you can't afford to edit the video once it's shot, you're going to be S.O.L. (which, of course, stands for "*sadly* out of luck").

SAMPLE MUSIC VIDEO BUDGET

PREPRODUCTION	NOTES	UNITS	RATE	SUBTOTAL	DISC. RATES
Director		2	400	800	600
Producer		1	400	400	250
Art Director		2	250	500	400
TOTAL PREPRODUCTION =				$1,700.00	$1,250.00

PRODUCTION	NOTES	UNITS	RATE	SUBTOTAL	DISC. RATES
Equipment					
HD Camera Package		1	250	250	150
Lens Kit		1	489.38	489.38	489.38
Camera Expendables		1	50	50	50
Lighting Package		1	250	250	150
Grip & Electric		1	317.50	317.50	317.50
Playback/Sound		1	150	150	150
Monitor		2	150	300	300
Crew					
Director		1	600	600	400
Producer		1	500	500	300
D.P.		1	400	400	250
Asst. Director		1	250	250	200
Art Director		1	250	250	200
Grip		1	200	200	200
Prod. Assts.		6	150	900	300
Stylist		1	200	200	150
Art Dept. Materials					
Water Guns		30	25	750	750
Paints		5	10.75	53.75	53.75
Costumes		1	200	200	200
Misc.		1	100	100	100
Travel & Expenses					
Craft Services		1	$500	$500	500
Crew Meals	$18 meals, 1 meal a day for cast and crew	40	18	720	720
TOTAL PRODUCTION =				$7,430.63	$5,930.63

POSTPRODUCTION	NOTES	UNITS	RATE	SUBTOTAL	DISC. RATES
Edit Suite Rental		2	200	400	0
Editor	Based on a 10 hour day	2	250	500	500
Director		2	250	500	500
Color Correction		1	250	250	250
File Compression		3	10	30	30
Uploads for Review		3	15	45	45
DVD Stock		5	1	5	5
HD Archival		1	300	300	300
TOTAL POSTPRODUCTION =				$2,030.00	$1,630.00
CONTINGENCY	NOTES	UNITS	RATE	SUBTOTAL	DISC. RATES
Additional Edit Day		1	400	400	200
SUBTOTAL =				$11,160.63	$8,810.63
Machine Man Inc.					
Management Fee				$1,762.13	
GRAND TOTAL =					$10,572.76

Dreaming

To write a budget, you need to know what the idea for the video is! This process needs to be a give and take, though, since the final idea you propose has to be something you can afford to do. To this end, I recommend you develop your treatment in tandem with your budget.

Creative processes are wildly different from person to person, but sometimes I find it helpful to learn exactly how someone else works. I met a feature film writer who, when he's hired to write a script, checks into a hotel room for three days and doesn't come out until he has a script. He just brews pots of coffee and writes and orders room service and writes and sleeps and writes. That's insane but kind of inspiring to me. I'm going to share my process with you here. Yours may end up baring no resemblance to it, but hopefully you will find some of this useful.

> Read the lyrics as you listen. Try to notice things in the song that you didn't know were there before.

Get to Know the Song Super Well

I recommend you take a pad and pen and your iPod to a quiet place like a local coffee shop or a park, outside of your own personal space where you can distract yourself, and listen to the song over and over. Read the lyrics as you listen. Try to notice things in the song that you didn't know were there before.

Take notes and try to brainstorm the visuals that you will be coupling with the song. Really push yourself. Try to brainstorm past the point where you think you have everything. Try to really zone out and write down nonsense. See what comes out! A lot of it won't make any sense when you look at it later, but you get some cool, weird ideas this way that you might never have otherwise hit upon.

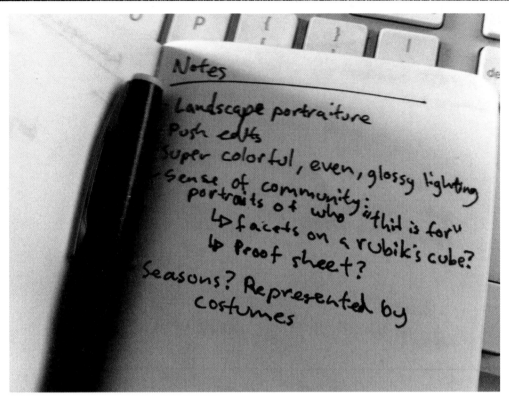

...I can't even remember what song I was developing a pitch for when I wrote these, but I found them in a notebook and thought they might be worth sharing. Let's break them down.

Some Things I Did Well When I Wrote These Notes:

• Thinking in terms of color and lighting.
• Developing themes. "This is for" is probably a lyric and I'm trying to pull visuals out of it.
• Not trying to get too fancy too early. Letting the song tell me its story and not the other way around.

Some Things I Could Have Done Better:

• Some of my jargon doesn't mean anything to me anymore. I don't know what a "push edit" is.
• I may have gotten too hung up on punctuation to be writing fast enough.
• Ideas like "seasons represented by costumes" aren't necessarily specific enough to be of any use to me when I'm trying to remember exactly what I was thinking later.

An Aside

I have almost always developed my concepts after hearing the song I was pitching for. I know directors who work the opposite way: they come up with an idea and then try to find a song to pitch it for. Sometimes this works out, and sometimes it doesn't. Don't be too eager to shoehorn an idea into a song that it doesn't necessarily work for.

Distill Your Ideas

Once you have all your notes and a deep, intimate understanding of the song, it's time to write a treatment that you will include, along with your budget breakdown, to show to the artist. Unfortunately, this is real work that takes a lot of time, and nobody ever gets paid for it. However, it's worth doing right because it shows the act that you are a professional who takes them seriously, and it gives you that much greater of a likelihood that you'll get the gig–if you are competing for it.

Your Treatment

Take all those notes you wrote and try to pull the juiciest ideas out. Form them into a coherent idea in your head. Are you going to tell a story? Are you going to make a parody of a film? The treatment is a two- to four-page document that describes, in detail, what your goal is for the video; what happens in the video; and tone, color, and inspiration.

Treatments are a highly variable type of document from director to director, but essentially you're trying to sell the artist on your idea and actually to clarify the idea to yourself as well. This will be what your D.P. and art director read as they begin to work on developing the visuals in the video, so you need to write something that has enough detail for everyone to really get a hang of your vision, but in an interesting way that will excite the artist and record label enough to hire you.

Most treatments I have seen spend a few paragraphs talking tone and inspiration and then break the song down by section– first verse, first chorus, second verse etc.–and describe the action beat-for-beat. Generally, it's good to include pictures for visual references, and more and more I see people including YouTube links to this end.

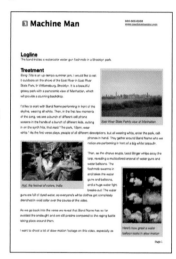

Check out the special Superfly Illmatic Bonus website for this book to download this sample music video treatment and other extras.

Put It All Together

Put everything in a proposal document for the band to go through. Spend some time laying it out nicely and make sure it looks professional. Here's what I include:

Cover Sheet

Has the song name, my name, the band's name, and the date. Possibly dressed up with a photo of the band.

Treatment

One to four pages, with photos and possibly video links describing in detail, what the video is about.

Budget

Broken down on a spreadsheet.

Production Timeline

Your best estimates on how long everything will take. If you put it in a calendar format, it will give you and the artists a very clear *visual* picture of what needs to be done and when.

Expectations and Questions

A clear discussion of what is expected of both parties. Format of deliverables? Payment schedule? Make sure everyone is really on the same page on this stuff. Do you have any questions or concerns? If so, this is a great place to spell them out in writing.

Your pitch packet has been reviewed, and your proposal has been approved. Now the work *really* starts!

Unfortunately, you probably won't be getting the kind of budget that would enable you to hire an entertainment attorney to craft a contract for you and the client to sign, but I recommend that you spend some time writing down everything you have agreed upon with the act, their manager, or their label, and have each party sign it. This may prove to be extremely useful down the line if disputes arise over who said what. It's really nice to be able to fall back on a contract and say, "Hey, this is what we agreed upon at the outset, and here's your signature to prove it!"

What You Should Stipulate In Your Contract

❏ **Song title and general description of the project:** For example, a music video for the song "Love Is a Rose." This way, if the client decides to change songs on you, you've got grounds for renegotiating. You can get even more detailed and list that they are hiring you for preproduction, production, and postproduction.

❏ **Who owns what:** Usually, the client retains the rights to the song and gets the rights to the video. I usually specify that they do not have the rights to the raw footage or edit project files. This protects me from being pushed out of my own video in the editing process.

❏ **Payment amount and payment schedule:** You should know when you're getting the money and how much.

❏ **Project deadlines:** I usually leave the delivery date as TBD because editing can often take longer than anticipated and I don't want to breach my contract because of that.

❏ **Who pays for what:** My normal contract includes a clause about client assets (the song, wardrobe if they're providing it), my assets (any equipment of mine that we're using), and third-party assets (anything we're renting). Sometimes the client gives me a fixed budget but agrees to pay for food for the crew on top of that budget. That would go in this section.

❏ **Format of deliverables:** I usually deliver a few DVDs for DVD players and one DVD that includes a high-res master file and a few different compressed files for uploading the video to YouTube and all those sites.

❏ **Deposit amount:** I always get a deposit from the client at the contract signing. Generally, I ask for the entire sum of the preproduction and production portions of the budget, leaving the contingency and the postproduction for final delivery.

What Do I Need to Do to Prepare?

It's time to start locking down dates, booking your locations, hiring your crew, and deciding what equipment to rent. Start having conversations with your D.P. about what you want the video to look like. Give your art director and costumers their budgets so that they can start to get their ducks in a row.

It's also time to turn your treatment, a few pages of descriptive writing, into a shootable script.

WARNING

Don't do *any* work on planning the video until you get a *deposit*. On one of my early projects, I told a client that they could bring the first check to set on our shoot day. I reserved equipment at rental houses, rented a studio space, paid for production insurance, and had a crew ready to go, when two days before the shoot, the music artist broke ties with his managers who were funding the video. They had to scrap the project. My crew had turned down other work for the days I had hired them for and now had nothing to show for it. My reputation with the studio and equipment rental place went in the toilet. I would have lost my shirt on the production insurance, but the managers were kind enough to cover that. Get the money ahead of time and avoid disasters like that.

The Patent-Pending Benjamin Ahr Harrison Music Video Scripting Process

Music videos are distinct from films and can't really be scripted in the same way. With a film, you have a script, which is a standard format, and then you have conventional shooting techniques, like the master and two singles shooting setup that typifies 90 percent of all dialog scenes. A film script is easy to line and distill into a shot list. Music videos do not have standardized scripts for a lot of reasons. The logic that informs how they play out is totally different from narrative films. They often change locations, costumes, and scenario in split seconds. Music videos are naturally hard to plan for.

This is a system I developed in order to address this problem. It's not for every music video, and you should take from it only as much as is useful to your project. I have found that this system is immensely helpful when my videos follow a structure that includes a narrative storyline or some sequence of events. When the videos are largely just intercuts between different performance shots, this system is sort of overkill.

Fundamentals of the Process

Most music videos are some combination of performance and storyline. To make best use of your time on set, I recommend you plan to shoot the musician(s) performing the song all the way through, many times. That way, if all else fails, you at least have a performance video in the can. Then you shoot the isolated storyline portions of your video strategically and efficiently. In preproduction I plan my music videos down to the second. This is tedious, weird, and *totally worth it.*

In Preparation, Hire an A.D.

You should definitely do the planning of your video with the help of an assistant director. I cannot recommend highly enough that you have someone on set who knows the script and shot list as well as you do, and is keeping track of what has been shot and what remains unshot. On my third music video, I didn't have an A.D., and after finishing up at a location, I announced to the crew that we were wrapped and that it was time to move to the next location. One of my actors pointed out that I'd forgotten a shot! I consulted my clipboard, and sure enough he was right. It was embarrassing, and it would have been a huge pain in the editing room if I hadn't gotten the shot. Normally, you don't have a big enough budget to do reshoots and pickups later on. Solve that problem in advance by hiring a responsible person to keep track of these things for you. As a director, you are going to have a lot on your mind. An A.D. will make your job that much less stressful and save you money in the long run.

The Four Key Documents

This stage of the process is all about trying to figure out the answer to the following question: "What happens in this music video?" Fortunately, you have your treatment there to help you get the ball rolling, but you also need an outline, location-based outline, shot list, and shooting schedule as described in the next few pages.

Outline

The first thing you're going to do is translate your treatment into an outline, broken down second by second, that says what is happening on-screen at any given instant. This is the most tedious part of the process, and it involves sitting with your recording, playing it, pausing it, rewinding it, and playing it again. As you move through the song, you visualize your music video as you go and write it down. Presented here is an example of an outline from one of my music videos.

Sample General Music Video Outline

Music Video Outline—Draft #3

0:00–0:05 A single black dot appears on a white plane, then a second, then halftone spots flood out of the first two;, we pan down as they fill the frame.

0:06–0:08 The dots resolve describe rooftops in Manhattan, the camera's pan continues down and rests on Sanjay, the only part of the image that is not a black-and-white halftone. Intercut with a slow push in on a scattering of black-and-white photographs of Sanjay with the leading lady.

0:09–0:23 The camera-move holds on Sanjay, singing directly to the camera.

0:24–0:55 A series of shots of Sanjay against a seamless white background intercut with the camera moving in on one of the black-and-white photographs and resting on it.

0:56–1:07 A photograph of Sanjay and the leading lady fills the frame; they slowly start to move and he is singing to her.

1:08–1:29 The photograph goes up in flames and we return to the rooftop, where Sanjay is singing to the camera, but the camera pulls back and away, and we see the leading lady standing across from him.

1:30–1:41 Sanjay against the seamless white background, which fades and turns into a field of stars. Intercut with the camera pushing in on a different photograph.

1:42–1:52 Sanjay sings to leading lady in the second photograph.

1:53–2:13 Camera on jib, moves past Sanjay and lady on the rooftop. With each cut they are further apart. The background is now simply black and white.

2:14–2:37 Close portraits of Sanjay and lady on seamless white background.

2:38–2:58 Jib shots on the roof. A slight tint of color comes into the background. With a little regret in her face, the leading lady's feet leave the ground.

2:59–3:04 Sanjay against seamless white as we intercut with the photographs and push into a new one.

Location-Based Outline

The next step is to break this outline up and break it down into locations. In the same way that each scene in a film script takes place at a specific location, break your outline down into its locations so that you can easily shoot each location out before moving to the next one. As the director, this document will be your main reference on set. Include the same, down-to-the-second time information, as well as the lyrics you're covering, and number each beat. Following is an example of a location-based outline.

Example location-based outline

Location 1: Rooftop			
Grab	Time	Scene	Lyrics
I	0:00–0:23	A single black dot appears on a white plane, then a second, then halftone spots flood out of the first two, we pan down as they fill the frame. The dots resolve describe rooftops in manhattan, the camera's pan continues down and rests on Sanjay, the only part of the image that is not a black and white halftone. Intercut with a slow push in on a scattering of black and white photographs of sanjay with the lead lady. The camera-move holds on Sanjay, singing directly to the camera.	Can't believe it would've come to this We don't even hug, much less kiss All we do, is reminisce Long gone are the days of bliss Slip pin ur slip pin ur slip pin
II	1:08–1:29	**The photograph goes up in flames** and we return to the rooftop, where Sanjay is singing to the camera, but the camera pulls back and away, and we see the leading lady standing across from him.	I feel u slippin away,slippin away, slippin away...way Slowly slippin away, slippin away, slippin away And though I try and try and try I feel it inside ... Your slipping away
III	1:53–2:13	**The photograph burns away.** Camera on jib, moves past Sanjay and Lady on the rooftop. With each cut they are further apart. The background is now simply black and white.	I feel u slippin away, slippin away, slippin away...way Slowly slippin away,slippin away, slippin away And though I try and try and try I feel it inside ... Your slipping away

Shot List

Now that you have your outline broken down into locations, you need to break each beat down into shots, since each beat might represent more than one shot. This is also a great time to stop, take a breath, and remind your brain to come up with as many fun, creative solutions as it can.

I number my shots by location and letter, and include a note about which beat they belong to in the description, so that I can easily reference them to my location-based outline and keep track of where each shot falls in the context of the video. I also like to include a little thumbnail on the page so that I can draw a storyboard if I need to. I tend not to do a lot of storyboards, but some people find them very helpful, and they're a great way to show your crew exactly what you're talking about.

Example shotlist

Loc.	Shot	Description	Storyboard
1	A	GRAB I: Long jib shot down from slightly overexposed sky, past building, resting on Sanjay as he starts to sing	
1	B	GRAB II: Start with the same framing as IA, swivel out and back to reveal lady	
1	C	GRAB III: Pan past each character	
1	D	GRAB III: Pan past each character. They are slightly farther apart than IC	
1	E	GRAB III: Pan past each character. They are slightly farther apart than ID	
1	F	GRAB IV: Medium two, horizontal camera move past the two characters	
1	G	GRAB IV: Plate covering the ground where her feet lift off, raise camera up to edge of railing	
1	H	GRAB V: Medium OTS on Sanjay singing, then left alone on the roof	
1	I	GRAB V, XI: Medium OTS on lady floating away	
2	A	GRAB VI-IX: MCU on Sanjay (Cover entire song)	

Shooting Schedule

Now you *really* need to get your A.D. involved in this step. You want your A.D. to have as good an understanding as anyone on set as to why you're shooting in the order you're shooting in. They will be on much firmer footing if they are involved in the process of figuring out what to shoot when. They'll also be much more invested in the schedule and keeping you and your crew on it. In this step you're taking into consideration:

1. The amount of *time* you have at each location
2. The amount of *time each shot* will take to set up and shoot
3. The amount of *time* you will need to *wrap* each location
4. The *availability* of your *cast* and how long they will need to spend in *costuming and makeup*
5. Breaks for *meals*
6. Any *transportation* considerations, such as how *long* it will take for company moves
7. What *cast* will be in each shot

Scheduling for any production is hard. It's a real balancing act between shooting out locations, shooting out cast, feeding everyone on time, and completing any number of other variables. Do your best and try to be very honest with yourself about how long each shot will really take to get in the can. Be pessimistic, because you *don't* want to find yourself unable to make the day when you get on set and every setup is putting you further behind.

Sanjay-slipping away-shoot schedule

SAT 10/11	START TIME	ACTIVITY	DUR.	LOCATION	CAST	NOTES
	10:00 AM	CALL	45m			ACTRESS IN MU
	10:45 AM	1A	30m	ROOF	SANJAY	
	11:15 AM	1B	30m	ROOF	SANJAY,ACTRESS	
	11:45AM	1C	15m	ROOF	SANJAY,ACTRESS	
	12:00PM	1D	10m	ROOF	SANJAY,ACTRESS	
	12:10PM	1E	10m	ROOF	SANJAY,ACTRESS	
	12:20PM	1F	15m	ROOF	SANJAY,ACTRESS	
	12:35PM	1G	10m	ROOF	SANJAY,ACTRESS	CALL FOR LUNCH
	12:45PM	1H	20m	ROOF	SANJAY,ACTRESS	
	1:05PM	1I	20m	ROOF	SANJAY,ACTRESS	
	1:25PM	LUNCH	60m			
	2:25PM	3B	20m	INT/POHTO	SANJAY,ACTRESS	
	2:45PM	3E	15m	INT/POHTO	SANJAY,ACTRESS	
	3:00PM	3A	15m	INT/POHTO	SANJAY,ACTRESS	
	3:15PM	3C	15m	INT/POHTO	SANJAY,ACTRESS	
	3:30PM	3D	15m	INT/POHTO	SANJAY,ACTRESS	
	3:45PM	3F	15m	INT/POHTO	SANJAY,ACTRESS	
	4:00PM	3X	20m	INT/POHTO	SANJAY,ACTRESS	
	4:20PM	Loc change	25m			
	4:45PM	2D	10m	GREEN	SANJAY	
	4:55PM	2E	15m	GREEN	SANJAY	ACTRESS WRAP

A Few Things to Consider as You Prep Your Shoot

If your experience is anything like mine, you will be doing a lot of projects that don't really have any money behind them. Early in your career, you won't be able to pay your crew great money if you're lucky enough to be paying them at all. Keep that in mind as you write your schedule. It's a bit uncouth to ask people who are volunteering their time and services to work a 14-hour day. Schedule easy days so that your crew stays happy and you keep your reputation as a reasonable person to work for.

When it comes time to go to set, you and your AD should both have copies of the location-based outline, the shot list, and the schedule. Keep your copies close at hand when you're on set and use them to make notes to yourself for postproduction. Like the second take better than the third? Write it down next to that shot on your shot list and you won't forget!

Locations

Book your locations well in advance. This can be a tough issue for music videos because of several factors that all link to your lack of funding. Many locations ask for insurance, which isn't always a realistic option. You may not have much money in the budget for location fees, but even if you're just paying a location owner a dollar, I highly recommend that you make a written agreement with any location owner you deal with, because talking about a music video is one thing, but a crew with equipment and musicians with instruments is something else. Location owners have a way of being surprised at how much equipment shows up, and it's not unusual for people to panic and kick crews out. Nip this problem in the bud by making some sort of financial agreement with them.

Some locations will need proof of insurance if you're going to shoot in their space. Generally, you can purchase insurance for shoots on a per-day basis. Call around to rental houses, production companies, and other filmmaking resources to get the best price on insurance. This is something you should get figured out a few weeks in advance, as insurance companies are often slow in turning around paperwork for you to show to location owners.

Try to shoot after hours or during off-hours if your location is a busy
business or count on a slower production.

Studio Space

Having a film studio at your disposal is a wonderful thing, but studios often cost several thousand dollars per day to rent. In the past I have gotten into studios in a couple of different ways. I shot one video where I spent half my entire budget on a greenscreen stage because I needed a huge space and there was no other way to do it. I have gotten discounted and free studio days by making friends with stage managers. Many studios are sympathetic to the plight of broke filmmakers and will give you a break on weekend days. Tell them your

No studio? No problem. You can shoot greenscreen outside and save on lights.

situation and see if they'll hook you up. It couldn't hurt. From their perspective, if they give you a deal the first time and then you go on to land projects with better budgets, you're more likely to bring your business back.

You may, however, not have any luck in finding a studio you can afford. Don't let that discourage you, though! How about building your own? Really, you just need space, a bit of creativity, and a few simple tools. See if a local school will let you get into their gymnasium on the weekend. You can buy seamless set paper in 9' and 12' rolls, and they make for excellent greenscreens or white cycloramas in a pinch. You can light your makeshift stage with halogen work lamps with their safety grilles removed. It's a little harder to get the lighting even, but it's totally doable. It's worth noting that big-box hardware stores like Home Depot and Lowe's have very liberal return policies. (I'm just saying.)

One last tip is to think about doing greenscreen scenes outside. If you can set up your seamless fabric facing south, where it won't be disturbed by wind, you can often get great results, and it's much easier to make the lighting on your subjects match an outdoor environment if that's what your **background plate** will be.

Test Shooting

If you are planning any special effects that you haven't done before, I *highly* recommend that you shoot tests of these. You may learn crucial things that you will need to know for your real shoot that you hadn't anticipated. This is an easy thing to write off, but it's worth doing if you're at all uncertain about something. If you don't have access to a camera, call up your rental house and see if they will allow you to do a test shoot. Sometimes you can do the test in the rental house itself. This is an especially good move when you're planning something with a piece of equipment that you aren't used to using, or if you are using an unusual configuration.

Test shooting special FX scenes ahead of time will help you discover and solve problems before the shoot.

The Day Before

Hopefully, you've had enough time to fully prepare. Here's a checklist to go through:

✓ Are your notes and documents prepared and printed?

✓ Have you confirmed with all your locations?

✓ Has your A.D. sent out the call sheet?

✓ Is your equipment good to go? Batteries charged?

✓ Have you confirmed that the band knows where they need to be and their call time?

I have a few rituals that I would like to recommend here. They are not necessarily specific to music videos, but music videos have been my training ground, so that's where I learned this. Production can be super fun, but it's a physically and mentally draining enterprise, and as the creative visionary, you need to be on your game when you are directing, and this is especially true when you are directing a project that has been funded with someone else's money. Take good care of yourself, and your work will improve in quality and focus.

Eat plenty of protein the night before the big shoot. You're gonna need the energy.

✓ Be ready **early**. Don't procrastinate and have tons of work to get done the night before the video. Get your work done ahead of time and spend the night before getting *relaxed*.

✓ Eat protein. Protein will load up your brain with endorphins and energy.

✓ Get great sleep. Production days often start at weirdly early hours in strange parts of town. Turn in early and just chill, even if you can't sleep.

The Day Of

You've made it to set, and you are suddenly the big cheese. Yesterday you were nobody's boss, but now you're everybody's boss. This is a startling transition. Next up? Some tips for dealing with this transition to a managerial role.

Don't procrastinate on your video prep. The night before, all you should be doing is *eating well, relaxing,* and *sleeping*.

5 THINGS TO ALWAYS DO ON SET

1 Delegate

Hopefully, you hired a competent crew you can trust. Even though this is your creative endeavor and it's hard to trust others with your vision, you *have* to do it. If you have any experience as a crew member, or any experience in any other industry for that matter, you know how much it sucks to be micromanaged. You may not be used to having people whose job it is to do what you tell them, but music videos are a great way to start to get the hang of it.

2 Dress the Part

One of my most embarrassing moments in my early career was when I was working as a P.A. on a commercial. I had to move a bunch of heavy equipment from the back of a truck to the set. I noticed a scruffy guy in a shabby hooded sweatshirt and jeans who was standing around with a cup of coffee just watching me. "Hey, buddy," I said. "Can you spare a hand?" He declined, and later I worked out that he was the director of the commercial. My mistake was to be presumptuous, but had he worn a collared shirt and shaved that morning, I might have taken a cue that this guy wasn't just any old crew member. Dressing like a professional will reinforce your authority on set, and it will make you feel more in control. Your goal is not to alienate your crew, but to help them.

3 Learn Names

This is especially hard for me because I have a tough time remembering names under the best of circumstances. But I often find myself on set with 5 or 10 crew members that I've never met before. I've worked for a few very accomplished film directors in my day, and I've casually met several others. An ability to remember names is something I've noticed is an astonishingly common trait among successful directors. I doubt that they're successful *because* they remember names, but rather have noticed that keeping track of the names of even the lowest crew members on the totem pole inspires loyalty and solidarity in crews. Your work will improve if your crew perceives that you respect them and don't consider them the anonymous "help."

4 Pitch in Where Reasonable

Back to the example of the schlubby director that I related earlier: what was he even doing? If he didn't have business on set, and all he had to occupy himself was drinking some coffee and watching me move crates, what was stopping him from helping me? At least with one crate? Nothing. Obviously, you should limit the amount of equipment you're moving around as a director, but if you have a moment, there's no reason you

shouldn't pitch in and help your crew. Again, they will see that you aren't some entitled jerk who thinks you're above them, and this will command their respect.

5 | Have a Diverse Crew

The film industry is full of all kinds of interesting people. Don't hire homogenous crews. Crews of all one gender or another can get too much like one thing or another, so too can crews of all one ethnicity or another. If your crew is made up of a range of interesting people, the ideas that they bring will be more interesting, and your work will benefit from it.

1 Slate Your Shots

How do you get the lip sync to be perfect when you're shooting a music video? By slating your shots. This allows you to perfectly match the timecode of each shot to the timecode of your music track when you get into editing. In the old days, you used to need an SMPTE slate and a DAT playback rig. Cheap, abundant digital technology has changed all that.

Here's what I do: I take the music into Final Cut Pro (FCP), put a **Slug** layer above it, and apply the "Timecode Generator" effect to it, being careful to set the frame rate to match the frame rate I'm shooting at. This gives the video nice big

An iPod (above) used as an SMPTE timecode slate by importing a video of the "Time Code Generator" effect in Final Cut Pro (below) using the artist's song as audio.

timecode numbers. I then export this video and load it onto an iPod Touch. This iPod is now my SMPTE slate AND my playback device! I plug the audio jack into some loudspeakers and hold the screen up to the camera before each shot with the video playing back. Once I do that, I have a frame-accurate reference point for where to put each shot. It takes out all the guesswork.

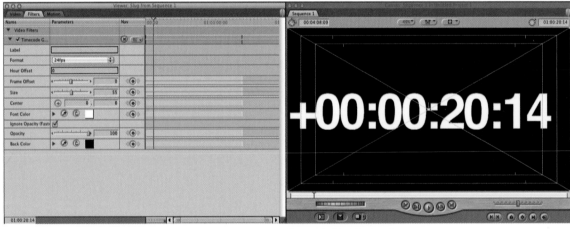

The Time Code Generator Effect as in Final Cut Pro 7

2 No Faking

Lip sync looks way better when the artist is really singing or rapping out loud. On every shoot I do, one of my main directions to the act is to perform the song like they would perform it for their biggest concert ever. Musicians are performers, and if you can help them get into the right mindset, they can really light up the screen. There are a few exceptions to this rule. After all, rules are made to be broken, and in music videos, that's doubly true. Take a look at some of your favorite music videos. See if you can spot this taking place, and if it works, try to analyze *why* it works for that video.

3 Get Full Performances at Every Location

If you have four locations on your video, go ahead and get a few run-throughs of the entire song with the full band in each one. You might as well, since an entire run-through costs you only a few minutes. This is a trick I learned the hard way when I got into the edit bay on one or two of my early projects and didn't really have as many performance takes as I wanted. This is a great way to cover your butt in editing, and it's way cheaper than reshoots.

4 Film a Concert

This tip is closely related to the previous one. If you have concert footage, you don't have to use it, but you can if you need to. If you're filming a concert, make sure the act is performing an arrangement of the song that matches with the cut you're making the video for. Also make sure that they perform it at exactly the same tempo. This is easier to accomplish with rappers, who

often perform to the instrumental version of the album cut, whereas rock bands are generally playing the set live. You can usually find a workaround if you talk to your band about it in advance. Attending a concert or two before your shoot, whether or not you're filming the concert, is a great way to get to know the band's stage persona. You're attempting to translate that persona to video, so it's going to be hugely beneficial if you know what that persona is beforehand. You can also get valuable insights into the act's audience, who in large part will make up the audience of their video.

5 Get a Great Performance

You generally have enough money for only one shoot. If you get into the edit room and find out that the band was kind of mailing it in on-screen, or couldn't overcome the distractions of the set to focus on their performance, that's what you're stuck with. You will know in your gut whether a shot is or is not working when you're on set, but it's tough to learn to listen to your gut. You'll have a lot of distractions from your instincts on set. You'll be under time and budgetary constraints. Balance the importance of the shot against these constraints. If a mission-critical shot isn't working, then the video isn't working, and you need to do whatever needs to be done to make that shot work because you will not have another chance.

> Don't lose focus on the most important thing you came to get: a good, energetic, on-screen *performance* of the song.

6 Be a Good Communicator

You can't be a good director if you can't convey your ideas to your cast and crew. That's true of any project, not just music videos. Make sure you talk to the performers after each take. Did they feel bad? Did they feel good? Why? Talk to them about how they are framed. If they aren't too self-conscious, you can probably get away with showing them playback.

Tell your key crew about each shot and what you're trying to accomplish with it. They will set things up with far greater artistic integrity if they feel as though they have a stake in the concept.

Sometimes words fail. When this happens, it's great to have a storyboard handy, or at least a pen and paper and a passable ability to draw a stick figure. I've been on sets where directors even fire up YouTube and show shots from other music videos or films that they were using as reference. There is no shame in this. You're the visionary, and you should use whatever tools are at your disposal to convey that vision to the people who are helping you to execute it.

7 Use a Field Monitor

A relatively inexpensive rental, field monitors are a great way to make sure the video you're shooting is looking the way you want it to look. Obviously, your D.P. is a talented visual artist in whom you can place a lot of trust, but your working relationship with your D.P. should be a collaboration. Additionally, your camera and lighting crew will be glad of having a screen they can all look at the same time in order to converse and really nail the shot. There have

been plenty of shoots in my short career where a monitor wasn't in the budget, but often I could borrow a TV set to work in a pinch. This is one of those line items that is tempting to cut when you're trying to save money, but think twice before you do. Having a monitor is usually way cheaper than correcting a mistake that a monitor would have enabled you to spot.

8 Drink Water and Eat Fruit

This point is often met with a laugh, but hear me out. Directing is a super stressful enterprise for a lot of people, especially beginners who feel that a lot is on the line for each shoot. This often translates into loss of sleep, bad hygiene, and poor eating habits. Being sleepy, scruffy, and underfed are all major contributors to incompetence. Fortunately, if you make a point of taking good care of yourself, you can avoid these problems and be a better director as a result.

Fruit is cheap, high-quality, brain-enhancing energy food. Never has having an apple in hand slowed a director down. Drink lots of water. You might have to take more bathroom breaks, but taking quick breaks is a great way to reflect on how your shoot is going, and that momentary objectivity can often contribute to important insights. Have a bottle of water close at hand at all times for the sake of your video.

9 Maintain Your Composure

A director has two jobs: (1) make a vision a reality and (2) incorporate the unexpected into that vision with integrity. Obviously we spend a lot of time in preproduction covering our bases and setting our house in order so that we can have a smooth shoot, but when the snags inevitably hit, you need to be able to cope. So hope for the best, but prepare for the worst, and have some levity about the sustained chaos that is filmmaking.

> Murphy's Law:
> "Anything that can go wrong, will go wrong."
> Flanagan's Precept: "Murphy was an optimist."

On a recent music video, I was lucky enough to borrow a modest lighting package. I had a bunch of Fresnel lights for one location and a bunch of Kinoflos for the other. Somehow when we got to the second location, we realized that we had somehow left all of the ballasts for the Kinos at the studio we had borrowed them from. We had no soft lights for the entire second half of our day. But we didn't panic. I kept the possibility of sending a P.A. across town to grab the ballasts if I needed to, but my lighting team spent 15 minutes trying to set up the same shot with the Fresnel lights and a lot of diffusion. What we ended up with, in my opinion, looked *better* than what we would have gotten with the Kinos. If I'd gotten all bent out of shape and started yelling at my crew, some of whom were no doubt at fault for spacing out on the ballasts, we would have wasted a lot of time and probably wouldn't have even arrived at the creative solution to the problem that we did. As a result, I would have had to wait around for an hour while someone got the ballasts and then rushed through the rest of my day and gotten crappier footage as a result.

Be cool. Roll with the punches. In every catastrophe lies an opportunity.

10 Know When to Quit

With the previous tip in mind, sometimes things just don't work out the way you imagined. For one reason or another, shots just don't come together sometimes. You can avoid a lot of this by having a great battle plan and testing everything in advance, but everyone fails at least some of the time. Sometimes admitting defeat is the best thing you can do for a shot that won't cooperate. Try to re-imagine the scene. Is there a simple alternative to what you were trying to accomplish? Can you cut away here? I can offer only the most abstract of suggestions here, because every shoot is different, but keep this in mind: you aren't Stanley Kubrick, and you don't have a bottomless budget to draw from while you try take 35 of shot two. At the end of the day, it's just a music video. Be real with the musician and their label or manager. Let them know that there's a problem with the shot and that you'll do your best to make up for it. Remind them that you want the video to be awesome too.

FREE! Bonus Tip!: Have Fun

We got into filmmaking to have fun! We're serious about our work, but we would be working in a bank or a coal mine or something if all we cared about was money or hard work. This is a passion, and if you aren't enjoying it, then you're playing yourself. Besides, having fun stimulates creativity, and creativity begets more interesting music videos. Filmmaking is a grind, but it's also mad rewarding.

Always back-up your project and raw footage on at least one other hard drive....ALWAYS.

Introduction

Editing is the major distinction between filmmaking and all the art forms that came before it. In some ways it's the most important part of the process. I've seen a lot of videos that consisted of extremely compelling and interesting visuals that didn't manage to come together in a coherent way due to poor editing. At the same time, I've seen average visuals that came together in a big way due to excellent editing. Editing is a talent, but it's also a muscle, and the more you do, the better you'll

get. I got into filmmaking thinking I wanted to be an editor. I had my first professional editing job the summer after high school and consistently edited my own work all through film school and afterward. Here are some pointers that I've picked up over the years.

Kill Your Baby

Editing is fraught with pain and regret. If you don't walk out of an edit session with a sense of loss, you probably weren't doing your job. You will always have to leave shots and takes that you love on the editing room floor. Obviously, I'm being hyperbolic, but what I'm trying to convey is the fact that you need to dispassionately select the shots and cuts that best serve the story and rhythm of your music video. That's not easy for most directors because we tend to fall in love with our footage. That's why I recommend that all directors, especially first-timers, do at least the assembly edit on their own videos.

Editing your own footage is the best film education you will ever get. As a director, you will make mistakes, no matter what, and in editing your footage, you will be confronted with those mistakes and forced to reflect on them. My editing room nightmare is to come to a clip that I'm excited to see, realize that it doesn't really work on camera, and hear myself giving directions that are the root cause of *why* the clip doesn't work. It's a painful thing to go through, but you can bet I don't make the same mistakes ever again.

If you can get through the assembly edit of your video, you will be a better director for it. If you do it every time, you'll be a Jedi in no time. If you don't want to do the whole edit, you can pass off the project to an editor at this point, and you'll be that much more conversant in the material so that when you talk to them about it, you'll know what you're talking about.

Notes on Media

If you're new to postproduction, you need to be aware of the problem of hard drive failures. If you don't have your project on more than one hard drive, you might as well not have it. Obviously, drive failures are rare, but when you're working with other people's money, risking data loss is unacceptable. Keep a *complete* copy of your project on a second hard drive. That includes save files from your editing software, comps from After Effects, the raw footage, the music, everything. Fortunately, hard drives are getting cheaper all the time.

If you are shooting HD, your hard drives should be a minimum of 500GB each.

You should use FireWire 800 drives. FireWire 400 and USB 2 are okay, but you will get far better performance out of the high throughput of FireWire 800 or the even faster eSATA connections if your computer is equipped with an eSATA port.

Save frequently, and make sure that you back up your saves as you go. Never edit footage on the boot disk of your computer. ("Macintosh HD" is *not* a good place to keep your footage.)

A major issue in any creative field is the client-review process. I talk to graphic designers, advertising executives, photographers, writers, and other filmmakers. Nobody can avoid it. Unless you have some unbelievable creative cachet, they're going to make themselves a part of the postproduction process and have you make lots of changes.

This is a balancing act because editing a music video is a ton of work. As a form, music videos tend to be the most editing-intensive kinds of films, and often involve lots of compositing, titles, and effects work. If I've spent two days rotoscoping and applying effects and rendering to get a 30-second sequence just right, the last thing I want to hear is that the client wants to make changes that will cost me all that work.

I could charge them more, but usually music video clients have very tight budgetary constraints, and overages are generally tough to get approval for.

Furthermore, the more a client gets involved in the post process, the more input they will tend to give, and the more back and forth you'll have, the more disagreements will arise, and generally you will have to do more work without making any more money.

So what's the solution? I recommend a three-review edit process. I recommend that you establish this up front, before you even sign a contract. The idea is that you show your client the video in three, progressively more refined cuts which they may give notes on. If they feel like they still need to see more cuts before the video is finished, then they agree, in advance, to pay for the extra work that it costs you to do more editing.

> Music videos are much more editing intensive than other genres and usually involve a lot of cuts, special FX, and compositing.

This process is a great compromise to keep the client involved in the edit, which will generally be to a video's benefit, but not so much that they make a ton of extra work for you, or get too micro-managerial over the edits and actually make the video worse. Below is the basic format I use.

This process can be tough because while you are dialed in on killing your baby and realizing your vision, confronting the limitations of the footage you got, and vying against all odds to make your video great, you *invite* someone to look over your shoulder and second-guess you the whole time. Don't lose faith, though. Everyone that makes money from their creativity has to go through with this. It's frankly the price we pay until we're on James Cameron's level and we can get away with telling the studio executives that are bankrolling our next blockbuster to go get bent.

It is the rare client, in my experience, that actually pays attention when I tell them what to expect in the editing process. This can be a very stressful time. Try to keep a cool head and remember: everyone is here to make this music video as awesome as possible. You and the client are working toward the same goal, and the review process is about reconciling your perspectives on how best to achieve that.

The 3 Review Edit

Review #1

A rough assembly edit, generally without any effects work or composites finished.

Review #2

A refined edit with some composites and effects completed and all of them started.

Review #3

As close to a final edit as I can get without final notes.

Setting up your project and getting organized are the first orders of the day.

The best editors in the business have this down to a science. The idea is that you want a well-thought-out system for keeping track of the changes you make over the course of a project and that your system is understandable to other people with whom you are collaborating. If you do the assembly edit and then pass off the project to someone else for the fine cuts, or if you do the editing and someone else does the graphics, those people need to be able to find all the media on your edit disk easily. I have a template folder structure that I keep on my hard drive for this very purpose:

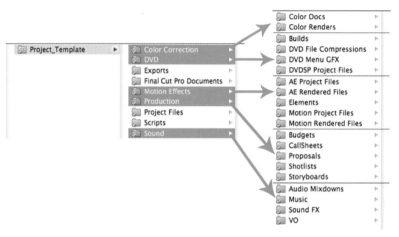

Keeping a standard project template like this for postproduction will help keep your project organized and standardized, especially when working with collaborators.

Generally, instead of continuing to edit and save in the same Final Cut Pro document (or the save file of whatever nonlinear editor you are using), I save a new version of the document for each day that I work on the project. For each review cut, I make a new copy of my sequence file within my editing software. In this way, I retain access to old versions of my project in case I need to turn back the clock. Maintaining a consistent scheme for tracking changes will also help you avoid confusion if you ever need to go back to an old project and re-export it for some reason.

Make sure that as you ingest your footage into your NLE, you also name clips and organize them. This is boring, but later in the edit you will have a much easier time finding the second take of the wide performance shot if you name it "Wide Perf. 2nd Take" than if it's still called "4JKV06N" or whatever your camera decided to call it. This will also obviously make it easier for your collaborators to find footage. This is tedious at first, but it's totally worth it.

Getting Synced

Now that you have your clips organized and named, it's time to start getting them synced up with the song. If you followed my advice and used timecode, this will be a snap. If you didn't, this will be a tricky and time-consuming process that will generally result in at least a few imprecise syncs. Drop your clips in and line up the timecode in the video with the timecode of your sequence. I like to drop everything in at first. Then as I work toward an assembly edit, I cut out the parts I don't like.

Getting Rhythmic

Music videos are generally most effective when the cuts have a feel for the rhythm of the song. Here's a tip on how to accomplish nice cuts on the beat.

Beat Markers

Before I do any cutting, I usually like to give myself some beat markers to work with. In FCP, the best way to do this is by highlighting the audio track and playing through the song tapping the "M" key to the beat. With hip-hop and rock, which are almost always in 4/4, you can usually hear whether it will sound best to tap on the ones and threes or the twos and fours. Use your best judgment, or if you have no rhythm, get someone to do it for you. As you play through the song, FCP will put a mark on the audio track every time you tap the "M" key. You can then use these marks as guides when you make your edits.

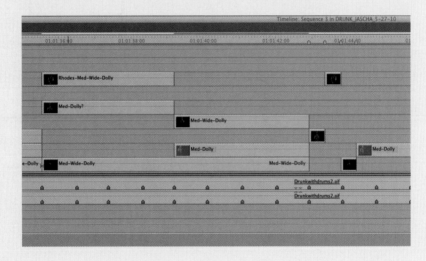

Send It to the Client

This is a tough one because generally the video is barely together at this point. I like to show a very early cut. Mainly, I want to make sure that the performances that I have selected are the ones the client likes. If any shots need to be nixed from the cut, I want to know early so I don't spend a lot of time adding effects and color toning to things I'm not going to end up using.

I make sure to ask the client for very detailed notes. To this end, I usually burn timecode into the video so that (a) they can give me notes that refer to specific shots, and (b) they can't really release the video before they pay me. If the client returns vague or confusing notes on the edit, tell them to redo them. One of the easiest ways for your relationship to sour with a client is if they feel that their input is being ignored during this process. Don't ignore them and also don't let their communication infect the discourse. If their notes are unrealistic, talk to them about alternatives.

Horror Story

I shot a music video for a client that had big, effects-driven sequences involved. I sent a very early cut to the client for approval on just the performances before cutting in any of the greenscreen shots that we would use to make the storyline components. The artist's manager sent back the notes for the first review. They were three very general notes, one of which simply said something about cutting in the storyline stuff, which was already on the agenda. I found out during the second review that the other two notes she had sent were basically the opposite of what the artist had wanted.

The artist wasn't communicating well with the manager, and the manager wasn't communicating well with me. There were numerous instances of this in a long and arduous editing process that culminated in the video coming out inferior and quite different from what anyone had intended, and my relationship with the client having completely soured to the point that we were having shouting matches on the phone. Was this all the client's fault? You could make the case for that, but I think that a lot of the bad communication could have been avoided if I had been more clear about what I needed from them with that first review edit. If I got those notes on a project today, I would send them back and ask for more detail.

Years later, the client released another music video for a different song that used a bunch of the footage that I had shot for him intercut with clips he had lifted from popular TV shows and movies. I learned a few things from this: I will never let a client have the raw footage from a shoot ever again, and I will be more realistic about how well I am communicating with a client before I embark on a big project with them.

Review Edit #2

Presumably, the client has given you very useful notes. Maybe they like the performance selects in the second verse but want to change the ones in the first verse. Make all the changes you can, treating their notes like a checklist, and then wade in to any comps or special effects you might have. In my process, the second review cut I send to the client incorporates their notes and includes partially complete comps throughout the video, and ideally one or two that are complete so that I can show the client what I have planned for all the incomplete comps.

In this section I'm going to give a rough overview of some essential compositing techniques, but this book isn't intended to be a postproduction manual, so I recommend you check out other resources such as **Lynda.com** if you're interested in learning more about special effects work.

The Basics of Compositing

Compositing is simply the act of putting two or more pieces of visual media together. Often, this is done with greenscreen or chroma keying. The invention of chroma keying dates back to the 1940s, but music videos have been an incredibly important driving force in developing and democratizing this technology. A huge percentage of music videos employ chroma-keyed visuals. Every filmmaker should have at least a basic understanding of this technique and its capabilities. Fortunately, with the advent of HD cameras with deep color spaces, keying is now easier and cheaper than ever.

"Color space" is a term used in video compression. I won't bore you with too much detail, but you can read up on it by looking up "Chroma Subsampling" on Wikipedia. Essentially, different cameras produce images with different levels of color detail in the footage they produce. You will encounter the following color spaces in modern cameras: 4:1:1, 4:2:0, 4:2:2, and 4:4:4, which ascend in level of color detail and also in file size. The RED ONE camera uses a 4:4:4 color space, and the Panasonic HVX-200 uses a 4:2:2. These are great cameras for shooting chroma key. The Sony EX1 and Canon 7D cameras shoot a 4:2:0, which I have found to be inferior to the HVX-200 for keying, though these cameras have many advantages over the HVX-200 in other scenarios.

When it comes to compositing and special effects, you need to know what you're doing going in. If the previous paragraph looks like Greek to you, you might want to exercise caution before planning that major effects sequence. I highly recommend test-shooting before you even propose SFX-driven videos to clients.

Mere mortals are generally going to have access to either Adobe After Effects or Apple Motion for compositing. Here's how they break down:

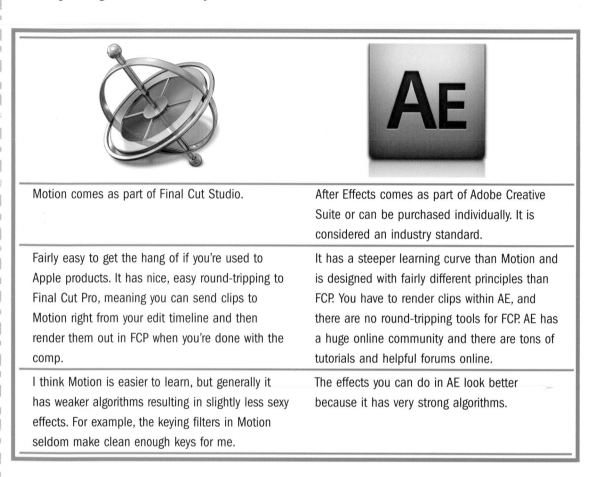

Motion comes as part of Final Cut Studio.	After Effects comes as part of Adobe Creative Suite or can be purchased individually. It is considered an industry standard.
Fairly easy to get the hang of if you're used to Apple products. It has nice, easy round-tripping to Final Cut Pro, meaning you can send clips to Motion right from your edit timeline and then render them out in FCP when you're done with the comp.	It has a steeper learning curve than Motion and is designed with fairly different principles than FCP. You have to render clips within AE, and there are no round-tripping tools for FCP. AE has a huge online community and there are tons of tutorials and helpful forums online.
I think Motion is easier to learn, but generally it has weaker algorithms resulting in slightly less sexy effects. For example, the keying filters in Motion seldom make clean enough keys for me.	The effects you can do in AE look better because it has very strong algorithms.

Here's a basic graphical breakdown of what's happening in a normal **comp**.

We start with a flat shot of the character against a greenscreen; in this case, I used a cheap piece of bright green fabric and made sure to light it well. (I could've done a better job of getting the wrinkles out here.)

I used Adobe After Effects' Keylight plug-in to key out the background, leaving me with a "matte" of the foreground. Notice that the green in the fish necktie has been dulled by this process. Sometimes it is necessary to mask out problem areas like this. Generally, your subject should not be wearing green.

Now the keyed subject is layered in with some graphics to make him look like he's in a newsroom. See the next section for an explanation of how those layers break down.

Layer 3: Graphics/Lower thirds

Layer 2: Keyed matte

Layer 1: Background

Review Edit #3

You should once again work to incorporate the notes the client gives you for Review Edit #3. For this review, I like to get the video to what I consider to be a broadcast-ready state of completion. Something I would be happy to release. That means a finalized picture edit, finalized comps and graphics, and color timing.

Intro to Color

I love digital filmmaking for its flexibility and the relative inexpensiveness of trying new things. One of my favorite parts of making a music video is playing with the color.

A professional photographer was showing me some tools for adjusting the colors of RAW photos in Photoshop. I complained that I felt like jazzing up an image with contrast and color was cheating. He disabused me of this notion quickly by reminding me that with film, photographers always had control over these aspects of their image when they went into the darkroom. He told me that if I didn't adjust my images I was leaving major aesthetic decisions to whoever designed my camera. The same is obviously true of motion pictures. Music videos are about making bold decisions. Camera manufacturers design their cameras to capture very flat images with lots of range to appeal to the broadest possible market. It is on you, as a filmmaker, to decide what to do with those images.

Enter color timing. With film, you do this in a darkroom by exposing your emulsion to different chemicals for different amounts of time. With digital, you do this by adjusting sliders and applying effects.

If you have Final Cut Studio, you already have a very good color timing program, called Color. If not, there are lots of color-correction tools in almost every nonlinear editor. If you use them, you can make your images look great. If you hire a professional colorist, they can make your images look *amazing*.

My Approach to Color

I always wait until I have my entire music video cut, with the effects finished and client-approved, before I start color timing. My reasoning is that when I apply a color effect to the whole music video, that effect works on the digital effects and the live footage at the same time, creating a more cohesive aesthetic.

Nota Bene

Obviously, you should be thinking about color all the way through the process of making a music video. You should have a color palette in mind when you write your treatment, and talk to your art department and D.P. about what colors you want. Much of what is done in color timing is fixing things, but a good D.P. can achieve a lot of what you want in-camera, which is a great time-saver. If you are working with a colorist or editor, it's always advisable to check with them *before* shooting to determine which looks are best achieved in-camera and which are best achieved during the color-correction or visual FX phase of post.

Here are just a few key terms you should know before wading into color correction.

Bleach Bypass: In the old days, skipping the bleaching part of color film processing meant that the silver molecules stayed on the emulsion. The practical upshot: a black-and-white version of the image overlaid on the color image, meaning less saturation in the color, higher contrast, and more graininess. Gives a very edgy look to film.

Contrast: The difference between the tones in an image. High-contrast images will have sharply distinct brights and darks.

Cross-Process: When you process one type of film with chemicals intended for another. Generally, you would do this with reversal film and negative developing chemicals. This gives you a unique look in your image, generally at the cost of some vividness in colors. The Son of Sam sequences in Spike Lee's *Summer of Sam* are a great reference for what this looks like.

Curves: Many color correctors represent colors on a diagonal line. You can, for example, make medium-bright red tones a little brighter, and thereby add some redness to your image, by curving the reds up a bit. You can add contrast by lowering the bottom and raising the top of the luma curve.

Day for Night: Usually a preset, this lets you make footage shot outdoors during the daytime look like it was shot at night. This is something that can look great if you really know what you're doing, but can look awful too.

Gain: The whiteness of the whites. Raising gain usually brightens images while leaving black tones black. Generally, this results in noisier images.

Gamma: The overall brightness of the image. Raising or lowering gamma makes whites, blacks, and everything in-between brighter or darker. Generally, I avoid playing with the gamma.

Hue: Messing with the hue of something just means changing what color it is. Usually, if you shift the hue of something, you're shifting the hue of everything else too.

Saturation: How much color is in an image. A black-and-white image is totally desaturated.

Vignette: Old cameras made images that were less bright toward the edges of the picture. Some modern lenses do this too. A vignette effect will let you darken the edges of your image—or occasionally brighten them if you are trying to counteract an in-camera vignette that you don't want. This is a good effect if you are trying to mimic an old film look or to really make the center of the image pop.

COLOR GRADING OPTIONS

Here are your software options for color grading. There is some higher-end stuff, but generally that is software you hire someone to use for you because it usually requires specialized control equipment and specially calibrated monitors.

Color: The best option at the prosumer price point. Color ships with Final Cut Studio and produces very pretty images. It includes lots of filter presets too, which will enable you to mimic lots of classic film processes. Color has a bit of a learning curve and its interface is decidedly tough to grasp, but once you get going with it, it's very powerful.

After Effects: Adobe's motion graphics and compositing has a lot of good color-correction tools built right in. These will be very easy to get the hang of for anyone familiar with Photoshop.

Final Cut or Other NLEs: Generally, you'll find that editing software has some color-correction tools, but my experience is that these tools never produce images that look as good as specialized programs. I do some light color-correction work with the Three Way Color Corrector, but that's about it.

Before

After

This is some fairly intense color adjustment. We filmed the subject, the very talented rapper Jake Lefco, with the sun at his back. His face was too dark, and the sunset was too bright. Using curves, we managed to bring out detail in both his face and the background. If I had had more time and a bigger budget, it might have been worthwhile to rotoscope the buildings and river behind him and use the original image settings for just the buildings and river, then only adjust the details of the sky and his face. Also note the vignette effect added around the edges.

Before

After

Here's another shot from the same music video. I wanted the blacks to be blacker and his face to be more distinct. I increased the contrast and saturation and added vignetting around the edges. The overall changes are subtle but definitely affect the feel of the video.

Before

After

We wanted the images in this music video to have a dreamlike quality, so we shot this dancer in slow motion. Unfortunately, the colors were muted, and the whites weren't glowing as much as I wanted, so we bumped up the saturation, gained up the red tones to give that warmth to the image, and then added a subtle glow filter.

Before

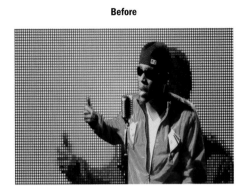

After

Here's a greenscreen shot that I added color grading to. You'll notice the vignette and the glows of the bright parts of the image bleed from foreground to background in the graded image, which helps to make the digital background feel more cohesively a part of the image.

Before

After

Color grading is also when you want to go from color to black and white if that's what you're going for. Black-and-white images have a lot to offer in music videos, but bright and dark areas behave differently when they have no color in them, so it's best to do this all at once. I also cropped this video to wider 2.35:1 aspect ratio.

THE END OF THE EDIT

So once your Review Edit #3 notes come back from the client, what's next? Well, the notes should be something you can execute within the prearranged edit time. If it represents a ton of new work, you should discuss that with the client and come to an agreement on how to proceed. This can be a touchy conversation because you are basically telling the client that they need to settle for the video in something close to its current state or spend more money to continue editing. Obviously, most clients are not psyched about the idea of expanding their budget, and what this scenario usually boils down to is that either their notes weren't clear enough in the earlier reviews, or that there has been a fundamental misunderstanding between you and them the entire time. That's why you need to be super careful to communicate well with your clients all the way through the process. Don't make any assumptions about what they're thinking.

Get used to it, though. This is one of those areas in which music videos are a microcosm of the film industry. When you turn in a commercial spot or a cut of a feature film, you will always receive notes from nonfilmmakers on the client side or studio side, and you won't always agree with those notes or find them easy to incorporate into your thinking. I cut a commercial for a department store once, and while I was editing, they decided that the male model should be wearing blue socks. The only problem was that their stylist had put him in white socks and there wasn't a frame of film featuring blue socks. In the end I had to rotoscope his socks and tint them blue.

Clients are going to give you crazy notes, and it's a skill to incorporate these dispassionately and in a way that honors your original idea. It's best to get good at this skill now while the stakes are fairly low. Remember, as a director, your job is to deliver quality work with a consistent vision, despite the inevitable setbacks and compromises that happen in all filmmaking. Crappy notes from the client side are just another obstacle like a finicky location owner or a burned-out bulb on a light you need to use. Improvise and power through. You were hired because you can handle it. You were hired because of your skill at creative problem solving.

You may not think of promoting the video as part of your job, and in some cases it might not be, but if you're working on tiny budgets and don't have a major record label's PR firm pushing your video, you should be doing everything in your power to give your video a chance to make an impact. Not everything goes "viral" or needs to. But your career will benefit from a run on MTVU or a lot of YouTube hits, so don't take the exhibition phase lightly.

Television

Unfortunately, there isn't much of a life for music videos on television these days, and in my experience, to get on television you either need to be working with a label that can do the legwork or know someone who programs music videos at the network in question.

That said, there are a few things you need to know.

The digital revolution is changing these rules, but as of this writing, generally you submit your music video to the network for review on Beta tape. They usually have review screenings once a week, and if they want your video, they'll generally send you a list of edits for S&P (Standards and Practices). This includes bleeping out language and cutting around racy or illegal subject matter (sex, drugs, guns). Don't get too married to one particular cut. I was once shown the S&P edit request sheet for Drake's "Best I Ever Had" music video directed by Kanye West, and it looked like a letter to Penthouse Forum. There were literally dozens of edits necessary to get a music video that was already blowing up on the Internet onto a major television network.

Once you've complied with the puritanical censors at the network, you resubmit, and pending final approval, you submit again on Digi-Beta or an HD format. They may also require that your final deliverables include a closed-caption track.

If you've never messed around with these pro tape formats and don't have access to the decks that play and record on them, you should know that they are expensive. You can expect to spend hundreds of dollars having tapes made in this part of the process. Check with your local postproduction houses to get an idea of how much this will cost. They usually charge for the media and the time it takes to record onto the media. If you have to submit closed-captioning, that costs as well.

As a rule, I talk to prospective clients about the process of getting on television before we even shoot the video. It's often not a priority. Usually, the cost of doing this is not in the budget up front. It's something that they decide to do later, but you can protect yourself from a misunderstanding by having this conversation in advance. It's better not to surprise a musician with another thousand dollar's worth of expenses before she can see her video on MTV.

The Internet

YouTube is the traffic king. Vimeo is the quality king. You need to be on Twitter and Facebook to smash the video out. By the time you read this, all of this may have changed. What probably won't change, though, are some general rules of thumb about releasing a music video on the Internet:

Know Your Release Date: This will probably be selected by the artist or label, but you should know about it too. Send an email out to everyone you know that would be interested and tell them that the video is coming soon and that you'll really appreciate their help in spreading the word when it does. If you tell 10 people about the video, and each of them tells 10 people and so on, that begins to translate into a lot of views. If you have a blog or a social network profile, use that as effectively as you can to build hype surrounding your upcoming video.

Blogs: Take aim early at the biggest blogs in the genre you're working in. Some blogs like **Pitch-fork** and **Paste Magazine** will occasionally partner with artists to release music videos, and since they're such popular websites, this can translate into a lot of views and reblogs.

To identify blogs that would like your video, try to think of bands that are similar to the one you're working with and then search for blog posts about those bands. Generally, blogs have an easy way of getting in touch with their editors through a contact form. If that doesn't work, try getting their attention on Twitter or Facebook.

Reddit/Digg, etc.: These social content aggregation sites are a great way to steer traffic to your video, but don't get tripped up. People who are active users on these sites generally want to be the first to post something cool, so if you don't have any followers on these sites, don't just post the video yourself and hope it goes somewhere. Your best hope would be to find someone who is already a power user and see if they would post it. If not that, then hope it gets submitted through the link-sharing widgets that most blog posts these days are spangled with.

Getting a video to go viral can be one of the biggest thrills of a filmmaker's early career. Going viral is as much alchemy as it is science, but there are some best practices you should observe:

- **First and Foremost, Have an Awesome Video:** The videos that do the best have the most original ideas, the best music, and the most arresting visuals. If you can do something legitimately incredible, that's going to be the single most important factor in going viral.

- **Tags:** You need to have tons of tags to make your video as searchable as possible. Don't just tag it with literal descriptors, but with the names of similar artists. If your band is the next White Stripes, go ahead and tag it White Stripes.

- **Title:** Think about who will be in your target audience. Is the band already well known? If not, there might be no advantage to putting the band's name in the title. Put it in the description instead. Try to make your title the kind of thing you would click on if you knew nothing about the video you were about to watch.

- **Timing:** Many experts agree that the first 48 hours of a video's presence on YouTube are the most important. You should really have a battle plan figured out for your digital premiere if you want to get a viral hit going. Basically, you're going for 50,000 to 60,000 views as quickly as possible, which is when you start to catch the attention of YouTube's servers, and your video starts to get placed on the front pages of categories. It's important that it happens early, and it's important that you do everything you can to drive those views up with every tool you have (see above for tips on email, social networks, blogs, and social bookmarking sites).

- **That Certain Something:** A truly viral video has its own momentum. You can only do so much in getting the views up, but what really starts to increase the numbers is when people who don't even know you start sharing the video with their friends. What causes people to do this? There's something wild or outrageous or amazing about the video that they feel the need to share it. In that way, a viral video is like a joke that, when you hear it, you immediately want to tell to other people. Factor this into your thinking about the video from the earliest planning stages, and you will have a better chance of making a hit.

- **Follow Through:** The day of the release, send out a second email to the same group, announcing the release! You can also move eyeballs to your video by emailing the link to popular blogs whose viewership might enjoy the music. Blogs are generally desperate to publish as much cool content as they can, and you'd be surprised at how many will be happy to post your music video if it will appeal to their demographic. This is good stuff to think about in the planning phase: what visuals can I add to this song to get the most people excited about it?

Things spread through the Internet for all kinds of reasons, but if I had to put my finger on what makes one thing more likely to become popular than another, it's having a *hook*. If you can figure out a way to describe your video in terms of having a hook, you're going to be way better off. Here are a couple examples of that.

Okay, Go!—"Here It Goes Again"

Their breakout hit music video was a choreographed dance on treadmills. The hook was that the guys doing the dancing were clearly amateur dancers, and they didn't fit the profile of the people you normally see dancing *at all*, much less in music videos. It was just weird enough to inspire people to send the link around.

Beyoncé—"Put a Ring on It"

Not to knock Beyoncé, who I think is one of the greatest living musicians, but this is an example of the video making the song. The song is catchy in a few parts, but ultimately kind of repetitive. But the dancing and the styling of the video are so incredible that it's spawned thousands of homages and imitations on YouTube and television. Everyone knows that scissor-kick/ground punch dance move and the weird wrist-twist move she does. It's an incredible video.

Rebecca Black—"Friday"

The song is garbage, the video is super literal to the plot of the song, and the editing is weird. Nevertheless, this video was cresting 10 million views within a few days of going up on YouTube, and it took a 13-year-old girl into the stratosphere, if only for a moment. What's the hook? Cynically, you could say that it's the badness of the song, but take a closer look, and I think you'll notice that the video has something to it that makes you want to watch to the end. YouTube doesn't count the views of people who open a video and watch for 10 seconds and then close it before it's over. You keep watching the *Friday* video because it keeps surprising you, and because Rebecca Black is actually really engaging on camera. There are a bunch of little moments in her performance that are extremely endearing. Partly, you watch it because you want to see what the next crazy turn is going to be in the video, but partly you watch it because you *like* it…. I just blew your mind.

The animated video I directed for Jascha Hoffman's, "Some Hungry Guy" based on the artwork of Windsor Mckay, went viral with more than 16,000 YouTube views in less than a month thanks to aggressive follow-through promotion and write-ups from notable blogs.

In Conclusion

Music videos are an incredibly challenging part of the film industry to work in, but I think of them as trials by fire. If you direct a few music videos, I guarantee that you will be a better filmmaker. They can totally suck up all of your time, but when you start down the path of making a music video, you come out on the other side with this perfect little four-minute movie that puts your skills on display to the whole world. Music videos can lead to bigger and better things, like feature films and commercials that pay big money, and getting paid to do what you love is an incredible feeling. I hope this chapter helps you to create killer music videos and stay sharp as a director.

I'm going to turn the book back over to Anthony now. You can check out my music videos, marketing videos, and other work on my page at **Double7Images.com**. Good luck!

–Benjamin Ahr Harrison

A $150* Music Video
Project: "Bluffin' Ain't an Option"

Hard Costs*:

1 Enhancing Filter	$80.00
2 Day Meals	$40.00
Still Film Prints	$10.00
Boombox Batteries	$ 5.00
Gas Money	$15.00
Total	**$150.00**

Preproduction:
1 Day Location Scouting
Storyboards
Meeting with artists to discuss concept

Equipment:
Beta SP Camera (Borrowed)
Tripod (Borrowed)
Enhancing Filter (Purchased)

Playback Boombox (Owned)
Video Projector (Borrowed)

Artists: Black Tongue
Director/Producer: Anthony Q. Artis
Music Genre: Conscious Hip-Hop
Web: vimeo.com/20323676

Crew:
1 Director/Producer
1 D.P.
1 Editor

Labor Costs:

Director/Producer	$300.00
D.P.	$150.00
Editor	$200.00
Total	**$650.00**

Postproduction:
Media 100 NLE System
2 weeks cutting part-time

Transportation:
Crew Car (personal vehicle)
Talent Car (personal vehicle)

Schedule and Locations:

DAY 1
Inner-city Baltimore (Stolen)
- Various Urban Locations (B-roll)
- Billy Holiday Mural
- Modern Art Mural
- Abandoned Pier
- Playground

DAY 2
Studio (Borrowed)
- Projection Scenes
- Constructed Set

Inner-city Baltimore (Stolen):
- Howard Street Bridge

Project Details

Budget: This is the very first freelance video job I ever did for pay. *Okay, as you can see, the actual cost was $800, but that's only because I chose to pay myself and the two people working with me. So discounting labor, which I could have easily gotten (and given) for free as most of my filmmaking colleagues were as young and eager to shoot a music video as I was at the time, the hard costs to actually realize this video were about $150. Some 15 years later, I think the Down and Dirty production values still hold up well, and I'm still very proud of the end product (which I definitely can't say about everything I shot in my formative filmmaking years).

The Artists: One of the artists was the brother of a good friend whom I'd known for many years. He was trying to take his hip-hop career to the next level but didn't have much money. I was young and hungry to direct and I liked the song and always wanted to make a music video, so I was more than willing to work for peanuts. I also honestly didn't know if I could even pull it off, so I didn't want to charge much anyway so that there would be no real pressure or guilt if I screwed it up.

Concept: The concept was pretty simple and in keeping with other music videos of the time. It was a straightforward performance video set in hometown urban environments juxtaposed against a few cool visuals created during a studio performance. To make the video a little more dynamic and gritty, I wanted to intersperse documentary-style street scenes of everyday people in the 'hood.

Crew: I hired my friend Jason, who was a camera intern at my day job, to be D.P. He was still in school and it was his first music video, so he was more than happy to shoot for cheap to build his D.P. reel. A good friend who worked for a small production company in L.A. connected me with an assistant editor on a TV show who aspired to be an Editor-editor. He also had never worked on a music video before and was looking to build his professional reel and do something more exciting than logging reality TV footage.

Preproduction: After spending a Saturday scouting the locations and taking pictures of potential camera angles, I drew up simple stick figure storyboards and diagrams for every setup and then reviewed them with the artists. I also did a quick test shoot to see if I liked the look of the enhancing filter and my "ghetto film-look" technique. (See next section for details on these.)

Production: We shot run-and-gun over two days, about 75 percent on location and 25 percent in the studio. To save travel time, I chose all the locations within 15 minutes of each other. I scheduled most of the performance shots for early in the morning, so there would be minimal foot and street traffic and fewer chances of being hassled while shooting in the rougher neighborhoods that were the backdrop for half the video. We pulled up to each location ready to shoot, so all we had to do was hop out of the car, frame the shot, and start rolling. We used a battery-powered boombox for playback and did two to three full song takes at each location, getting a few different angles and camera moves for each take. For the documentary street scenes, we just drove around and asked random people in the 'hood if they wanted to be in the video, and most were flattered. The rest of the video we shot in a small studio where we could get free access during off-hours.

Postproduction: The video was cut on a Media 100 nonlinear editing system (state-of-the-art in 1995, particularly for its ability to achieve a film-look before 24P cameras were prolific).

I shipped the tapes off to L.A. along with full notes and storyboards for the editor, whom I spoke to further by phone. He mailed me a first cut on VHS. I typed up and sent notes via mail, and he made the appropriate changes before sending me a final version.

Establishing Shots—Adding Movement

Shooting a music video with your camera locked in place on a tripod is a recipe for boredom. Even for the simplest shots such as establishing shots, think of ways to add some *movement*. Dolly and crane moves are great when you can get them, but more difficult and time consuming to pull off, especially under guerrilla conditions with limited manpower. However, there are many ways to organically add movement and energy to a shot beyond a dolly. One of the easiest flashy video moves is a **whip pan** or **whip zoom** like the one here. Beyond that, there are infinite possibilities when it comes to **visual effects (VFX)** in postproduction. (See "whip zoom" on page 296.)

The Bridge—Enhancing the Look and Fixing My Screwup

We did two setups on Baltimore's Howard Street bridge. The first setup we shot with the camera at a low angle, shooting close-up shots with the upper bridge girders and blue sky as a background. The second setup we shot shooting down the length of the colorful orange and blue bridge as traffic drove by. It was one of my favorite shots of the video. Unfortunately, it was ruined by our failure to check or clean the lens, which was filthy. So when the camera was pointed directly toward the beams of sunlight on a wide shot, every speck of dust and crap on the lens was illuminated and looked awful. In post, we were able to get away with using only some of the footage from this setup because the editor warped the shot with a fish-eye lens effect, put it and black and white, and added some video noise, which kind of gave the feel of looking through a dirty video camera viewfinder...rather than a dirty novice filmmaker's lens.

All of the exterior location performance scenes were shot with two in-camera FX to enhance the look. First, we were shooting on a standard definition Sony Beta SP camera before the proliferation of low-cost 24P cameras, so we needed a Down and Dirty solution to achieve a more filmic and less video "broadcasty" look. Before 24P, there was "24 Knee," as in sheer knee-high pantyhose, which could be cut and stretched tightly over the lens mount with a few rubber bands to hold it in place for a softer more filmic look. The second in-camera effect was the single largest cost to the production: an enhancing filter. The enhancing filter made reds and browns "pop" much more on video. I wanted the performers brown skin tones to look richer and more saturated so they'd stand out more from the backgrounds, as I knew we wouldn't be using any lighting. This filter also made many of the murals we were using as performance backdrops appear brighter and more vibrant.

The Murals—Adding Production Value with Location

I scouted these colorful art murals as some of the most visually interesting locations in the inner-city neighborhood that also spoke to the uplifting urban themes of the song. No matter what you're shooting, the easiest surefire way to add some production value is to find a cool-looking place and stage your scene in front of it. Far beyond these simple murals, the possibilities to add production value and give your project a big-budget look with a visually striking location are endless.

If it looks beautiful or cool in person, it will look even better on camera. A vista with a great cityscape, a giant mansion, a carnival, the edge of the Grand Canyon, a rooftop view of a skyscraper, the beach, a rolling field of wildflowers are all camera-ready premium locations that can make your video look a lot cooler than something you just shot in your garage or next to your house. Do a quick test shoot beforehand to find just the right camera filter and/or color treatment in postproduction, and you can make the most striking visual features of any location stand out even more. And the best part of all, most of these places can be accessed (with or without a permit) totally for *free*.

Documentary Street Scenes—Film Look

You can't really do a hip-hop music video without *some* shots of the 'hood. In this case, after we got all the more complex performance scenes for the day, we drove around the same area looking for interesting scenes of life in the neighborhood. Once we found them, we approached the people to see if they would let us include them in our video. Most people obliged and were excited to be part of a video project. We got permission from an urban motorcycle club, a group of kids playing, some teenagers on a stoop, and even some corner hustlers. Some subjects we posed portrait-style as we panned across them, and others we shot as they went about whatever they were doing when we first saw them.

All the doc footage was treated in post with a 8mm-style film look by adding grain, slowing down the frame rate, and desaturating the vibrant colors—all courtesy of the then-revolutionary Media 100 editing system. We also shot some general street scenes of the neighborhood courtesy of a "Nissan Sentra Dolly" (otherwise known as shooting out the window of my mom's car while driving at a slow pace). We did this to add some more movement to the visuals and to also keep it moving in a rough area once there were many more people on the street, so it was both an artistic and practical choice.

The Studio Scenes—Projection FX

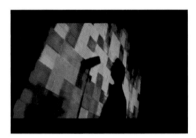

I wanted some slick and colorful animated lighting FX that would dance and change to the rhythm. Traditionally, to achieve this, a director lacking in Down and Dirty imagination might employ a stage lighting designer, a nightclub VJ or video artist, or maybe even a computer animator or special FX artist. They'd have meetings and sketches and multiple screen tests, etc. And none of it would be fast or cheap. So how did I pull it off here? With an early model of the Sony PlayStation 1, which I discovered quite by accident one day has a video animation mode that activates and responds to any music CD played in the system. Even cooler, the animations could be manually changed and altered using the PlayStation controller.

This funky little feature made for some trippy fun on my TV when entertaining friends at home, but when hooked up to a video projector (borrowed for free) and screened on a 20' wall in the studio, it made for a very cool MTV-style nightclub video stage FX. We did one round of takes staging the artists in front of the projector to shoot their sharp silhouettes as they performed with the animations in the background. Then we did a second set of performance takes shooting close-ups of the colorful lights as they shifted on the artists' faces (left). Total setup time was about 15 minutes. Total cost was zero. Total production value bang for the buck: incredible.

As I pointed out in *The Shut Up and Shoot Documentary Guide,* the greatest asset of a Down and Dirty filmmaker is imagination. Where others see an ugly white wall, we see a white cyc. Where other people see a surveillance camera, we see the perfect camera to cover the robbery scene in a wide shot. Where they see a rock, we see a tripod. They see a forklift; we see a crane shot. They see a motorcycle gang: we see cheap extras and motorcycle rentals. I'm telling you: tools, locations, collaborators, special FX—*the resources* we need are all around us. The shots here are all cases in point. It's all about your perspective. What free and cheap otherwise-overlooked resources could you put to filmmaking use with a little more imagination? Break out your Down and Dirty goggles, find the answer to this question, and put it on the screen, baby! Free your mind and your budget will follow every time.

Special FX in Postproduction

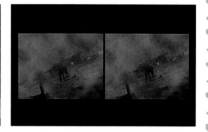

The final little bit of pizzazz was added in postproduction with color correction to make some scenes a little more saturated and some simple but effective video FX. Motion trail was added to some of the studio close-ups to produce overlapping images of the artists as they moved. Split screens and digital smoke were used for some of the pier shots, etc. All the doc footage (center) was treated in post with an 8mm-style film look by adding grain, slowing down the frame rate from the video standard of 30fps to 24fps, and desaturating the vibrant colors—all courtesy of the then-revolutionary Media 100 nonlinear editing system.

The key to post FX for your freelance projects is to employ FX that aren't totally gratuitous and enhance the visual storytelling on-screen. However, I think music videos are perhaps the one genre (other than experimental film) where FX *can* occasionally be totally gratuitous—meaning you can do something just because it *looks* cool. And we certainly took liberties with that exception on this project.

The Abandoned Harbor Pier—Baltimore Money Shot

No film or video shot in Baltimore is really complete without some shot (if not an entire scene) at the Inner Harbor. It's the centerpiece icon of the city. The problem with shooting there is that, well, it's the centerpiece icon of the city. So it's always buzzing with tourists and cops and not the type of backdrop where you can *easily* stage a guerrilla music video with no permits or permission. However, for me as a director, completely omitting the Inner Harbor was not an option for two hip-hop artists trying break out and represent Baltimore on the national scene. (This was long before *The Wire*.) I scouted an abandoned pier just off the main area of the harbor with a perfect view of the gritty old Domino Sugar factory in the middle of the harbor, a well-known Baltimore landmark. We shot the scene in less than an hour without incident, thanks to a little extra preplanning, scouting, and forethought to pull off this money shot. (See "HOT TIP: ~~Stealing~~ Borrowing Locations" on the next page.)

STEALING BORROWING LOCATIONS

L.A. nightscape as seen from the hills.

The secret to shooting in more high-profile places is to find just the right nook, corner, or hidden little area that allows you to still have the iconic location of your desire framed in the background of your shot, but at the same time to keep your camera position obscured from easy public view. Private rooftops and balconies are great for this purpose, if you or a friend has access to them. I've also stealthily shot some quick scenes in Times Square and Venice Beach, as well as some beautiful scenes on the waterfronts of New York and Baltimore by finding old piers, loading docks, or hidden nooks and crannies in otherwise public places—all with prime views of the cityscape or waterfront which helped me "open up" the look and add some production value to my low-budget production.

In other situations, it might be shooting with your camera under a pier at Venice Beach, shooting through an open side door with your camera hidden inside a minivan, setting up your camera close to and just behind the massive beam at the base of the Brooklyn Bridge, just down a hill off the roadway with a beautiful vista of the city below. In almost every town I've ever been to, there are little hidden nooks and crannies with beautiful views of famous landmarks, mostly around abandoned structures of one type or another known to the locals but otherwise unnoticed by everyone else. It's generally the type of place where locals go to smooch or party (perhaps both) on Friday nights.

A perfect shooting spot to capture the waterfront and breathtaking Manhattan cityscape in a "borrowed" location in Brooklyn. Notice the embankment on the left shielding us from easy public view.

The key to shooting there is careful location scouting beforehand, taking pictures to decide exactly where you want to set up, and going there already knowing and prepared to shoot exactly what you came for in the minimal amount of time, just in case you do get kicked out. In every case that I've done this, I've always got my money shots and left before anyone even knew I was there. One big caveat here is that you always make safety a top priority when shooting anywhere near abandoned structures. (They are usually abandoned for a reason.) There are often rotten beams of wood, broken glass, tight squeezes through barbed-wire fences, etc., that must be navigated just to gain access to these hidden urban oases. Use a little common sense and caution here. It's best to go with a local who knows the place already. No shot, no matter how cool or beautiful, is worth 12 stitches and a tetanus shot.

CHAPTER 6
WEDDINGS

Know this: the video *is* the memory. Weddings are seminal, life-changing events for people. Their whole life has been spent dreaming, imagining, wondering what this day would be like. And now some 20–30 years later, the big day is finally here. All the plans, meetings, tastings, and arguing over details are done, and this is the big reward...and it goes in a whirlwind. In a few quick hours, all the people the couple know and love most from all over the country—maybe even all over the world—gather in their honor to celebrate. The happy couple will be carefully groomed to look their very best. The place will be decked out to their specifications, and perhaps tens of thousands of dollars may be spent on a lavish half-day party. The cruel twist to all this joy and expense is that the happy couple at the center of it all will probably remember very little of it. (If you're married, you already know this.) The day is just too emotional, too full of event details, expectations, ceremonies, old friends, and new relatives, not to mention a hundred whirlwind conversations, toasts, and well wishes that the couple simply can't process and retain most of it. And yet it's "the most important event" in their lives.

So you have to be there to capture it in all of its love, hope, and glory. They are counting on *you* to capture all the tender and fun moments they missed or won't remember. They want you to hone in on the people they love most and show them at their best. They want you to show them all the fabulous food and atmosphere that they paid an arm and leg for. They want you to capture their memories. And not necessarily the reality of the situation, but rather the fantasy, the fairytale of the wedding.—Everyone looking and feeling their very best gathered in the spirit of everlasting love and family.

Find out your bride and groom's "fairytale" vision of their wedding and then capture that story on video, put it to music, and make them fall in love all over again. That to me is what a good wedding video should do—not just reflect the events of the day, but actually make people remember why this day was so important to them, who came to celebrate with them, how much fun it was, why they fell in love in the first place. Show them at their very best surrounded by the very best. Sell them their wedding fantasy in pictures, words, and music. If you can make the couple and their families laugh and cry several times throughout the video, you've done your job well.

> Wedding days come and go in a flash of emotion and activity.... In the end the video *will be* the memory.

Remember, ultimately, the video and photos are the record of what happened, regardless of what *actually* happened. As time passes, what people are going to remember most is what's in the video and photos. Capture the whole experience in its very best light. The theme of any wedding video is always "Love and Happiness." *That's* the story you want to tell.

IN THE BEGINNING

The Golden Rule of Wedding Videos

There are a number of participants and people involved in the planning and execution of a wedding–the wedding planner, the bridesmaids, the celebrants, the groom and best man, etc.–but make no mistake about it: weddings are all about the bride. Don't be confused by anything else you may hear. *Their* special day is really *her* special day.

> **Rule #1:**
> It's *all* about the BRIDE.

She is the star of the show and will ultimately call the shots on everything that happens. If you have a bad angle and can get only one person's face in the shot, make sure it's the bride. If you get conflicting instructions from the bride and groom, listen to the bride. I assure you that the groom will ultimately lose the disagreement in the end...if he's smart. (Whether he's actually right or wrong is irrelevant.) If you make her happy, everyone else will be happy too. *Why?*–Because **it's all about the bride**. Get it? Got it? Good.

The "How They Met" Montage

Nowadays a wedding video package routinely encompasses more than just video of the event itself; it can also include other events that help to tell the whole STORY of the happy couple's life from childhood to engagement. You can tell this story simply as a short musical montage of still photos. Or, if they are really paying the big bucks, you can make a mini-documentary with still photos; home movie clips; and interviews with the couple, friends, and family with tender and humorous anecdotes about how they met.

  This video is usually screened for the wedding guests at the rehearsal dinner or reception. And it can later become the opening minutes or a separate chapter of the full wedding DVD. A photo montage is a fairly simple affair that can be put together in an hour or two if the photos are already digitized, longer if you need to shoot them or scan them into your computer. The particular goal with this part of the process is to visually tell the story of the couple's backgrounds, how they began dating, and to make the couple fall in love all over again.

  Your fondest wish when creating a wedding story is that one day, years after the initial romance has given way to daily routine and the hard work of marriage, the couple will pop in this video and remember and *feel* why they fell in love with each other in the first place. You're creating video foreplay of the best kind...love.

Keys to Make 'Em Cry

1. Ask the bride and groom for photos from their childhood, teenage years, dating years, and a few recent photos. Having 20–40 is a good range. It's also important to get the couple to date the pictures as best they can so that you can edit them in chronological order.
2. In addition to pictures of the couple with each other, make sure you include a few photos of the prospective bride and groom with their best friends, favorite relatives, pets, cars, and places...whoever or whatever has played a major role in their lives.
3. Add just the right tender music for the final touch of sentiment and edit the pictures together using slow dissolves and other appropriate transitions.

Hear this: Shooting a wedding video is no different from approaching any other documentary shooting. All you're doing is telling the *story* of what happened on that day. You want to cover the whole story from beginning to end starting off with preparations to the final farewell at the end of the night. Always ask yourself, "What images and sounds best capture the *story* of the day?" And the story of weddings is always love. Love between the bride and groom. Love between family. Love between friends. It's just a big room full of love and well wishes…and even if it's not, your job as the wedding video director is to make it *look* like it was. Use your awesome skills of observation and filmmaking prowess to craft the narrative of the wedding.

> **Rule #2:**
> Your job is to visually tell the story of the wedding.

What Style of Wedding Video Will You Create?

❑ **Documentary**—Polished documentation of the story, generally edited in order of continuity. A documentary approach produces a polished retelling of the wedding day events.

❑ **Cinematic**—This style of videography and editing captures the event with a particular eye toward dramatic storytelling and artistic flare. Shallow depth of field, soft FX filters, special FX transitions and creative camera moves are all more cinematic storytelling devices.

❑ **Experimental**—Experimental wedding videos get funky with it. They may be nonlinear, shot in black and white, involve re-enactments or fantasies, or they might be impressionistic wedding music videos. They are, in short, experimental artistic impressions of the wedding that usually reflect the personality, style, and/or sense of humor of the lucky couple.

❑ **Traditional**—This is your standard old-school wedding video shot and edited from beginning to end. Usually in linear order with minimal editing used mostly to cut out moments when nothing is happening. Most events are shown fully intact from beginning to end, except the reception, which is usually condensed to key moments.

❑ **Short Form**—Short form videos condense the wedding day down to a tight 2–15 minute piece that captures the highlights and essence of the day.

WEDDING VIDEO APPROACH

VASIA MARKIDES, DOCUMENTARY FILMMAKER/FREELANCE VIDEOGRAPHER (www.vasiamarkides.blogspot.com)

APPROACH

I'm a documentary filmmaker in origin. I think of wedding videos in terms of creative documentation, not trying to make it something more flashy and exuberant than it is, but by capturing the moment depending on how the couple organizes their wedding. If it's something lighthearted, then I would make the video cater to that style. If it's something more formal like a Catholic wedding in a church that's really extravagant, I would tend to make it more formal and less whimsical. I read the couple and what their style is and I cater my own aesthetics to that. For a beach wedding, I would try to be more experimental with the shots. For a traditional Jewish wedding, I would focus on the dancing, the ceremony, and the ritual and all the things that are important to that type of ceremony.

THE INITIAL MEETING

The first contact comes mostly from word of mouth, friends of friends, or Craigslist ads. They contact me or my business partner, who is also the photographer. We'll arrange to have coffee with them and get a sense of what type of people they are. During that initial meeting, we'll talk about what they're looking for. We'll show them some of our work samples and go from there. Usually we only meet with them once and then arrange the date, and we'll continue to be in contact via email or phone. We tend to be more drawn to relaxed clients, so it's usually not an intense process. We've been pretty lucky in terms of it being an easy and a very smooth process. They trust that we'll do what we'll do, and they usually just want us out of the way. They don't want us to be a distraction to the ceremony or ordering the wedding party around. That's how we advertise ourselves—as inconspicuous—documenting the event, but we're not there to *orchestrate* the whole thing.

THE CONTRACT

I didn't always use a contract, but then I realized that it's a necessity, because it helps avoid misunderstandings and extra unpaid work. Make sure that you get a down payment— 1/3 up front, and 1/3 the day of the wedding. Then collect the balance when you deliver the final product to the clients. Make sure the contract includes the number of DVD's you'll deliver and whether or not you will be giving them the raw footage as well. (Usually, I'll keep the original master recordings.) I typically deliver 4 DVD copies with menus.

For one of my first wedding videos, I made the mistake of not including a menu. Not surprisingly, the clients brought it back and requested a menu. These are small, but really important details. You want to establish your clients expectations early on, so they don't come back to you and ask for extra copies or a new version. If they do, remember to factor in the extra costs in the contract. For example, "There's a charge of $50 per extra DVD after the four initial copies." Also include any charges for making additional changes once the final product is delivered. You could charge an additional $50 an hour (or whatever your rate is) for editing; this rate should be specified in the contract.

Typically, I offer a 10-minute version and an hour-long or full-length version of the video. The short version is for friends and quick viewing. The longer piece is for the family and really close friends who want all the intimate details. Make sure the contract clearly spells out the final deliverables.

EDITS

If there is something blatantly wrong with the video, I would fix that for free. However, this shouldn't happen all that often if you're a professional and know what you're doing. If the clients are nit-picky, and they want a small change (for example, if they don't like the song), I'll change it at no charge. Before the event, I usually ask them for samples of music that they like; music tastes are so particular. I ask them to send me their favorite songs, or choose music based off the soundtrack from the reception. If they don't have suggestions or samples, sometimes I add my own experimental music; I tend to prefer instrumental tracks.

CAMERA LIGHTS

I don't use camera lights because we want to be as unobtrusive as possible. However, it can be too dark in the reception room to capture footage very well. If you're not using camera lights, you need to have a good camera that performs well in low light.

I may mask the low light issue by making the reception images black and white and popping up the contrast. Otherwise, it can look like crap. It's also in keeping with my more artistic style. I have the freedom to do more creative things like that, and my clients have always responded well to it.

AUDIO

I may position mics on stands nearby and do a sound test at the venue. The ceremony is usually projected through speakers, so it sounds pretty loud. If I also attach a shotgun mic to my camera, I can capture audio from the camera's perspective.

If it's an outdoor ceremony and the audio is trickier, I'll put the mic on a stand closer to where the ceremony is happening, and I'll stand back with the camera. I've also recently started using wireless mics which are ideal for wedding ceremonies.

SCOUTING THE WEDDING VENUE

✓ Always try to scout the venue ahead of time.

✓ Try to check the lighting conditions at the same time of day as wedding.

✓ If you can't get in, try to at least look in from outside.

✓ If you can't get to the venue beforehand, try to get digital pictures of the venue from the venue's website or have the clients email them via smartphone.

✓ Look for the best camera positions and electrical outlets if you will need them.

✓ Check to see if you can get an XLR audio feed from the P.A. system. Even so, have a backup audio system, such as a wireless mic or hardwired mic on a stand, as the reliability of audio systems and technicians can be hit or miss from venue to venue.

✓ Draw a simple diagram of the layout and wedding party positions. Use it to plan camera placements and audio coverage.

> It's important to scout the wedding location ahead of time, preferably at the same time of day.

✓ Go over any video "house rules" for the church or venue and plan accordingly.

Get a Point Person

You want to have a point person, someone other than the bride or groom, who can act as their representative and a tour guide to who's who and which elements of the wedding are most important to the happy couple.

Typically, this person may be a bridesmaid, an aunt, or other relative of the bride or groom, a wedding organizer–pretty much anyone who's not as occupied as the wedding couple that knows the crowd or couple's wishes well. This person doesn't need to stick by your side, but just be your go-to person when you have questions about who or what to shoot.

In the best-case scenario, these people will keep you informed of what's coming up next on the schedule and help make sure that you're in place for the various ceremonies, traditions, and preplanned surprises. Ask the couple ahead of time to appoint a point person who can assist you with information, particularly during the reception.

Identifying Key Characters

There may easily be anywhere from 50–200 people at any given wedding. In reality, the bride and groom may only actually *care* about a handful of people in the whole crowd.

Your job is not so much to capture everyone who's there, as it is to capture all the people who are *most special* to the clients and give a general sense of everyone who was there. To capture the best product for the bride and groom, you need to identify who the "key characters" are in the story of this wedding. Get these names from the bride and groom in your initial meeting with them; then have the point person point them out to you at the ceremony and reception.

Get lots of shots of the crowd, but make sure that you get these key characters in action–dancing, laughing, hugging, etc. Look for and try to capture those golden moments with these people from across the room. These are the moments that the bride and groom will cherish: their father dancing with the flower girl, Uncle Al doing his famous

> Get a "point person" to help you identify key characters and keep you updated on the program.

Al Pacino impersonation from *Scarface*, Aunt Ida nodding off at the table. Apart from the ceremony, these are the moments that will make your clients laugh and cry, and recommend your services to their friends. These are the moments *they* most want to remember. Give them as many as you can get, and you'll have very happy clients who will send you even more clients to make happy!

The Rehearsal

Attending the rehearsal is very wise and valuable for anyone shooting a wedding. Although the basics are often the same, ceremonies, house rules, lighting, audio systems, and blocking are always a little different from wedding to wedding, church to church, and clergy to clergy. Everyone does things a little bit differently and likes to add their own little twists. If your client is adding a twist, it's going to become apparent at the rehearsal.

Look for lighting issues and potential shooting problems during the rehearsal.

In fact, if almost anything of significance is going to happen during the ceremony, it will come up during the rehearsal. This is your best time to ask questions, plot camera positions and coverage, anticipate surprises, test the audio system, check the lighting, and go over anything else of importance before the crucial day. This is when you solve production problems by *anticipating* them. If you wait until the day of the wedding, you may find yourself dealing with all sorts of nasty surprises from unprogrammed performances to audio interference to giant balloons blocking your camera position. You can easily avoid or plan for many of these issues ahead of time by attending the wedding rehearsal and going over the program with the organizer, point person, and/or bride and groom.

The Celebrant

An often-overlooked consideration in shooting wedding videos is the preacher, priest, pastor, or person conducting the ceremony otherwise known as the "celebrant." In the case of traditional weddings in churches, synagogues, or other houses of worship, make no mistake about it, these are the people in charge. You, the bride and groom, the wedding party, and the invitees are all simply *guests* for the day in that house of worship. It is not just a wedding venue, but a holy place to the people who worship there, and especially the celebrant.

In a place of worship, there may be certain areas or aspects of the ceremony that may be off-limits for you to shoot or to shoot from. Most notably, you may be banned from being on the dais or altar where the celebrant and bride and groom are standing during the ceremony. You also may be banned from shooting any "calls to worship" where the audience is invited to come up front and pray.

Again, every church and celebrant is different. Your job is to find out any special rules or considerations of the church *ahead of time* and stay on the celebrant's good side. Ask the celebrant about where other videographers have set up in the past and get their input on camera positions. Often, they will be the most familiar with the best places to catch the action, and they may even suggest some angles you may not have thought of. Remember, they've already done this countless times over in that location. Don't reinvent the wheel. Tap into their previous experience of what's worked best for other videographers in the past. If you shoot at the same church more than once and/or make a good impression, the celebrant may even start recommending your services to future brides and grooms. Always focus on the big picture.

*All wedding photos by **Vasia Markides**, **Sonya Artis** and **Anthony Q. Artis**.

WEDDING LIGHTING CONDITIONS

Another important consideration is the lighting conditions of the church or wedding venue. Lighting in churches can vary from full beams of heavenly sunlight blasting through massive sky light windows above to dim, moody candlelit chapels. It's important to get some idea of the lighting in the wedding location beforehand. Observe, shoot tests, and/or ask about lighting conditions during the rehearsal to avoid surprises.

However, if the rehearsal is not near the same time of day as the wedding, it's a good idea to try to stop by the church for a few minutes during the actual time of day as the wedding. You also want to check with the organizers or celebrant for any special lighting, such as candles or theatrical lighting, that might be planned for the wedding day.

Most importantly, you want to make sure that the camera you are using can handle the lowest lighting conditions you will encounter during the wedding. While wedding ceremonies vary from bright to dim, receptions are much more likely to be more low-key romantically lit evening affairs.

It's not uncommon for reception halls to have no windows and to be completely lit by artificial lighting, which is frequently set at a level that's less than ideal for video recording. If this is the case, you should see if the couple is willing to compromise on the lighting and raise the levels a little more, so that you can better capture the action. (Some will and some won't, depending on how much they value the live experience vs. the video memory.) If they'd rather keep the lighting low, make sure you explain how it may look on video, so there won't be any disappointments at delivery. Better yet, try to shoot a little footage in the low light conditions and play it back for them to make sure it's a look they can live with. Remember, your ultimate end goal is **happy clients** and occasionally that will mean *not* getting the best shot, but rather the best solution that works for your clients.

However, there are a few different tips and tricks you can use to get better results under low lighting conditions listed on the following page...

Check the lighting conditions of the church or wedding hall beforehand. Use a camera that's good in low light.

Add More Light

One of the unavoidable realities of shooting wedding videos is low-light situations. Here are several ways to overcome low-lighting issues. The easiest and most practical thing you can do to deal with a low-light situation is to add more light. This can often be accomplished by turning up dimmed lights or turning on additional lighting units if they are off. The big problem with this solution is that it might also compromise a carefully planned low-key romantic mood that the organizers planned to set. Your best bet is to discuss the lighting with the couple and/or organizers well ahead of time and try to work out a compromise that will preserve the mood but still provide you with enough light to get a good video image.

Shoot Wide

 Telephoto lens settings suck up more light. Shooting with your zoom lens at the widest setting is also another way to get more light into the camera. Rather than zooming in and out to adjust your frame, move the camera closer or further away from your subjects to reframe shots.

Decrease Your Shutter Speed (Slightly)

Taking your shutter speed down a setting or two from the normal 1/60 will increase the amount of light going into your camera, which will brighten your image. Normal settings are 1/48 (for 24fps) or 1/60 (for 30fps). However, it's common for shooters to use shutter speeds a notch or two lower than these (i.e. 1/32 or 1/24) to let in more light. The trade-off with using a slower shutter speed is that faster motions will appear blurry or surreal if the shutter speed is lowered too much.

Use the Gain Function

The 3-chip prosumer cameras have a gain function that artificially brightens the image. The gain can be adjusted in steps from very little brightening (3dB–6dB) to major brightening (12dB–18dB). However, the big trade-off that comes with gain is video noise, which is a lower-quality grainier video image. Use only as much gain as you need.

Use a Camera Light

Onboard camera lights are small battery-operated lights that mount on top of a camera to illuminate subjects' faces. They are commonly used in broadcast news and in event videography. They are ideal for subjects 5–10 feet away from the lens, so they work best for medium shots and close-ups. The downside to the onboard camera lights is that they do look less natural and call more attention to the camera. Dimmable LED lights are your best most natural-looking option.

Use a Fast Lens

If you are using a DSLR or other camera with an interchangeable lens, use only a **fast lens** that can shoot at f-stops of 2.8 or lower for the best low-light results.

POSITIONING YOUR CAMERA

One of your primary considerations when scouting the wedding venue will be to find the best position to plant your camera to capture all the action…and most importantly, the bride's and groom's faces. Your best available camera angle will be affected by factors such as the "blocking," or staging, of the wedding party; how many cameras you're using; the number of camera operators; and "house rules" about videography.

If you are shooting a single camera on a tripod, look for an angle that will allow you to get the bride's and groom's faces and still pan over to get shots of performers, readers, and guests. This could mean shooting the couple and celebrant at a slight profile, shooting over the shoulder of the celebrant, or shooting the couple with audience in the background. It's always easier if the couple stands facing each other at the altar (Example A), but they may also be staged facing the guests (Example B), or with their backs to the guests (Example C). Some people don't like to face the guests because it makes them more nervous. Still other people consider it rude to turn their backs on the guests.

Example A:

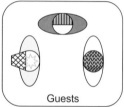

Guests

Example B:

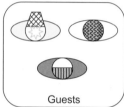

Guests

Example C:

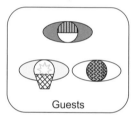

Guests

PRO: You can get the bride's, groom's, and celebrant's faces in the same shot.

CON: You will get only a profile of the bride or groom.

PRO: You can get the bride and groom in full frontal shots.

CON: You will mostly get the back of the celebrant's head.

PRO: You can get the couple's faces and the audience *from the altar.*

CON: You will be shooting the backs of the celebrant's, reader's, and musicians' heads.

Generally, the blocking or staging of the bride and groom will largely be a matter of factors beyond your control. The trick is to understand how to get the best camera angle no matter how the wedding party is positioned. As with everything else when it comes to weddings, remember Rule #1: *It's all about the bride.*

So when in doubt, first choose an angle that will give you a clear shot of the *bride's* face and most or all of the groom's face; then worry about getting the celebrant, readers, and other subjects in the room. Avoid shooting the couple dead-on. Instead, shoot at a slight angle because this will make for a more interesting composition, and you will be able to get a better angle that show's all of the bride's face and all or most of the groom's face and even a bit of the celebrant's face.

In the worst-case scenario where you are not allowed to shoot from the altar and the bride and groom have their backs to the guests, you may be able to compromise with the celebrant to place an unmanned camera on the altar to get clean shots of the bride's and groom's faces. Remember, this camera will be unmanned, and you probably won't be able to check on it during the ceremony, so framing is crucial. I recommend setting the focus manually for the position they will be standing at. While autofocus might seem like a good idea here, if an altar boy or celebrant steps near the bride's and groom's position, it could easily throw off your shot. You'll have more latitude with manual focus on a wider shot.

If your shot is too tight and your subjects move just a foot or two off their original positions, they could easily go (and stay) out of frame. You could also inadvertently end up with a 45 minute shot of an altar boy's back on an unmanned camera. Make sure politely notify anyone who may stray into the shot where the camera is, so they can avoid this. If you do see it happen *during* the ceremony, try to give them a subtle visual cue to move over as discreetly as possible. To help avoid this amateur nightmare, set this camera on a medium to wide shot with a little "breathing room" for the bride and groom to shift around. And equally important when using unmanned cameras, don't forget to hit the record button just before the ceremony. A remote control is a big help when using unmanned cameras.

Anatomy of a Good Camera Position

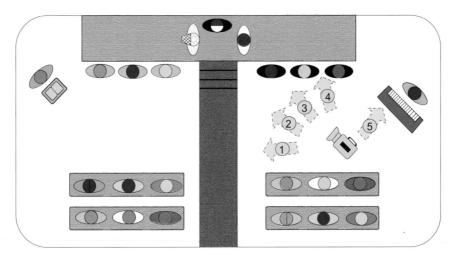

1 – Family and Guests

2 – Bridesmaids/Poems and Readings

3 – Bride, Groom, and Celebrant

4 – Groomsmen

5 – Musicians and Singers

The Establishing Sequence

One important element of the video that shooters often neglect is establishing shots. The irony of this neglect is that establishing shots are so easy to get and can add a much more professional feel and production value to a finished video. You can pop off five or six quick shots in just a few minutes to get enough material to create a nice poetic opening sequence that sets the romantic mood for the entire event. If you want to make visual poetry, don't just shoot an establishing shot–shoot an establishing *sequence*. This is one of the areas where you can really get creative and show off the skills you've honed in your personal work: smooth camera moves, artful composition, macro-videography, clever editing, and juxtaposition. Get busy with it and show your clients that you aren't just another cookie-cutter hack with a camera, but a straight-up visual artist who deserves a professional rate. (And if you *are* just another cookie-cutter hack with a camera, creative establishing sequences are your first chance to start to change that.)

Setting the Mood

Rather than avoiding the seemingly drab visuals of a rainy day filmmaker, Vasia Markides, embraces and incorporates the details and natural splendor of raindrops on leaves, a cloudy sky, and an empty swing set in artfully composed shots.

The Bride's Preparation

As with all events, the wedding is not just what takes place at the altar and the reception. Telling the *whole* wedding story encompasses many other significant moments before and between the main events–from bridal prep to guests arriving to a jovial groom cracking jokes with his groomsmen. These are special moments that the bride or groom may not be physically there to share in, so it's part of your job to capture those moments on video and show them the *whole* story.

Candid Interactions

Supportive best friends complimenting the bride.

Fussing over the flower girl.

A last minute lip gloss check...perfect.

More so than the ceremony, the candid conversations, loving greetings, and rituals before the event are the things that many couples will cherish seeing and remembering. For reasons of budget, transportation, and the logistics of setup, it's not always possible to shoot these moments, but it's worth trying to get even just a few quick minutes of the bride's prep, guests' interactions, or the nervous groom waiting so you'll have yet another important element of the story to help you create a full and vibrant edited video. If you can't be there yourself, splicing in a few still shots from the photographer (or even home video) of these wedding moments can help you visually craft a narrative of the whole event.

The Guests

Wedding guests greet one another at the door and sign in.

The groom's bachelor buddies give him a little good-natured ribbing on camera.

The pews fill up as guests anxiously await the nuptials.

STEALING CUTAWAYS AND REACTION SHOTS

One of the greatest challenges of shooting a live event like a wedding with a single camera is getting enough coverage or different shots and angles of the unfolding action. It's boring to just stare at the bride and groom in the same medium shot for 15 minutes straight. Not only that, but if there is a camera bump, a temporary audio mistake, or a tape change, you will need another shot to cut away to so you can smoothly cut out the bad part of the video. Shooting lots of cutaways will make your end video 5 times better and editing will be 10 times easier. Time and again, having enough good cutaways has saved my butt in the edit room.

But if the action is up at the altar, how can you get a cutaway and *still* cover the bride and groom? Simple, "steal" them and "cheat" them whenever the opportunity presents itself.... Before the ceremony, grab lots of shots of the details in the wedding hall: flowers, fountains, stained glass windows, décor, statues, chandeliers, etc.

> Cheat and steal cutaways and reaction shots whenever the opportunity presents itself.

As the pews start to fill up, go in tight for neutral close-ups and tight group shots of family and friends smiling and looking toward the altar. Whenever there is a switchover or pause in the action for 15 seconds or longer, quickly pan over to the audience to steal cutaways. Get fancy with some pans, tilts, zooms, "walk-bys," and other creative camera moves. Later, you can strategically cut in all these shots to help you condense time, smooth over problem shots, and ultimately create a more dynamic visual story.

Teach yourself to *think* like an editor. Constantly ask yourself, "What visuals or angles will make this scene complete?" For example, a sequence showing the cutting of the cake could involve a single medium or wide shot of the whole four-minute affair from beginning to end... lame. Or with a little foresight, creativity, and camera hustle, you could shoot and edit the sequence like this:

Dynamic Single-Camera Scene Coverage

1. CU–The cake on the table next to flowers and ceremonial cake knife.
2. WIDE–The MC announcing the cutting of the cake.
3. MED–The bride and groom smiling as they approach the table.
4. MED–The happy guests' faces as they look on.
5. MED–The bride and groom make the first cut.
6. REVERSE ANGLE–The bride and groom place the cake on a saucer.
7. CU–Members of the wedding party egg them on.
8. CU–The groom feeds the first piece to the bride.
9. CU–The bride smashes cake in the groom's face. PULL OUT to
10. MED–Bride and groom with the crowd laughing behind them.
11. WIDE–The couple kiss as the bride cleans up the groom's face.

SMOOTH MOVES: THE REVEAL

One of the things that really adds elegance and a feeling of professionalism and production value to a wedding video is having lots of nice, smooth, well-conceived camera moves. By "well-conceived," I mean they have a point, a juxtaposition, a payoff. Having a series of random gratuitous unmotivated pushes, pans, and tilts done simply for the sake of moving the camera is the mark of a first-year film student. But having a series of well-timed camera moves that aid in setting the mood, teasingly reveal new information, and *visually* helping tell the story is the mark of a camera pro. (Yes, the word "story" will appear on almost every page of this book.) As often as possible, every camera move should be crafted to have a payoff by revealing new visual information to the audience.

The Pull-Out Reveal

We start off on a nice close-up of the bride's face as she puts on an earring. We pull out to reveal it's actually her reflection....

...We continue to slowly and smoothly pull out to fully reveal the graceful curls of her hair and just hints of an elegant wedding dress....

...We continue that butter-smooth camera move to reveal a more full picture of the bride. BAM! That's the "visual payoff," baby!

The Rack-Focus Reveal

Look at this fine champagne being poured in a sharp, clear close-up in the foreground....

...We begin to rack focus from the golden glasses of bubbly in the foreground to some fuzzy figures in the background....

...We complete the move to reveal the loving bride and groom snugly nestled in each other's arms in the corner. BAM! Payoff.

Your camera moves should not be gratuitous but should always have a visual payoff.
Visual Payoff = Video Pay Day.

If you are shooting the bridal prep, you will have a move from her house or hotel to the ceremony and, more often than not, there will also be a move from the ceremony to the reception. Many wedding videographers just fade down from one and fade up to the other in the edited video, which is *okay*. But wouldn't it be a lot more cinematic storytelling if we included some nice creative shots to *get* the audience from point A to point B? (The correct answer is "yes.") If you aspire to make documentary and narrative projects beyond just weddings, I say take every opportunity you have to hone your storytelling craft and approach by treating every wedding as if it were a straight-up cinematic documentary that's going to play on HBO next week. How would you should shoot it if you *knew* it was going to premiere on HBO next week with your name on the front credits as director?...Well, that's exactly how you should shoot it right *now*. I say play for keeps, every time. It's how we get better.

Even if you don't aspire to greater filmmaking heights, surely you aspire to greater client referrals and making more money. The key to both goals is creating a final product that's a step above the generic wedding video competition. When you can consistently create a better, more creative, more well-rounded custom story for your clients, you can raise your rates and still get regular bookings. Again, just like establishing shots, these transitional shots don't have to be a lot of work; they just require a little forethought before you leave the parking lot. The basic elements are the couple's departure, the journey, and their arrival. You can always throw in some establishing shots, too.

A Simple Transition

The wedding party boards a trolley to the reception.

The camera points out the window as roadside greenery whizzes by in a blur.

Still shooting out of a moving vehicle, we see the sign establishing our new location.

The bride's face close up as the criss-cross textures of the Brooklyn Bridge whiz past on the way to her wedding.

The bride finally arrives.... Always a good "money shot" if you can get it and still get back inside ready to roll before she comes down the aisle. (Hint: Have your assistant shoot it.)

By running a little ahead and walking backward with an assistant spotting you, you can get a nice moving shot of the bride and groom walking to or from a location.

A DOZEN WAYS TO GET ARTSY WITH IT

A lot of filmmakers dismiss shooting weddings as a boring and predictable endeavor that's beneath their skill set. I say, if the video is boring, it's because it was shot and conceived that way. Instead, constantly focus on how you can show things in a way that *is* fresh, visually interesting, and gives your skills a workout. If you're such a creative artist, you should be able to paint any scene and make it look hot. Show and prove it. Grab your brush (camera) and get to work creating *art* in the medium of wedding videos.

Black and White

Editing some sequences in black and white is a classy touch that can also help mask problems such as low light or poor color.

Low Angles

This low angle offers a different and dramatic viewpoint. The blades of grass in the foreground also add a real sense of depth.

Through Curtains

This handheld shot taken through a sheer curtain gives it a voyeuristic feel and creates a dreamy, romantic look akin to a soft filter.

Lens Flare

Shooting on a wide lens and pointing your camera toward the angle of the sun can create some beautiful natural lens flare.

Translucent Foreground

Translucent materials such as glass and fabric can be employed to artfully play with light, color, and composition.

Silhouette

Shooting and exposing for a bright background when your subject is in low light will create a sharp, well-defined silhouette.

Frame-in-a-Frame

Look for opportunities to compose a
frame-within-a-frame shot as a creative way
to isolate and highlight people in your scene.

Split Screen

Split-screen editing is a fun way to convey multiple
scenes in a short time frame. Several simple shots
are combined to create a single screen that is
much more visually engaging and complex than any
of the source material that makes up this edit.

Converging Lines

Try to create as many shots as you can like a master
painting by using the rules of composition to complement your subjects and draw the audience's eyes where
you want them to look. Here, converging lines lead us
straight to the bride and then the bridge.

Extreme Close Ups

Here, the scene shifts from black and white to color just
as the bride slips the ring on the groom's finger,
signifying a colorful new beginning. These techniques
aren't used just for the sake of doing something cool...
they are used for the sake of *storytelling*.

Color Shift

A simple way to get artsy is to look for extreme close-up
details that reveal setting, texture, or little magic moments
that otherwise set the mood. A single bead of wax dripping
down a candle or raindrops on a leaf as the sun breaks
through are visual verses in the cinematic language of film.

Dutch Angles

Just as the camera shouldn't always remain locked down, it
shouldn't always remain level. Twist your wrist and capture
a few Dutch (diagonal) angles to add a little energy and
perspective to an otherwise ordinary shot.

DETAILS DETAILS DETAILS!

Capturing the moment is doing your job. Capturing the *fine details* is doing it well. The moments make up the story, but the details make up the story of the moment. (Yes, it's like the movie *Inception*–there are stories within the story. Am I totally blowing your mind?)

How do you capture details? By developing a filmmaker's observant eye. You should always be scanning for the interesting within the mundane, the beautiful within the plain, the micro within the macro...the extraordinary within the ordinary. These little shots not only aid in your storytelling, but also aid in your editing by always giving you something interesting and artistic to cut away to whenever you need to condense time or cover up a visual mistake.

The wedding program that just happened to be next to a flower.

The pouring of the bubbly before the first toast.

An ancient statue looks on the proceedings.

What an immaculate and unique table-setting.... Good thing you remembered to shoot it.

Every element of the bride's outfit deserves a video moment...even the shoes.

A family heirloom bearing a tiny "M" charm—the first initial of three generations of women.

A stained glass window casts a purple glow on a flower arrangement.

A close-up on the dish as rose petals are sprinkled down the aisle.

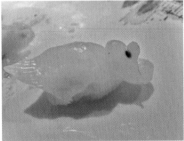
Some crafty chef took the time to make a dumpling that looks just like a swan. The least you could do is *shoot it*!

CAPTURING THE KEY MOMENTS

VASIA MARKIDES, DOCUMENTARY FILMMAKER/FREELANCE VIDEOGRAPHER (www.vasiamarkides.blogspot.com)

THE MONEY SHOTS

I try to get a few shots of their dinner the night before. I'm always there to capture the bride getting ready before the ceremony... doing her hair, makeup, the excitement of her friends. I try to get the little rituals, the bride and her mother...all the little moments of anticipation building up to the wedding. Then I meet with the groom and do a quick interview while he's putting his tie on. I get a few shots of people arriving and waiting around for the ceremony. Another important thing to get are details such as the flower arrangements, the post cards, the invitations, guest book...all the little details they put so much energy into. They are really proud of all these custom touches, so I make sure to incorporate them into my shots.

To me the whole ceremony is a "money shot," so I have to get everything. I definitely don't include everything in the edit, but I want to capture it all so I have plenty of choices. At the reception, you want to shoot: the eating of the cake, the first dance of the bride and groom, bride and father, groom and mother...that whole sequence. I try to at least make sure I get a snippet of all the speeches given by friends. I will usually record most of the reception, but you have to learn how to filter what you shoot, because it's a lot more work editing the footage down in post. With weddings, it's always nerve-racking because you want to make sure you don't miss anything important. But after you get the ceremony and all the money shots, there's the dancing! I love shooting the dancing! That's usually what clients want to see most. That's when people start getting more relaxed and silly. I'll have fun with different angles depending on what song is playing, and I can get more experimental with my shots. You can start having more fun at that point.

In the final edit I include the important moments, but usually leave out a big chunk of the ceremony, because it becomes very dry and repetitive after a while. I'll include anything the bride and groom say. I'll cover any extra readings they might have chosen themselves, especially if it's less traditional or if they have someone come up and do a special reading. I try to not include the entire ceremony unless my clients specifically ask for it all in the final video. (I want to be sure to meet their expectations). Most of my clients are relaxed, and just want something that captures the day and the important moments. I deliver the final video on DVD. Some clients also want the master recordings, which is always going to be pre-stipulated in the contract. However, most just want a DVD with a menu. And now with social media, including short digital versions is also a common practice.

The Rites and Rituals

Traditional American weddings will generally have a number of little rituals and traditions that take place during the larger ceremony—from the lighting of candles to the exchange of rings. Depending on the couple's ethnicity and religious practices, there may also be a number of other rituals that may be unfamiliar to you. Make sure you ask in advance about every little candle-lighting, glass-breaking, broom-

jumping, ring-passing, tea-drinking, henna-tattooing, goat-giving, or other special wedding ritual that will take place so that you can be prepared to capture it in just the right way. Try to find out which traditions are most significant to your clients, so you can make sure you cover them well and put them in the final edit. This is where having a designated "point-person" who knows the customs and bride and groom well can really payoff.

The Vows

The vows are the most important part of the ceremony. It's where the promise of marriage is made. Whenever they happen in the ceremony, just make sure you are on a rock-steady shot where we can see the bride's and groom's faces. (Of course, if for any reason, you can only get a clean shot of one face... make it the bride's. Remember Rule #1.) And equally important, make sure that your audio is crisp, clean, and audible.

The Kiss

The vows are important, but the kiss is the real "money shot." Don't screw it up. It's where the wedding deal is sealed, and it's the moment that everyone is waiting for, because immediately after that kiss, the whole church—bride, groom, wedding party, mothers, fathers...everyone—breathes a collective sigh of relief. It's now official. The ceremony is over and everyone survived. The party is about to begin. Just like you do with the vows, you've got to get this moment in your frame perfect every time. Get a nice medium or close-up shot of this moment.

Why You Should Use a Tripod

Ceremonies may be really long, and a tripod can keep your picture rock steady the entire time. You can pan to quickly follow action as it shifts to different parts of the room to cover various readers, singers, and parts of the ceremony. It's much easier on the back and knees. Your hands can be free to write, signal an assistant, or swap out media cards. You can tilt and pan smoothly around the room or just chill and relax a little when the action is stationary.

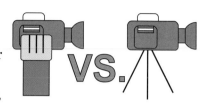

Why You Should Go Handheld

Rock steady can be boring and formal. Handheld is much more dynamic, personal, and subjective. As the action shifts around the room, you can quickly shift with it. You can quickly change positions to cover the action from a reverse angle. You can really "shoot for the cut" and capture a more dynamic scene by grabbing full coverage from multiple angles. You have greater options to get creative with camera moves. A nimble and skilled cameraperson can make it seem like there were three cameras recording any given event of the day with a little forethought and hustle. (One note of caution, if you're going handheld during the ceremony, it's best to have a second camera on a locked down tripod shot, so you don't miss any action while you're moving and resetting your position.)

Why You Should Split the Difference

If you have decent handheld camera skills, I recommend that you switch back and forth during the course of a wedding. (If you don't have handheld skills, read the mini-tutorial on the next page to get you started.) Try going with a tripod for most of the ceremony, which is more formal, and go handheld for most of the reception, which is always more relaxed. Remember, good handheld camerawork takes a steady hand and plenty of practice. And, as I learned the hard way, it's not a good idea to down a big can of energy drink right before you are about to do handheld camerawork.

> Tripods will allow you to get steady, clean shots when necessary, but handheld camera work is more dynamic.

Another challenge of shooting events with an audience is finding a camera position that offers you a great view but does not completely block someone else's view. To avoid audience issues, try to set up your tripod early, so people will know where the camera will be and can sit accordingly. You may also be able to negotiate blocking off a certain section of the seating just for you and the camera. If so, bring up this issue at the rehearsal. When you're going handheld, just keep it moving, changing positions regularly to get the best angle, and you won't block anyone else's view for long.

There are a number of different ways that you could cover audio at a wedding, depending on your particular resources, location, skill level, and the wedding ceremony. It is absolutely *vital* that you get good, crystal-clear audio when recording people speaking. If you record the vows so low that they can't be heard or so loud that they are overmodulated (i.e., distorted, rumbly, and unintelligible), you are going to have some very disappointed clients.

Wireless Lav Mics

The single most valuable accessory you can get to enhance your audio when shooting weddings is a wireless lavaliere (aka "lav mic"). If you mount one of these tiny, unobtrusive mics onto the groom's lapel on the side closest to the bride, you will be able to pick up every word of the vows and every whispered "I love you" crisply and cleanly. Not only that, but you can also pick up the celebrant on the same mic since they will usually be projecting their voice out to the audience (or their voice will be amplified if they use a P.A. system).

Sennheiser Evolution G2 and G3 wireless mics are a reliable option for event videography. They go for about $500 per unit.

Plugging In

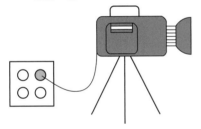

The ideal situation to capture audio from readers at a podium and musicians is if they are using microphones that are plugged into an in-house P.A. system or mixer. You can then plug into their sound system using XLR cables to run the same audio feed going to the speakers *directly* into your camera. This situation is ideal because (a) the necessary mics will already be provided and placed in their ideal location—close to the subject—and (b) all you have to provide is XLR cables and preferably a mixer, but you can get away without a mixer just fine. If you are fortunate, there may be an audio tech person to assist you with setting up a sound feed to your camera. You may also have to switch between mic and line levels or adjust the trim level on your camera's audio input to find the right type of signal. (See also **pg. 282 "Plugging Into a Soundboard"**)

Placing Hardwired Mics

Handheld mics can be placed on a mic stand to pick up speakers, musicians, and/or the celebrant and vows. Similarly, hardwired lavaliere mics can be mounted or taped into position and used for the same purposes. This may require a considerable bit of XLR cable if your camera position is far from the action you're recording. Take note that in some cases, the church or wedding hall where you're shooting may already have microphones that they will let you use. Yet more good reasons to scout your location ahead of time.

Wedding videos are all about emotions and feelings: love, happiness, romance, togetherness, friendship. If you've done your job well, you've managed to capture all these warm and fuzzy feelings in your images, but nothing drives emotion more effectively than the music. What better easier way to conjure up instant sentimental feelings of love and happiness than a familiar romantic tune like, say, "Love and Happiness" by Al Green?

"Love and Happiness" may be the *perfect* song, but it ain't perfectly *legal* to use.

However, while Al Green, The Beatles, or Shania Twain may be the couple's favorite artist, you cannot *legally* use *any* of this music in their wedding video. The second you add copyrighted music to a video, it's called "syncing" (as in "syncing the sound with the picture"). And syncing requires a **sync license.** And, as you may guess, synch licenses are not cheap or even easy to obtain for that matter. So even if your clients were extremely wealthy and willing to pay double the cost of production just to have a single song, chances are you'd still spend many weeks, emails, and phone calls trying to track down the rights and get permission from the publishing company. The general rule of thumb for using popular music in any type of film–narrative, documentary, or corporate–is **DON'T**, unless you've already researched and secured permission.

However, I wouldn't be being straight with you if I didn't also tell you that many people who shoot wedding videos for hire commonly edit in popular copyrighted music–*illegally*. I suspect it's probably as common as shooting without permits. However, just like shooting without permits–it's still *illegal*. And although it does not appear that the music industry is overly concerned with the practice, there's nothing to say that they can't or won't just one day up and decide to mass-prosecute wedding video creators for copyright violation and theft. So proceed with caution if you decide to take this risk. (Remember all the teenagers and college students who suddenly found themselves being sued for tens of thousands of dollars by the music industry for uploading songs to Napster and torrent sites?)

> Although many people do it, it is *illegal* to edit copyrighted music into a wedding video.

If making wedding videos is a big part of what you do (or all you really do) to make money, it's probably not worth the risk to use copyrighted music. Although I was captain of the mock trial team in high school (we got to the state finals), I'm far from a lawyer (we lost). Nevertheless, I imagine it'd be pretty hard to discover and prosecute some guy in suburban Ohio who put Billy Idol's "White Wedding" in his friend's wedding video and then handed it out to close family and friends. Not to mention the bad publicity for the record company and music artist that would ensue. So I suspect that's why it's still a common, if illegal, practice. To play it safe and professional, consider some of the many legal sources for quality music for your productions: royalty free libraries, your friend's bands, licensing sites, live recordings from the wedding band, etc. (See the Superfly Illmatic Bonus Website (www.freelancevideoguide.com) for links to some popular sources of legal production music.)

The Most Important Part: The Vows and Kiss

The entire event is important to the bride and groom, but the vows and kiss are particularly important. No matter what happens, you've gotta get the vows from beginning to end, every word recorded clean and clear, every loving look in sharp focus and rock steady on a good frame. You need to anticipate when these important parts of the ceremony are going to happen. Tape the wedding program to your tripod so you'll know exactly when the vows and kiss are coming up.

Make sure that you still have a clear line of sight to the bride and groom and that no one standing near the altar has shifted position in front of your camera. Check that you have enough battery power in your camera, mixer, wireless mics, or any other accessories to last through this crucial part of the ceremony. Equally important, make sure you have enough record time on your digital media or tape to record all of the vows and the kiss and the newly married couple walking back down the aisle.

Tape and Media Card Changes

Depending on the ceremony, the saying of the vows might be short or run long. A little sermon or drawn-out anecdote thrown in by the celebrant can eat away the minutes. You want to change your media cards or tapes well before it's time for the vows to give yourself at least 30 minutes of recording time. Always keep empty media cards or fresh unwrapped tapes ready to go. Try to change tapes during a *transition* in the program (i.e., changing speakers at the podium, etc.). If you're using

tape, it's also a good idea to prelabel them beforehand or at least as soon as possible after you eject them. Lastly, every time you eject, don't forget to put the record tab on the media card or tape in "save" or "protect" position to avoid accidentally erasing your footage.

Getting Establishing Shots

One of the first things you want to get as soon as you arrive are establishing shots of the church, wedding hall, home, or wherever the wedding is taking place. Get pans, tilts, slow zooms in and out, and close-ups of details such as signs, landscaping, exterior decor, etc. (I often get these as soon as I get out of my car.) Once you get the exterior establishing shots, walk around inside the wedding venue and grab details of the décor and flowers. If the chance presents itself, go back out to get the guests and then bridal party arriving in the limo or at least a nice shot of the limo in front of the venue. Grab video of smiling faces and warm embraces wherever you see them. (See also **Establishing Shots** pg. 254.)

10 WEDDING VIDEO BEST PRACTICES

VASIA MARKIDES, DOCUMENTARY FILMMAKER/FREELANCE VIDEOGRAPHER (www.vasiamarkides.blogspot.com)

1 Roll the whole time. Stay alert and pay attention, so you don't miss an important moment.

2 If you need to go to the bathroom or step away, have your assistant or second camera person cover your camera. Also try to check with the organizer to make sure nothing big is happening within the next few minutes.

3 Before you begin, make sure you talk to the point person or bride so you know who all the important people are that need to be captured on video. (I once had a friend who didn't get shots of the mother-in-law. That was a big mistake.) If you miss the mother-in-law or their favorite little cousin, they're going to be upset when they see the edited video, and you won't have any footage to fix it. There are so many people at a wedding that you might miss that one person that means a lot to the bride. So, make sure you know who all the important people are.

4 Always have fully-charged batteries, backup AC adapters and extra tapes or media cards.

5 You're working in a very tight time frame, so you want everything easily accessible. I recommend a fanny pack so that you're wearing everything you need on you, and don't have to keep running back to your bag and risk missing important moments.

6 Have a good organizational system when shooting weddings, because it's different from anything else you'll shoot. Things happen very quickly, especially at ethnic religious weddings where you may have 10 rituals take place in a single wedding. You don't get many breaks.

7 Make sure you know how to spell the bride's and groom's names correctly.

8 Always send a thank you note with the DVDs to show your appreciation. They entrusted you with a really important task, so extending that gratitude is important.

9 Let them know in advance and incorporate it into the contract if you're going to use an image or a short clip of the video on your website for marketing purposes; you need to have permission to use their footage.

10 In addition to the DVD, it's smart to send them a QuickTime file of the short version of the video, so they can email or post it online. It's just a nice extra little thing to do.

CAPTURING INTIMACY

Once the tension and pressure of the wedding ceremony and formalities have subsided, the happy couple usually starts to relax some and just enjoy one another's company. As the realization that "Wow, we're really married now" starts to settle in, they often begin to dote on each other, gaze into each other's eyes, or steal away for a few moments alone. These first few hours of marriage are full of *visual signs* of love and closeness.... Hang back with your finger on the record button and capture as many of these intimate moments as you can.

Look Out for the Little Tender (Semi) Private Moments

You should always be *fully observing* the scene around you for all the little moments that visually portray the love between the new husband and wife....

Get tight shots of hand holding.

A bride lovingly pats her husband's forehead on a hot summer day.

The bride-to-be greets her groom for the first time.

Love can always be captured in the eyes...no words needed.

The relief and joy of being married start to settle in.

A beautiful bride-to-be quietly contemplates the day as she gazes out the window.

Hang Back and Zoom In

An easy way to capture unguarded intimacy between the happy couple is to plant your camera in some inconspicuous place and zoom in from afar. If you still have the groom on a wireless lav mic, you may also capture their first candid sweet nothings as husband and wife.

Their first few minutes alone.

A romantic stroll through the scenic reception site grounds.

A stolen kiss captured through a sheer-curtained window.

The Groom Awaits His Bride-to-Be

The bride descends from the bedroom room to her waiting groom and family.

A beaming groom sees his bride-to-be all done up for the very first time.

She descends the stairs and greets him with a sweet kiss as the family looks on.

The New Couple Steals Away for a (Semi) Private Walk

We open on an establishing shot of a wet and empty swing set just after the rain.

We tilt up from the sand as the bride and groom walk away in the distance.

We cut to away to a shot of a small boat putt-putting by on the water in the distance.

The camera hangs back as the bride and groom share a waterfront kiss.

We push in close as the newlyweds laugh to realize they are not exactly alone.

We cut to "the payoff" shot revealing a whole gang of groomsmen comically posed and staring from afar.

Bridal Prep Close-up Montage

Here, we dissolve through a series of short close-ups of key moments in the bride's prep—final application of lipstick, the tying of the bow on her dress, and fastening of her shoes. This whole prep sequence may make up only a few seconds in the final video, but it adds so much to the... (I don't even have to say the word now, do I?).

Capturing the Fun

We open on a curious shot of the groom with bouquet in mouth and arms wide. A second later his new bride playfully takes a flying leap into his arms as the two burst out in laughter.

Sure, weddings have their fair share of nervous tension, solemn ceremonies, and serious religion, but most weddings also have a healthy dose of fun. There are two surefire signs that you've made a good wedding video: (1) people watching your video get teary-eyed or cry from some sentimental tender moment you've edited just right; (2) the people watching your video laugh out loud at some fleeting humorous moment that you've captured at just the right time. And the surefire sign that you've made a great wedding video is that it will make your audience laugh *and* cry...and fall in love all over again before it fades to black.

Making your audience cry is mostly a matter of using the right tender music and good editing. However, making them laugh is more about good timing and a little good luck. Always be vigilant for passing humorous moments, happy accidents, and the jokesters in the crowd. There is almost always a good-natured wisecrack from the groom or his buddies, and a few spontaneous and funny mishaps are bound to occur somewhere during the course of the day. (After all, wedding videos are the lifeblood of *America's Funniest Home Videos*!) These fleeting moments of humor and good times are pure wedding video magic....

The new groom rocks a little air guitar for the crowd before leaving the ceremony.

A cute joke gift of his-and-her rubber duckies.

Seeing his bride-to-be, a groom jokes, "She looks even better than on the Internet!"

The camera rolls on a locked-down shot as a cute little flower girl happily runs into and across the frame...

...a few steps later she does a complete face-plant in the dirt. (Guarantee you, they replayed this moment again and again!)

Some videographers charge by the hour, some charge a flat rate, and many offer several different package deals. It's important that you are very clear about exactly how much of the wedding and ceremony you will cover, the cost of additional hours, how the video will be edited, and other basic details. The best way to do this is with a simple contract that states all of these things and the costs to the clients.

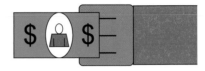

I also highly recommend you request half payment up front and half on delivery. Or you could break it into thirds: one-third due at contract signing before the wedding, one-third due on the wedding day, and one-third due on delivery. Either way, be weary of giving over master tapes or DVDs until you have *the final payment in hand.* Sometimes weddings can go over budget, and you don't want to be left holding part of someone else's bill, so protect yourself with a simple contract signed by yourself and the clients and some money up front.

You may wish to screen a first cut for the bride and groom's approval before making a final cut. If there are any spelling mistakes in your titles or parts of the video they'd like edited out (or back in), music they can't stand, etc., you can fix it and deliver a finished product that you know your clients will be pleased with. Every market is different depending on geographic location, competition, and local cost of living. Research the rates of wedding videographers in your area and price your services accordingly.

> Use a contract to clarify your services
> and prices. Request half payment up
> front and half on delivery.

The reception is a much more relaxed affair. You'll probably want to switch to handheld coverage for most of this part of the wedding. The reception, like the ceremony, has its own distinct script. Consult with the wedding planner ahead of time and write down the order of events if they don't email it or give it to you on paper. This is also where a good point person really comes in handy to help keep you abreast of what's coming up next.

Covering the Spread and Decor

The first thing you should shoot when you arrive at the reception hall is the food and decorations. These will be the first things to lose their screen appeal as soon as the room fills up with hungry and thirsty people. Your clients (or their families) paid lots of dough for the décor and food being served. Get plenty of shots of the details that have gone into making the day special. This means close-ups and smooth moves showing off the flowers, lighting, food, place settings, open bar, colorful decorations, linens, ice sculptures, guest gifts, guest books, and anything else that will help communicate the general flavor of the affair.

How long do you really think this Royal Lobster dish is gonna sit on the table before hungry guests devour it? (I give it less than a minute.) Get the shot!

Traditional Wedding Reception

There are a handful of things that are going to happen pretty much the same at any traditional American wedding. **You should get a copy of the reception plan ahead of time and think through how you will shoot each of the following.**

- ❏ Couple arriving in limo
- ❏ Intro of wedding party
- ❏ First dance
- ❏ Best man/bridesmaid toasts
- ❏ Celebrant's prayer/grace
- ❏ The dinner
- ❏ Dinner speeches
- ❏ Dancing

- ❏ Special presentations
- ❏ Dessert
- ❏ Throwing of the bouquet
- ❏ Throwing of the garter
- ❏ Presenting of the cake
- ❏ Cutting of the cake
- ❏ Changing outfits
- ❏ Bride and Groom address guests

INCORPORATING THE PHOTO SHOOT

Generally, the bride and groom will shoot photos with the wedding party and family immediately after the wedding ceremony. It's probably the only time that all of these particular people—multiple generations, both sides of the family, best friends from out of town—will all be together in one frame and all smiling and still looking fresh. In editing, incorporating "still shots" from the photo shoot will also make for a nice little end montage to transition over to the reception.

Simply position your camera on or near the same axis as the photographer's camera and frame up the shot like a still photo. In postproduction, you can freeze-frame on these poses and add in white flashes and "camera shutter" sound effects to transition from photo to photo. To make it more interesting, throw in some still frames from highlights of the ceremony. Add a touch of appropriate music, and you've got a very nice little creative segment to wrap up the ceremony and lead us into the reception.

A

PRODUCTION

Wedding Videographer Checklist

Before the Wedding

1. __Meet with bride and groom
2. __Get signed contract
3. __Get a deposit
4. __Scout wedding venue
5. __Scout reception venue (if possible)
6. __Attend wedding rehearsal
7. __Check and test record all equipment

Wedding Video Shotlist

Preparation

1. __Shoot bride getting ready
2. __Shoot groom getting ready
3. __Establishing shots of church/venue
4. __Guests arriving and greeting one another
5. __Groom arrival
6. __Bride arrival in limo

The Ceremony

1. __The wedding party procession
2. __The groom awaiting bride
3. __The bride coming down the aisle
4. __The sermon
5. __Readings
6. __Musical performances
7. __The vows
8. __The kiss
9. __Bride and groom exit aisle
10. __Wedding party exits aisle
11. __Bride and groom exit church
12. __Guests throwing rice, blowing bubbles, etc.

The Reception

1. __Announcement of the bride and groom
2. __Best man's toast
3. __Bridesmaid toast
4. __Family and guests' toasts
5. __The cake
6. __The food spread
7. __Cutting of the cake
8. __First dance
9. __Father/mother dance
10. __Apron dance
11. __Throwing bouquet
12. __Throwing garter
13. __Guests dancing

Post-Production

1. __Review footage for highlights
2. __Select Music
3. __Edit long version
4. __Edit short version
5. __Initial screening of 1st cut for client
6. __Edit 2nd cut with corrections
7. __Design DVD menu
8. __Design DVD case and cover
9. __Deliver final DVD(s)
10. __Deliver digital video files
11. __Collect final payment *on delivery*

CHAPTER 7
LIVE EVENTS

Of all the various things you can shoot to put bread on the table, often the most fun and engaging are live events. In the best-case scenarios, these gigs can be easy money in your pocket with minimum setup, little audio hassle, and only a few hours of work. And in the *very* best scenarios, you can get a great seat to a coveted show. (Attention Alicia Keys' tour manager—I'm available.)

However, in the most *challenging* scenarios, live events can be fraught with unpredictable problems, complex audio setups, and coverage nightmares for the uninitiated and unprepared shooter.

The main challenge, regardless of the type of event, is that often this will be a one-time only never-to-be-repeated-in-the-history-of-mankind special live event. So you've got only *one chance* to get it right. You are the main historian, and whatever you don't get on camera effectively *didn't happen* as far as everyone who views the video will be concerned.

And believe me, if you miss a highlight of a live event such as a spontaneous joke, great entrance, pyrotechnic explosion, or standing ovation, your clients—the people who put bread on your table—will notice, and they will most likely be very disappointed. So we always have to make sure that we get a clear sense of what the most important aspects of the event are ***to our clients.*** In my book (you're holding it in your hands right now), happy clients count above all else. Because a happy client is a returning client and a client who spreads word of mouth and makes it possible for us to actually make extra money or maybe even make an entire living making video and getting paid to perfect our real craft: creative filmmaking.

> **You only have one chance to get it right live, so *think* and *plan* ahead.**

5 QUESTIONS TO ASK THE VENUE

Producing a video can make you feel very important, but don't ever forget that you are shooting in someone else's house, and just like at your house, they have their own house rules and way of doing things. When the situation is handled correctly, in the best-case scenarios, the venue workers can be like having extra crew members, but when it is handled incorrectly, the same people can become video saboteurs who make your shoot difficult if not impossible. Here are five critical questions to ensure a smoother gig and enlist the venue's cooperation.

1 WHO ARE THE LIGHTING AND AUDIO POINT PEOPLE?

This question is vital. You simply cannot effectively do your job shooting a live performance without some (if not a whole hell of a lot of) input from the lighting and audio people to find out

crucial information that will help you with the job at hand. Here are just some of the many duties, tasks, and everyday filmmaking problems that these techies can assist you with:

- Plugging into AC power
- Storing and staging your gear
- Borrowing accessories (i.e., adapters, extension cords, etc.)
- Giving advice on specific performers, plus all of the following...

2 CAN I PLUG INTO THE MAIN MIXING BOARD?

It's not always possible, but if the venue already has multiple microphones set up and running into a big, professional 30-channel mixing board with all the levels meticulously adjusted during a sound check, why reinvent the wheel? Just very politely ask if you can get an audio feed of "the mix" to your camera. This one is HUGE on three accounts: (1) it saves you an incredible amount of time setting up the most complicated component: audio; (2) you can get the use and benefit of a few thousand dollars' worth of pro audio gear for free; (3) it will generally sound way better than any of the standard options you could pull off as a micro-production. (See "Plugging into a Soundboard" in the Live Event Audio Cookbook on page 282.)

3 WHERE DO PEOPLE NORMALLY SHOOT FROM?

Don't approach every gig as if you are Christopher Columbus discovering a strange new land and a strange new people. You are not the first person who has ever covered this territory. (Neither was Chris.) While it may be your very first time working in the venue, *other* video crews have shot there before. The venue staff have observed and assisted those crews as well, so chances are that they know which camera positions work best and how to best manage audio and other practical shooting issues. You may also want to ask if they have or know where you can acquire any DVDs or footage of previous shows recorded at the venue. While you may not necessarily want to do things the same as the crews before you, simply knowing, and if possible—*seeing*, what they did could be tremendously helpful in deciding how you wish to approach your shoot.

4 WHAT'S THE LIGHTING GOING TO BE LIKE?

Musical and theatrical lighting schemes in particular can be full of nasty surprises that can make shooting considerably more difficult than you planned. Performers often enter in total darkness and suddenly appear onstage in a place you didn't expect, a portion of a scene could suddenly be lit entirely by bright flashing strobe lights, the area you've set up in under house lights may become pitch black so that you suddenly can't see any of your gear or camera controls...like I said—nasty surprises.

How can you minimize these unexpected obstacles to shooting a good show? You got it: simply ask the people who are behind the controls what to expect and look out for so you can plan accordingly and take appropriate measures. For example, you might need to switch your camera to autoexposure if you know there will be some quick and hard-to-predict lighting changes, bring along a flashlight or set up a small work light in your shooting area, or have your camera pointed in the right direction to catch an actor who magically "appears" on stage. These moments should be a surprise to the audience, but never to you. Occasionally, you may even be able to get the lighting people to adjust the lighting to be more video-friendly, such as leaving the house lights up for a few minutes during part of the show so you can record decent shots of the audience. (Is it starting to become clear why these tech people can be your best friends at a venue and why you should suck up your pride and even kiss their butts a little if necessary?) You really **need** these people to be successful in your job.

Most live music shows will have less-than-ideal lighting conditions. Try to reach a compromise with the act and manage their expectations on what you'll be able to capture well on video.

5 ARE THERE ANY SPECIAL RULES I SHOULD BE AWARE OF?

This is a question that mostly comes into play in larger venues in major cities, which will often tend to be union venues, as in all the employees are required to be unionized workers. This is an area where you should tread very lightly. If you are shooting in a unionized venue, it means that there will be a number of very specific rules (some very impractical and a little silly) that will strictly govern who can do what and when. Simple things like who can unload a truck in the rear of a building or who can touch a light switch are often regulated by union rules. And I can tell you from experience that these guys don't usually take such violations lightly or with much humor. (No joke. I once got scolded for pushing my own button in a freight elevator.) When working in a union venue, make sure you've talked to the supervisor and ask before you do anything. If you willfully disregard these union rules, however nonsensical or trivial they may seem to you and end up pissing these people off, only bad things can happen. (I got two words for you: Tony Soprano.) When it comes to union and house rules, just be deferential and straight up, respect their house and work with them, and they will generally work with you. Keep your eyes on the prize you came for—a smooth and successful live shoot. Follow the rules and do whatever you have to do to pull it off and collect your check.

The Performance vs. The Video

The needs of video and the needs of putting on a good live performance can often be at odds. Some examples: ample light vs. moody dark, camera position vs. audience experience, a clean stage vs. cameras onstage, etc. Bands and musicians often end up effectively sabotaging the quality of their own live performance video by refusing to compromise on things like lighting design or camera position. "Yes, I know you always do that song with all-red lighting onstage and then the two-minute drum solo in complete darkness, but it's going to play like crap on the finished *video*."

Should you ever find yourself saying something like the above, make sure that your clients clearly understand how some of their artistic choices will negatively affect the video product they are paying you to produce. (That way if the video comes out sucky or unusable, they can't fault you.) The best way to avoid this dilemma is to manage clients expectations and clearly spell out what lighting, audio and shooting conditions will work best for the project at the initial client meeting. Stress the importance of the conditions that matter most and educate them on why those things are important for quality. Whenever possible, I like to include it in my **statement of work**.

Audio Quality

One of your primary concerns when covering musical performances will be the quality of the audio. If you read *The Shut Up and Shoot Documentary Guide*, you already know my mantra: "Your audio is MORE important than your video." Well, that's doubly true when recording a band or musical artist doing their thing onstage. If this is a recording that will be sold to fans, act as a demo of their live performance, or become part of a larger film project, the quality of the audio should be as professional and clean as possible.

One of the many reasons I say that your audio is more important than your video is that there are almost always multiple ways that you can record a given situation—each with pros and cons that are often understood only with experience. The size of your crew (often one to three people for these types of gigs), your equipment package, and your time frame will all dictate which audio strategy you use to pull off a live event recording. The next few pages are my recipes for dealing with some common audio strategies for music venues and other live events.

DIFFICULTY: Easy
PREP: 10–15 mins.
CREW: 1 person

Venue
Mixing Board

XLR Cable

Plugging Into A Soundboard

The easiest way to get quality audio is not to do a complicated setup of mics and mixers and leveling everything out, but rather to take advantage of a venue's pre-existing layout of carefully placed mics, mixers, and pre-amps by simply "plugging in" to their sound mix.

More often than not, the people running the show, be it the venue or the act itself, already have every instrument and vocalist miked up, leveled out, and fed into a large, professional mixing board that will be manned (or womanned) by an audio engineer or sound mixer whose fondest goal in life is to make live music sound good. These people are your very best friends at a shoot like this, and you definitely want to stay on their good side because in the best-case scenarios they can (a) make your job twice as easy and (b) make your audio twice as good.

"How do they do this?", you ask. By simply handing you the other end of an XLR cable that is plugged into the output of their giant master mixing board. So whether it's a 30- piece Mexican mariachi band, a 6-piece jazz ensemble or a solo violinist, the audio will be premixed (i.e., levels set precisely for each instrument or vocalist), crisp and clean, and set at just the right level *before* it even gets to your camera.

All you will usually have to do is set the input at the proper level—mic or line. Generally, it will be line, as that's the stronger of the two types of audio signals. Also, if you pick the wrong one, it will sound like total garbage—way too low or way too hot—so it's not hard to figure it out even if you don't already know. There can sometimes be slight variations in how different audio devices process and handle a given signal, so you may need to adjust things on your end for the best results. If you can listen to the sound from the house mixer on headphones, then compare it to the sound you get when plugged in. If your camera has a trim setting for the audio inputs, you may need to adjust it to find just the right level that sounds best on *your* equipment. Similarly, if you are using a mixer with a gain adjustment for the audio inputs, such as the Sound Devices 302 mixer, you may need to tweak the gain level to decrease or increase the strength of the incoming signal until it sounds strong and crystal clear with no distortion.

DIFFICULTY: Hard
PREP: 1hr min.
CREW: 1–3 ppl.

INGREDIENTS:

Multiple
Microphones

Field Mixer

Multiple
XLR Cables

Individually Mic The Instruments

This will usually be your next best *quality* option to plugging into a pre-existing audio setup. However, it's by far your least practical and most expensive and time-consuming option because it gets 10 times more complicated and requires that you have enough mics to cover the size of the performance, as well as your own quality mixer with enough mic inputs to cover the band. So, a one-woman performance on acoustic guitar is no problem. A six-piece rock band, on the other hand, is a big pain in the butt.

Ideally, you would use a separate mic (or sometimes two mics) to record each instrument and vocalist, run it back to your own mixer—which would need to have an equal number of inputs, and then go out of your mixer's left and right outputs into your camera's XLR ports. Just as when recording dialog, you'd have to set the level of each instrument so that it's not too soft or too loud in comparison to the other instruments. Unless you are already well-versed in audio, individually miking an entire band or any setup beyond one to three instruments is probably a task best left to an audio professional who is well-versed in the sound qualities and specific strategies for recording various types of instruments and genres of music. There's a lot to know and consider for each type of instrument and genre of music if you really want to do it right. Alternatively, you may also be able to find a member of the group or a veteran musician who can assist and guide you with the complex task of properly miking the band. (See "Miking Instruments" on page 288 for some basic guidance on miking several specific types of instruments.)

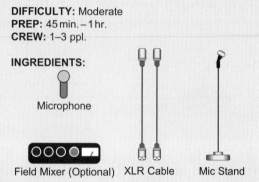

DIFFICULTY: Moderate
PREP: 45 min. – 1 hr.
CREW: 1–3 ppl.

INGREDIENTS:

Microphone

Field Mixer (Optional)   XLR Cable   Mic Stand

Miking The Speakers

If you have only one or two external mics apart from your camera's built-in mic, you're really not set up to get a good audio recording of a musical performance unless you can plug into a clean sound feed from the venue's mixing board. However, taking "no" for an answer is just not the Down and Dirty thing to do, especially if there's money on the table.

So one option that may work for gigs where crystal clear audio is not going to make or break the project is to simply mic the speakers themselves. Again, this is not preferable, but it's a workable solution that can be made to sound fairly decent with a little bit of know-how and a good live mix and speaker system to work with.

To pull off this grimy solution, you'll need to (a) place your mic on a mic stand about a foot or two away from the main speaker and (b) run the XLR cable back to your camera's audio input. Make sure it's taped down and secure. The speaker will be very loud compared to normal audio you would get, so this will generally only work best with:

a) less sensitive dynamic mics
b) a good mixer or pre-amp
c) cameras that have adjustable audio trim, such as the Sony EX-1 and EX-3 models
d) camera models that have a mic attenuation feature which dampens the sound coming into the camera.

The mic attenuation switch is usually found with the mic line switches and indicated by a "–20dB" symbol to indicate the amount of audio level cut down by that switch. The other Down and Dirty solution that may work is to just set your camera's audio inputs on autogain, which will adjust the levels automatically. If your sound is still blown out and overmodulated after trying this fix, try moving the mics back a little farther from the speakers and experiment with your camera or mixer's limiter feature if it has one.

DIFFICULTY: Moderate
PREP: 10–15 mins.
CREW: 1 person

INGREDIENTS:

Shortly
XLR Cable

Shotgun Mic

Shotgun Mic Mounted On Camera

Okay, this is as whack as it gets for recording a musical performance, but *something* is always better than nothing. (I've had both, so you'll have a damned hard time convincing me otherwise...I *know* something is better than nothing.) To be clear here, any of the previous Live Event Audio Recipes should really be your first option if you have the resources to do any of them, but I'm assuming if you're reading this part that that's not the case.

Recording a musical performance from a shotgun mic on the camera (or the internal shotgun mic, even worse) is a real makeshift solution, but there are some things you can do to make it suck a little less than it already does. Here they are in order:

1. Try to use a good external shotgun mic mounted on the camera. (Almost any third-party mic will be better than using the camera's internal mic.)
2. Use the mic attenuation feature if your camera has one to avoid rumbly overmodulating audio (see previous page).
3. As best you can, try to position yourself in a "sweet spot" of the venue where the speakers aren't too far away or too close to the camera to get a good live room sound.

Apart from that, if you are stationed in the audio sweet spot of the club, there's a very good chance that the patrons of that club are also stationed there... and dancing there... and bumping you and your camera there. I recommend standing in front of a wall, column or pole for a more defensible position from the crowd. An assistant could also be useful for guarding the camera position from errant thrashers and drunken "bro's."

RECORDING AND MIXING LIVE MUSIC

JOCELYN GONZALES, FREELANCE AUDIO PRODUCER,
NEW YORK TIMES (JocelynGonzales.net)

The first thing I do is scout to see how big the club is and whether they have their own house sound system. I always try to catch whoever the engineer is and speak with them beforehand. For instance, we are going to record a live set at a venue next week. Thankfully, they have an in-house system. They've got an engineer who is going to be taking all of the different mic inputs and making a nice mix for P.A.s. All I am going to do is take a "feed" off that mix, which is an easy gig. Otherwise, you set the mics up yourself, or you record the room sound. There are different ways you can do it.

If I'm trying to record a band in a decent-sized club, or even if it's small—you can still move around—I usually get a portable stereo digital recorder with two mic capsules on the head to record in stereo left and right. Then you basically want to find a spot in the audience—a chair or table—set it up, tape it down, and make sure that it's not going to vibrate and that no audience members will be coming into contact with it. You can also change the angle of the mic capsules on some models. They are generally set at 90 degrees, but they can be adjusted depending on how wide or narrow the stage is. I try to just get an "audio snapshot" of the stage and the way that the musicians are positioned on stage. You want to pay attention to the digital readout to make sure that the levels are good. (Yes, people can bump into you every once in a while with this method, so you want to try to guard the space around the recorder if you can.) The club is mixing for the center of the room where you are stationed, so it's pretty accurate to what the live listener would get.

The other thing that you can do, if you have a little bit more control, is put up two cardioid condenser mics. (They should be directional, but not quite shotgun, quality music mics.) Place them on stands on either side of the stage about 8 to 10 feet above the stage pointing downward. Then those two separate condenser mics can be fed into a camera or digital recorder by XLR cable. That will give you a closer and more focused sound from the musicians because now we are not *in* the audience, but we actually are up there with the band, so the sound will be more focused, and it's still a stereo image. It's live, so you will still be able to hear the audience behind them, but the sound from the stage will be a bit more isolated.

The third way you could approach it, if you are really in on the planning, would be to be behind that P.A. mixing desk *yourself*, helping to select all the microphones that will go in front of the drums, in front of the singer, etc.; deciding what line inputs you are getting from the keyboard and other electronic devices; and then feeding all those sources into a big mixing console. Now you have individual fader control over each element during each song. Then you can either feed that to a multitrack recorder, or you can take the stereo feed off that mixing console and feed that to your camera or record it separately to a good professional audio recorder and resync it later. You would still record a "dirty" audio track using the camera's built-in mic, but that "dirty" audio would be your guide so that you can sync the picture to your higher-quality audio track later. The audio sync might drift off a little in post, but it's nothing a little bit of compression here and there won't fix.

GETTING THE LIVE MIX RIGHT

How I mix live music depends on what type of music it is. If there are a lot of vocals, the main thing for me is to make sure the vocal track is present on top of the mix, but not sticking out there so far that the band feels diminished. Similarly, I don't want to have the opposite problem where the band sounds big and the singer is buried inside it. The second thing that I find challenging is making sure guitars don't pop out. The guitarists can be somewhat "hammy" and feel the need to be up front. There is ego involved, and they often don't sound check at the same level they intend to play live. They are usually a lot louder live. So when a sound check happens, you usually want to set it and then turn it down some and hope that it's okay. (It's often the same with actors' performances as well.) So we usually mix that stuff quite conservatively because we just know that when the adrenaline kicks in performers put out a lot more energy than in the rehearsal. Or, quite frankly, they cheat in sound check, turning themselves up when the sound person isn't looking. So that's usually the hardest thing, and you always mess it up the first song. So that first song is spent trying to figure out where everyone's real levels are going to be for the show and setting them there. One other thing I would add is that when doing live music, you start to notice that very few vocalists actually understand professional mic technique. There are a lot of bad habits they have picked up from music videos that might look cool but that lead to inconsistent tone, breath distortion, and handling noise.

AUDIO POST ON LIVE MUSIC

With live music, we don't really fix much in post except to maybe redo some of the peaks and put light compression over everything. The compression is just to smooth out the high and low points—the dynamics of the piece where the music gets soft and where the music gets loud. It's just to make them more even, so that if you are listening on your iPod or your computer on a DVD, you won't have to keep turning the volume up and down to do it. If we got a clean signal, usually all I will do other than that is balance the left and right levels so that one is not heavier than the other. I might also **EQ** (**equalize**) a little bit, but I don't really mess with live audio tracks a lot because live music to me is best recorded the way it was. I don't want it to sound like a record.

MIKING INSTRUMENTS

Miking individual instruments is a job best handled by a professional audio engineer, but in many cases due to your budget level and Down and Dirty circumstances, you may find that you *are* the de facto audio engineer. That being the reality, I want to at least offer some basic guidance to help you pull it off.

There aren't too many strict rules when it comes to recording instruments because it all depends on the sound and feel you want. However, your goal should be to strive for the most faithful and natural recording of the instrument. The more you understand about how various instruments create and give off sound, the better you'll be able to find an optimal mic and mic position.

Miking individual instruments takes more time, expertise, and equipment.

Different mic positions will yield different results with regard to elements like room ambiance, bass, or instrument handling noise...it's all situational. Your best bet is to experiment with different mic placements, record, and then listen back to the results. Here are some mic placement basics to keep in mind as you try different techniques.

VOCALS

Vocal mics should be no more than two feet away, but not closer than two to three inches from the singer, depending on the strength of their voice. Too close and it will sound excessively "breathy" or muffled, but too far away and it will sound weak and distant. A windfoam or pop filter can help avoid "popping p's" and "hissing s's," a common problem when people perform close to the mic.

STRINGS

Violins, cellos, guitars, and other acoustic string instruments actually give off sound from the sounding boards (body) and not the strings. The higher frequencies also travel up, not out, so a mic placed at about eye level is ideal for many instruments such as guitars.

WOODWINDS

You can get good recordings from most woodwind instruments by placing your mic several inches from the sound holes. In the case of some instruments, such as flutes, you can avoid excessive noise from fingering of keys and breathiness by placing the mic behind and slightly above the instrument. A windscreen or pop filter can also be useful to minimize breath noises from playing woodwind instruments.

HORNS AND BRASS

Placing the mic just off-axis about one to two feet from the bell (front) of the horn will usually result in a more natural sound. Several instruments can all play into the same mic at once. Recording directly into the bell of a horn will tend to pick up more high frequencies. Backing off the mic some will give you a more full and dramatic sound. Similar to drums, horns are particularly prone to sudden loud blasts, so it helps to know the music so that you can have your finger ready on the **fader** at the right time.

PIANOS

There are many considerations and techniques to record a grand piano, and no doubt entire chapters have been written just on this subject, but for our purposes, I'm gonna stick to the basics. For a simple single-mic setup, you can place the mic facing the rear open end of the piano at about a 45-degree angle. Aim the mic toward the middle of the strings, making sure that it's placed high enough so that there is a direct "line of sight" from the mic to all the strings on both ends. For more emphasis on the low notes or high notes, simply move or aim the mic closer to that end of the strings inside. The farther away you move the mic, the higher it should be.

ELECTRIC INSTRUMENTS

You can mic an electric instrument by simply miking the speaker as described on page 284 in this chapter, or you can use a device called a direct box that allows you to plug an electric instrument directly into a mixer or camera's XLR port. The speaker method allows the musician more control over audio, but distortion is a big potential problem. The direct method puts you in greater audio control but at the complete expense of the live room ambiance.

MIKING THE AUDIENCE

If you're recording a live performance, one often-overlooked aspect of the audio is the *audience* itself. We see and hear the band rocking out, but we also need to hear the crowd's claps, cheers, roars, and catcalls: "We love you, Jay-Z!" The crowd is what makes a live performance LIVE. The crowd is the very energy that the band is feeding off, and if you don't capture their audio as well, you are really capturing only half of the performance. A live show is a collaboration. That's why bands and comedians put out live albums and studio albums; they are two different animals. Ideally, you would dangle a mic (or two) somewhere over the middle of the audience to capture the 'live' element of the show. This is how TV shows with live audiences pick up audience laughter and verbal reactions. A more grimy guerrilla solution that can also pick up the audience would be to use your camera's on-board mic, assuming that the camera is somewhere mid-venue to capture the natural live sound.

For more info on mic placement, see this detailed article on the Shure website:
www.shure.co.uk/support_download/educational_content/microphones-basics.

You're in the Band Now, Baby!

One of the most common mistakes I think new shooters make is shooting a musical performance with a static, mostly locked-down camera. A musical performance really calls for

When shooting live music, your camera is *your* instrument... play it for all it's worth and make that song come alive visually.

fluid and dynamic camerawork to catch the live energy being emitted from the stage. (Actually, it doesn't just call for it–it screams out loud for it!) Good camerawork really becomes *part* of the recorded performance. Although you may not be able to afford a 30-foot long sweeping jib like the ones used to shoot big-budget concerts, with a little practice, know-how, and creativity, you can still pull off a variety of interesting dynamic moves while handheld or from a decent **fluid head tripod**.

It's always best to be as familiar with the music as possible so that you can anticipate (there's that word again) where to place the camera for a cool move. But the reality is that you will often *not* know much more than the type of music, number of people playing onstage, and a set list beforehand. Nevertheless, even if you've never heard the song before, you can still *listen* and *look* carefully and actually *feel* where the song is going. Your handheld camera is your instrument, and you are improvising to the song being played. You are now in the band, baby! Have fun and play *your* instrument along with them. Your camerawork should always strive to complement the tone and rhythm of the music being played.

If you pay careful attention to the rhythm of the music, gestures, eye contact between musicians, body language of the performers, and even the sheet music, it's much easier to tell when the horns are about to blast their chorus or when the drummer is gonna break down the beat to just a snare roll or when the singer is gonna belt out the big finish. And when they do, you're gonna be right there with a nice whip zoom into a 3-shot of the horn section, a smooth tight push-in on that snare drum, or a pull-out from a close-up of the singer's face to a full-stage wide shot as the band plays their heart out and the audience goes wild for the last few notes of the last number of the night.

Over time as you shoot more musical performances, you will develop your own unique vocabulary of live music performance camerawork, and many of these moves will be just like dancing; you won't really think about them as much as feel them and go with them when the music dictates. And in the best-case scenario where you are actually familiar with the music going in, you will be able to plot and plan out where the camera needs to be to get the best angles and coolest creative moves to really create a visual interpretation of the performance. If you do your job well, your camerawork should perfectly dance with and complement the music. You're like the fifth Beatle now! Play your part and show 'em what you got. Study live performance videos and concerts on TV and learn to make your camera do what it do to the rhythm of the music, and your musical clients will take notice and call you back for more. The next few pages are some of the camera moves I think you should add to your live event repertoire.

Pull-Out from Instrument CU

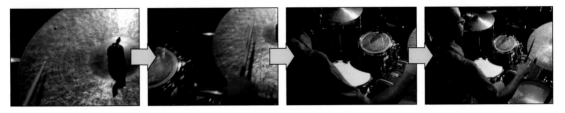

Here, we pull out from a close-up of the drummer gently tapping a solo cymbal to a wide overhead shot as he lets the sticks loose across the entire drum kit. POV (point of view) close-ups like the starting shot here really help put the audience right in the middle of the performance and get a sense of what it *looks and feels* like to be up on that stage. A few well-timed close-ups of the action can go a long way to boosting your production value and breaking up static camerawork.

Push-In for Solo

Whenever one instrument plays a solo or becomes the focus of a certain part of the song, you want to focus in on that particular instrument (rather than the drummer readjusting his snare). A slow, steady push-in will usually do the trick. It's called "directing" because you are directing the audience's attention to the most significant elements. It makes little sense to remain on a wide shot of the full band when only one or two instruments are actually playing.

Push-In from Performer's POV to Audience

Above: A push-in from a wide **OTS** (over-the shoulder) shot of jazz pianist virtuoso, ELEW, to a close-up of his private audience during a preshow warmup.

Remember, your video audience is most likely to be people who weren't at the actual live event, so one of your primary objectives is to re-create the energy and feel of that live event as much as possible. Composing shots that help capture the energy and emotion of the live crowd and their interaction with the performers will help you with this goal. Your camera moves should never be pointless; they should always be timed in response to and/or complement the music or the action in front of you.... Bust a move, don't bust the groove.

Handheld High Angles

Above: All of these dramatic high angles were pulled off by simply raising the camera high above my head.

Raise It Up

Avoid just shooting everything from straight eye-level. Just like a static camera, a static viewpoint also gets old after a while, especially when you're shooting a full concert, so you also want to vary the camera height. From time to time, as the performance, music, and/or your stage position dictate, you will want to try to get some high and low angles. The simplest way to get these is by raising the camera high above your head and tilting the LCD viewfinder about 45 degrees down, facing the ground, so that you can still see the screen from below. You'll also probably get better results by

switching to auto-focus for this type of tricky camerawork. It takes some practice and a steady hand, but using this poor-man's crane position, you can get more dramatic overhead angles, as well as push-ins and pull-outs to and from closer shots. In addition to adding some dynamic movement, executing a camera move while in this position will also help cover up much of the extra shake that may result from holding the camera in this more awkward position. This position will also be necessary at times to shoot above the heads of a rowdy crowd when you are on the floor. As the opportunity presents itself, you may also want to take advantage of ladders, open staircases, catwalks, and balconies to get more dramatic high angles. (Always watch for wires and be *very* careful walking around dark backstage areas.)

Showing Off Technique

Above: Showing off the technique as ELEW plays the piano inside and out.

Any time a performer does something particularly unique or impressive, such as play the guitar with their teeth, spin their drumsticks in between beats, or in the case here—reach inside the piano to dampen the strings for an original sound—you want to make sure you highlight that on video. These moves are demonstrations of showmanship and/or extraordinary talent that often come only with hours of practice and planning. Improvise cool camera moves that complement and show off these crowd-pleasing tricks, and your client and audience will be equally impressed with *your* ability to capture the moment.

Lens Flare

Nothing says showbiz like bright lights. Lens flare is often something we want to avoid, but in the case of music, it often works well as a cool stylistic visual touch. You generally don't have to do much more than zoom out wide, then frame your shot with the stage lights aimed into your camera to get this funky dramatic starlight/flare effect. It will often occur organically, particularly when you are shooting reverse shots from the performers perspectives, since the lights face the stage. It gives the audience a real sense of what it *feels* like to be on the stage—in "all of the lights," as Kanye West put it. Make sure that your lens is clean when you use this technique because light shining directly into your camera will reveal every speck of dirt or dust on the lens and ruin an otherwise slick and glamorous effect.

You can also purchase star filters that really play up this effect, but for most documentary-oriented projects, this would probably be overdoing it. If you do use star filters, I recommend using them for only a handful of shots. Like anything else, lens flare and starry lights are cool only when used *sparingly*. If every other shot has lens flare in it, it gets stale in a hurry like a day-old donut.

Rack Focus to Pull-Out

To set up this move, zoom close up onto an object or subject and defocus; then start the move by (1) bringing the subject back into sharp focus and then (2) pulling out smooth and easy to reveal the full scene in a wider shot. (If you're feeling really wild and crazy, you could also pull out with a quick and flashy whip zoom instead.) Going from a rack focus to a smooth pull-out is a great technique to hold an audience's attention on a shot a little longer as you reveal the out-of-focus image and show the full scene. This technique also adds a little cinematic drama to a scene as the audience waits for the visual payoff.

Whip Zoom

The whip zoom is a staple of MTV, sports shows, and other high-energy stylized video segments. It's the video equivalent of popping a wheely or doing back flips down the middle of the block...completely unnecessary, but nonetheless attention-drawing, cool, and fun to do. To pull off this flashy move, you need a camera with a manual zoom lens. Many higher end prosumer cameras can be switched to manual zoom mode, allowing you to pull (or in this case, "whip") the zoom ring on the camera instead of using the smoother automatic rocker zoom control.

How to Pull Off a Whip Zoom

1. Look for a switch on the camera somewhere under or near the lens that says "Servo" or "Auto"/ "Manual" and put your camera's zoom lens in the "Manual" mode.

2. Move the zoom lever on the lens all the way up and all the way down to find where the lens stops on its widest shot and tightest shot. Take note of the stopping point of the lens and make sure you use just enough pressure to zoom the lens quickly to the end shot you want. Practice the move once or twice.

3. Hit the "record" button. Quickly flick the zoom lever **down** to zoom in tighter or **up** to zoom out wider.

Whip Pan

The equally flashy cousin of the whip zoom is the whip pan, which is so fast that it blurs the scene. To pull off a whip pan, loosen the pan tension on your tripod so that it moves very loosely left and right. Frame your starting shot; then frame your exact end shot and practice swinging your camera quickly from the start shot to the end shot. One way editors use whip pans is to transition between scenes by cutting from the beginning of one whip pan move to the end of another, with the blurry middle of each whip pan masking the transition from one scene to another.

Getting Up Close and Personal

One mistake that I also think a lot of shooters make, especially when they are just starting out, is not getting enough close shots. Close-ups reveal new information, focus the audience's attention, and add drama by bringing us in closer to the details of a scene, cutting away the clutter of a room, and showing the emotion on subjects' faces. They also come in very handy when editing.

Detail Close-ups

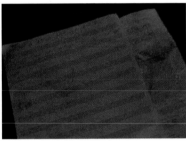

Above: Close-ups (CUs) on details of the space and performance help tell the whole story and give the audience more detailed visual information.

Emotion Close-ups

Above: CUs on performers' faces bring the audience on the stage up close and personal and reveal emotion and magnify the drama of the moment.

Action Close-ups

Above: CUs of performers' fingers strumming, plucking, striking and playing their instruments put us in the action and show off talent and technique.

Make sure you shoot enough close-ups to reveal greater detail, emotion, and action.

MOUNTING SHOTGUN MICS

One of the very first things you'll want to add to your equipment package after purchasing a camera is a decent shotgun mic. I recommend also purchasing a good shockmount accessory like the one here with a "shoe" to mount it directly on the camera and minimize handling noise, especially when you are shooting handheld.

On the cheaper side, you can always use the camera's standard mic mount, but one common problem you may find is that these simple mounts are too big for the particular mic you are using and the mic will not sit still or even stay in the mount once you start moving. A simple broke filmmaker's solution to this problem is to just use some nonsticky gaffer's or camera tape to form a cushion around the mic and hold it tightly in place. This poor man's solution will also act as a very minimal shockmount to absorb *some* of the camera noises and bumps.

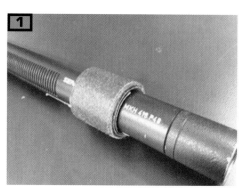

Determine where the mic needs to sit to be balanced in your mic mount; then use gaffer's tape or camera tape to build up a cushion around that section.

Place the mic in the mic mount, adding or removing a few layers of tape as necessary for a snug fit.
(A wadded-up paper towel held on with tape can also be used in a pinch.)

Make sure you've got a snug fit and can securely close and fasten your the mic mount.

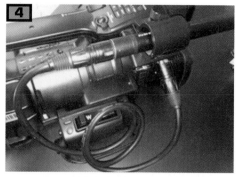

Make sure the tip of the mic is not visible when your lens is on its widest shot. Use a "shorty" XLR cable to connect to the mic to the camera.

Similar to groundhogs, if a cameraperson sees their *own* shadow, it's going to be a long edit session! Stay vigilant of *everything* in your frame.

Try to frame, pan to/from, or zoom in/out to reflections to add some more playful visuals and "payoffs" to your coverage.

A good low angle can be just as dramatic as a high angle and make performers appear larger than life on camera.

Tilt your camera sideways to capture some Dutch angles to add more energy to a shot.

Composing some shots as a "frame within a frame" can also make for more dynamic coverage.

Use foreground objects to add a sense of depth to otherwise plain shots. You can also rack focus to spice it up even more.

Making Single-Camera Coverage Work

The hardest part of covering a live one-time-only event is getting enough interesting shots to cover all the action. To do this the easiest way, I highly recommend doing multiple-camera recordings for any live show or event, whenever possible. However, if you're a broke guerrilla filmmaker (or my *main constituent*, as I prefer to call you), you are probably very limited in your resources and fortunate to have one working camera, least of all several of them.

Perhaps this section of the book should more aptly be called "Attempting to Make Single-Camera Coverage Work" because it's not something that's easily done. In this case, the two biggest challenges you'll face in covering live events, shows, and performances with a single camera is (1) making it *not* look like a single camera shot from a single viewpoint and (2) covering all the action adequately.

> Shooting with multiple cameras is *always* the easiest and safest way to cover live events.

You essentially have to learn to "edit" the sequence in your head as you are shooting it, better known as "shooting for the cut" or "shooting for the edit." The best way to learn to do this is through shooting and editing similar sequences. This is one of those filmmaking skills that you are really going to understand only after some trial-and-error shooting and then editing material together.

After the first few times you attempt to shoot a show with a single camera, every shot you really needed when shooting will become painfully obvious during the editing process as you're trying to make the sequence work. Make it a habit when editing to make mental (better yet—*written*) notes on the shots you "should have" gotten to make the sequence cut together effectively and make sure you get those shots next time out shooting the same type of material.

Once you've burned yourself a time or two by not shooting things that would've taken you an extra 30 seconds on location but now cost you several hours to work around, you'll start to pick up the vital skill of *shooting for the cut* more quickly.

> You have to learn to "shoot for the cut" to make single-camera coverage work.

NEUTRAL SHOTS AND CUTAWAYS

We know that "**shooting for the cut**" is the secret to effective single-camera coverage, but the secret to shooting for the cut is getting enough neutral shots that can be inserted almost anywhere to cover up repositioning the camera, missed moments, and other inevitable **holes** in your coverage of live events. Here's what to shoot and when to steal the shot.

What: A close-up of a performer's face
When: Anytime

What: A foot on a piano pedal
When: During warmup, a less-important song, re-create after the fact

What: Over-the-shoulder reverse angles
When: Anytime

What: A close-up of audience reaction
When: During warmup, a less-important song, re-create after the fact

What: Details of the room décor
When: Before the show, during intermission, after the show, a lull in the action

What: Signage and exterior of the venue
When: Before or after performance—whichever best matches the time of the show

Do One Just for the Camera

Because of these classic conflicts that come up, it's always worth considering a special performance *just for the camera*. Often, this can be done during a final dress rehearsal. While you may not capture the extra energy that comes with a live audience, you could get your camera in places you wouldn't normally go during a live audience performance—like directly in front of the lead singer's face—and steal some good close-ups and reaction shots onstage without worrying about blocking anyone's view or taking the performers "out of the moment" because the performance will now be entirely about doing whatever is best to capture the event on video. So you can cross the stage, get reverse angles, shoot close-ups of fingers on the keyboard, or even have the performers repeat certain actions or parts of their performance, or even repeat the whole perform, if necessary.

THE ANATOMY OF "SHOOTING FOR THE CUT"

So let me try to break down what shooting for the cut actually looks like in a finished sequence. On the next page is a line-by-line illustration of an edited live performance sequence that was shot with a single camera. To pull this off requires great documentary camera skills—essentially getting as much usable real-time footage of a live event as it unfolds while simultaneously changing camera angles and techniques. The goal is to make the finished product a visually dynamic representation of the live event...with the understanding and application of some standard editing trickery.

KEY		
COLOR	**SHOT DURING**	**EXPLANATION**
	■ Realtime like live TV.	These shots are from the actual performance as it unfolded live in realtime.
	■ The same song/scene ■ Another song/scene	These shots are from a different point of the actual live song/scene or even from another song/scene, but "cheated" (i.e., used twice or moved to a different point) to appear as though they occurred at the same moment of the performance that they are edited in. The main requirement is that performers be in the same clothing, lighting, and setting to sell the illusion. (*Switching to a different camera angle makes it much easier to "sell" these edits.)
	■ Anytime the same night ■ Anytime another night	These shots are completely **neutral cutaways** that can be inserted anywhere they are needed to cover up a **hole** in the footage or to make an edit work.

Note: The sequence on the next page reads in rows from left to right.

THE ANATOMY OF "SHOOTING FOR THE CUT"

*Sequence reads left to right.

COVERING THE WHOLE PERFORMANCE

One mistake that some freelancers make is telling only part of the performance story–the part that takes place when the curtain opens and when the curtain closes. A little forethought can go a long way to creating a classy three-dimensional project that tells the whole story of the event instead of just what happened when the curtain went up. "What is the *whole* story?" you ask. Here's just a *partial* breakdown of everything you could shoot:

- ✔ Establishing shot of venue
- ✔ People buying tickets
- ✔ Setting up the venue tables
- ✔ Testing the lighting design
- ✔ People in line
- ✔ Preshow interviews
- ✔ The band warming up
- ✔ Backstage joking around
- ✔ Getting dressed
- ✔ Sound check
- ✔ Audience taking their seats
- ✔ Bartender pouring drinks
- ✔ Tech crew prepping equipment

There's hell of a lot more that goes into a performance than just what occurs on stage. You can always choose to leave out this footage, but you *can't* use it if you never shot it to begin with. Keep your options open in the edit room. This can also be bonus web content or even an effective way to convince clients that they might benefit from hiring you for a larger project, such as a behind-the-scenes doc or an EPK, instead of just a one-time concert video. Always think of the **BIG** picture and how you can entice clients to hire you for more services.

The scene out front

The coveted sold-out ticket

The venue exterior

Backstage arrivals and greetings

Warming up the pipes

The final tech adjustments

THREE SINGLE-CAMERA COVERAGE STRATEGIES

If you've got only one camera shooting a one-time live event from only one angle at a time, you've probably got a real editing challenge ahead of you. You have three basic choices—and all three are difficult, but they can be done with some extra planning and forethought:

1 Shoot for the cut

This is probably the most common way to approach single-camera coverage and best suited to experienced shooters as you have to always be thinking about how everything you shoot will fit into a smooth, cohesive, edited piece with no holes. The problem is that as you move the camera, you will be creating holes in the edit. For a few seconds here and a few seconds there, footage will be unusable because the camera was unsteady, you had to reposition the camera, your view was obstructed, or you needed to switch handheld techniques or clean the lens during some part of the performance, etc. That's why it's always easier to have at least one other camera rolling.

2 Let the whole event play out in realtime in one long well-shot master take

This probably works best when shooting cinéma vérité for more private performances that lend themselves to an intimate in-the-moment documentary feel. The real key to making this work is hiring (or being) a good documentary cameraperson with a steady hand and an understanding of editing with an eye for real-time visual storytelling. Basically, you have to pretend that the camera is shooting a live broadcast. This essentially means that the camera has to always have a good shot and remain fluid. Shooting an entire master take from a locked-down tripod has the strong potential to suck all the energy out of the performance and bore your audience to sleep. If you must use a tripod, keep the tripod head loose and get in as many *smooth and fluid* tripod camera moves as you can—pushes, pulls, pans, and tilts. You need to really control the camera so that you can seamlessly transition from one move to the next without jarring the audience.

3 Shoot a section of the event and shoot cutaways plus neutral and reaction shots during *another* part of the same performance

This is a strategy that you would use when you are short on time or know you'll just be using a representative clip of a performance for something like a band **EPK** or actor's highlight reel. You know the edited version won't include the whole song or scene but needs to showcase some of the highlights.

So if the performance were a play, for instance, maybe you'd shoot just the first 10 minutes of the best and most visual scenes—maybe the introduction of a major character, a funny bit of dialog, etc. Then during the second half of the same scene, you'd get some reverse angles showing the other characters' reactions to the main performer and get some close-up audience reaction shots as people laugh, applaud, gasp, etc. It doesn't have to be their *real-time* reaction to that part of the show, just appropriate to the part of the scene you already shot. (If it were a sad scene, then you would look for audience shots of people looking engrossed or teary-eyed.)

It's also worth noting that if you are covering a major recording artist or a Broadway or off-Broadway production as press, you will often only be allowed to shoot 2-5 minutes of the show, so think carefully about what you wanna capture and what shots you can get from wherever they allow you to place the camera. Make sure you are clear on any shooting restrictions beforehand so you can plot and plan accordingly.

SHOOTING THE AUDIENCE

In addition to miking the audience, you also want to make sure that you get some decent shots of the crowd enjoying the show. This is another one of those elements in the final edit that will communicate the energy and excitement of being there live. Keep these basic considerations in mind:

1 Permissions

It should be standard practice when shooting these types of events to post a group release prominently at the entrance to the venue as well as in noticeable places throughout the club like near the coat check, bar, and bathroom entrances. A group release is simply a large (and preferably colorful) sign in big, bold print informing all the attendees that the entire event and everyone in it will be videotaped and simply by *entering* the venue, they are giving you permission to videotape them as they enjoy the show. This is necessary just in case you inadvertently shoot someone that doesn't want to be seen on video (ex. someone caught dancing wildly who's also in the midst of lawsuit over their back injury). If they decide to sue you, they can't later say they weren't informed they were being taped. It is also a good idea to have the performers themselves announce this near the start of the show to make sure everyone knows what's up with the video crew.

> **NOTICE!!!**
> Plain Jane Productions is shooting a **music video** of The Aperture tonight. By entering this event you are giving **permission** to be **videotaped**. Have fun!

2 Energy

You want to pick and choose which people you shoot in the audience and when. I usually wait until a little into the show to start grabbing most of my reaction shots, because by then the crowd is warmed up and it's clear which audience members are the most animated and into the show. There's always that one dude who's just smiling and bobbing his head to every song and that one chick who's dancing freely in a trance to the music. Find these people and get good close-ups. People often get self-conscious about being videotaped, especially when they are dancing or getting loose, so you might try positioning yourself somewhere in a shadowy corner of the room and zooming in to get the best close-ups of people genuinely enjoying themselves. On the flip side, if you are in a situation where people may be more prone to complain about being taped, you can simply approach and ask their permission beforehand or go in much closer so it's completely obvious that they are being shot. Believe me, they'll stop whatever they were doing or move away if they *don't* want to be on camera. Others still will ham it up for you, so going in close can work both ways.

3 Audio

We don't just need to see the crowd, we also need to hear their screams, applause, and shout-outs. "Freebird!!!" "We love you, Weezy!" "Brooklyn!"...If the viewing audience doesn't *hear* it, then nobody *said* it as far as they know. I said it before and I'll say it again: the video *is* the reality, baby. Use your camera to capture the reality for the audience. **(**See "Miking Instruments" on page 288 for tips on how to mic an audience.**)**

4 Lighting

Probably the trickiest part of shooting an audience at most shows is actually *seeing* them. Generally, the stage will have ample light on the performers, and in the better venues with bigger bands, there may even be an intricate lighting design that dances and changes with the music. However, the audience is often in almost total darkness. In these cases, you have three basic choices: (a) shoot only the first row of the crowd who are usually lit by some of the light spilling from the stage; or better yet, (b) ask the venue if they can turn up the lights some just for a song or two so that you can also get some decent reaction shots of the crowd that came for the show; or (c) crank up the **gain** and try to get some decent (but grainy) shots of the dark crowd.

5 Size

Remember earlier when I said it's your job to capture the reality of the event? Well, that's true except when the reality *sucks*. When the reality of the situation is less than flattering to your clients, such as the band you came to shoot had almost as many people onstage as there were in the audience, well, that's when your job shifts to *enhancing* (and when necessary, *completely altering*) reality. Nobody wants to stare video in the face that is documented proof that their band is lame and actually has no fans.

This means every shot of the audience is composed to make it look as crowded and dense as possible–even if it's not. You can accomplish this by (a) shooting only tight clusters of people or (b) shooting individual close-ups so there are multiple audience shots of different people to cut in later. (c) If you have room in the venue, move the camera as far back as you can to get the deepest composition and shoot the crowd on a longer lens (i.e., zoomed in), which will make it appear more crowded and dense. And lastly, (d) if diversity–in race, sex, age, or otherwise–is a goal, then make sure you get at least one single shot of each *type* of person in the room and two or more shots of the most desirable types. If there are 50 guys at a show and only one group of 4 women shows up, I'm gonna make sure I get four individual shots of four different women, plus a few group shots of just the women jamming to the music, so in the edited version it won't seem like the "sausage factory" that it actually was at the show.

Look for deep shots of the crowd that make it appear as crowded as possible.

The clients will always appreciate the extra steps you take to make their show look good, especially when it really wasn't that good. Whoever or whatever is most important to your paying clients to foster their desired image is exactly what you want to try to include each and every time you shoot. The only people that were there and the only things that happened in the end are the ones you *choose* to edit in. Make sure you have appropriate footage to paint the picture you need to create. While it's similar, this is a whole other ballgame from documentary filmmaking. Remember, you are being paid to make someone look good, and the perception *is* the reality when it comes to a finished piece of video.

1 Learn to anticipate actor movement

One thing you'll have to contend with when shooting plays, more so than other types of live stage events, is unpredictable actor movement. In an ideal world, you'd be able to attend rehearsals and become intimately familiar with the full blocking of the play, but just like in real life, you will rarely find yourself in that *ideal* situation. Even if you are able to attend a rehearsal or two, chances are slim that you'll be able to note all of the moments when actors stand up, sit down, dash across stage, or otherwise may move out of (or into) your shot. And even if you do take careful notes, keep in mind that actors don't always do things the same way twice.

The smart solution here is to be as familiar as possible with the general blocking, but you also want to learn to read an actor's *body language*. Reading body language is a sort of "sixth sense" you will develop over time shooting documentary footage and other unpredictable situations. Through careful observation, you will discover that most people will **"telegraph"** their moves by body language, like looking in a new direction, uncrossing their legs, pulling in their feet, leaning forward, or otherwise subtly physically indicating the way they are about to move. With experience, you will come to *feel* movement coming and react accordingly without missing a beat.*

A 2-shot covering two characters sitting on sofa talking to another character off camera.

The actor off-screen walks into the shot as the actor in the center stands up.

The camera quickly tilts up to cover the two standing actors and still includes the seated actor.

The other important part of anticipating people's movement is to always keep the pan and tilt tension on your tripod loose enough to quickly and easily follow actors as they rise, sit, and move around the stage. Similarly, you want to be prepared to quickly (but always *smoothly*) pull out to keep the action in frame as necessary if the actors interacting in a scene spread across stage like they do here.

An actor "telegraphs" his impending move by uncrossing his legs, providing the crucial warning needed to adjust the shot as he starts to move.

Thanks to her "sixth sense," the camerawoman is prepared to simultaneously widen the shot and pan right to keep the action in frame.

* All play images in this section were captured by Lauren Fritz.

2 Shoot with multiple cameras

Just like other live performances, stage plays are difficult to cover adequately with just a single camera. Single-camera coverage limits you to staying on fairly wide shots for most of the performance–static, boring, and lacking in detail. Even if you stay on tighter shots with single-camera coverage, you still risk missing the crucial actions (and reactions) of other characters on other parts of the stage. Adding even just one more camera to a live play setup will make it possible to cut together a much more interesting and fluid video. A multicamera shoot will allow you to **punch in** on details, reactions, and emotional moments in a scene; or **punch out** to cover all the action and better orient your audience to the position of relevant characters, props, and settings in a scene. One potential solution for those with only one camera is to shoot the same play twice in a row–once favoring all safe wide shots, then again favoring medium and close shots. You could now intercut the two different performances together as if they were one.

As the actor on the right suddenly grabs and then dramatically slaps the hysterical actor opposite him...

...we punch in to a close-up to show the actual slap and her comical reaction to it.

Another point to keep in mind is that when editing multiple camera shoots, you always want to try to cut on the action when switching between camera angles. So this means cutting to the other angle in the middle of some physical action when possible. Apart from just making for a less jarring and smoother cut, this practice can come in handy to help mask slight inconsistencies in continuity when splicing in shots from two different performances as noted earlier.

Camera 1–The actor begins her leap to pounce on the man on the sofa.

Camera 2–Mid-leap we cut to another camera with a tighter shot and better angle to capture the other actor's reactions.

3 Don't forget about reaction shots

Obviously, you want to cover the actor speaking most, if not all, of the time they are delivering their lines. However, just because they are speaking doesn't mean that they are the *only* person onstage who's acting and communicating to the audience. Everyone onstage is acting the whole time they are visible to the audience–whether their lips are moving or not. Just as with any given scene in filmmaking, a HUGE part of the story being told at any given moment is *nonverbal;* it's in the facial expressions, body language, and small gestures of the other actors in the scene.

Those little curls of the lip, wrinkles in an eyebrow, and coy grins are the stuff that stage acting is made of. Such subtle and delicate feats of nonverbal communication are often lost in a wide shot, so it's crucial to make sure you find a way to include the relevant reactions of the other actors in the scene. This is one of the ways that multiple-camera shooting and being familiar with the material really pay off. Reaction shots are especially important for comedic plays where so many of the jokes and comedy aren't actually in what is being said, but rather in how other characters *respond* to it. No matter what we're shooting, we're always storytellers behind the camera. And any good story always says as much *between* the lines as it does in the script. Reaction shots are the important things being said between the lines.

4 Get close-ups to show detailed action and emotion

Make sure you get plenty of medium shots and close-ups of the action onstage. Close-ups better reveal the emotion in an actor's face and really bring home the horror, hilarity, excitement, fear, joy…the emotion of the moment. You can heighten the effect of any actor's performance by choosing a tighter shot. Tighter shots also draw the audience's attention to the actions of individual actors. This can be simply to show them the details of what's going on onstage. (Audience: *"That guy is pouring a very strong drink for his friend. He's definitely going to get tipsy drinking that."*) Or close-up and medium shots can be used to add an element of suspense, misdirect the audience, or give them clues to the story unfolding onstage. (Audience: *"When the other character's back was turned, that character accidentally dropped a knife out of her pocket. I wonder what she's planning to do with that?"*) The most crucial act of directing a video involves *choosing* which shot will cover which action; you are literally *directing* the audience's attention to the most important aspect of a scene that you want them to notice. Don't neglect your role in the video retelling of a stage play. Know when to get close and do it.

This actor's comic "surprise" hairdo begs for a close-up.

Bring the audience in close to share in a warm embrace.

Some small actions can be missed if not seen up close.

5 Be prepared for dramatic entrances

One thing you can count on during a play is that there will be some, if not many, dramatic character entrances. Often these entrances can be quite sudden, back to back, or from multiple places onstage. There are only two ways to make sure you never miss the dramatic injection of a new character into the drama: (1) shoot with multiple cameras so at least one camera is always covering the main entrances onstage or, more preferably, (2) know exactly when the most dramatic entrances will take place. You generally want to try to get a tighter shot whenever a new character is introduced. Similarly, be aware of entrances that take place when the stage is dark and the lights suddenly come up to reveal that a character (or characters) has now "popped up" in the middle of the sofa or around a dinner table. This will usually happen right after intermission or before a new act, but could also occur mid-play. The only way to be prepared...is to *be prepared*. Ask the director or stage manager about any sudden entrances you should be aware of. If you do find yourself in a situation where you are caught off guard by a sudden stage entrance or appearance, whatever you do, *don't* suddenly jerk and swing the camera wildly across stage to pick up the action. (If you do that, you may as well shout out loud in the theater, "Oh $#!+! I just &@*%-ed up!") Instead, don't sweat it. Just smoothly and deliberately pan over to where the action is. Never let the audience feel your panic. All good filmmakers screw up sometimes, but we sweat and panic only on the *inside*. (That's why the most successful directors always gain weight after a few films–Lucas? Jackson? Coppola? That ain't fat, baby! That's the long-retained sweat of a filmmaking professional who always plays it *cool* when the unexpected happens.)

Always get a good shot when a new character enters.

Don't miss the fun surprises that pop up at the door.

Go wide for the curtain call as all the actors take a bow.

6 Shoot above the audience

Whenever possible, I advise you to try to avoid shooting the heads of the audience in the theater, as I think it tends to makes your video look like a bad bootleg DVD. You can usually push in to a little tighter shot to crop out unwanted noggins. Unfortunately, you are mostly at the mercy of the design of the theater when it comes to this issue. When you're scouting the theater beforehand (you are doing that *already,* right?), I recommend choosing camera positions that give you a clean shot of the stage over the heads of the audience. Stylistically, some directors may want to include shots of the audience's heads because it is "live" theater after all. But even then, I think it's distracting to do any more than sparingly throughout the shoot. But that's just me. You do what you want. If you shoot live events regularly, you might also consider investing in a portable shooting platform that will raise your position a foot or two off the floor.

Some directors like the "live" feel of audience heads in the foreground.

I prefer clean shots of the action onstage.

7 **Know your stage directions**

Just as there is certain language specific to filmmaking, there is also certain terminology specific to the world of theater that you'll want to be familiar with if you are going to be shooting stage productions. We have **"C-47's"** and **"inkies"** in filmmaking, but in theater they have stage directions, such as "right wing" and "upstage left," that you had better become familiar with if you want to pick up the main character's surprise entrance in act 2 or understand what the director's talking about during rehearsal. Some of it's a little counterintuitive, but pretty easy to figure out once you take a few minutes to familiarize yourself with this chart.

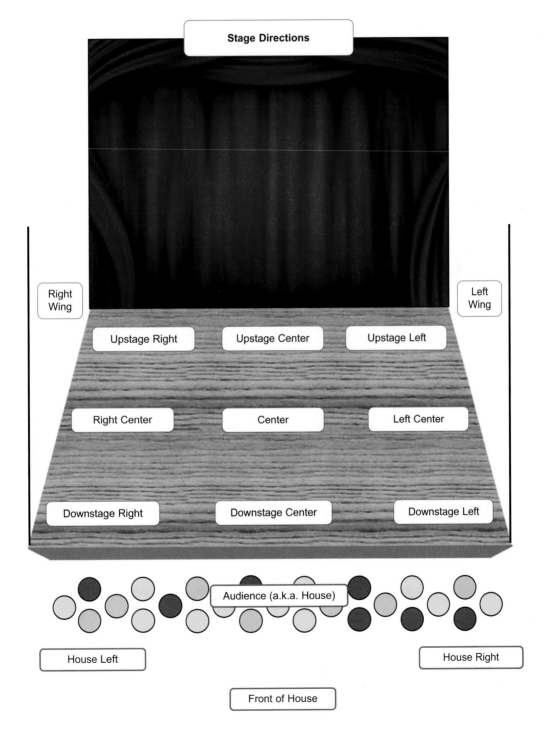

SHOOTING PROJECTED IMAGES

Projected images always present exposure and framing challenges during live events. You'd have to be very wide to get this high screen and a speaker at the podium below in the frame at the same time.

A common element of all kinds of live events is projection...and it's always a pain in the butt. There are a few challenges to successfully capturing video or slides being projected on a screen that you must resolve if you want to have a professional-quality video, rather than something that looks like what someone's mom shot from the fourth row of the theater. Specifically, these challenges are that the image on the screen is way brighter than the live shots of the speaker, so both can't be exposed well simultaneously. You are not sure exactly when the video projection is gonna start or stop, so you may miss part of the projection. You have a mic on the person onstage, but the projected audio is actually coming from speakers in the room and sounds like doody. And last but not least, people in the seated audience sometimes take advantage of the lights going down to slip out to the bathroom and stand up right into your previously clean shot of the screen. But I don't want to harp on just problems. Let's talk about some *solutions*.

1 EDIT THE SOURCE VIDEO

The *very best* way to handle projected images and video is to get your hands on the actual digital source material for the projection, which will generally be a DVD, digital video file (i.e., H.264, QuickTime, Windows Media, etc.). Once you have the projected video in the highest-quality digital format you can get, all you have to do is import it into your editing program, and you can then treat it the same as any other video clip on your editing timeline.

2 EDIT THE ORIGINAL SLIDE PRESENTATIONS

In the case of slide presentations, you will most likely be dealing with a PowerPoint (PC) or Keynote (Mac) source file. It's generally preferable to get the original PowerPoint or Keynote files so you have the option to tweak colors or fonts that aren't video-friendly. However, some speakers (such as myself) may be reluctant to release their original presentation source files and will prefer to give you a TIFF (.tiff), JPEG (.jpeg), or PDF (.pdf) file export of their presentation. TIFF files are preferable as they are the highest quality for video editing.

3 SHOOT IT LIVE STRAIGHT TO CAMERA

This is the *least* preferable way to shoot projection, but when caught off-guard, we gotta do what we gotta do, so here's how to make the most of a crappy shooting situation. (1) Shoot with your camera on auto-iris, so that it automatically adjusts the exposure for whatever it's pointed at. This way, when you tilt up from the live talent onstage to a slide above their heads, the projected image won't be blown out. (2) Try to get an audio feed directly from the source video, so at least your sound won't be as lame as the video you are already shooting off-screen. If this is not an option, try to set up a separate mic to pick up the speakers and manually adjust your levels. Or (least preferable), (3) shoot with the camera's onboard mic picking up the sound in the room, which will also pick up audience reaction, which may or may not be desirable, depending on your video.

The biggest challenge with a live speaker using projection is that you can only properly expose for the speaker *or* the screen, but not both at the same time.

CHAPTER 8

HANDLING YA BUSINESS

Once you get serious and decide that freelance producing is something you are going to continue to do, there are some business basics you'll need to take care of to look and operate as a legitimate business entity. I highly recommend that you set aside some time to thoroughly research setting up a business because the process involves several steps, can be confusing, differs from state to state, and will have a major impact on how you file taxes. I recommend consulting an accountant, lawyer, and/or friends who have already set up production companies in your state. Nevertheless, I don't want to leave you totally high and dry, so I'll outline the basic steps to start you on your merry way to collecting cash as a legitimate business.

Get an Employer Identification Number (EIN)

Getting a tax ID number is a good simple starting point. An employer identification number (EIN), or tax ID number, as it's often referred to, is like a Social Security number for your business. It's used to register for federal, state, and local taxes. When companies write you big checks or when you open a bank account, they will ask for your tax ID number. Getting one is simple. You can apply online at **http://IRS.gov** (enter "EIN" in the search box on the site for info and forms) or apply by phone by calling **1-800-829-4933**.

Form a Business Entity

The most important and involved part of becoming a bona fide production company is forming a business entity or corporation. There are several different types you can go with, and each offers different levels of legal protection and tax advantages (and hassles). Your choice of business entity determines whether you are personally liable for debts, damage, or other things that may happen during the course of operating your business, as well as which tax forms and corporate paperwork you must file and how often you file them.

From my observations, limited liability companies, better known as LLCs, are a popular choice among small production companies because they offer a good deal of protection from liability and have comparatively simple and straightforward tax requirements. However, some states may charge annual fees and taxes for LLCs that make them a much less attractive option for a small business. (For example, at the time I'm writing this, California charges LLCs an $800 annual fee.) Sole proprietorships are also a common choice for forming a production company because of their simplicity, but they offer considerably less legal protection. There are also some other types of entities to consider.

So as you can see, this is where it starts to get more complicated, and this is the part that requires a considerable amount of homework and research.

Fortunately for you, there is an abundance of information on setting up a small business available online from a wide variety of sources. The Small Business Administration (SBA) at http://SBA.gov is a good online starting point. The Small Business Administration also has local chapters in every state that offer free small business workshops that cover starting up. An online search for the terms "starting a small business" or "forming a corporation" will yield literally millions of online articles on the subject. I also recommend a trip to the business section of your local bookstore or library. It's definitely the kind of information you want to be able to pour over and keep on hand during the process.

Although you can file the paperwork to set up a corporation by yourself, I think it's a good idea to seek the help of a legal professional or company that specializes in setting up corporations in your state. If you're willing to spend the money, you can hire a small business lawyer to create or help you create a business entity. This is the absolute safest way to go, but by far the most expensive. Alternatively, you may wish to prep as much as you feel comfortable doing by yourself and then just have an attorney look over your paperwork before filing.

Another popular route these days is to form your corporation through any one of hundreds of online companies that will create and file your corporation for you, such as **Incorp.com**, **LegalZoom.com,** or **BizFilings.com**. These companies offer online convenience, can clarify some of your questions, and most notably, charge a much smaller fee than the average attorney would charge to file corporate papers.

Bank Account

Next up, you want to open a small business bank account so that

- Your business appears legitimate to your business clients. Clients, especially other businesses, are generally uncomfortable writing a check to an individual person for business services. (That's fine for the kid who mows your lawn, but not for a professional video production who's billing for thousands of dollars.)
- You don't want your serious small business to look like what the IRS calls a "hobby business." You can deduct business expenses for a small business but not for a "hobby" business. A separate bank account for your business transactions is a big legitimizer for clients and the IRS.

Comingling personal and business expenses become a nightmare to untangle at tax time. Skimming through a year's worth of purchases and expenditures is a tedious, frustrating, and inefficient exercise that will probably also result in your missing out on many legitimate tax deductions because you simply won't remember what that $137.57 purchase was really for 10 months after the fact.

Production Insurance

One of the final business frontiers you will cross will be acquiring some type of insurance to protect your business. At the very simplest level, you want to make sure your equipment is covered for theft. Apart from financial protection, you will usually need insurance to do two other important things: (1) get a shooting permit in most cities and (2) rent equipment from a rental house.

As you are forming a production company, production insurance is ideal, but it is not cheap. (That's the main reason I name insurance as the "final business frontier.") Production insurance covers your company for all the everyday disasters that can occur when you're shooting a project, such as personal injury, fire, theft, lost or damaged footage, lawsuits filed by clients, etc. For just about anything that could go wrong during a production, there is some type of production insurance, so there is a maze of options to consider. It's also not easy to figure out exactly what *type* of production insurance and how much you'll need.

Unfortunately, the subject of production insurance will probably require just as much, if not more, study than setting up your corporation, and the nuances of production insurance are well beyond the scope of the information that I intend to provide in this book. However, I will point you to some resources where you can dig much much deeper.

Video University's Excellent Production Insurance Primer:

videouniversity.com/articles/how-to-buy-video-production-insurance

Some Production Insurance Providers:

FilmEmporium.com

ProductionInsurance.com

FilmIns.com

A Legal Book for Filmmakers

...And you may also wish to check out *The Pocket Lawyer for Filmmakers: A Legal Toolkit for Independent Producers, Second Edition,* by Thomas A. Crowell for more info on forming a production company and purchasing insurance.

A common question that many people have when starting out in the world of corporate and freelance video is, "How do I find clients?" The short answer to this is to simply be damned good at what you do. If you are good (damned good) at what you do, the clients will almost always find you. And the way that they'll find you is from word of mouth from all the people who've hired you before who are showing off the hot video you did for them to their friends and colleagues. It's a beautiful and profitable cycle when it gets going, but how do you get it going to start with? Here are a few of my suggestions:

1. Do the First One for No Money

The primary strategy that I use when I want to branch out into a new area of video or when things are slowing down is to do the first one for "no money" with a client that I've strategically chosen because I like their company or their company's position in the marketplace. The client may not have a video budget or may not be ready to pay me for my services, but they may have *other things* that can be very valuable to a budding freelancer, such as international recognition, a half-million eyeballs watching their website, or perhaps they are poised to be the next big thing in their market. (Just imagine if you had done the first video marketing for Facebook or Netflix and the clout that one little video on your reel would buy you later.)

I have a saying: "I've never worked 'for free' in my life. I've worked for *no money*, a hundred times over, but it was never 'for free' ". Money is not the only value in shooting a job, especially when you are not that experienced or you're just starting out in a new marketplace; credibility, visibility, and the opportunity to expand into a new area are all great reasons to shoot for free. (Just imagine if a young struggling Mariah Carey asked you to shoot the music video for her first demo song before she had a record deal? How many others would later enlist your services based on that one video alone?)

The informal deal I usually make is that if they like the job I do for them for no money (or severely discounted), then they must bring me back when/if they need more video work, but more importantly, they must *refer* me and talk up my company to their industry peers and colleagues (of course, never revealing that my work for them was actually for free).

This strategy does three key things for me: (1) I get more video practice and a new demo piece without the pressure because it's free anyway; (2) it generates incredible goodwill and loyalty with the client getting free/discounted services; and (3) it usually gets me at least two paying clients over the course of a year as a result of their recommendations. In one case in particular, using this strategy has yielded me five new paid jobs (and counting) with several different clients who were referred to me, plus new well-paid jobs with the original "free" client.

Of course, there's obviously the risk that the client could just take the video and never refer anyone, but even then, the way I look at the situation is I have more experience in this genre now and a new demo piece, so I'm never actually walking away empty-handed, even when shooting for no money. (For the record, this worst-case scenario has *not* happened to me in several executions of this strategy; I've always gotten at least one job out of it within a year's time.)

2. Develop Strategic Partnerships

You may also want to consider forming some strategic partnerships with event photographers and other service providers to the same people you wish to be hired by. In the case of weddings, you could offer a 15 percent discount for all clients of a certain wedding organizer or photographer with whom you have a relationship. For live events, you could offer a discount to any clients that rent stage equipment from a certain vendor or play at certain venues. By using this strategy, you are creating a win-win scenario: (a) the company or person you partner with has a little bonus to offer their clients in the form of a discount and convenient "one-stop shopping" for their services plus your video services, and (b) you will be getting more work and a new client. Always approach these situations looking to form a win-win scenario. Come up with a proposal where the partner you seek has something of equal value to gain by promoting your video services.

3. Offer a Kickback

Another twist on this same idea is to offer other vendors, friends, and other contacts that help you land new clients a referral fee (or as politicians call them, "kickbacks") of between 5%-15% of the budget of any work you get through them. Hey, money talks and is always a powerful incentive for people to promote your services. This is the type of deal you would offer to the movers and shakers in your networking circle. This is also a deal you could offer to regular clients who refer new clients to you in the form of a cash payment or, better yet, the equivalent cash discount on your services the next time they hire you. So if you had a deal with an existing client for a 10 percent referral fee, and that client hooked you up with a new client who pays you $1000, you would give the referring client $100 credit toward their next video job. Again, use your imagination to find ways to incentivize others to promote your services. I have both given and collected several referral fees over the years, and they are beautiful thing for both parties involved.

4. Hand Out Cards and Brochures

Good old-fashioned cards and brochures are still a viable way to entice and educate people about your video services. Do not be cheap when it comes to cards or brochures. They are both seen as direct reflections of you and your services. Your card and brochure are people's first visual impression of your business. They must be tight and professional looking. Avoid printing your own cards on an inkjet printer. Such cards scream

"amateur hour" and point out that you are not serious enough about your business to invest in real business cards. You can pick up a decent set of color business cards for less than $100 in most places. Make them glossy and full-color and have them professionally designed. If you have a talented niece or friend who's in art school or graphic design, you may be able to save a few bucks on design. If you are really tight on cash, you can order decent (but not premium) "free" business cards, postcards, or brochures for very cheap from a company called **Vistaprint. com**. The catch is that they print their logo on the back of all the cards, which certainly takes away from the professional appearance. However, for a little bit more money, you can get business cards, brochures, etc., without their logo. (Don't expect premium-quality cards or cardstock here; this is just something that's a step above the old inkjet printer cards to get you started if you're broke.)

Similarly, **Overnightprints.com** is also another popular choice for ordering cards online. In my opinion after having used both companies, I think the cards from Overnightprints.com are of a higher quality than the Vistaprint.com cards, which is reflected in the price difference. Nevertheless, both of these companies offer a variety of affordable premade designs that you can customize by changing the text and fonts and adding and removing certain design elements and colors to create a semi-unique card for a reasonable price compared to that of your local printer. You can also upload your own custom design and logo and have those printed as well.

5. Create a Website

Even more important than your "paper presence" is your web presence. Let me break out my bullhorn here for a minute:

YOU *MUST* HAVE A GOOD WEB PRESENCE!!!

The very first thing that anyone is going to do, often before they even contact you, is look up your company online. They want to see an official website that looks professional and offers some visual and written proof that you actually do what you say you do. Hopefully, you are also able to offer that visual proof in the form of a demo reel and/or previous videos you've shot. You don't have to include all of these things on your website, but here's a breakdown of what to strive for:

- ✓ **Web address**
- ✓ **Contact info: email, phone, fax**
- ✓ **Physical location (city, state) or address**
- ✓ **Demo reel**
- ✓ **Full videos of previous projects**
- ✓ **Types of videos you do**
- ✓ **Your unique approach**
- ✓ **Equipment package**
- ✓ **Client testimonials**
- ✓ **Standard rates**

Unless you've got deep pockets, I would not go the route of hiring a designer to create a site from scratch. Instead, the easiest and cheapest way to create a professional-looking website quickly is to use a website template. If you aren't already down with them, website templates are premade websites that you can buy for very little (in most cases, $30–$100) and customize with text, colors, design

My own Down and Dirty DV website (DownAndDirtyDV.com) was customized from a WordPress template. I had a web designer change the background and color scheme, customize the rotating banners on the front page, and import my blog. I just added the written content and some pictures.

elements, and widgets to your own liking. Although you can get them in a variety of formats, templates for the **Wordpress.org** blog platform are probably the most popular, because the Wordpress.org blog platform makes it fairly easy to customize your website and update content, pictures, and video after the site is up.

(Note that there are two types of WordPress blogs: those installed and hosted on your own server via Wordpress.org and those hosted on the WordPress server at WordPress.com.) Two popular sites that I've used to purchase web templates are **ThemeForest.com** and **TemplateMonster.com,** each of which offers hundreds of different web templates that can be completely customized. Both of these sites also offer affordable template customization services via third-party web design companies that specialize in templates.

If you are somewhat HTML savvy or have previous web design skill, you can probably install and customize many of these templates yourself. However, every premade template is different, and some are much more user-friendly than others. I recommend hiring a designer to install and/or customize the template for you, which involves putting out some money, but still *much* less than you would spend for a custom site made from scratch. It's very easy to get lost in endless days and weeks of laying out and troubleshooting web design issues that a professional could navigate in a fraction of the time. (Remember, your time and sanity have a value, too.)

Again, if time and money are of the essence and you don't even want to deal with the limited hassle of customizing a template, you could set up your website on any of several free blogging platforms, such as **Blogger.com** or **WordPress.com** or **Typepad.com**. And although it's not free like the others, **SquareSpace.com** is a commercial blog/website hosting service worth researching as well. Ignore the fact that these companies are "blogging" services. You do not have to use them as blogs. (Although that would not be a bad idea at all to increase your web presence and lure clients.) Instead, you can use these blog platforms as many people do–to host your static website.

Why choose a blog platform for a static website? Using simple blogging platforms is the most versatile, user-friendly, and easy-to-update way to maintain a website. The design stays static, but you can update the text and swap out pictures and video instantaneously, without having to rely on a web designer. So whether you use a custom template or one of the services I just named, it's always easy to update, change the information, and add or remove pages from your site without having to know HTML. The free blogging platforms also offer a variety of templates that you can customize to your specific needs and color scheme, although there are considerably fewer template choices, and they usually aren't as professional looking and versatile as the customized templates you can buy online.

THE CLIENT "DANCE" AND CRAFTING A PROPOSAL

PETE CHATMON, CEO, DOUBLE7 IMAGES—MEDIA AND MARKETING COLLECTIVE (Double7Images.com)

The dance begins when someone's interested. Somebody emails you. You meet them at an event or whatever. The first thing you do is contact them and begin to see what their needs are, at which point you put together a proposal. That proposal should be reflective of your conversation with them and how you think you can meet their needs creatively. You go back and forth on that proposal until you come to an agreement. At some point that proposal also graduates to include a budget.

After the proposal is agreed upon, you should create a statement of work. That is going to be basically more of a business document reflecting what you agreed upon in the proposal, but on paper you clearly delineate "This is the payment schedule. These are the contact people from each side. This is the production and delivery schedule. These are the delivery modes, whether it's QuickTime, DVD, whatever it might be."

Now you have a road map that both you and the client can refer back to that minimizes miscommunications and controls expectations. If you're doing a project that requires a lot of shooting and editing, I would advise as you move through every part of the process that you have new **sign-offs**. When you send them a new cut of the video, provide a question-naire to help them provide feedback in a way that fits your needs. Rather than say, "Please provide your notes," say, "We would like to have your notes within 36 hours. Please provide notes on pacing, shot selection, graphics…" because they may not be able to voice those things or pinpoint them in an itemized way unless you specify exactly how you need them to frame their input.

This helps you avoid getting notes on a second cut that you could have gotten in the first cut because your clients didn't know how to give feedback from the start. When you have people sign off, there's no going back. Well…they can always go back, but they should understand that they will be charged more to do so after signing off.

If you ever have a freelance job or have clients that end up becoming a nightmare, chances are that you share a good deal of the blame for not planning and communicating everything properly at the start. Almost anything that becomes a source of extra work or expenses on a freelance gig will most likely be something that *you* failed to think through and/or communicate clearly to your clients beforehand. Make absolutely sure that you and your clients are on the same page before a single frame of video is ever shot. The following items should be discussed in conversations and emails beforehand and appear in any estimate or contract that you present so that you don't end up doing 30 extra hours of unplanned work or spending an extra $250 on delivery items you didn't budget for.

1 Will You Just Shoot or Also Edit?

This is a huge factor in the ultimate amount of work involved, which means it's a huge factor in what you should charge a client. Gigs that require you only to shoot a performance or event are by far some of the easiest and fastest money you can make. You show up, shoot for 2 hours, and hand over the footage to the client at the end of the gig; in turn, the client hands

you a check or cash. Everyone's happy. Done deal. (For obvious reasons, these are often my favorite jobs.) However, if you also have to also edit that same 2 hours of concert footage, you will likely be putting in another 8–20 hours of work—if you do it right. There are many little considerations here that add up, so think it through carefully and do all of the mental math. (Also see "What Should You Charge?" on page 326.)

2 What Is the Rate?

Make absolutely sure that before you shoot a single minute of footage, you and the client both clearly agree on the final costs of the production itself, the schedule of payment, plus any extras they may want later, such as additional edited versions, extra copies, publishing to sites such as YouTube or Vimeo, etc.

Make sure you have communicated this rate in writing, whether it be a contract, written quote, email, or text message. The more formal, the better. Just make sure that if there's a misunderstanding later you can quickly pull up your written communication and enlighten the client as to what they agreed to pay.

3 When Is Payment Due?

This is entirely up to you, but make sure it's something you can live with. Probably the most common option is half up front and half on delivery. You could also do a third up front, a third at time of shooting, and a third due upon delivery. With my regular bigger-budget clients, I sometimes structure things so that everything is due upon delivery to simplify the paperwork, because I know I'm gonna get paid by these big companies, based on past dealings with them.

4 What Will You Shoot?

Another thing you want to have clear is exactly what you'll be shooting. Are interviews part of the project? If so, how many interviews will you shoot? In how many different locations? This simple question alone could easily expand the scope of the project three-fold. There's a big difference between shooting three back-to-back interviews in the same room with the same lighting setup and shooting three interviews on three different days in three different places. Again, think the whole shoot through step by step and quote your rate accordingly. If you don't clarify little details like this ahead of time, you could easily screw yourself into working for minimum wage (or less) without even realizing it.

5 What Do *They* Have to Do?

Hey, you aren't the only one with responsibilities on these jobs. There are certain things that you are going to need or want the clients to do to make your life easier. Specifically, some of the routine things I often ask of clients on a job are securing shooting spaces, getting the okay to shoot from venue owners, selecting interview subjects, arranging interview times with subjects, providing hard drives, etc. Often my clients have pre-existing relationships with the other parties involved in a project, so it makes more sense to have them handle certain phone calls and emails that can burn up a lot of my time. Arranging even a single interview can often take four to seven emails and/or phone calls before it's all said and done. Give them the shoot date and time frame and let the clients arrange the interviews and some locations because the interviews and locations are usually going to be with their own people and facilities anyway.

Since I first wrote *The Shut Up and Shoot Documentary Guide* a few years back, we've moved into a brave new world where almost every camera is tapeless and records images on some type of data card (i.e., **P2, SxS, SD card, flash card**, etc.). This means that we've also moved into a brave new workflow that requires our media to be stored and archived on hard drives. So one thing to decide early on is who will provide these hard drives—you or the client? If the answer is you, remember you'll need to make the time to purchase a hard drive and put out a little more money ahead of time, so don't forget to bill the client accordingly.

If the client will be purchasing or handing over their own hard drive, make sure they have a hard drive suitable for high-speed data transfer, which means it should have an eSATA port, FireWire 800 or 400 port, or at the very least a USB 2.0 port—preferably all four. An even faster option is Apple's new Thunderbolt ports which reportedly blow all previous transfer speeds out of the water, but have yet to be released and in wide use as I write this.

Little portable USB-powered bus drives are a good choice to deliver and store footage for your client.

Compact mini-hard drives that hold as much as 500 gigabytes to 1 terabyte (i.e. 1000GB) are a popular choice among video freelancers, as they are small and easy to transport or ship and can be powered entirely by a laptop without the need to plug into a power outlet. So in addition to their tiny size, these drives are great for offloading camera data cards in the field.

WHAT SHOULD YOU CHARGE?

One of the great things about being a freelance video producer/shooter with your own equipment is that you have very little overhead. Once you own some gear, your main cost outside of paying any crew you bring on is *your time*. Remember, your time is a very real and valuable resource that should be managed carefully. The first thing that you'll probably want to consider when it comes to rate is whether you'll be simply shooting the project or also conceiving and editing the final piece. Editing will typically be twice (or even four times) as much work by the time it's all said and done.

So as a general rule of thumb, my rate is *at least* double for jobs that also require editing. However, for more complex editing jobs that involve elements such as using multiple cameras, creating fancy titles and graphics, creating and reviewing transcripts, having a stylized look, compiling different edited versions, etc., you may want to charge triple (or more) the total that

you charged just to *shoot* the event. While live events that require editing are a lot more work, I should point out that I also find it quite satisfying to be the one who get to shape the final product, since I always shoot with the final edited piece in mind anyway.

Think the whole process through carefully before quoting a client a rate to shoot *and* edit. I thought I was getting good money for the first weddings I shot, but once I got down to the process of actually editing a good two-camera video, adding in music and titles, making dubs, etc., the rate that I charged actually turned out to be well below *minimum wage*. I suspect that this is a common mistake among those just starting out freelancing. Fortunately, it's a lesson you need to learn only once. One way to avoid this amateur scenario is to figure out what you want to charge per hour of your time. Then you can think it through and write out all the steps required in the postproduction process, from downloading P2 cards to making final dubs, and estimate the hours it will take for each and then multiply that times your hourly rate.

So what to charge clients often comes down to making an accurate estimation of how much **time** you will ultimately spend on the project. Guess right and you can make a handsome profit to put toward that hot new camera you've been eyeing. Guess wrong and you'll be making less per hour than the fry boy at Burger King. The key to guessing accurately, just like any other filmmaking budget issue, is to try to take into consideration all the many tasks that you will have to take on to deliver a finished product.

Next is a simple chart of common tasks that you should assign a time and value to. I often just assign a set charge for each service, as some things (like backing up footage) don't actually require much effort beyond a few keyboard strokes, even though they do take a certain amount of time to complete. Similarly, I like to include a few lines in my cost itemization for clients for simple tasks that say "Gratis" or "Free" so that they'll know my time was involved, but I'm not actually charging them for every little thing. However, there's nothing wrong with just multiplying the total hours for *everything* times your hourly rate as long as you think the final price is competitive with your market and you can get it.

SETTING YOUR RATE

SETTING AN HOURLY RATE

Your hourly rate is a personal choice of what your services are worth based on your own skills and the particular market you are in. If you have no clue what to set as an hourly rate, I suggest starting no lower than double the rate you get (or feel you deserve) for your current or last day job and no more than the highest going rate of your local competitors, which can often be found online or with a little sniffing around with your video clients and colleagues. I say double your day job rate, because creating (good) videos requires specialized skills and knowledge that should command more than private jobs that don't require specialized training.

SETTING A FLAT RATE

Unless you're a lawyer, it may not always make sense to charge a client for every single minute you spend on their project. You could probably easily price yourself way out of the market if you billed clients for every moment of mental or physical energy you put out to realize their project. For larger jobs, you may wish to charge a flat rate just for certain parts of the job, such as research, designing titles and graphics, preproduction, etc. and still charge your hourly rate for shooting and editing. For simple jobs such as shooting a two-hour speech or B-roll of a company outing, you may want to just make a simple mental calculation of how much work the job will be and/or how much you need or want the money and the client's business.

FAVORED NATIONS

A common method to deal with negotiating crew rates is called "favored nations". This simply means that everyone at the same crew level is getting the exact same pay, whether it's a flat fee or hourly rate. So there are still different rates, but not for similar jobs with the same level of responsibility. So the department heads (D.P., Audio, etc.) would work at one rate, the crew under them (A.C., grips, assistants, etc.) would all work at another. And the actors would all be paid the same fee across the board regardless of role. This is helpful in negotiating low budget project rates with crew, because it values everyone's contributions equally and eliminates back and forth negotiations.

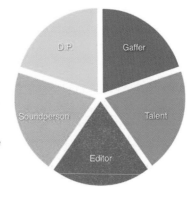

SAMPLE RATES FOR A LOW-BUDGET SHOOT

The below chart represents many of the common tasks that you will have to execute over the course of a typical project from start to finish. These are all the time and energy-consuming tasks that you must take into consideration when giving a quote for a job whether you perform them or hire someone else to. You don't have to necessarily share all of this minutia with your clients, but you should figure it out for yourself and decide which tasks you are going to charge them for and how you are going to charge them—flat rate, hourly or no charge. I typically provide clients a simple budget broken down by prep, production and post-production and provide more details, if requested.

RATE CALCULATION CHART

TASK	RATE	X	HRS / #	=	CHARGE
Preproduction meetings/planning	No charge	x	1 meeting	=	0
Attending rehearsals	No charge	x	1 rehearsal	=	0
Location scouting	No charge	x	1 scout	=	0
Travel time	No charge	x	1 hour	=	0
Offloading media cards	$50	x	1.5 hours	=	75
Backing up footage and edits	$50	x	1 hour	=	50
Logging footage	$50	x	4 hours	=	200
Designing titles and graphics	$200	x	Flat rate	=	200
Making transcripts	$150	x	Flat rate	=	150
Choosing sound bites from transcripts	No charge	x	2 hours	=	0
Picking out production music	No charge	x	2 hours	=	0
Locating archival footage	None	x	1.5 hours	=	0
Shooting additional B-roll/footage	$100	x	1.5 hours	=	150
Designing a DVD menu	$100	x	Flat rate	=	150
Designing DVD labels	$100	x	Flat rate	=	100
Transfers to other formats	No charge	x	.5 hours	=	0
Burning DVD copies	$20	x	5 DVDs	=	100
Total Pre/Post Tasks					**$1,175**
Total Crew Costs*					**$1,955**
Total Job Estimate:				=	**$3,130**

*See "Sample Crew Rates Chart" on next page for breakdown.

Now that you've figured what you need to make to make the job worthwhile, you need to figure out how much you need to pay your crew. Crew rates will vary widely depending on your local market, the nature of the project, experience level, and your personal relationships to crew members. Some quick examples of situations that will affect how much you pay for any given job: (a) Your film school friend who's an experienced sound mixer is more likely to cut you a break if she owes you a favor from the last time you worked below your rate when *she* was directing a project. (b) That whiz kid D.P. fresh out of film school is happy to work on a project of this stature for half of what an experienced pro would charge just to build his reel. (c) This project has a tight deadline and really needs some slick After Effects work and a lot of greenscreen compositing, so you need an experienced editor who also is also skilled at special FX and titles. The list goes on and on. Nevertheless, what I recommend you do is create a personal rate card for all the people you work with (or hope to work with regularly). That way, when a new gig does come your way, you have a starting point to draft a budget based on the needs of the job.

One thing I've learned the hard way is that experienced crew are almost always worth paying for. This is a very competitive business, so most professionals I've come across command a day rate that is in line with the skills, value, and speed they bring to the set. I've been burned (or just burned out)

> **NEVER** hire anyone unless someone you know and trust is willing to **VOUCH** for that person as a crewmember.

many times by trying to save a few hundreds bucks by hiring a less experienced crew member who made some rookie mistake that ultimately cost me more than the difference of their rate in time and/or money spent fixing or reshooting their mistake. To be fair here, I've also saved plenty of money by giving motivated film students and self-taught amateurs an opportunity to work at a higher level for more pay than they usually get but still less than I would pay to a veteran. These people I try to choose very carefully based on attitude, ambition, and, most of all, word of mouth. And in most cases, they worked for me in some smaller capacity before I hired them for the real deal. Word of mouth and personal observation are king here.

SAMPLE CREW RATES FOR A ONE-DAY SHOOT

CREW	#		RATE	X	DAYS		TOTAL
Director	1	x	$400	x	1	=	400
Camera operator	1	x	$300	x	1	=	300
Digital assistant	1	x	$150	x	0.5	=	75
Audio person	1	x	$300	x	1	=	300
Editor	1	x	$400	x	2	=	$800
Crew meals (flat)	1	x	$80	x	Flat	=	$80
Production assistants	0	x		x		=	0
Miscellaneous crew	0	x		x		=	0
Total:						=	$1,955

CALCULATING YOUR CREW'S RATE

PRESENTING THE BUDGET TO CLIENTS

PETE CHATMON, CEO, DOUBLE7 IMAGES—MEDIA AND MARKETING COLLECTIVE (Double7Images.com)

Too often we get scared to present the reality of how much something costs. With every proposal I send out, I say to myself, "I hope they don't roll their eyes when they get this one." Well, they never do. In actuality, your first volley at the budget is merely a negotiating tactic. You're saying, "Here's what it costs" in anticipation of the client's response being "Here's what I'm willing to pay." It's not necessarily fair, but it is what it is. That's why it's important to protect yourself in this exchange by not making assumptions on what *you think* a client is willing to pay. On rare and monumental occasions, you will come across clients who have budgeted more than you might have expected, and cutting your rates in that first budget volley might just cut serious dollars out of your project that they would have willingly shelled out.

Now, in regards to rates, it's important that you make an honest assessment of your own experience and abilities. You also have to look at the experience of those around you and put a realistic cost on their services, multiplied by the amount of time it's going to take. You should have a day rate and a week rate that allows some minimal discount as a benefit of locking you in for so long. Trust me, there will be months you don't work at all, so to get a job that pays you for multiple days can be a blessing. To be specific, if you're making $1,000 a day, you may say your five-day week rate is not $5,000, but maybe $3,750 or $4,000. It's all up to you, but the same percentages should be applied across the board for all folks on the project.

If you find that the client's budget is just waaaaaaay too low and impossible to pay even a portion of a half day rate or whatever the cost, you still have options (if the project is exciting and of interest). In this case, you can offer a flat rate. For example, if you have a $5,000 project that requires several team members who won't get anywhere near their quote, an agreed-upon flat rate allows people to be compensated with something while you all get to knock out an exciting project that can lead to bigger, better campaigns and some awesome content on your reel.

Lastly, when you're using a discounted flat rate, after all of the negotiating is finished, do yourself a favor and provide the client with a two-column budget that shows what you are doing the project for *as well as* the budget with fully realized rates. They'll see the discount, but they'll also have a document reflecting your standard rates so that, moving forward, they can budget accordingly.

WORKING REMOTELY WITH AN EDITOR

One of the many convenient things that digital technology offers us is the ability to collaborate with our team from just about anywhere in the world with a decent Internet connection. Whether it's a cowriter, storyboard artist, producer, or any collaborator in between, we can easily share scripts, files, videos, and more with a few keystrokes. However, of all of these technological mini-miracles, none is more practical and mutually convenient than the ability to collaborate remotely with an editor. Once upon a time, you had only two choices: sit in the edit room with your editor for nights on end until the wee hours of the morning or leave your baby in the arms of another and hope that it's still on track when you view the next cut. Now, with recent online technologies (and a few twists on old ones), you can instantaneously check in with your editor, review a cut, give notes, or sign off on a final edit even if you're in New York and the editor is halfway around the world.

1 EMAIL

The most primitive form of online collaboration is still good old-fashioned email with a slight twist. Even a three-minute video compressed for the web will often be too big to email using the most popular email providers, which often tap out when it comes to attaching files larger than 25MB (which is *nothing* when we're talking HD video). Fortunately, there are a number of online services that specialize in storing and delivering large files. Many of them are free as long as your files aren't *too* big. If you do need to transfer larger video files, then you can pay for a subscription to these services, which will allow higher file limits and more frequent uploads as well as certain other conveniences, such as long-term file storage. However, if you need to send more than a few minutes' worth of raw (uncompressed) HD footage, you'll need to upload it to a server and **FTP** it.

Services like Dropbox.com allow you to easily share large video files back and forth with collaborators.

I commonly use file services such as **Pando.com, YouSendIt.com** and **Dropbox.com** to receive new cuts from my editors, transfer raw HD footage to them, and deliver final versions of video to clients.... And the best part is that you can do it all from your laptop without ever leaving the warm snug butt-groove of your living room sofa. Which is probably not a good thing for your waistline, but extremely quick, easy, and convenient for everyone involved. If you provide your editor with detailed notes as to what changes you want and also speak on the phone to make sure those notes are clear, this method can be simple and effective. The only downsides to this method are the upload and download times for large files, which can often take a half hour (or more) for a five- or six-minute video file at good quality and much, much longer for a lengthier high-quality video. Of course, the faster your web connection and system, the faster the download, so actual download times will vary. I find email best for reviewing cuts of short video projects.

2 SKYPE, ICHAT, AND OTHER STREAMING VIDEO PROGRAMS

On the simplest, most primitive level, using any of the popular videoconferencing applications such as **Skype** (free download), **iChat** (pre-installed on Mac computers), or **Windows Live Messenger** (pre-installed on PCs), you can videoconference via a built-in video camera or external webcam or camcorder hooked up to your computer. Your editor would just need to have an external webcam or any old camcorder hooked up to their computer with a cable long enough to point at their computer screen and/or monitor. Establish a

web connection, and you can have all the convenience of being there in person, with none of the smells of being cooped up in a cramped editing space. You can "sit in" on the whole session cut by cut or just check in periodically and have your editor show you the latest progress and run questions by you. Obviously, you'd both need to register for a (free) account with the respective software company, and the video quality of pointing a camera at a computer screen will be low, but it's fine for judging pacing, what shots work, music placement, titles, and all the most important elements of bringing a piece together. Some alternative programs your editor can use to share their computer screen are **ShowMyPC.com**, **WebEx.com**, and **GoToMyPC.com**, which all have various fee structures for their services.

3 FINAL CUT PRO/ICHAT THEATER PREVIEW

If simply pointing a camera at the screen is too primitive for you, you may want to check out **Final Cut Pro 7**. FCP version 7 has a remote collaboration feature built right in that works with a program called **iChat Theater Preview**. If you have the latest **iChat** program and your editor has

the latest version of iChat and FCP 7.0 also installed on their computer, your editor can remotely stream the video output from FCP 7.0 *directly* to your computer screen. Not only that, but you can videoconference at the same time and have multiple clips streaming at once, so you could compare two different versions of a clip. I suspect more and more NLEs will be coming out with their own modules for collaborative editing. Apple has replaced FCP 7 with the controversial FCP X which has a drastically different interface and does not (yet) have such a super-convenient remote editing sharing feature. So

you may be limited to trying to track down a copy of the older and more popular FCP 7 if you want to use iChat Theater Preview.

GLOSSARY

1-shot	A shot with only one person in frame.
3-point lighting	Traditional lighting setup using three lights: key light, fill light, and hair light.
4-point lighting	Traditional lighting setup using four lights: key light, fill light, background light, and hair light.
720p	High-definition (HD) video that has 720 lines of vertical resolution. The "p" refers to progressive scan HD video.
1080p or 1080i	High-definition (HD) video that has 1080 lines of vertical resolution. When followed by "p," it refers to progressive scan HD video. When followed by "i," it refers to interlaced scan HD video.
access	Your ability to get up close and inside the world of your subject. This is the golden ticket to documentary making.
ADR	Acronym for "additional dialogue recording," which refers to the technique of having on-screen talent lipsync a section of their dialog in postproduction because it was not captured well during location recording.
AGC	See **auto gain control**.
ambassador	Another term for a "stringer." Someone who acts as a liaison between your production and another community or culture. Someone who knows their way in the society you wish to film.
amp	A unit that measures electricity. Most household circuits are 15–20 amps.

anamorphic — A technique for capturing a 16:9 widescreen picture on standard 4:3 aspect ratio camera. Uses an electronic process or a special lens that squeezes the 16:9 widescreen image into a 4:3 aspect ratio, which can be later unsqueezed in postproduction.

aperture ring — The spinning ring on a camera lens that controls exposure. Prosumer camera models may have a small aperture dial instead of an aperture ring.

approach — How you choose to tell your documentary story. Using re-enactments, your style of camera work, narration, editing techniques, viewpoint, etc., are all parts of your overall approach.

archival footage/photos — Any footage/photos that you use that was not originally shot for your documentary. This includes news segments, movie clips, etc.

aspect ratio — This is a ratio that simply refers to the shape of your image. In video there are two aspect ratios to choose from: 4:3 = standard TV and is more square; 16:9 = widescreen and is more rectangular. The numbers represent units of width:height.

audience — This is the people you are actually making this film for. Don't ever forget about them.

autogain control — Commonly abbreviated as "AGC." This is a camera feature that automatically adjusts sound levels for you.

A/V screenplay format — Industry script format that splits picture and audio into two columns so that visuals can be described with their corresponding dialog, music, and sound FX displayed side by side. Commonly used for corporate video and commercials.

Avid — One of the leading professional computer editing programs available for PC and Mac.

back light — A light usually placed above and behind your subject, used to separate them from the background by using a rim of light to outline them. Also synonymous with a hair light, which is positioned the same but focused more on the hair.

background plates — The scenes, photos, or animations that are to be inserted as the background when compositing a greenscreen scene.

barn doors — The metal flaps mounted on the front of professional film lights that open and close to control the shape of your light and prevent unwanted light from spilling in undesirable places.

bars and tone — The industry standard reference tools for adjusting color and audio: SMPTE color bars and 1 kilohertz audio tone. It's important to include bars and tone at the beginning of every media card, tape, and every finished project so that editors, projectionists, audio engineers, and other film and TV professionals know how to adjust your color and audio to accurately reproduce what you intended.

black wrap
Extra heavy-duty aluminum foil coated in a special heat-resistant black paint. This is used to shape and control light much like barn doors, but black wrap is completely customizable.

blown out
Overexposed video. This is the video kiss of death. If important parts of your video such as your subject's face or the entire background are blown out, it sucks to be you. Blown-out white blotches in video simply can't be fixed in post. Use zebra stripes to avoid this issue.

BNC
Video cable commonly used to connect cameras to monitors, projectors, and other A/V equipment.

breakaway cable
Special sound cable that combines two XLR cables and a headphone cable into one cable that connects between the camera and the mixer or microphone. There is a twist-apart connector in the middle to allow camera people to quickly "break away" from sound people.

bus drive
These are small high-capacity mini-hard drives that are powered by plugging them into a computer via a USB or FireWire cable. Because they don't require AC power, they are an ideal choice for offloading HD video footage at remote locations and run-and-gun shooting.

C47s
Common, ordinary clothes pins. Used to secure gels to the barn doors of lights.

character studies
Films centered around a single person. The content is heavily driven by that person's personality and character traits.

cheat
To move a prop or person to a new or staged position for a more favorable shot.

chimera
Special heat-resistant tent-like housing for light instruments that provides soft, evenly diffused light. Popular for interviews.

China ball
See **Chinese lantern**.

Chinese lantern
Common, round household paper lanterns that produce soft, warm light. Often used as soft key lights and as fill lights for interviews. Also known as "China balls."

circuit breaker
An automatically operated electrical switch designed to protect an electrical circuit from damage caused by overload or short circuit.

clapper board
Also known as a "slate," this item is used to mark the beginning or end of each take, but more importantly the clapper board is

used for syncing up visuals to sound by using the exact frame where the board claps as a visual and audio reference point in editing.

closing down See **stopping down**.

CMOS chip CMOS stands for "complementary metal oxide semiconductor."

coaxial Type of video cable used to connect cameras, decks, monitors, and other video equipment to each other. Most commonly recognized on your cable box, VCR, or TV.

compact flash card Digital media card used by some cameras including the RED camera.

contingency This is all-purpose emergency money that is built into your budget. Industry standard is 15 percent set aside for contingency. Don't shoot without some amount of contingency money.

cookie A cutout pattern used to cast interesting shadows that add texture to the background of scenes. A cookie may also mimic the pattern of light shining through a window or blinds.

craft services The snacks, drinks, and sometimes food department on a film set. These people are responsible for keeping caffeine, sugar, and nourishment flowing at all times.

crane Piece of equipment used to raise a camera and/or camera operator to get high-angle shots and cool swooping camera moves.

crop out To adjust your frame by tightening a shot or panning or tilting the camera so that an undesirable element such as a sign or jerk waving at the camera is no longer in the frame.

CTB gel Stands for "color temperature blue." Put this gel on a light source to make it appear the same color temperature as daylight.

CTO gel Stands for "color temperature orange." Put this gel on a light source to make it appear the same color temperature as tungsten (indoor) light.

dailies Refers to the footage shot the previous day (i.e., the crew's daily output). In an ideal world, this footage is viewed by the director, cinematographer, and other crew members to make sure that everything is coming out okay and all necessary shots are being covered.

DB Stands for "decibel." These are units for measuring sound levels.

dead cat Film slang for furry coverings used to block wind noise from boom mics. Also known as "windjammers."

depth of field	A term that refers to how much of your frame is in focus at any given time. If your subject is in focus and the background and foreground are out of focus, then you have a shallow depth of field. If everything in the frame is in focus, then you have a deep depth of field.
digitize	To convert video into a digital format so that it can be edited. Done by hooking up a camera or tape deck to your computer and importing the video footage in a nonlinear editing program such as Final Cut Pro, iMovie, Premiere, or Avid.
dimmer box	A small electrical accessory that uses a dial or sliding switch to quickly control the brightness of any light instrument plugged into it.
dirty track	A low-quality track of audio that is not suitable for the final project, but recorded just for reference, so that better quality audio from a separate source can be synched up or recreated in post-production.
dolly	Any camera movement or piece of equipment used that rolls the camera. If it has wheels and you put the camera on it to shoot, it's a dolly.
double system audio	Audio that is recorded with a separate audio recorder apart from the camera. When shooting double system, the audio is synched up with the picture by using a clapper slate, so the sound of the clap can be aligned with physical clap seen on camera. It is also common when shooting video to record a "dirty" reference track with a camera mic to assist with synching.
dramatic reading	Storytelling convention where actors are used to read a document and/or portray the voice of a subject. Used to breathe life into letters, diaries, or other documents.
dramatic zoom-in	The act of zooming in or out slowly on a subject to give dramatic emphasis to what is being said. These are generally done at the most important or compelling parts of an interview to bring the audience physically and emotionally closer to the subject.
dropouts	Apart from people who quit film school early, this term also refers to breaks and omissions in the audio, usually caused by a cable short, wireless interference, or power issues that result in no sound being recorded for a few seconds here and there. This can't be fixed in post.
DSLR	Short for digital single lens reflex camera, which is a popular form of professional still camera. The "single-lens" part simply means the picture you see in the viewfinder is the actual picture

the camera is taking through the lens. The important distinction about these cameras is that they are basically *still photo cameras* that have *added* HD video capability. However, they were never meant to be dedicated video cameras so lack some common (and vital) professional features found even in dedicated prosumer video cameras.

Dutch angle
A shot tilted diagonally to communicate tension or an edgy extreme attitude.

DV Rack
PC-only computer software that can record live footage directly to a hard drive via a laptop computer. Also has other features for image analysis and color correction.

end roll
The term for the wise practice of letting the camera roll for an extra few seconds after each take so that there is adequate room at the end of a scene for an editor to make a cut without losing the end of the take.

equipment package
The entire list of equipment that you need to make a film. Includes your lights, camera, sound, and all the trimmings.

fast lens
A fast lens refers to a lens that is capable of opening to a very low f-stop, generally lower than 2.8, and therefore let's more light into the lens. Fast lenses can better handle low-light shooting situations and are generally more versatile and faster to shoot with, since you have less lighting hassles and can use filters more freely. Naturally, fast lenses are more expensive than other lens.

filament
The little delicate spring that glows hot to produce the light inside light bulbs.

fill light
A light whose function is to bring up the light level some to fill in dark shadows so that details are visible on a subject's face or a lit scene. Fill light should be soft and even. Fill lights are often bounced off a wall or ceiling.

Firestore
A particular brand of small battery-powered camera-mountable hard drives that capture live video via FireWire as a DV camera records it. The captured video files are immediately ready to be edited, saving you tons of time digitizing and logging tapes.

FireWire 400/800
Also known as "IEEE 1394" and "iLink," these are super-fast connections for transferring video data to or from a camera, computer, or hard drive. FireWire 800, used in computers and hard drives, is about twice as fast as FireWire 400, which transfers data at 400MBps. At the time of publication, DV cameras only use FireWire 400.

flood	To widen a beam of light so that it is less intense and more diffused and even. Focusable professional film lights have controls to allow you to flood or spot the light beam.
fluorescent light	Long tubular mercury-vapor lights that require a ballast to regulate the flow of power. Professional fluorescent lights such as Kinoflos may come as tungsten or daylight balanced. However, most household and industrial fluorescents give off light with an unattractive green or bluish tint.
follow focus	A device that attaches to a lens focus ring that's used to more smoothly and precisely focus shots. Using the dial on a follow focus, an operator does not have to touch the lens and can accurately repeat focus moves by marking focal points directly on the dial. Very useful for controlling cameras with very shallow depth of field.
format	Refers to the type of video you are shooting as expressed by vertical pixels and frame rate, typically in terms such as 1080/60i or 720/24p. May also be more generally referred to as "standard definition" or "high definition" as determined by the lines of vertical resolution.
frame line	The imaginary line that marks the top of a framed shot. If a boom mic drops below this line, it will be in the shot.
frame rate	Refers to the number of frames of video you are shooting each second. Frame rates are usually shown in camera specs followed by a designation of "p" for progressive or "i" for interlaced scanning. Typical frame rate specs are expressed in terms such as 24p, 30p, and 60i.
frame-within-a-frame	A shot composition that includes some other element of a scene, such as a doorway or window, that forms a second "frame" around a subject already in the camera's frame.
Franken-Camera	Slang term for DSLR cameras that have been outfitted with all the third-party accessories necessary to make them fully functional for professional video shooting. Includes any combination of support rods, a field monitor, follow focus, audio recording device, matte box, and more.
f-stop	F-stops are numbers that refer to the size of the hole that lets light into the lens, otherwise known as the "aperture." It's counterintuitive, but the larger the f-stop number, the less light is allowed in the lens, the darker the image will be.
gaffer's tape	Professional film industry tape, which is easy to rip by hand, but still very strong. It is also designed not to rip off paint or leave a sticky residue. This is a must-have for any shoot.

gain	This is just another word for "level." There are two types of gain in video: audio gain and video gain. Audio gain adjusts the volume level of audio signals. Video gain adjusts the voltage of the video signal to make an image brighter.
gels	Transparent or translucent sheets of material used to color lights or correct the color of lights.
ghetto-flectors	Homemade reflectors fashioned out of cardboard, aluminum foil, and paper. They aren't pretty or impressive, but reflect light just as effectively as their $30–$100 "professional" reflectors.
HDMI	Stands for "High Definition Multi-Interface." A connection or cable that allows you to hook up video devices such an HD camera and monitor to transmit high-quality high-definition images. Look for these on high-definition cameras, monitors, and TVs.
iMovie	Simple easy-to-use, but powerful editing program that is bundled standard with Mac computers.
in point	The starting timecode point of a shot or edit.
incandescent	An incandescent light passes electricity through a thin filament that heats up inside the vacuum of a bulb to provide light. Most household and professional film lights are incandescent. The other common type of lighting is fluorescent.
insurance certificate	An insurance certificate is a representation of the insurance policy that covers a particular project or production company. At your request, your insurance company will issue certificates naming locations and equipment rental houses as "additional insured" as proof that they are also protected by your insurance policy.
intensity	A term that simply refers to the quantity of light. Light intensity can be controlled in a number of ways, including moving the light closer or farther away, using ND or other light-reducing filters, or spotting or flooding the light beam.
interview subjects	The people who will be interviewed for your project.
interlace	Refers to how a video picture is captured or displayed. Interlaced scanning skips every other vertical row of pictures–making one pass on the odd-numbered pixel rows (1, 3, 5, etc.) and then a second pass on the even-numbered pixel rows (2, 4, 6, etc.) and alternating between these two half images known as video "fields" to form a single interlaced frame of video. Interlaced video is not as detailed and smooth as progressive video.
jam sync	Jamming sync is the act of using a SMPTE time code generating device to send continuous matching free run timecode to one or multiple cameras or recorders. Time code is fed from one device

(the master) to a second device (the slave), which then synchs up to the master device's time code so they are exactly the same. The time code generating device may be an electronic smart slate, time code generator or other video or audio recording device capable of sending time code.

jib
A mechanical arm balanced with a camera on one end and a counterweight and camera controls on the other end. Often mounted on tripod legs. Works similar to a seesaw, but the balance point is closer to the end with the controls so that the camera is at the long end of the arm and can make sweeping vertical or horizontal moves.

jump cuts
Refers to a cut made in editing where two shots of the same subject, but taken from different angles, are cut back to back to create a jarring "jump" in screen composition.

jump-cut style shooting
My own terminology for the "jumpy" style of cinematography most popular in some reality, music tv, and mockumentary projects that consists of rapid manual zooming (i.e. push-ins and pull-outs) to switch composition from a wide shot to close-up, or vice-versa, during a scene. "The Office" is a popular American show that's shot in this style.

Ken Burns Effect
A popular visual effect for animating digital still photos that smoothly pans, zooms in, zooms out and otherwise adds life by performing digital "camera moves" on simple still photos. It was popularized by documentary filmmaker, Ken Burns. It's commonly found on many non-linear editing programs, photo slideshow programs like iPhoto and mimicked on computer screen savers.

Kinoflo
Popular brand of professional fluorescent lights used in filmmaking. Known for their light weight; soft, even light; and low power consumption and heat output.

kit rental
A standard industry "rental fee" charged by professionals who also provide special equipment or supplies, such as makeup artist or sound, camera, and lighting people with their own equipment. They get their day rate for their labor plus a smaller kit rental for use of their gear and/or supplies that you would otherwise have to rent or buy separately.

lavs (aka lavalieres)
Small mics designed to be worn close to the body on the chest or neck. Because of their small size, they can also be hidden on location to pick up sound in wide shots.

location
Any real-life environment not created specifically for film production, such as an office, a park, or someone's home, where you are shooting.

location release	Legal agreement between a location owner and filmmaker that grants a filmmaker permission to shoot in and publicly show a location in their film. Also spells out any fees and obligations to the location owner in the event of damage or injury.
lock down	To secure a tripod's pan-and-tilt function so that it does not move and keeps the shot on camera locked into place.
log sheet	A form used to make notes about the location of scenes and quality of your footage. A log sheet typically includes information such as timecode, scene description, length, and whether a shot was good or bad.
logging	Going through all your footage to note the starting timecode, contents, and other vital information that will be necessary for locating scenes and making decisions during editing. Usually written out in a log sheet (see **log sheet**).
MCU	Shorthand for "medium close-up." Basically a shot from the shoulders up.
Magic Lantern	Third-party firmware that can be installed on some models of DSLR cameras to add some basic video camera features such as zebra stripes, audio meters, etc.
mark slate	To call the information on a slate out loud, typically including title of the production, scene number or name, and take number.
matte box	A box-like apparatus that mounts onto the front of a camera lens used to avoid unwanted lens flare from the sun and artificial lights. Matte boxes also allow you to mount multiple filters on the front of the lens.
metadata	Information about your video that is embedded within a digital file that can be accessed in playback mode or in post-production. Typically includes things such as important camera settings, date, time or day, or custom information that a user enters via the menu. Some new cameras can even include geographic location.
mini-stereo connector	Another term for an 1/8" stereo sound connector like the one on your iPod.
money shots	The most important shots of a given project that will have the most impact on your audience. The shots that mean you are screwed if you don't get them. For a wedding, it's the kiss; for a race, it's the winner crossing the finish line; for a concert, it's the moment the lead singer leaps into the audience to crowd surf in the middle of the finale. These are the most iconic shots that tell the story of the scene or event almost by themselves. Know what they are ahead of time and be ready to capture every one.

monopod	A device that serves the same function as a tripod but is made up of only a single extending and locking leg. Monopods are highly portable and easy to move and reset quickly.
Movie Magic Budgeting	A powerful and widely used software program designed specifically for budgeting movies. MMB makes it easy to create, rearrange, and compare different versions of a budget.
narration	The oral telling of a story. In documentary filmmaking, narration is often laid in as a voice-over the picture.
narrative filmmaking	Filmmaking genre that tells a story. Narrative is almost always scripted but can be improvised as well. If there are actors and a script, it's a narrative.
ND gel	Clear gray lighting gel used to cut down the intensity of lights.
neutral cutaways	Very useful shots that can be inserted almost anywhere in a scene because they aren't very time or action specific. For example, a cutaway to a picture on the wall, a subject's hand gestures, or a reaction shot of someone listening are all examples of neutral cutaways that could be used just about anywhere in a scene to help you condense time, cover up a mistake, or just make it more visually interesting.
NLE	Short for "nonlinear editor." Final Cut Pro, Avid, Premiere, and iMovie are all NLEs.
noise	Video static and artifacts caused by using the camera's gain, digital zoom feature, or other electronic function that results in poor image quality.
on the D.L.	Short for "on the down low." Means to travel and shoot as low-key as possible and not draw any unnecessary attention to yourself when shooting without permission or in hostile areas.
open up the lens	To increase the camera's aperture so that more light comes into the lens.
out point	The ending timecode of a shot or edit.
overmodulate	When sound levels are set so high that they distort, sound rumbly, or are unintelligible. Overmodulation can't be fixed in postproduction.
P2 card	Digital media cards used by some Panasonic cameras including the Panasonic HVX-200.
paper edit	A preliminary editing of material by cutting and arranging sections of transcripts into the order they will appear in the film and then using this paper version of your project to make the rough cut.

pelican cases	Popular industry-standard hard plastic cases designed to store and protect film and video equipment during transit. Pelican cases are water resistant and are typically used with foam.
pickup pattern	Outlines the direction(s) in which a microphone best captures and records sound. Common pickup patterns are cardioid, hypercardioid, and omni.
pixels	The little red, green, and blue microdots that make up the image on a TV or monitor screen. The more pixels there are, the sharper and clearer the picture will be.
Plan B	This is what you plan to do when your first idea doesn't work out. To be successful at guerrilla filmmaking, you always need a Plan B, C, and D when things go wrong.
play back	The act of viewing or listening to previously recorded video or audio.
pots	Another name for the knobs on audio gear. If someone says, "Turn up the pot on channel 2," they are not referring to the drug.
practical lights	Any lights that appear on camera as part of your scene. They may or may not actually be contributing to the main lighting of your scene.
pre-amp	An audio device similar to but simpler than a mixer that is used to boost, control, and/or transform audio signals.
preproduction	All the thought, preparation, planning, and budgeting that takes place before you start to shoot.
pre-roll	Refers to the few seconds of tape that need to roll off before a camera or deck is up to proper recording speed.
production insurance	Insurance that covers you and your crew from liabilities as a result of any property damage, theft or loss, and personal death or injury caused by your production.
production value	The professional look or polish of a production. Production value is affected by such factors as the quality of your lighting, video, audio, camerawork, sets, graphics, and number of mistakes. The term "putting your money on the screen" means raising production value wherever possible.
progressive	Refers to how a video picture is captured or displayed. Progressive video scanning goes straight down the vertical rows of pixels to form a complete picture on each frame of video. Progressive cameras and TVs have smoother, more film-like images.
raccoon eyes	The effect created when you're shooting subjects in bright daylight when the sun is high in the sky, which puts their eye sockets in complete shadow.

rate cards	A rental house's or other vendor's price list.
RCA	Also known as "phono." The very common yellow, white, and red cables/connections used with video equipment. Yellow=Video, White=Left, and Red=Right. However, they are completely interchangeable.
rack focus	To shift focus either to or from a person or object in the foreground to or from another person or object in the background of a shot when shooting with a very shallow depth of field. This move forcibly shifts the audience's attention from one thing to another.
reaction shot	A shot showing how another participant is responding to an event. In interviews, this is the occasional shot of the interviewer responding to the subject. For a performance, a reaction shot would focus on audience members.
re-enactments/ re-creations	A dramatic acting out of some significant event. May be performed by actors or the actual persons involved in the original event. Often presented in documentary style similar to flashbacks in narrative filmmaking. Re-enactments are common in crime and historical documentaries.
refresh rate	The number of times per second an image is scanned on a screen to form the picture. This number is measured in units called Hertz (Hz). A screen with a 60Hz refresh rate scans the image on-screen 60 times per second to form an image.
research	Any and all work you do to learn more about your subject as you prepare to shoot your documentary. Research encompasses reading books, surfing the web, watching videos, visiting locations, talking to experts, etc. Research is doing homework on your subject.
resolution	The size of the image in pixels. In camera and TV specs, resolution is listed as the number of horizontal pixels x vertical pixels. For HD, there are usually 1080 or 720 vertical pixels.
reverse shot	Very similar to a reaction shot, a reverse shot is just the same action captured from the opposite angle to show another viewpoint.
rolling shutter	Rolling shutter refers to the method that CMOS cameras use to scan an image by "rolling" or moving the shutter across part of the image, so that not all part of the image are recorded at the same time, even though they are played back as a single frame. Issues that commonly result from rolling shutter particularly when the camera or objects move quickly are smears, diagonal skews or bending of images, and wobbly images known as the "jello effect".

rotoscoping	The technique of manually creating a matte for an element on live-action footage so it may be composited over another background. The matte masks certain parts of the image on a layer of video allowing you to show just a single object or person from a scene and then lay that object or person on top of another scene. You are essentially "cutting out" parts of a video or still photo and putting them on top of another scene.
rove	A loose style of handheld camerawork, most common in reality TV and some scripted dramas where the camera is continually moving and shifting slightly (as if hovering) as opposed to traditional handheld camerawork where the objective would be to hold the camera as steady as possible. Also a common technique for POV camerawork to give the psychological feeling that we are watching through someone else's eyes.
rule of thirds	Rule of composition that dictates if the screen is divided into thirds horizontally and vertically forming a tic-tac-toe pattern, your subjects should be framed so that they are positioned on the intersection of any two or more lines.
run and gun	Guerrilla shooting style that generally refers to any hectic, unpredictable, fast, and unfolding shooting condition that requires you to cover a lot in a little time often at various locations. Local news is almost always a run-and-gun shooting situation.
S.A.G. paperwork	The simple, but very important forms required by the Screen Actors Guild (aka S.A.G.) whenever an actor in their professional union works on a production. This paperwork verifies the hours they worked, rate agreed upon and that S.A.G. rules regarding lunch breaks and turnaround were followed by the filmmakers.
SxS card	Digital media cards used by some Sony model cameras, including the Sony EX-1, Sony EX3, and the Sony F3.
scene detection	The ability of some edit programs to automatically divide footage into video clips by detecting the timecode when the record button was pressed to start each new shot.
screen captions	Titles placed at the bottom of the frame to spell out dialog or subtitles.
scrims	Specially fitted round metal screens of various thicknesses that come as full or half circles placed in front of a light to reduce intensity.
SSD	Stands for solid state drive. These are hard drives that use flash memory similar to P2 and SxS cards. They have no moving parts, so they are sturdier and not as susceptible to the malfunctions

that can more easily occur with hard disk drives which have spinning disks and moving parts.

SDHC card
Small, relatively inexpensive reusable flash media cards used to record audio and video. Common media for many models of consumer and prosumer video cameras.

short
A loose or bad connection in any cable that results in the cable not clearly and consistently carrying an audio or video signal, which generally will result in static, pops, and dropouts of the signal.

shotgun
Another name for hypercardioid mics, which have a very narrow pickup pattern and focus only on sound in the direction they are pointed.

shutter speed
This term refers to the amount of time the camera's shutter stays open to expose each frame of video. Shutter speed affects how motion is portrayed—sharp or blurry—and how much light enters the lens.

single system audio
Audio that is recorded on the camera at the same time as picture.

slate
This is a device used to synchronize picture and sound and mark particular scenes and takes recorded during production. Can be as simple as someone clapping their hands in front of the camera or as complicated as a battery-operated slate with electronic timecode display. Also commonly used as a verb. Alternatively known as a "clapper board," "marker," or "smart slate."

Slug:
Text that is edited into a project as a note or reminder for those working in post-production, projection or broadcast usually to denote things such as titles, audio tracks used, or unfinished elements. Slug text is not intended to be ever seen by the audience.

SMPTE
Pronounced /simp-tee/. Stands for the "Society of Motion Picture and Television Engineers." This long-standing group of film and TV engineers develops industry standards. Best known for their SMPTE color bar test pattern, which is used to adjust video colors on monitors.

spill light
Any excess, unwanted, or uncontrolled light that appears in a shot. Barn doors, flags, and black wrap are all common tools for blocking spill light.

snoots
Can-like cylindrical inserts that go in front of lights to reduce the width of the beam to highlight a specific subject or object in a scene.

sound blankets
Thick quilted movers' blankets used to dampen echoes caused by hard room surfaces.

speed	Term referring to the moment a second or two after you press the record button when a camera has finished its pre-roll and reached the necessary speed to properly record video and audio signals.
spill	Undesired light that is illuminating any area other than the targeted area. Barn doors, black wrap, and snoots are used to control excess spill light.
spot	To adjust a light's spot/flood control so that the light is at its narrowest, most intense beam.
staging area	An area set aside on a set or location for a department to exclusively use as homebase to store and set-up all their equipment and supplies. Camera, audio, make-up, etc. all need separate staging areas.
statement of work	A document that describes the work that you are proposing to do and clearly spells out what you will do as a producer/director, the basics of how it will be accomplished (such as locations, number of shooting days, etc.), and how much it will cost your clients. Presented after you have an initial meeting or conversation with a client to discuss their needs.
SteadiCam	An industry standard and very expensive camera-stabilizing device used to get smooth, fluid, handheld camera shots. The professional models require a trained operator.
sticks	Another word for "tripod."
stills	Refers to digital or film still photographs.
stock footage	Stock footage is essentially any footage that was not originally shot for your documentary. It can be anything from relevant stills from a local newspaper to clips of old movies that deal with your topic. Stock footage houses sell historical and current video footage.
stopping down	To make a shot darker by closing the lens aperture so that less light comes into the lens.
style sheet	A general term for the written description of the look and feel of various visual and graphic elements such as lower thirds and main titles, transitions, on-screen graphics, how interviews are framed and lit, color palette, style of cinematography, etc. This simple document ensures that your project has a consistent look and style throughout.
surveillance video	Video that is recorded without a subject's knowledge. Usually done from afar using telephoto lens or with hidden or unmanned cameras to capture criminal activity.

S-video	Analog connection/cable used to transmit high-quality video signals between cameras, monitors, and videotape decks. Does not carry audio.
tally light	The little red light that comes on whenever the camera is recording. Found on the front and sometimes also on the rear of video cameras.
take	Every time you call "cut" or start a shot over again is considered a take. To successfully capture a single shot, you may do multiple takes.
telephoto	The longest lens setting achieved by zooming all the way in to a subject. Subjects that are very far away will have to be shot with a telephoto lens to get a medium or close-up shot.
timecode	A digital signal recorded as a track on a DV tape that maintains consistent playback by digitally marking the precise time and tape position down to seconds and frames (1 second = 30 DV frames). This is what editing programs use to mark the exact start and stop points of an edit.
timecode break	The common anomaly that can occur when there is an error in recording that results in the timecode track not recording.
tone	See bars and tone
transcript	The line-for-line written conversion of a videotaped interview or conversation into a "script." For doc filmmaking purposes, transcripts should also denote the timecode of interview questions and dialog so they can be easily located during editing.
translucent powder makeup	Makeup used to smooth and even out complexions as well as diminish the appearance of common blemishes such as wrinkles, acne, freckles, and moles. Particularly useful for counteracting the unflattering effects of HD video on close shots.
tungsten	Light that is orange in color temperature. Most quartz bulbs and standard household lights are tungsten.
USB/USB 2.0	Stands for "Universal Serial Bus." These data cables/connectors are used to connect digital equipment such as cameras, computers, and hard drives.
USB drives	Also known as "thumb drives," these are popular, sturdy flash media storage devices a little bigger than a pen cap that plug into a computer's USB port. USB stands for "Universal Serial Bus."
verbal release	Recording a subject giving you verbal permission to use their image in your project. Not as trusty as a written talent release but will still offer some proof of a subject's cooperation and consent

should there be a legal dispute in the future. This is a runner-up when you can't get a written release right then.

video noise Undesirable static, dots, and graininess in a video picture. Most common when shooting in low light or with the gain turned up.

VFX Short for "visual effects."

visual FX General term used to describe a wide array of special effects accomplished using computer software such as Adobe After Effects or Apple's Motion. Spinning metallic text, muzzle fire added for a fake gun, or digital snow are all examples of common visual FX.

warm cards Special pale green or blue "white cards" made to give your image a warmer look when you white balance your camera on them instead of pure white.

watts A unit used to measure electricity. Typical household light bulbs are 40–100 watts. Professional film lights are typically 250–2000 watts.

whip pan A quick pan move that's so fast that it causes the image to blur in the middle of the move until the lens rests on the final shot.

whip zoom A quick manual zoom move in or out that's so fast that it causes the image to blur in the middle of the move until the lens rests on the final shot. This move is common in reality, sports, music videos and other high energy productions.

white balance A video camera function that adjusts your image to correct variations in color temperature.

white cards A special pure white card used as a reference to set a camera's white balance function to adjust for the lighting conditions. Pure white sheets of paper or T-shirts are a common substitute for white cards in the field.

wild sound Recording of the natural sound of a room or environment to help you smooth out audio problems and re-create the original sound quality of the location during postproduction.

wind shield/windjammer Also known as a "dead cat." A faux fur cover that's custom-fitted to a mic or zeppelin (aka blimp) and used to provide significant reduction of wind noise above and beyond a zeppelin or wind filter alone.

wipe To erase a digital media card by reformatting it which clears all video and or audio clips from the card... *forever*. This function is usually found in the camera's menu and likely at the very bottom of the menu set. Never wipe a card until you've verified your footage by playing it back and listening to it.

wrap out	When everything is packed up and put back in place at the end of a shoot.
XLR	The most common high-quality sound cables/connectors used for professional sound applications. The connectors are three-pronged (male) or three-holed (female).
zebra stripes	Vibrating diagonal stripes that are superimposed on the overexposed parts of the image on a viewfinder or LCD screen. Zebra stripes are not recorded to tape.
zeppelin	A microphone housing that resembles its namesake, designed to shield boom mics from wind noise.

Anthony Q. Artis is a 19-year veteran of the film and TV industry and the author of **The Shut Up and Shoot Documentary Guide, The Shut Up and Shoot Freelance Video Guide**, and co-host of **The Double Down Film Show** podcast.

Anthony produced director Benno Schoberth's indie feature, **Shelter**, which won the grand prize at the 2003 IFP Feature Market as well as several other festival awards. He was also Associate Producer and Gaffer on the hip-hop documentary, **Paper Chasers** (IFC) which premiered at the Tribeca Film Festival, and he was a Segment Producer for the popular MTV reality series, **Flipped**. Over the years he has worked professionally in positions as diverse as producer, cinematographer, gaffer, special-fx make up, sound mixer as well as location manager.

Apart from professional film and television production, as CEO of **Down and Dirty DV, LLC** Anthony has created dynamic attention-grabbing video projects for a variety of clients and institutions. Additionally, his company has produced a slew of original guerrilla filmmaking seminars, DVD's, and educational products, including **Indie Film Boot Camp**, an intensive 8-hour workshop of practical filmmaking seminars.

Anthony currently teaches lighting, camera and audio seminars as an adjunct instructor at the **N.Y.U. – Tisch School of the Arts Kanbar Institute of Film and TV**, where he also manages the Production Center which coordinates the equipment for all Film and TV students. See some of Anthony's freelance video work at: double7images.com/author/anthony-artis.

Photo by: Leyla T. Roasario

END CREDITS

Project Coordinator
Anthony Q. Artis
Project Consultant
Pete Chatmon
Literary Agent
Jan Kardys
Music Video Chapter
Benjamin Ahr Harrison
Interview Subjects
Pete Chatmon
Jocelyn Gonzales
Alexander Houston
Vasia Markides
Chris Chan Roberson
Lighting Article
Steven Bradford
Models
Sonya Artis
Danny Be
Robert Blake
Gian "Gynus" Bravo
Mary Schmidt-Campbell
Maurice Carr
Debra Church
Eddie Cunha
Dre
Eliza McNitt
Sam Laidlaw
Julie Hackett
Ina Franck
Sorayya Kassamali
Ian Kim
Maggie Langlinais
Lucas Lee
Julio Macat
Sean "Golden Child" Mangan
Julian Muller
Kian Najmabadi
Tristan Nash
Kevin Patrick
Keri Patrick
Sam Pollard
Leyla T. Rosario
Kwabena Shango
Jenny Chun-Ossowski
Peter Ossowski
Jasmin Saudi
Giga Shane

Axuan Vrolijk
Crew as Themselves
Live Event Subjects
ELEW
Roy Hargrove
Tina Sugandh
Cliff Charles
Wayne McElroy
Tristan Nash
Stage Play
Transatlantica, by Kenny Finkle
Finkle
The Operating Theater
Keith Chandler
Pierre-Marc Diennet
Tim Donovan, Jr.
Lauren Fritz
Mathieu Lorain Dignard
Eben Moore
Dori Ann Scagnelli
Jason Schuler
Evelyn Sullivan
Anna Wilson
Researchers
Greg Payton
Nicole Sylvester
Audio Consultants
Maggie Langlinais
Lucas Lee
Videography for Photos
Matthew Ahl
Anthony Q. Artis
Pete Chatmon
Benjamin Ahr Harrison
Tristan Nash
Max Nova
Giga Shane
Additional Crew
Additional Photos
Snowboarding - Alex Houston
Mexico - Linda Maxwell
Rebecca - freakyfrugalite.com
Storyboard - by Clark
   Huggins, storyboardinc.com
Icons
T-Ski's Ghetto Graphix
D&D Website Design
Cidney Hue

D&D Logo Design
Brian and Sarah Gallarello
Ian Kim (hand/camera graphic)
Additional Photos
Sonya Artis
Canon
"Paper Chasers"
Storyboards Inc.
JVC
Lowel Lighting
Pando.com
Panasonic
Skype.com
Sony
Interview Transcripts
Shayla Williams
Legal Counsel
Ralph DePalma
Special Thanks
NYU Film & TV Community
Double 7 Images
The Down and Dirty DV Nation
Storyboards, Inc.
Mordy Steinfeld
Zully Moore
Paul Coy Allen
Rebekah Sindoris
Sheril Antonio
Lou LaVolpe
Rosanne Limoncelli
Dave DiGioia
Dan Shipp
Inspiration and Motivation
Sonya Artis
Charles Blackwell
Pete Chatmon
Maxie Collier - Son #1 Media
The "Paper Chasers" Crew
My Mom and Family
My Production Center Familia
All the Playa Haters
Bennie Randall "The Motivator"
Johnny Rice II
Kristin Wynn
Fat Joe
God

INDEX

Page numbers followed by *f* indicates a figure and *t* indicates a table.

A

Action close-ups, 295–296
Additional dialog recording (ADR), 101
After Effects, 154, 157, 171, 221
Analog meters *vs.* peaking meters, 77
Analog mixer, 71*t*
Animatics, creation of, 138
Anticipate actor movement, 307
Apple's iPad, 148, 148*f*
Apple's Motion software, 157
Apron, 57, 57*f*
Audio, 246
 bracketing, 81, 81*f*, 81*t*
 frequency, 96, 96*f*
 levels, setting, 80–81
 measurement, analog *vs.* digital, 78–79, 78*f*, 78*t*
 monitoring
  selection, 92*t*
  setup, 92
 point, 279
 in post, 94
  fixing location, 95–96, 95*f*
 quality of, 281
 strategy, 176
 trim, 92
Audio cookbook, 282–284
Audio recording
 location issues, 93
 pattern, 75, 75*t*
 position, 75, 75*f*
 secret to, 102
 strategy, 74–78
Audio trouble spots, 92–94
Audio troubleshooting guide, 87–91, 87*f*

Autogain audio, 20
Auto-white balance, 49
A/V screenplay format, 136–137

B

Beachtek box, 71*t*
Beat markers, 217, 217*f*
Beep function, turn off, 142
Beware shorts, 85
BizFilings.com, 317
Bleach bypass, 224
Blimp, 70*t*
Blogs, 230
Boom mics, 142, 146*t*
 avoiding, 142
Boom operator, 72, 72*f*
Boompole, 70*t*
Bracketing, 81, 81*f*, 81*t*
Brainstorming notes, 193, 193*f*
Brass, 289
"Breaking the fourth wall," 153, 153*f*
Bride's preparation, 243, 255, 255*f*
Broad lighting, 60
Broadcast, preparation for, 164
Broadcast standard, 165
B-roll, 154, 154*f*, 158
 buying, 160
 clients for, 159
 recycle/borrow, 160
 shooting, 158–159
 still photos, 161
Brush
 cleaner, 57, 57*f*
 premium, 57, 57*f*

Budget, 187–189
    sample music video, 190–191
Business bank account, 317
Business entity, 316–317

C

Camera
    angles, multiple, 149, 149f
    audio levels, 90, 90f
    3-chip prosumer, 251
    headphone level, 91, 91f
    lights, 246, 251
    mic/line setting, 90, 90f
    phantom power, 90, 90f
    position, 252
        anatomy of, 253, 253f
    shotgun mic mounted on, 285, 285f
Camera guide, 7t
Candid interactions, 255
Canon camera
    5D model, 150
    7D model, 150, 219
Casting, 97
Ceremony money shots, 244
Chroma subsampling, 219
Chromatte greenscreen, 112
    setup, 121f, 122f
Cinematic videos, 244
Circuit box, 106f
Circuit breaker, 105
    switching, 106f
Circuits
    crash course in, 105–107
    definition, 105
    lights plug into, 105
Cityscapes, 43–44
Clients, 317
    for B-roll, 153
    dance and crafting proposal, 323
    staying on same page with, 144
Clients' problems, solving, 124
Clive Davis Institute of Recorded Music, 128
Color
    correction, 226–227
    grading options, 225
    terminology, 224
Color bars, 159, 159f

Color shift, 260f
Color slash setup, 119f
Color space, 219
Color wheel, 32, 32f
Commercial videos, format for, 130
Commercials, 143
    common mistakes, 156
    experience vs. process, 157
    rules of, 144
    testing spot, 158
    workflow, 156–157
Compact mini-hard drives, 325
Composing shots, 291
Condenser mics vs. dynamic mics, 76
Contrast, 224
    extreme color, 120
Converging lines, 260f
Corporate video, 49
Craigslist.org, 182, 182f
Crappy notes, 228
Crazy notes, 228
Crew's rate, 327, 329t
    calculating, 330
CTO gel, 57, 57f
Cutaways, traditional, 147, 147f

D

Danger spots, 102
Daylight shots, 46
Dead cat, 69t, 84
Depth of field (DOF), 19
    shallow, 17, 33, 33f, 36, 44
        super-duper, 21
Desk setup, 121f
Detail close-ups, 295
Detecting shorts, 85–86
Dialog recording, 100
Differenter campaign, 145, 146
Digital file chart, 24–25
Digital media chart, 26–27
Digital meter, 79
Digital mixer, 69t
Digital single lens reflex (DSLR), 22, 251
    audio limitations, 17
    cameras, 150
    DOF, 19
        super-duper shallow, 21

Franken rig, anatomy of, 23
Franken-camera, 17, 20
  low-light sensitivity, 21
  multicamera shoots, practical options for, 20
  overheating and 12-minute clip limit, 18
  rolling shutter speed, 18
  soft-focused shots, 17
  super-duper stealth mode, 20
Disruptive technology, 21
Documentary videos, 244
DOF, *see* Depth of field
Double7Images.com, 233
Downanddirtydv.com, 321*f*
Dropbox.com, 331, 331*f*
DSLR, *see* Digital single lens reflex
DSLR Cinema : Crafting the Film Look with Video
  (Lancaster), 17
Dutch angles, 260*f*, 297*f*
Dynamic mics *vs.* condenser mics, 76
Dynamic single-camera scene coverage,
  256

E
EIN, *see* Employer identification number
Electric instruments, 289
Email, video files transfer in, 331
Emotion close-ups, 295
Employer identification number (EIN),
  316
Entertainment TV setup, 114*f*
Establishing shots, 267
Expanded focus, *see* Focus assist
Experience commercials, process *vs.*,
  157
Experimental videos, 244
Extreme color contrast, 120

F
Facial issues and fixes, 56–62
Fast lens, 251
Favored nations, 327
FCP, *see* Final Cut Pro
Field monitor, 210, 210*f*
Final Cut Pro (FCP), 151, 208, 208*f*, 216
  version 7, 332
Fish-eye lens, 44
Flash card, 325

Fluid head tripod, 290
Focal length, 43–44, 150*f*
Focus assist, 36, 36*f*
Frame rate, 3
Frame-in-a-frame shot, 260
Frame-in-frame setup, 120*f*
Franken camera, 17, 20
Free run timecode, 5
Freelancers camera guide, 7*t*

G
Gain, 6–16, 6*t*, 30, 30*f*, 31, 31*f*, 224
  function, 251
Ghetto-flector, 110
Giant master mixing board, 282
Graphic equalizer, 96, 96*f*
Graphic text, 163
Green screen interview, anatomy of,
  47, 47*f*
Greenscreen lighting, 121*f*
Group interviews, shooting, 167
  audio strategy, 170
  camerawork, 168–169
  casting, 167
  interview, 167
  lighting, 168
  staging, 169
  technique, 170

H
Handheld camerawork, 264
Handheld high angles, 292
Handheld recorder, 69*t*
Handheld technique, 34
Hard-and-fast rule, 79
Hardwired lav mic, 69*t*
Hardwired mics, 265
Harsh hyper-realities of HD, 50
HD, *see* High-definition
Headphones, 69*t*, 100, 100*f*
Hertz (Hz), 3
High-definition (HD) cameras, 35
High-definition video, low definition of, 2
Horns, 289
Hue, 224
Hypercardioid mics, 69*t*
Hz, *see* Hertz

I

iChat, 332
   theater preview, 332
Incorp.com, 317
Interlace scan lines, 3f
   progressive vs., 3
Internet, 230
Interval recording mode, 48
Interview space, constructing, 51
Intimacy videos, capturing of, 269
iPad, 148–156, 148f
iZotope, 94

J

Jam timecode, 5
Juiced link, 69t
Jump-cut style, 42

K

Ken Burns effect, 161
Keying, process of, 221–222
Kickback, 320
Kinoflos, 125
Kit rental, 56

L

Laser printers, 111
Lav mics, 142
LegalZoom.com, 317
Lens
   fast, 251
   fish-eye, 47
   normal, 47, 47f
   telephoto, 46, 46f, 251
   using different, 156f
   wide, 46, 47f, 61
Lens flare, 259f, 293
Library bookshelf setup, 122f
Lighting, 36, 37f, 279, 280
   safety of, 112
   short, 60
   simple, 141
   turn off record, 142
Lights, plug into circuits, 109
Limited liability companies (LLCs), 316
Live music, audio post on, 287
LLCs, see Limited liability companies

Load-in procedure for shooting, 143–144, 143t
Low-angle setup, 127
Low-budget shoot, sample rates, 328
Low light, 113

M

Massify.com, 182, 182f
Media card, 267
Menu settings, 4
   timecode, see Timecode menu settings
   for video format, 4
Mic, 86, 100
   attenuation switch, 284
   back-up strategies, 86f
   condenser vs. dynamic, 76
   hardwired lav, 69t
   hypercardioid, 69t
   pickup pattern on, 75, 75t
   support, 69t
   switch, internal/external, 91, 91f
Microphones, 69t
Miking instruments, 288
Mixers, 69t
   battery power, 89, 89f
   and boom position, 73, 73f
   headphone level, 90, 90f
   mic/line in switch, 89, 89f
   mic/line out, 90, 90f
   phantom power, 89, 89f
   pot
      input, 89, 89f
      output, 89, 89f
Mixing live music, 286–287
Money shots, 262
Monitor set up, 120f
MTV-style camerawork, 37
Multicamera recording, 5
Multiple camera, 308
   angles, 36, 36f, 155, 155f
Murphy's Law, 185, 211
Music videos, 169, 180, 196–197
   Ben's final thoughts on, 233–240
   dreaming up, 192
   exhibition, 229–230
   before gig starts, 185
   good reasons to make, 181
   project, 234–236

details, 235
  documentary street scenes, 237–238
  enhancing the look, 236–237
  establishing shots, 236
  money shot, 239
  murals, 237
  special FX in postproduction, 239
  studio scenes, 238–239
sample budget, 190–191
scripting
  location-based outline, 200
  outline, 199–200
  process, 198
  shooting schedule, 202
  shot list, 201
shooting
  locations for, 203, 240
  preparation for, 203–204
  tips for, 208–211
things to do on set, 206–207
tips for finding first act in, 182–183
tools of trade, 220
treatments, 194–196
Musical lighting, 280
Musical montage, 243

N
Narration, directing, 98
Natural lighting, 141
ND gel, 52, 52*f*
Neutral cutaways, 153
Neutral shots, 299
Normal lens, 47, 47*f*

O
Ohm's law, 109
On-screen talent, 148
Original slide presentations, 312
Outline, of video
  detailed, 134
  simple, 133
  starts with an, 133
Overnightprints.com, 321

P
P2 cards, 325
Panasonic HVX-200 camera, 219
Peaking meters, *vs.* analog meters, 77

Peaking on camera, 39, 39*f*
People's psychology, 54
Photo montage, 243
Photo shoot, incorporating, 274
Piano, 289
  recording, 76–77
Pitch, 186
Pixels, 2, 2*f*
Plugging in, 265
Point of view (POV), 291
Pop filter, 98*f*
Postproduction, 152, 189, 212–213
  process managing, 214
  tool, 94
Powder makeup
  applying, 58
  translucent, 55, 57, 57*f*
Pre-amp, 69*t*, 91, 91*f*
Preproduction, 152, 189
  budget, 187–188
  pitch, 186
Process commercials, experience *vs.*,
  163
Production, 152, 189, 205
  insurance, 317–318
Professionalism, 54
Progressive scan lines, 3
Promo videos, project details, 168

R
Rack focus, 293, 297*f*
Radarmusicvideos.com, 183, 183*f*
Rate, 324
  calculation chart, 328, 328*t*
Rate for capturing videos
  flat rate, 327
  hourly rate, 327
Reaction shots, 256, 308–309
Real people
  tips for working with
    avoiding boom mics, 142
    constant visual feedback, 141
    lighting, 141
    moving camera far and away, 142
    relaxed and informed, keeping, 140
    turn off the record light and beep, 142
    verbal feedback, 141
Record Run timecode, 5, 5*f*

Recorders, 69*t*

Recording, 286–287

  dialog, 100

  multicamera, 5

  pattern, 75, 75*t*

  piano, 76–77

  position, 75–77, 75*f*

  secret/sensitive, 103

RED ONE camera, 219

Referral fee, 320

Reflectorology, 114–117

Reflectors, 114

Refresh rate, 3

Rehearsal, 249

  procedure, 145, 145*t*

Retro film, 172

Review edit, 215

  compositing, 219

  final cut, 223

  rough cut, 216–217

Rocker zoom control, 42

Rolling shutter speed, 21

Room tone, 94

Roving, 153

S

Safe sets, 104–108

  first-aid kit for, 106

  hospital search, 107

  phone service, 107

  practicing, 104–108

  safety briefing, 108

  secure everything, 107

Saturation, 224

SBA, *see* Small Business Administration

Scan lines, 3, 3*f*

Scripting

  creating, 136

  location-based outline, 200

  outline, 199–200

  process, 198

  shooting schedule, 202

  shot list, 201

SD, *see* Standard definition

  Secret/sensitive recording, 82

Semi-automatically zooming method, 42, 42*f*

Setup procedure, 136*t*, 144

Shallow depth of field, 122, 126

Sheer curtains, 259*f*, 269*f*

Shockmount, 70*t*

Shooting

  locations for, 240

  low angle, 127

  low-budget, sample rates, 328

  low light, 251

  procedure, 146*t*

Shooting sports

  camera position and POV shots, 62

  lens choice, 61

  and narrative, 61

  snow and exposure, 64

  Sony EX-3, 63

Short form videos, 244

Short lighting, 60

Shorts

  avoiding, 85

  beware, 85

  dealing with, 85–86

  detecting, 85–86

Shotgun mics, 69*t*, 143*t*

  mounting, 296

Shut Up and Shoot Documentary Guide, The (Artis), 68, 325

Shutter speed, 43–45, 43*f*, 44*f*, 49, 251

Silhouette, 259

Single-camera coverage, 298

Single-camera coverage strategies, 303–304

Six-piece rock band, 283

Skype, 332

Slate screen, 165

  commercial, 166–176

Small Business Administration (SBA), 316

SMPTE slate, 208, 208*f*

Soft-focused shots, 20

Sole proprietorships, 316

Sony EX1 camera, 219

Sound

  department crew, 72–73

  level monitoring, 100–101, 100*f*

  locations for, 101, 101*f*

  rules, 100–102

  tools, 69–71

Sound devices 302 mixer, 282

Sound mixer, 72, 72*f*

Sound wild, recording, 101–102
Split-screen editing, 260
SquareSpace.com, 322
Standard definition (SD)
  cameras, 2
  cards, 325
Still photos, 161
Storyboard Quick, 139*f*
Storyboards, 138, 139*f*
  creating, 139
Storytelling, 149–150, 157–164
Strategic partnerships, 320
Streaming video programs, 332
Strings, 288
Student group interview, 166
Studio space, 204
Sunlight, 110
Super-duper stealth mode, 20
Switching, circuit breaker, 106*f*
SxS cards, 325
Sync digital recorder, 69*t*
Sync license, 266

T
Talent, 142
Tape, 267
Telephoto lens, 43, 43*f*, 251
Teleprompters, working with, 142–147
Television, music videos on, 229
TemplateMonster.com, 322
Test shooting, 204
Text
  and storytelling, 151
  treatments, 148, 148*f*
Theatrical lighting, 280
Theidealists.com, 182, 182*f*
ThemeForest.com, 322
Tighter shots, 309
Time intervals, setting, 45
Timecode break, 5
Timecode Display function, 6
Timecode Generator, 208, 208*f*
Timecode menu settings
  display, 6
  Free Run, 5
  gain, 6, 6*t*
  preset mode, 6, 6*f*

Record Run, 5, 5*f*
Timecode Display, 6
Timecode Preset mode, 6, 6*f*
video gain, 6, 6*t*
Timecode Preset mode, 6, 6*f*
Time-lapse footage, 45
Time-lapse shot, 46
Title screen, 159
Tone, 159
Traditional cutaway shots, 147, 147*f*
Traditional videos, 244
Transitioning, 258
Translucent foreground, 259
Translucent powder makeup, 52, 54, 54*f*
Tripod, 45, 45*f*, 264

U
Unmanned cameras, 253
Unorthodox two-camera setup, 117*f*
USB-powered bus drives, 325*f*

V
Video, 130*t*, 131*t*
  checklists, 275
  conceptualizing, 126
  fields, 3
  format, 4
  frame rate, 3
  freelance workflow, 171
  gain, 6, 6*t*, 30
  marketing, 125
  monitor, 35, 35*f*
  product, 281
  resolution, 2
Video format, menu settings for, 4
Vignette, 224
Viral video, 231–232
Vistaprint.com, 320
Visual FX
  illustrative, 165
  transitional, 164
Vocals, 288
Voice-over
  anatomy of down and dirty, 99
  narration, 97
  setups, 98, 98*f*
Voice-overs, directing, 98

W

Warming card, 32
Wedding audio strategies, 265
Wedding venue
　lighting conditions of, 250
　scouting, 247
Wedding video
　celebrant, 249
　in low light, 251
　music, 266
　style of, 244
Wedding videographers, 272, 275
Whip pan, 294
Whip zoom, 294
White balance, 35, 35*f*
Wide lens, 46, 47*f*, 61
Wild sound, recording, 101–102
Wind noise
　blocking out, 84, 84*f*
　filtering, 84, 84*f*
　taming, 84, 84*f*
Windjammer, 70*t*
Window view setup, 117*f*
Windows Live Messenger, 332
Windscreen, 70*t*
Wireless lav mic, 69*t*, 103, 265
Wireless mic, 82
　batteries, 88, 88*f*
　frequency, 87, 87*f*

"mute" switch, 88, 88*f*
　sensitivity, 88, 88*f*
　using, 82–83
Wireless receiver
　batteries, 88, 88*f*
　frequency, 88, 88*f*
　level out, 88, 88*f*
　Wiring, damaged, 111
Woodwinds, 288
Wordpress.org, 322
Wrap-out procedure, 147, 147*t*

X

XLR
　adapter, 91, 91*f*
　cables, 69*t*, 85*f*

Y

YouTube, 182, 182*f*

Z

Zebra stripes, 32
Zeppelins, 70*t*, 84
Zooming
　fully automatic, 42, 42*f*
　fully manual, 42, 42*f*
　pull out, 41, 41*t*
　push in, 40, 40*t*
　semi-automatically, 42, 42*f*

Down and Dirty Filmmaking: Guerrilla Tactics – Professional Results

An overview of guerrilla filmmaking philosophy, tactics, and procedures that can be applied to any budget, any camera, any time.

— Anthony Q. Artis

How To Make a $1 Million Video (…without $1 Million)

An overview of cutting edge digital tools, techniques, and practical strategies that can help you make low cost/high production value videos that blow away audiences and keep clients coming back.

— Benjamin Ahr Harrison

Documentary Interview Boot Camp

An A-Z crash course in the technical practices of camera, audio and lighting to the practical techniques of planning and conducting interviews. Perfect for aspiring documentary filmmakers, corporate videographers, and video journalists.

— Anthony Q. Artis

The Psychology & Technique of Directing

This seminar will arm you with the necessary tactics to manage any production and ensure that your creative vision is translated to cast, crew, and most importantly, the audience.

— Pete Chatmon

Raising Funds and Pitching…Effectively

Being able to secure financing means being able to sell your idea. This seminar will help you streamline your efforts, strengthen your proposals, and better speak the language of the investor.

— Pete Chatmon

Learn, Break In & Rise Up In The Biz

Attendees will get a no-nonsense 5-step blue-print for improving their craft, creating "luck", and parlaying an entry-level (or even temp job) in the industry into a major career break.

— Anthony Q. Artis

FILM BRICK: CHECKLISTS
a powerful new app for filmmakers